Using R:BASE®

Marva Dasef

que®

CORPORATION

LEADING COMPUTER KNOWLEDGE

Using R:BASE®

Copyright © 1990 by Que® Corporation.

Library of Congress Catalog No.: 90-62070

ISBN: 0-88022-603-X

93 92 91   8 7 6 5 4 3 2

Interpretation of the printing code: the rightmost double-digit number is the year of the book's printing; the rightmost single-digit number, the number of the book's printing. For example, a printing code of 90-1 shows that the first printing of the book occurred in 1990.

Using R:BASE is based on R:BASE Version 3.1.

DEDICATION

To my husband Jack, with love.

Publishing Director

Lloyd J. Short

Acquisitions Editor

Karen A. Bluestein

Product Director

Shelley O'Hara

Project Manager

Paul Boger

Production Editor

Fran Blauw

Editors

Sara Allaei
Kelly Currie
Jay McNaught
Dan Schnake

Technical Editor

Jim Carr

Indexer

Joelynn Gifford

Editorial Assistant

Patty Brooks

Book Design and Production

Dan Armstrong
Claudia Bell
Brad Chinn
Don Clemons
Sally Copenhaver
Tom Emrick
Jill D. Bomaster
Denny Hager
Tami Hughes
Bill Hurley
Chuck Hutchinson
Betty Kish
Bob LaRoche
Larry Lynch
Cindy L. Phipps
Joe Ramon
Dennis Sheehan
Louise Shinault
Bruce Steed
Mary Beth Wakefield

*Composed in Garamond and Excellent No. 47
by Que Corporation.*

ABOUT THE AUTHOR ▼

Marva Dasef

Marva Dasef lives with her husband Jack, son Mark, and various critters on a five-acre farm outside of Eugene, Oregon. She has given up the career chase in high-tech Seattle for a more serene life as a freelance writer and R:BASE programmer.

With 19 years of data processing experience, including five years working as a technical writer and documentation manager for Microrim, Ms. Dasef is uniquely qualified to write about this new R:BASE product. At Microrim, Ms. Dasef received five Society of Technical Communications awards for her quality Microrim manuals, most recently for the R:BASE Compiler manual. Prior to Microrim, Ms. Dasef worked as a programmer, customer support manager, and bookstore owner.

CONTENTS AT A GLANCE

TABLE OF CONTENTS ▼

II   Using Data Entry and Viewing Functions

III   Producing Forms and Reports

IV   Using Advanced Features

ACKNOWLEDGMENTS

Special thanks are due to Fran Blauw and Shelley O'Hara at Que Corporation for their hard work in shaping up the manuscript and, in particular, asking many annoying questions that made this a better book. Without them, this book would not be as complete and detailed, and it would probably also be about 100 pages shorter. I hope they both know by now that my sense of humor is a little off-base and will accept my appreciation for their good work. And, a hearty thanks to the rest of the editing and production team for a job well done. And, for his good eye for catching little errors, thanks to the technical editor, Jim Carr. I also owe a note of thanks to David Maguiness for letting me write this book for Que. Without his support, I'd never have had the opportunity.

I would also like to acknowledge and thank the documentation team at Microrim. In particular, I owe Merrie Schriro a special debt for her quick answers and patience with my many calls. I'd also like to thank Peter Hapeman and Joan Hammond for their assistance in my time of need. Also at Microrim, thanks are due to Mickey Friedman and Scott Fallon in Marketing for expediting product releases and to Monte Schlichter in Customer Support for answering my questions.

Finally, my heartfelt appreciation to my husband, Jack. He read the whole thing and didn't fall asleep once.

TRADEMARK
ACKNOWLEDGMENTS

Que Corporation has made every effort to supply trademark information about company names, products, and services mentioned in this book. Trademarks indicated below were derived from various sources. Que Corporation cannot attest to the accuracy of this information.

1-2-3, DIF, Symphony, and VisiCalc are registered trademarks of Lotus Development Corporation.

3Com is a registered trademark and EtherLink is a trademark of 3Com Corporation.

dBASE III PLUS is a trademark, and dBASE II and dBASE III are registered trademarks of Ashton-Tate Corporation.

Epson FX is a trademark of Epson America, Inc.

Microrim and R:BASE are registered trademarks of Microrim, Inc.

MS-DOS and Multiplan are registered trademarks of Microsoft Corporation.

Novell Netware is a registered trademark of Novell, Inc.

PFS:File is a registered trademark of Software Publishing Corporation.

PS/2 is a trademark of International Business Machines Corporation.

CONVENTIONS USED IN THIS BOOK

The conventions used in this book have been established to help you learn to use the program quickly and easily. As much as possible, the conventions correspond with those used in the Norton Utilities documentation.

You select menu options by highlighting the option and pressing Enter. Therefore, when this book tells you to select an option, you should highlight that option and press Enter.

Screen names, menu names, and menu options appear in headline-style format. For example, select Add and Duplicate Row.

Words or commands that you must type appear in italics. For example, type *prompt*.

Prompts or messages that appear on-screen are in digital type. For example, Do you wish to continue or stop? (Y/N)

Throughout this book, you will find references to the relevant command or commands associated with the menu options. The reference blocks look like this:

```
Command: RBDEFINE
```

These references tell you the underlying R:BASE command that executes when you choose a menu option, or an alternative command you can use instead of the menu option. You can find out more about the commands in Appendix C of this book.

Also, you will see notes offering suggestions, cautions, tips, or techniques. A tip section looks like this:

Tip: If you define a date or time stamp column, be aware that the date or time value changes every time you modify the data in the row. Rows that are not changed keep their previous date or time values.

Introduction

What is R:BASE?

Welcome to *Using R:BASE*. With this book as your guide, you will find out how to use R:BASE 3.1—a powerful microcomputer database management system. R:BASE's strong point in previous versions was its extensive command language. It was, until Version 3.1, a command-oriented system. Throughout the history of R:BASE, Microrim (R:BASE's developer), continually improved on the R:BASE engine and added features to make R:BASE even more powerful and easier to use, culminating in the R:BASE 3.1 design.

In the past, Microrim had a problem with the perception that R:BASE was simply too difficult to understand and use. People wanted a Moped with a Maserati engine. Now, R:BASE's complete menu system provides the majority of R:BASE's command power in point-and-shoot menus. Now that the ease-of-use issue is solved, R:BASE even enables the novice to quickly create a database and immediately start entering and using the data. Then, when the user gains knowledge and skills, R:BASE's robust command understructure simply outperforms any other database management system.

R:BASE is a database management system (DBMS) designed and developed by Microrim, Inc. The great-grandfather of R:BASE was a mainframe database system called RIM that was developed for Boeing Corporation by Microrim's founder, Wayne Erickson. Erickson obtained the rights to reproduce the RIM concepts on DOS-based microcomputers, and the R:BASE family began.

The earliest versions of R:BASE were hard to use—command-oriented with very few helpful guides. As later versions of R:BASE were developed— RIM:BASE, R:BASE 4000, R:BASE 5000, R:BASE System V, R:BASE for DOS

1

and OS/2, and now R:BASE 3.1—Microrim added features to the basic
command structure to provide easier ways to use the system. From
rudimentary form and report-development tools, a full-blown menu-driven
system was derived, culminating in R:BASE 3.1.

What Can You Do with a Database System Like R:BASE?

Because R:BASE's origins are from the mainframe world, it closely follows
the design features of the original concepts of database systems as applied
on large computers. Other products calling themselves databases are really
flat-file managers that have tacked on database features. A *flat-file manager*
deals only with a single group of data at one time. R:BASE is the real
thing—a true database system with a powerful set of user tools included to
make database processing easy.

Although flat-file managers have many uses and are the solution to many
users' needs, a database system enables you to relate data stored in several
areas. You cannot ask questions about data contained in more than one
file, for example, with a flat-file manager because it is not a relational
system. The idea behind a database—whether it is relational, hierarchical,
or tree-structured—is the capability to draw information from many
sources and to avoid the duplication of data.

Database systems are software products with functions and utilities
designed to help you keep track of data within a set of rules and
guidelines. The rules for database management systems were defined by
groups that define standards for software products. You will see the term
ANSI-standard (the American National Standards Institute standard) in the
descriptions and documentation on various software products. The concept
behind a standard is to make sure that a set of rules that apply in one
product also apply to similar products. A product must have certain
features to receive the label "database."

A database must be able to store different groups of data and then look at,
compare, and manipulate the data in one group depending on information
derived from another group. The concept of a database solves the problem
of data redundancy (having to input someone's name in more than one file
or table in a flat-file manager, for example), and the eternal problem of the
left hand not knowing what the right hand is doing.

R:BASE comes closer than any other database product in following the
rules defined by standards committees (such as ANSI standards). R:BASE

uses a set of commands called structured query language (SQL). A strictly-interpreted SQL does not mean much to the average user. By following the rules closely, however, Microrim ensures that you can use what you learn about R:BASE SQL commands elsewhere—on mainframe systems or other microcomputer database products that use ANSI-standard SQL, for example.

Generally, you can use a database whenever you want to store and retrieve data. Specifically, you can use a database to perform the following tasks:

- *Manage personal finances:* checkbooks, home inventory, and loan and mortgage data.

- *Keep track of personal items:* genealogical tables, baseball cards, stamps, coins, comic books, home video libraries, collectibles, and bowling team statistics.

- *Manage a business:* inventory control, order entry, accounts payable, accounts receivable, customer lists, general ledger, purchasing, and notes payable.

- *Perform statistical analysis:* consumer analysis, not-for-profit agency donor tracking, political polling, and surveys.

- *Create scientific and medical applications:* experimental data tracking and medical records.

If you need to store and retrieve any type of data in a meaningful form, you may want to use a database system.

What Is in this Book?

This book describes how to use R:BASE by using the menu system. In addition, Appendix C lists all R:BASE commands with brief explanations on how to use them.

Each chapter starts with an introduction and explanation of an R:BASE feature, tells you how to start a module or utility, supplies detailed explanations of how to use each feature, and finishes with a summary of what you have learned.

Part I: Using R:BASE To Build a Database

Part I begins with an overview of R:BASE modules and how to use the R:BASE menu system. In addition, you learn how to use the R:BASE command builder—Prompt By Example—and how to enter commands manually in R:BASE command mode. This part also provides the information you need to design and create a database structure to contain your data.

Quick Start 1, "Defining a Database Structure," teaches you how to start R:BASE, access menus, and get help. It then leads you through the process of defining a database with three tables and setting rules for data entry.

Chapter 1, "Introducing R:BASE," elaborates on using the R:BASE menu system and teaches you more about R:BASE command use in command mode. Chapter 2, "Designing a Database," describes the concepts behind a relational database—how to design a good database structure and ideas for making your database as useful as possible. Chapter 3, "Using the Database Definition Module," describes how to define your database structure in R:BASE.

Part II: Using Data Entry and Viewing Functions

Part II describes how to use the R:BASE Query By Example and Info—the R:BASE tabular data editor.

Quick Start 2, "Using Tabular Edit," shows you how to add and modify data with the tabular editor and how to create a stored query from multiple tables.

Chapter 4, "Entering and Editing Data," describes how to enter and edit data by using the tabular editor. Chapter 5, "Using Query By Example," describes how to create a stored query from multiple tables.

Part III: Producing Forms and Reports

Part III is devoted to customized forms and reports—how to create and use them.

Quick Start 3, "Creating Forms and Reports," leads you through the steps of defining a customized Quick form and teaches you how to edit data by using a form. You also define a Quick report and learn how to print it.

Chapter 6, "Building and Using Customized Forms," provides details on the Forms module. You learn how to use the Forms module to create data entry forms. Chapter 6 also shows you how to use Query By Example and how to relate and manipulate your data. Chapter 7, "Building and Using Customized Reports," describes the Reports and Labels modules. It provides full information on using both of these modules to create customized reports and label formats.

Part IV: Using Advanced Features

Part IV expands on your R:BASE skills with details on building customized applications, using some of the R:BASE commands, importing and exporting data, and managing your database files.

Quick Start 4, "Building Applications," leads you through the steps of creating a custom application.

Chapter 8, "Building and Using Applications," describes the R:BASE application-building module—Application Express. Chapter 9, "Using Relational Commands," tours the relational commands in R:BASE, including the SELECT command. Chapter 10, "Importing and Exporting Data," shows you how to use R:BASE's Import/Export utility. Chapter 11, "Managing Your Database," describes how to back up and restore your database structure and how to use the DOS commands in R:BASE.

Appendixes

Appendix A, "Installing R:BASE," takes you through the installation process on a stand-alone computer and on a local area network.

Appendix B, "Customizing R:BASE," describes the R:BASE features that enable you to manipulate and customize your R:BASE working environment.

Appendix C, "R:BASE Command Summary," lists alphabetically, within logical groups, all R:BASE commands, and briefly describes the purpose of each command.

Appendix D, "Example Databases," describes in detail the two example databases used in this book for the illustration of concepts. The first, a mailing list, illustrates basic concepts of database design. This database is used in Chapters 3 through 7. The second application, a checkbook, illustrates more complex database features, including application development, programming, relationality, and data import and export. This database is used in Chapters 8 through 11.

Appendix E, "R:BASE Version 3.0 Enhancements," lists features of R:BASE 3.0 and the enhancements of this version over previous R:BASE versions.

How To Use this Book

If you have experience with other *Using* books from Que Corporation, such as *Using PC Tools Deluxe* or *Using 1-2-3 Release 2.2*, Special Edition, you know that Que books provide hands-on experience in actually using the programs.

This book is designed in the same way—quick starts lead you through processes that you actually can perform with your new program, and the chapter text enhances the knowledge and experience provided in the quick starts.

In general, *Using R:BASE* is organized to be used from beginning to end. Nevertheless, if you feel comfortable with the basic concepts introduced in the first or second part, you can easily move on to the more advanced sections later in the book. You may not need to go through Part I, for example, to know how to build your own database. Instead, you can skip to creating forms or reports. Keep in mind, however, that Quick Starts 2 and 3 are designed to use the database you create in Quick Start 1.

Using R:BASE describes how to use R:BASE through the menu system with brief excursions into command language. In addition, Appendix C lists all R:BASE commands, with brief explanations on how to use them.

Each chapter starts with an introduction and explanation of the R:BASE feature, tells you how to start the module or utility, supplies detailed explanations of how to use each feature, and finishes with a summary of what you have learned.

Part I

Using R:BASE
To Build a Database

Includes

Defining a Database Structure

Introducing R:BASE

Designing a Database

Using the Database Definition Module

Quick Start 1:
Defining a
Database Structure

In this quick start, you learn how to start R:BASE, access commands, and get help. Later, you define the mailing list database structure. Appendix D contains a complete description of this database, in case you need to make modifications to the structure as you go along.

You define the following tables in this chapter:

- *Mail_list:* The main table containing the mailing list names and addresses.

- *Codes_mail:* A lookup table containing the valid mailing codes and their descriptions.

- *When_mailed:* A table containing names of persons to whom the mailing is sent, the type of mailing (based on a mail code), and the date of the mailing.

A *table* is the structure that divides the data stored in a database. A table holds information about one topic. The basic information about a customer, for example, could be in a table. A *column* is the way you divide all the information about each item in the table into logical parts. The customer table may have columns defined for the name, address, city, state, ZIP code, and phone, for example.

You also will set up a few entry rules to ensure that the data entered is valid. You will designate a column to be numbered automatically by the system when new rows are added.

If you have not done so, install R:BASE on your computer's hard disk or on the server of a local area network to which your computer is connected. See Appendix A in this book or the R:BASE documentation Installation Guide for instructions.

Starting R:BASE

To begin, create a new directory for your sample database. Most people like to keep their databases in a special directory for easier organization. You can store all your databases, for example, on a single directory named DATABASE. To create the sample database, follow these steps:

1. At the DOS prompt, type *mkdir samples* and press Enter. If you already have a directory with this name, choose a different name for the sample directory.

2. Make the SAMPLES directory the current directory. Type *chdir samples* and press Enter.

3. To start R:BASE, type *rbase* and press Enter.

R:BASE displays its main menu, which is a bar menu. The Databases option is highlighted.

You choose bar menu options by moving the cursor to options on the menu bar and then highlighting the option you want to use on the pull-down menus. You move the cursor to a bar option in any of these ways:

• Press a direction key (an arrow key or Tab) to move to the option you want.

• Use a mouse to move the cursor to the option you want.

• Press Alt and the first character of the menu option. To move the cursor to the Reports option, for example, you press Alt and R at the same time. A key combination such as this is shown as Alt-R in this book. If more than one option starts with the same letter, R:BASE highlights the next option beginning with that letter.

To practice displaying a menu, follow these steps:

1. Press Alt-I to highlight the Info option.

2. Press Tab four times to highlight the Applications option.

After you highlight a bar menu option, a pull-down menu appears with the first option highlighted. After you highlight a menu option, a description of the general use for the bar menu option appears at the bottom left of the screen and a description of the pull-down menu option appears at the bottom right of the screen.

If you change your mind about using an option, press Esc to abort the procedure.

Using On-Line Help

On-line help is available everywhere in R:BASE. To get help on the task you are performing, press F1. To practice using help, follow these steps:

1. Highlight the Databases option.

2. Press F1.

   R:BASE displays information about the highlighted option. Figure QS1.1 shows you this Help screen.

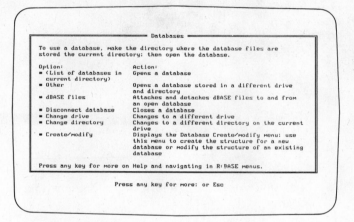

Fig. QS1.1

On-line help.

3. Press Esc to leave Help.

4. Press Shift-F1 to get another kind of help—a list of the function keys you can use while performing the current task (see fig. QS1.2).

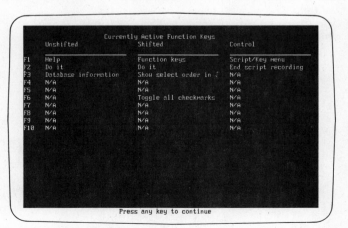

Fig. QS1.2

On-line help for the function keys.

5. Press Esc to leave the Function Key list.

Defining a New Database

To define the new database, follow these steps:

1. To start the Database Definition module, choose Create/Modify from the Databases pull-down menu, as shown in figure QS1.3.

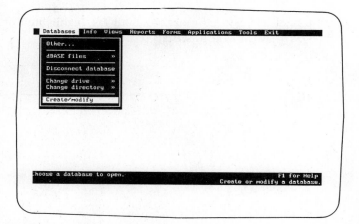

Fig. QS1.3

Choosing the Create/Modify option.

R:BASE displays the Database Definition main menu, as shown in figure QS1.4.

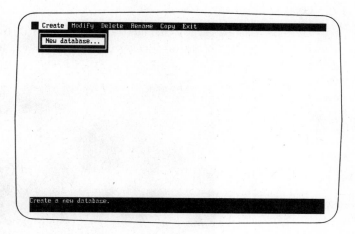

Fig. QS1.4

The Database Definition main menu.

You create a new database by adding the first table to the database. A *table* is a structure within a database used to divide the individual pieces of data into separate columns. Columns make handling data easier by giving parts of the data names and definitions of the type of data that will be contained in the database.

2. Choose New Database and press Enter to create a new database.

   R:BASE prompts you for the database name (see fig. QS1.5).

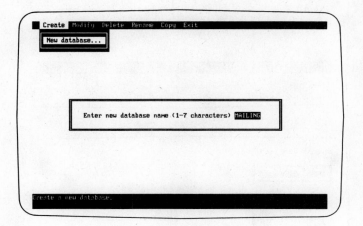

Fig. QS1.5
Naming a database.

3. Type *mailing* as the database name and press Enter.

Defining a Table Structure

After you type the database name, R:BASE immediately displays the Database Building menu (see fig. QS1.6). You use the Database Building menu to create a new table, modify the structure of an existing table, delete a table, rename a table, or copy a table. In this section, you define a new table—the first table in your new database.

To define the first table, follow these steps:

1. Choose Create from the Tables pull-down menu.

   R:BASE displays an empty Table Definition screen (see fig. QS1.7).

   This screen provides a table template, which is like a form you fill out. You fill in the names of the table and columns, and you tell R:BASE which type of data each column will hold.

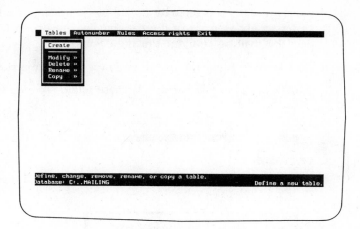

Fig. QS1.6

The Database Building menu.

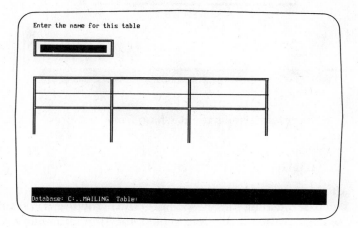

Fig. QS1.7

The Table Definition screen.

2. Type *Mail_list* in the table name box at the top of the screen and press Enter. Notice that you can use an underscore character in a table name.

   R:BASE prompts you for a description of the table.

3. Type *Mailing list master table* as the description and press Enter.

   R:BASE places the cursor in the first column name box.

4. Type *Idno* for the first column name and press Enter. This identification number column makes each row unique, serving as a good column for indexed searches. You find out more about indexing in Chapter 3.

   R:BASE prompts you for a description for this column.

5. Type *Id Number–Autonumber column* as the description and press Enter. You find out about Autonumber columns in Chapter 3.

   R:BASE displays a list of data types, which tells R:BASE what kind of data will be entered into each column (see fig. QS1.8). In this case, the ID number should be an integer (whole number) so that R:BASE can number the column for you. You can define the column for currency, dates, times, text, or one of the numeric types (decimal, double-precision decimal, or integer). Assign a data type that describes the data that will be contained under the column heading. For a name or address, for example, use a TEXT data type. Chapters 2 and 3 describe data types in more detail.

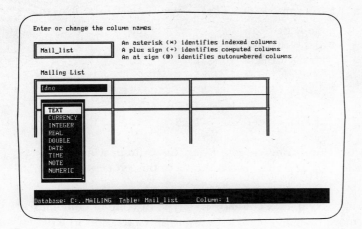

Fig. QS1.8
The Data Type list.

6. Choose Integer from the list of data types. To do this, press I to move the highlight to Integer and then press Enter to select it.

   R:BASE asks whether you want to make this column an indexed column. An index to a column is like a cross-reference in a library card file. An *indexed column* enables R:BASE to find the data quickly because the index marker describes the location of the data. This column should be indexed because it is the key to the data for each person added to the database.

7. Press Y and then Enter to make this column an indexed column.

   R:BASE places the cursor in the second column name box.

8. Type *Firstname* for the second column's name.

9. Type *Customer's First Name* for the second column's description.

10. Choose Text as the data type.

    For Text columns, you can set a maximum length for the data.

11. Type *30* for the column length and press Enter.

12. Highlight No and press Enter when you are prompted for Indexing. Because this column probably will not contain unique data, you should not define it as indexed.

    R:BASE moves the highlight to the third column name box. You can now define more of the columns in this table. Use the same techniques you learned so far. Define the columns as shown in the following list:

Column Name	Description	Data Type	Length	Indexed?
Lastname	Last Name	TEXT	30	N
Middleinit	Middle Initial	TEXT	2	N
Address1	Address Line 1	TEXT	25	N
Address2	Address Line 2	TEXT	25	N
City	City	TEXT	15	N
State	State	TEXT	2	N
Zipcode	ZIP Code	TEXT	10	N

R:BASE highlights the 10th name column box. This column will be a little different from the rest, so you may want to review this process step-by-step.

You will be creating a computed column. This type of column combines data from one or more defined columns by using an expression to tell R:BASE how to calculate the data. A *computed column* never holds data; its value is recalculated each time data in any of the columns used in the expression changes value. A common use of a computed column is to string together several text columns so that the data appears as if it were a single piece of data. In Chapter 2, you will learn that you should have only one piece of data (one address line, the city name only, and so on) in each column. A computed column combining several text columns is useful to pull together these separate pieces of data visually. You also can define computed columns to make arithmetic or mathematical calculations. You will learn how to do this in Chapter 3.

For this database, you will define the simplest type of computed column: a text-combining (concatenation) expression. To define the column, follow these steps:

1. Type *CSZ_line* for the column name.

2. Type *Complete City, State, ZIP* for the column description.

When you display this column, you want the result of a calculation to show.

3. For the data type, press PgDn to move the cursor past the bottom of the list until you see COMPUTED. Choose this for the column type.

    R:BASE asks for the expression for this computed column (see fig. QS1.9).

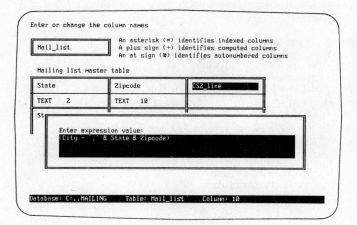

```
Enter or change the column names

                      An asterisk (*) identifies indexed columns
  Mail_list           A plus sign (+) identifies computed columns
                      An at sign (@) identifies autonumbered columns

  Mailing list master table

  State              Zipcode           CSZ_line

  TEXT    2          TEXT    10

  St
      Enter expression value:
      (City + ',' & State & Zipcode)




Database: C:..MAILING     Table: Mail_list     Column: 10
```

Fig. QS1.9

Defining a computed column.

4. Type *(City + ',' & State & Zipcode)* in the dialog box and press Enter.

    R:BASE knows that this expression will be text because you have included three columns that are defined already as TEXT columns.

5. Type *30* and press Enter when R:BASE asks for the length. This number is the total length of the three columns used in the expression plus two characters for spaces and one character for a comma.

    This column does not hold data. Instead, the column shows the result of the expression used to define it. In this case, the expression strings together the city, state, and ZIP code as a single piece of data and inserts a comma between the city and state. With this computed column definition, you can use the column on labels without having to link the separate parts again. You also may define a computed column linking the first name, middle initial, and last name in the same way. See Chapter 3 for more on the uses of computed columns.

6. After you enter the last column definition, press the F2 function key to end the table definition and save the database definition. R:BASE returns you to the Database Building menu.

Defining an Autonumber Column

Rather than having to remember what the next available ID number is, you can define the Idno column in the Mail_list table as an autonumber column. To do so, follow these steps:

1. Highlight the Autonumber option.

   You have three options: Create, Modify, and Delete.

   R:BASE displays the list of tables defined in this database (see fig. QS1.10). For now, Mail_list is the only defined table.

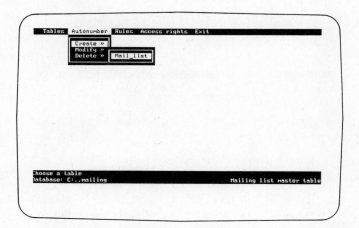

Fig. QS1.10

Choosing a table for auto-numbering.

2. Press Enter to choose Create.

3. Press Enter to choose the Mail_list table.

   R:BASE displays a list of the columns defined for the Mail_list table.

4. Choose Idno.

   R:BASE displays a dialog box asking for the autonumbering parameters, as shown in figure QS1.11.

5. Press 1 to enter the initial value and press Enter. Press 1 to enter the increment and press Enter.

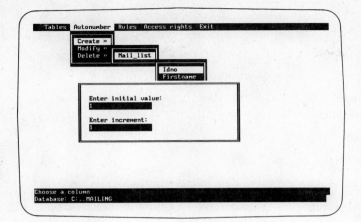

Fig. QS1.11

Defining an autonumber column.

R:BASE returns you to the Database Building menu. You have completed the definition for one table in the database.

Tip: As you define and modify tables, R:BASE moves the tables in its internal list. Your own table list may be in a different order each time you perform some action on the database. This change does not make any difference to R:BASE, but be sure that you read the table name before choosing the table to ensure that you are accessing the table you want.

Stay in the Database Building menu so that you can create more tables for this database. You use the Tables option to create the additional tables.

Completing the Database Structure

You now have added one table to your new database. However, a database by definition is a set of related tables, so now you should complete this database by adding the other two tables. Enter the following table definitions in the same way you defined the Mail_list table. The database described here will be used in examples in the next few chapters, so you should complete the database structure to follow along.

To add a table to the database, highlight Tables on the Tables menu and choose Create. The second table, Codes_mail, provides a description for each mailing type code:

```
Table Name: Codes_mail

Description: Mailing type codes and descriptions
```

```
Column Definitions:

Column Name     Description                  Data Type   Length Indexed?

Mailcode        Mailing Type Code            TEXT        2      Y
Maildesc        Mailing Code Description     TEXT        40     N
```

The third table, When_mailed, shows to whom a letter was sent, what letter was sent, and when the letter was sent:

```
Table Name: When_mailed

Description: Mailings by Id Number

Column Definitions:

Column Name     Description     Data Type    Length      Indexed?

Idno                                                     Y
Mailcode                                                 Y
Maildate        Date Mailed     DATE                     N
```

You do not enter descriptions or choose data types for the Idno and Mailcode columns in the last table because these columns have already been defined in previous tables. If you enter a description in a second table containing a previously defined column, the second description replaces the description you entered on the first table. R:BASE will not allow you to change the data type.

Linking tables by using a common column is part of developing a relational database. The easiest way to link is by giving each table a column with the same name, which is how linking was done here. R:BASE can, however, recognize links between tables using columns with different names if the data types are the same. That is, you can link a Text column with another table's Text column, but you cannot link a Text column to a Date column. See Chapter 5 for more information.

Defining Data Entry Rules

Now that all the tables are defined, you can create some data entry rules to ensure that your tables link properly. In this section, you define a data entry rule to require that the indexed column (Idno) always has a unique value. You learn more about defining rules in Chapter 3.

1. Return to the Database Building menu and highlight Rules.

   R:BASE displays a list of the rule options. You can create new rules, modify existing rules, delete rules, or list defined rules.

2. Choose Create.

   R:BASE displays a list of the types of rules you can define in the
   Database Definition module. Three standard rules and an option to
   define custom rules exist. Because you want to make sure that the
   ID numbers are always unique, you use the second rule in the list.

3. Choose Require a Unique Value.

   R:BASE displays a list of the tables in the database.

4. Choose Mail_list.

   R:BASE displays a list of the columns in the table Mail_list, as shown
   in figure QS1.12.

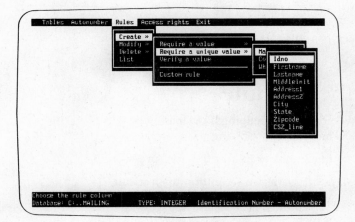

Fig. QS1.12

*Defining a
standard rule
requiring that
a unique
value be
entered for a
column.*

5. Choose Idno.

   R:BASE creates a rule with two requirements. The first requirement
   is that you must enter all ID numbers (this is an autonumber
   column), and the second requirement is that all ID numbers must be
   unique.

   Now list the rules to see what the rule looks like after it is defined.
   If you choose to create a custom rule, you need to enter your own
   rule definition in the same format.

6. Choose List. Figure QS1.13 shows you what the defined rules should
   look like.

```
( RULES   ) ON  Check data validation RULES
MESSAGE :  Value for Idno must be unique.
  TABLE :  Mail_list    Row is added or changed if condition SUCCEEDS
  WHERE :  Idno IS NOT NULL AND Idno NOT IN ( SELECT Idno FROM Mail_list )

Press any key to continue_
```

7. Press any key to return to the Database Building menu.

Leaving the Module

Now that you have completed defining a database, you can leave the Database Definition module by following these steps:

1. Press Alt-E to highlight the Exit option and press Enter.

   R:BASE displays the Database Definition main menu.

2. Press Alt-E again to highlight the Exit option on the Database Definition main menu.

3. Press Enter.

   R:BASE returns you to the main menu.

4. If you want to leave R:BASE, press Alt-E to display the Exit option's pull-down menu.

   The Exit pull-down menu has two options: Leave R:BASE and R> Prompt.

5. Press Enter to choose Leave R:BASE.

   R:BASE closes the database and returns you to the DOS prompt.

Summary

In this quick start, you learned how to use the R:BASE menus and how to get on-line help. You also completed the Database Definition tutorial. The rest of Part I describes how to create a good database design and how to implement that design in R:BASE.

1

Introducing R:BASE

R:BASE is a relational database management system. A *relational database* enables you to store and access groups of related data items stored separately in files or tables. A relational database is similar to a file cabinet. Different sets of files containing similar information are stored in separate files. Each set of files makes up a single database topic. These topics may relate to each other. A file containing basic customer data (name and address), for example, may relate to a file containing records of sales for the same customer. A relational database enables you to store the data separately, as you do in a file cabinet, but a relational database also enables you to bring together quickly the related information for viewing, manipulation, or editing.

You probably have some idea of what you want to use R:BASE for. Usually, people buy a database management system to store sets of related data and then use the management capabilities of the system to correlate the parts of the data into a meaningful form.

R:BASE is a superb database management system that is easy to use and powerful enough to meet the needs of any data storage and retrieval requirements. This book shows you how to use R:BASE's power through its *user interface*—a series of interrelated menus that provide all the tools necessary to create a database structure, enter data, and look at the data in a meaningful format.

After you become proficient with the R:BASE menu system, you will want to delve into the R:BASE command language. The R:BASE language is a combination of ANSI-standard Structured Query Language and a unique collection of programming, relational, environment, and data-manipulation commands. The purpose and use of these commands is described throughout this book. Appendix C briefly describes all commands.

This chapter provides an overview of the R:BASE features, system menus, and modules.

Reviewing the R:BASE Modules

R:BASE provides a single, cohesive set of menus, which you can think of as being individual modules. When you choose a menu option or type a command that starts a module, you remain in that module until you exit it. All modules have easy-to-find exit options.

R:BASE has the following modules, which you use constantly when working with your database:

- Databases
- Info
- Views
- Forms
- Reports
- Applications

These modules are described in the following sections.

Databases

Before you can do anything else, you need to define a structure to hold your data. This procedure is similar to setting up a series of file folders to hold different types of papers. At home, for example, you may have one file folder for receipts, one for bills, and one for product information on what you purchased. Together, these folders form a database of information on purchases.

The concept behind a computerized database is the same as a file folder system except that a database system, such as R:BASE, gives you the capability to look at the bill, the receipt, and the product information at the same time. This capacity is why R:BASE is called a relational database system—it forms relationships between separate sets of data. You can attach a dBASE file to your R:BASE database, giving you direct access to dBASE without importing or converting the data.

The Database Definition (Create/Modify) module enables you to create or modify a database structure, define rules for data entry, and assign passwords. See Chapter 3 for information on the Database Definition module.

Information

After you create a database, you want to enter the data and change the data as needed. R:BASE provides a default Edit screen. On this screen, the data that already exists is displayed for you to edit, or you can add new data by pressing a single key. The Info module presents data in a default tabular format for editing. See Chapter 4 for information on the Info module.

Views

Query By Example (the Views module) provides a quick method of requesting information from one or more sets of data. Views enables you to define special relationships between sets of data so that you can look at two sets at the same time (receipts and bills, for example). The Views module defines the information you want to look at or edit. See Chapter 5 for information on the Views module.

Forms

Although R:BASE offers a default data entry format through the Info module, you may want to customize the screen. You can create data entry forms that enable you to enter or edit data in as many as five separate sets of related data. The Forms module creates customized data entry forms.

Customized forms enable you to edit or enter data in as many as five database tables in one data-entry session. Further, a customized form gives you more leeway in ways to present data than does Info. With a customized form, you can display data without allowing the user to change it, customize screen colors, and even execute R:BASE commands directly from a form. These options are only a few of the features available with a customized form. You learn more about the power of a custom form in Chapter 6.

Reports

R:BASE displays data through the Info module, but you probably will need to create a customized output format. You can create customized reports that enable you to group data and calculate totals on the groups. The Reports module creates customized output formats.

Customized reports are especially useful for creating attractive and meaningful presentations. With a customized report, you can present your information in different styles to emphasize data. You can group and manipulate data, providing subtotals and grand totals, customize headings or cover pages, and even draw lines and boxes to make the format more attractive. See Chapter 7 for information on the Reports module.

Applications

Applications are customized menus and programs that operate on your database data and structure. Applications are useful especially if you are creating a database for someone else to use. An application structures how the data should be processed. From an application, you can use customized forms, reports, or programs that you write. The Applications module creates a set of menus and options for database access.

Applications are useful particularly when you want to control what another user can do in your database. By providing menu options that determine how the data can be manipulated, you control exactly what can be done and by whom. See Chapter 8 for information on the Applications module.

Getting Started

When you get your R:BASE system package, you first need to install R:BASE on your computer's hard disk. R:BASE operates only when installed on a stand-alone computer's hard disk or on a local area network's server drive. Appendix A provides system requirements and installation instructions.

When you start R:BASE, the R:BASE main menu appears automatically, unless you change the way the program starts when you enter the RBASE command at the DOS prompt. You can start the system at the R:BASE menu system, at the R> prompt, or from an application's main menu.

To start R:BASE at the R:BASE main menu, type

  RBASE

To start R:BASE at the R> prompt (Command mode), type

  RBASE -C

To start R:BASE and immediately execute the commands contained in the start-up file, type

  RBASE *cmdfile*

Start-up files (represented by *cmdfile*) are small R:BASE programs (called Command files) that contain one or more R:BASE commands. For the most

part, you do not need to know the commands to use R:BASE effectively.
You can define your database and create forms, reports, and applications
without ever typing a command. R:BASE has available a powerful set of
programming commands, however, which you will find useful as you
become more comfortable with the product.

A start-up file may contain commands to modify the R:BASE environment
for a particular database use, to execute another command file, or to start
an application. Application Express (the R:BASE application-building
module) creates custom start-up files for specific applications. You can
create your own start-up files. For more information on start-up files and
applications, see Chapter 8.

You also have these additional start-up options:

- *-B:*   Sets the start-up background color
- *-F:*   Sets the start-up foreground color
- *-P:*   Starts R:BASE in the default interface—the R:BASE main menu
  or Prompt By Example
- *-R:*   Suppresses display of the R:BASE logo
- *-T:*   Sets the terminal type if other than IBM
- *-M:*   Sets the monitor type (graphics) if other than IBM
- *-V:*   Defines high-level (over 640K) memory for use as a virtual disk

See Appendix A for a detailed description of each start-up option, a table of
available colors, and other information on installing and starting R:BASE.

You can combine these options by entering one after the other, separated
by spaces. The following command, for example, starts R:BASE in
Command mode and changes the default colors to black on red (the
R:BASE default colors are white on blue):

    R:BASE -C -F0 -B4

Notice that you use the number codes for the colors. These codes are
standard color codes for IBM color computers.

Using the Menu Systems

You can get to any module by at least three ways: the R:BASE main menu,
Prompt By Example, or Command mode. This book uses the R:BASE main
menu for the most part, with additional examples using Prompt By
Example and Command mode.

R:BASE provides two menu systems. The main menu is oriented to using the R:BASE modules and utilities. Prompt By Example is oriented to command structures.

Using the R:BASE Main Menu

The R:BASE main menu appears after you start R:BASE, unless you enter a start-up option to prevent the menu from appearing. Figure 1.1 shows the main menu.

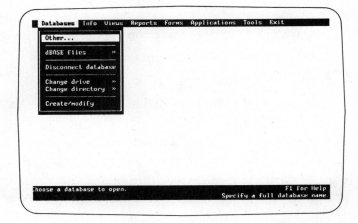

Fig. 1.1

The R:BASE main menu.

Notice that the Databases pull-down menu is displayed already. When you start R:BASE, it knows that you first need to tell it which database to use, so the program displays this menu.

Each main menu option leads to one of the following modules or utilities:

- *Databases:* Provides access to a database or a dBASE file, enables you to change to another drive or directory, or leads to the Database Definition module.

- *Info:* Leads to the default data entry and edit module (Info).

- *Query:* Leads to the Query Definition module (Views).

- *Reports:* Prints a custom report or leads to the Reports module.

- *Forms:* Starts a custom data entry form or leads to the Forms module.

- *Applications:* Executes a custom application or leads to the Applications module.

- *Tools:* Leads to a set of utilities useful for managing your database files.

You will use most of the R:BASE main menu options in the quick start sections of this book. Throughout the book, you will see instructions such as "Highlight the Views option," or "Choose the Create/Modify option." These instructions refer to how you use the menu.

You highlight menu options in any of these ways:

- Use the cursor-movement keys (remember to be sure that NumLock is not turned on), or use the Tab key to move the highlight to the option you want.

- Use a mouse to move the cursor to an option, and then press the left mouse button to highlight the option.

- Press the Alt key and the first character of a menu option's wording. Press Alt and V (Alt-V) to highlight the Views option on the R:BASE main menu, for example.

When you highlight an option, you move the cursor to the menu option. A highlighted option can be a pull-down menu option or a selection option.

After you highlight one of the menu options from the pull-down main menu, a menu immediately appears below the option, and the cursor (or highlight) is placed on an option in the pull-down list. The option highlighted on the pull-down list will be the first option on the list, or if you used an option previously in the session, that option will be highlighted.

Your selection will not execute until you press Enter. In this book, to choose an option means to move the cursor to highlight the option and then press Enter to select it.

After you choose an option, one of three things happens:

- The option executes immediately and does whatever it is supposed to do.

- The option displays a pop-up menu with further choices. Options that display a pop-up menu have a » next to them.

- The option displays a dialog box for entry of required information. Options that display a box have an ellipsis (. . .) next to them.

This general rule for menu displays has two exceptions:

- Listed database objects, such as forms, reports, or tables, do not execute like an option; they are selected as a part of the overall command you are executing.

- A dialog box can have a pop-up menu containing a list, (for example, of database objects). You can select a database object to insert into the dialog box prompt field rather than typing the object name.

Figure 1.2 shows the pop-up menu for the Disk Management option on the Tools menu, and figure 1.3 shows a dialog box for the Change Directory option.

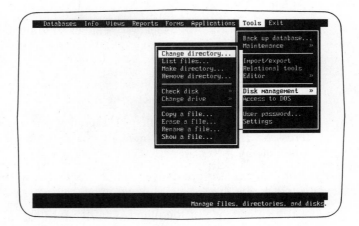

Fig. 1.2

An R:BASE pop-up menu.

The pop-up menu in figure 1.2 displays the options for managing your drives and directories while in R:BASE. Most of these options relate to DOS commands: commands you can enter at the DOS prompt to create or change directories, copy DOS files, list files, and so on. If R:BASE doesn't have room on-screen for a pop-up menu to appear to the right of a menu, the program displays the pop-up menus to the left.

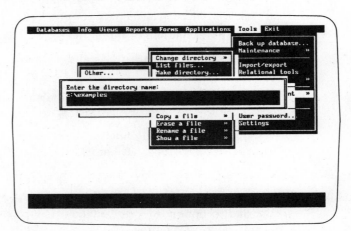

Fig. 1.3

An R:BASE dialog box.

The dialog box in figure 1.3 is a typical dialog box in R:BASE. In this example, a single entry is requested—the name of a directory to make the current directory. Dialog boxes in R:BASE can have multiple entry fields. Sometimes you type information as shown in figure 1.3, or occasionally R:BASE displays a pop-up menu from which you can select the item to be entered in the dialog box field.

Using the Keyboard in R:BASE

Regardless of where you are in R:BASE, the function keys operate identically in every module. Pressing F1, for example, always gives you on-line, contextual help. Table 1.1 lists the R:BASE function keys that operate in the same way, regardless of where you are in R:BASE.

Table 1.1
R:BASE Function Keys

Key	Effect
F1	Obtains on-line help.
Shift-F1	Displays the function keys you can use in the current context.
Ctrl-F1	Displays the Script/Key menu. This menu contains options for recording a series of keystrokes (called a script), defining a special use for a key (called a key map), or taking a snapshot of the screen displayed.
F2	Executes the action.
Ctrl-F2	Ends a script or key-map recording.
F3	Displays the Database Information menu. This menu contains options for selecting tables, columns, forms, or reports.

Each chapter in this book has a table of the function keys used in each specific module. R:BASE uses all function keys in addition to function keys combined with the Shift or Ctrl keys. The Alt key combined with a function key is available for your own key definition. See Appendix B for information on defining your own function keys.

Using Prompt By Example

Prompt By Example (PBE) is the R:BASE command-builder. It provides a stepping stone to learning R:BASE commands by prompting for parts of the command and showing the actual command syntax on-screen as the command is built.

Start PBE from Command mode by typing *prompt* at the Command mode R> prompt in R:BASE. You get to Command mode by pressing Alt-E to highlight Exit and then choosing R> Prompt from the pull-down menu.

After you start PBE, the Prompt By Example main menu appears (see fig. 1.4). You can work through the PBE menus to get to the command you want to build and execute. Each main menu option leads to a series of one or more submenus.

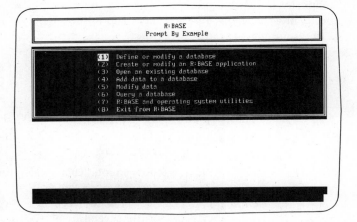

Fig. 1.4

The Prompt By Example main menu.

Suppose that you want to use PBE to build a command to edit data. The following steps show you how to use PBE with the database you will be creating in later chapters. You may want to return to this section after you create your database to go through these steps. For now, read the steps and follow the discussion.

In the following steps, you use Prompt By Example to create an Edit command. You tell R:BASE the table and columns to edit and the order in which you want to see the rows (sorting). You also limit the rows to edit to only those with *Chicago* in the City column.

1. First, start Prompt By Example by typing

   PROMPT EDIT

   Because you ask for a specific command's prompt screen, R:BASE immediately displays the Edit Prompt screen (see fig. 1.5). On this screen you select, in order, the parts of the command line that need to be filled in: the table, columns, and so on. (*Prompt* means that R:BASE displays a menu or dialog box requesting information needed to complete the command line.)

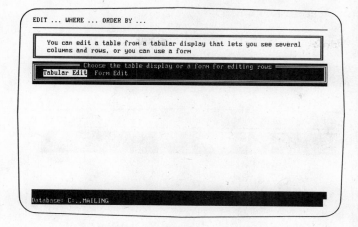

Fig. 1.5

Choosing to edit table data by using the default format or a form.

You can use the Edit command in three ways:

- To edit table data by using the default Tabular Edit screen
- To edit table data by using a customized form
- To edit variable data by using a Variable-Only form

2. Highlight Tabular Edit and press Enter to select it.

When you use the tabular format, you have a choice of displaying all rows or only unique rows (that meet conditions you set later). Figure 1.6 shows how PBE asks whether you want to edit only unique data or all data, even if duplicated.

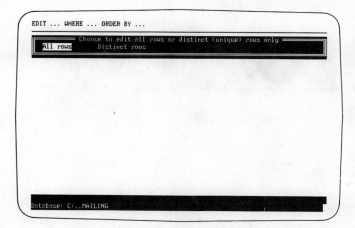

Fig. 1.6

Choosing to edit all rows or only unique rows in a table.

3. Press Enter to select All Rows.

   Prompt By Example displays a list of tables. Figure 1.7 shows you
   how PBE asks for the name of the table (set of data). As you
   highlight each table name, PBE displays any description entered for
   that table at the bottom of the screen.

Fig. 1.7

*Choosing the
table
containing the
data you want
to edit.*

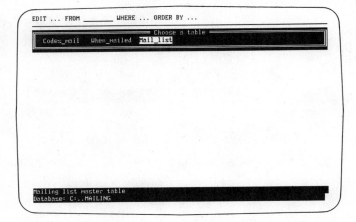

4. Highlight Mail_list and press Enter to select it.

   R:BASE displays a list of all the items stored in this table. Figure 1.8
   shows you how PBE asks for the names of the columns you want to
   edit. The descriptions of the columns that appear on the bottom of
   the screen help you determine which columns you want. You can
   select only a few columns or all the columns.

Fig. 1.8

*Selecting one
or more
columns that
identify the
specific pieces
of data to
edit.*

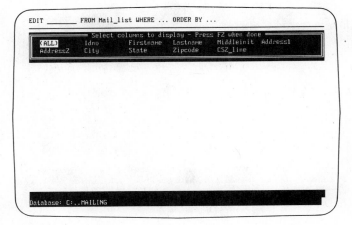

5. Press Enter to select (All) for all columns in the table.

   R:BASE now shows the Condition-Building screen. You now must choose a column with data to be tested.

6. Highlight City and press Enter to select it.

   Immediately after you select the column to test, R:BASE displays a list of comparison operators (see fig. 1.9). Comparison operators describe to R:BASE the type of test you want to make. If you choose the = EQUAL operator, for example, you are telling R:BASE that the data in the column you selected (City, in this example) must be equal to the value you will enter later. Because you will enter the city *Chicago*, R:BASE will enable you to edit only the rows where the City column contains the value *Chicago*. When you are comparing text values, you always must enclose the value in single quotation marks; otherwise, R:BASE assumes that the value is another column name—not a literal value. In other words, if *Chicago* is not enclosed in single quotation marks, R:BASE looks for a column named Chicago rather than looking at the data values in the City column.

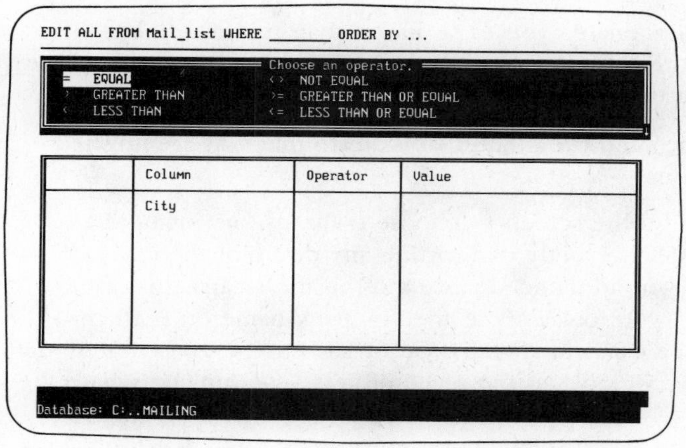

Fig. 1.9

Using comparison operators to compare the value of existing data to a value you enter.

The next three steps complete the condition. When you are finished (step 9), R:BASE displays the created condition following the word *WHERE* in the command line at the top of the screen. For more information on the condition builder, see "Using the Condition Builder," later in this chapter.

7. Press Enter to select = EQUAL from the comparison operator list.

8. Type the comparison value *'Chicago'* when the cursor is in the value box.

   R:BASE displays a list of connecting operators: AND, OR, AND NOT, and OR NOT (see fig. 1.10).

Fig. 1.10

Using connecting operators to specify several conditions for the comparison of data.

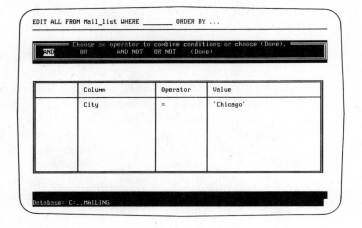

These connectors enable you to set more than one condition. In addition to limiting the people to just those in Chicago, for example, you also may want to limit the data in a second or third way.

9. Highlight (Done) and press Enter to indicate that you are finished setting conditions.

   Figure 1.11 shows the screen to choose columns for sorting data. Sorting in R:BASE is exactly like sorting any data alphabetically or numerically. If you are handed a stack of business cards to sort by company name, you look only at the company name on each card and then put the cards in alphabetical order. R:BASE does exactly the same thing. R:BASE looks at the piece of data (column) by which the program is asked to sort and puts the rows in order according to that piece of data. With R:BASE, you not only can ask that the data in a column be sorted; you also can instruct R:BASE to sort in ascending or descending order. Ascending is normal order (A, B, C, or 1, 2, 3, and so on). Descending is the reverse order (Z, Y, X; 10, 9, 8). See "Sorting Data," later in this chapter for additional information.

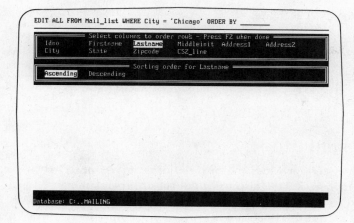

Fig. 1.11

Choosing a column containing the data to sort and the order of sorting— Ascending or Descending.

10. Highlight Lastname and press Enter.

    R:BASE asks for the sorting order—Ascending or Descending.

11. Press Enter to choose the sorting order—in this case, Ascending.

12. Press F2 to indicate that you are finished with sorting.

    Finally, figure 1.12 shows you the completed command and the Prompt By Example execution menu. The menu provides options for executing and editing the command, returning to the first command-building prompt, displaying help about the command, or exiting from command building without doing anything else.

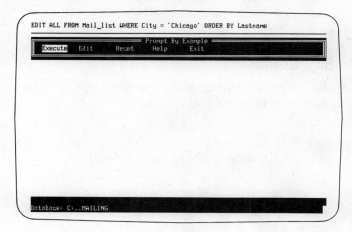

Fig. 1.12

Prompt By Example builds the command syntax for you and displays it at the top of the screen.

13. Press Enter to select Execute.

R:BASE executes the command and takes you to the Info module. To find out more about editing data using Info, refer to Chapter 4.

```
Command: PROMPT
```

Using Command Mode

Although the menu system provides the majority of what you need to create and use a database, R:BASE also has a full set of programming commands that add to the already powerful R:BASE capabilities. R:BASE Command mode is the third R:BASE mode. This mode is the power user's area because you need to know how to use R:BASE commands to operate in Command mode.

Command mode is identified by an R> prompt at the left side of the screen. From this prompt, you can use any of the more than 120 R:BASE commands. Many command functions are duplicated in the menu structure, so you may not need to use many of the commands in Command mode. To exit from Command mode, type *menu* and press Enter. To get to PBE from Command mode, type *prompt* and press Enter.

You also use commands when you write R:BASE programs (called Command files). R:BASE's programming commands provide all the programming power available in such high-level languages as BASIC. With the addition of the imposed structure intrinsic to a database system, the overall R:BASE programming capability can be as powerful as fourth-generation languages such as Pascal or C.

Entering and Editing Commands

You enter command lines by typing them at the R> prompt. You can edit a command line as you are entering it, or you can go back to edit it after you enter the entire command.

R:BASE provides you with the editing capability when you are entering commands in Command mode. Command editing has the following features:

- *Backing up:* You can back up through an entered command by using the Backspace or left-arrow key. Backspace deletes characters to the left, and the left arrow moves over characters without erasing.

- *Inserting:* You can insert characters at the current cursor position after you toggle Insert to the Insert mode (the cursor character is a block). To overwrite characters, press the Ins key to overwrite (the cursor character is an underscore).

- *Deleting:* You can delete characters by backspacing over them (this technique leaves extra blanks in the command, but R:BASE doesn't care about this), or you can press Del to delete the character at the cursor.

- *Recalling a command:* Use the following keys to bring back a previously entered command:

Key	Effect
→	Recalls the characters from left to right, one character at a time.
Ctrl-→	Recalls the entire command line.
Tab	Recalls the last 10 characters of a command for each time you press Tab.
PgUp	Recalls the last command line. You can page backward through the last 2,000 characters (approximately 26 single-line commands).
PgDn	Recalls the next command line if you paged up previously.
Home	Returns to the first character of the command displayed.

The editing keys are useful if you make an error when entering a command line. You can recall the command; move the cursor to the area that needs correction; type over, insert, or delete characters; and then execute the command again.

When you enter R:BASE commands that are longer than one line (75 characters), R:BASE automatically wraps the command line for you and inserts the continuation character (+ is the default) at the end of each line. If a command is longer than 75 characters, you need to have the continuation character at the end of the line. You can enter the character or let R:BASE enter it for you.

Enclose in single quotation marks any text strings embedded in a command.

Understanding R:BASE Command Syntax

Having the command syntax diagram in front of you is usually helpful when you start using R:BASE commands (see Appendix C). Figure 1.13 shows the format of syntax diagrams.

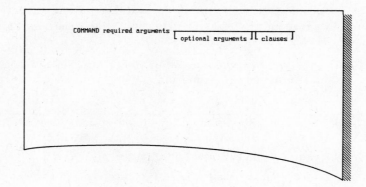

```
COMMAND required arguments ┌──────────────────┐┌─────────┐
                           └ optional arguments ┘└ clauses ┘
```

Fig. 1.13

R:BASE syntax diagrams provide the basic format of a command.

You always read syntax diagrams from left to right. The items on the main line of the diagram are always required. Items that are offset below the command are optional.

Because R:BASE is not case-sensitive, you can use any variation of upper- and lowercase letters. You can type a simple command in any of the following ways, for example:

    EDIT USING formname
    edit using formname
    EDIT using FORMNAME
    EdIt UsInG fOrMnAmE

The term *keyword* in this book refers to the words that are in R:BASE's vocabulary—that is, command names (for example, EDIT, SELECT, PROMPT). Keywords also can be words that tell R:BASE that something special is following, such as WHERE (a condition follows), ORDER BY (a list of sort columns follows), or USING (a list of columns follows).

In the syntax diagram in figure 1.13, COMMAND stands for the R:BASE command. R:BASE commands can be abbreviated to the first three or four unique characters. Three characters are sufficient for most commands (EDI for EDIT, INT for INTERSECT). If the first three characters are not unique, you must add a fourth character (PROM for PROMPT, PROJ for PROJECT).

Required arguments are parts of the command that you must enter. Most commands require the name of a database object—for example, table, form, and report. You also may need to enter some identifying keyword—for example, USING or FROM. The syntax diagram shows you what the keywords must be. You also can abbreviate keywords to three characters.

Optional arguments are parts of the command that you can enter but are not required for to the command to execute. Again, you may indicate a keyword. Optional arguments often are similar to required arguments; the requirement depends on the command syntax.

Clauses are modifiers for the command. The three R:BASE clauses are WHERE, ORDER BY, and SELECT. *WHERE* sets conditions that must be met before the command will act on the database. *ORDER BY* sorts the data output of the command. *SELECT* draws data from another area of the database for the command to use.

This standard format varies for some commands, as shown in figure 1.14. This structure means that you can take one of two paths—top or bottom—but one of them is required.

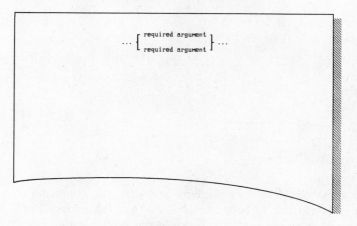

Fig. 1.14

Multiple-path diagrams give you a choice of two or more ways to use the command.

This type of path is similar to having two ways to get to the same place. If you want to go to work, for example, you may have more than one route. You need to determine which route is better. During rush hour, you may want to take the residential streets (everyone else is on the freeway); in the evening, the freeway is a better choice. The point is, you *must* take one route or the other; you cannot fly or teleport—you must drive. When a syntax diagram gives you a multiple choice as shown in figure 1.14, you must use one of the routes, but you do have a choice of which route to take.

One of the most common uses of a multiple-choice path is specifying columns to use in a command. One choice (the freeway) is to use an asterisk (*) or ALL to select all columns in a table. The other choice is to type each column name, separating the names with commas.

The structure shown in figure 1.15 is similar to the structure in figure 1.14. The structure is a required part of the command (because it is shown on the main command line). The difference is that you can enter more than one argument (all of the same type), as long as you separate the arguments with commas. In other words, the argument is repeatable. To belabor the figure 1.14 analogy, a repeatable argument is like making several trips to and from work, always taking the same street. The most common argument entered by using this structure is a list of columns.

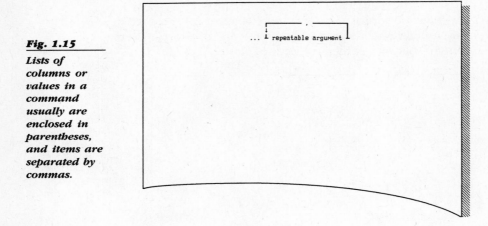

Fig. 1.15

Lists of columns or values in a command usually are enclosed in parentheses, and items are separated by commas.

Perhaps looking at some sample syntax diagrams and what the command line may look like will help you to better understand these structures. For now, don't worry about what the commands do. In the syntax in figure 1.16, the command is PACK. If you follow the syntax main line, you see that no other arguments are required. The one optional argument, dbspec, means to enter a database specification (drive, directory path, and database name).

In the syntax shown in figure 1.17, the command is PROMPT. Again, the command has no required arguments, but this time you have a choice of two optional arguments—filespec or command. A *filespec* is a file specification (drive, directory path, and file name) and *command*, in this example, is any R:BASE command available through Prompt By Example.

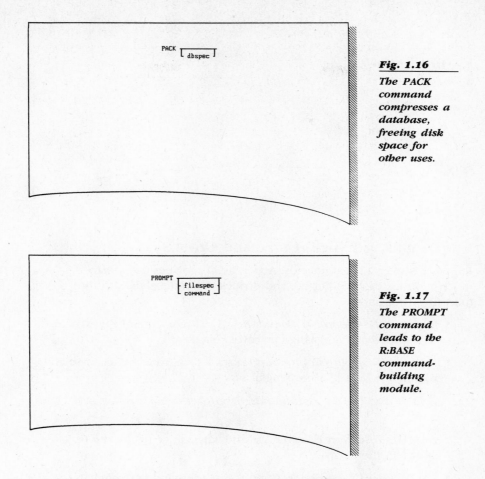

Fig. 1.16
The PACK command compresses a database, freeing disk space for other uses.

Fig. 1.17
The PROMPT command leads to the R:BASE command-building module.

In the syntax shown in figure 1.18, you see a variety of arguments, keywords, choices of required arguments, and clauses. PROJECT is the command. Required arguments include tblname1 (the name for the table being created by this command), the keyword FROM, tblview (the name of the existing table or view from which the new table is to be created), and the keyword USING. Next, you have a choice of entering a list of columns (collist) or an asterisk (*), which means all columns. Finally, you can enter one or both of the optional argument clauses—WHERE or ORDER BY.

The . . . at the end of the first syntax line means that the syntax is continued from the syntax main line, and the . . . at the beginning of the second syntax line means that this line is continued from the preceding line. This convention ensures that you do not think a second or subsequent syntax line is the start of a new syntax diagram.

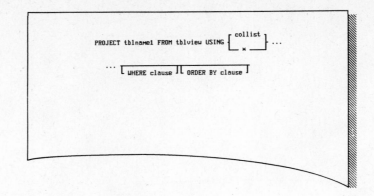

Fig. 1.18

A complex syntax diagram.

```
                     PROJECT tblname1 FROM tblview USING ┌ collist ┐ ...
                                                         └   *    ┘

                     ... ┌ WHERE clause ┐┌ ORDER BY clause ┐
```

Understanding R:BASE Command Groups

R:BASE has over 120 commands. Appendix C provides a summary description for each command, and divides the commands into the following 10 groups:

- *Structure Development Commands:* Create or modify the structure of the database, and assign or revoke passwords.

- *Select and Display Commands:* Extract data from the database and display the data in a meaningful way.

- *Printer and Output Commands:* Send data to the printer, screen, or a file.

- *Data Modification Commands:* Add, change, or delete the data stored in the database.

- *Environment Commands:* Control the operating environment for your database.

- *Backup and Restore Commands:* Make backup copies of your database structure or data and restore the structure or data if needed.

- *Housekeeping Commands:* Provide drive, directory, and file management.

- *Structured Query Language:* Provide the ANSI-standard set of structured query processing commands.

- *Programming Commands:* Provide programming structures for repetitive processing.

- *Multiuser and Transaction Processing Commands:* Handle processing of data-modification commands by multiple users or for batch-transaction processing.

As stated earlier, you can use the R:BASE menu structures instead of commands. Familiarity with using commands is useful, however, so that as your R:BASE skills increase, you can easily and comfortably start building more complex programs and procedures to use with your database.

Getting Help

Throughout R:BASE, you can obtain contextual, on-line help by pressing F1. When you are operating inside a module, such as Forms or Reports, the help screen that appears deals directly with the function you are performing.

If all you need is a list of the function keys, press Shift-F1. Figure 1.19 shows the function key list displayed when you press Shift-F1 at the main menu.

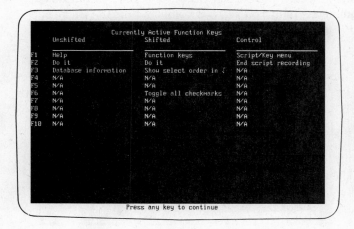

Fig. 1.19

A help screen showing you which function keys you can use.

Help screens usually cover the entire screen, and prompt you to press any key to return to processing. If the topic consists of more than one help screen, you press any key to display the second and subsequent help screens. In this case, you press Esc to return to processing.

Figure 1.20 shows the help screen that appears after you press F1 from the R:BASE main menu with the Databases option highlighted.

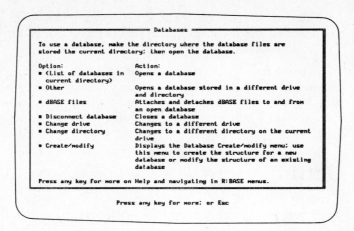

Fig. 1.20

A help screen explaining the function you are performing.

A second method of obtaining on-line help is through the HELP command. You can use this in Command mode. After you type *help* and press Enter in Command mode, the Help main menu appears, as shown in figure 1.21. From this menu, you can browse through the help screens. Much of the help obtained through the Help menu consists of help submenus. Choose options from the submenus until you reach a command menu. After you choose a command in Help, R:BASE displays the help information for the command and the syntax of the command.

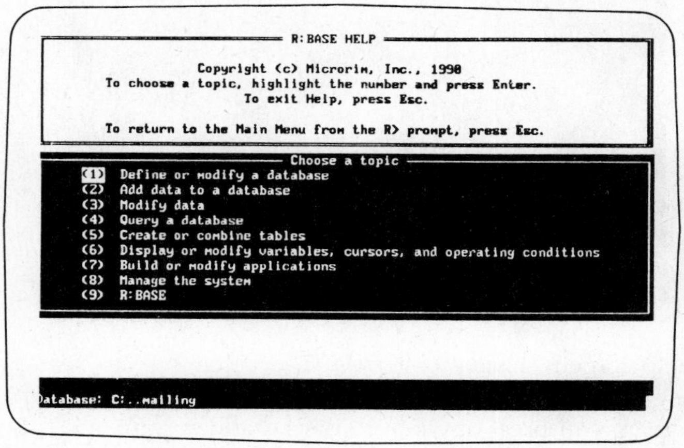

Fig. 1.21

The R:BASE Help main menu.

You also can get help about a specific command, including its syntax diagram, by typing *help*, followed by the name of the command when you are in Command mode. Figure 1.22 shows the Help screen that appears after you type *help intersect* and press Enter.

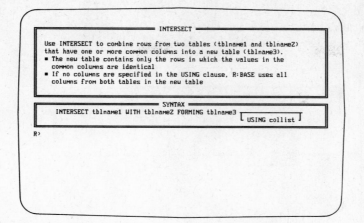

Fig. 1.22

The help screen for the INTERSECT command.

Using the Condition Builder

Throughout R:BASE, you will be using the R:BASE condition builder. The section in this chapter "Using Prompt By Example" gives you the steps to define a condition. Here, you learn about the condition builder in detail.

The R:BASE condition builder is a menu-driven method of selecting specific rows of data to include in the process you are executing. You use the condition builder to define views (see Chapter 5), edit with a form (see Chapter 6), print reports (see Chapter 7), and create applications (see Chapter 8). The condition builder steps through the process of creating an R:BASE WHERE clause (a WHERE clause is a set of conditions you type with a command).

Where a condition clause is allowed in a process, R:BASE automatically displays the condition builder on-screen, as shown in figure 1.23. If you do not want to set conditions (you want to use all the rows in the table), press F2 to bypass condition setting.

To use the condition builder, follow these steps:

1. Choose a column from the list to use as the condition criteria.

   A typical condition is to limit the rows of data by specifying a date range—use only the rows where the date column is within a date range. Another typical condition is to limit rows to only those where a specific column contains a value. Suppose that you want to make sure that each row has data in a specific column (everyone's first name column should be filled in, for example). Set a condition telling R:BASE to give you only the rows where no data exists in the column (by using the IS NULL operator). The possibilities are limitless and all depend on exactly what you want to do. (See table 1.2 for a complete list of comparison operators.)

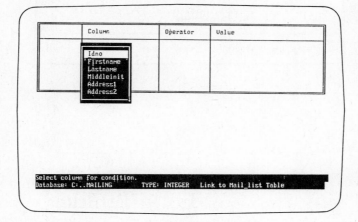

Fig. 1.23

The condition builder.

After you choose a column, R:BASE displays a list of comparison operators (see fig. 1.24).

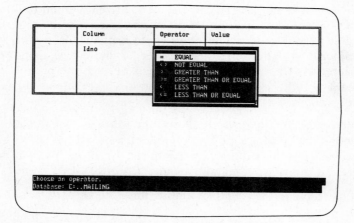

Fig. 1.24

Comparison operators enable you to compare the value of existing data to a value you enter.

You use comparison operators to specify to R:BASE the type of comparison for the column. If you want to specify only rows that have a certain value, for example, you can use the = EQUAL comparison operator. To tell R:BASE to use only rows where the date is in a certain range, you use the BETWEEN operator.

2. Choose the comparison operator you need for the type of comparison you want to make.

R:BASE then prompts you for a comparison value (except where a comparison value is not needed, as with IS NULL and IS NOT NULL).

3. Enter the comparison value or a range of values if you selected BETWEEN or NOT BETWEEN (see fig. 1.25).

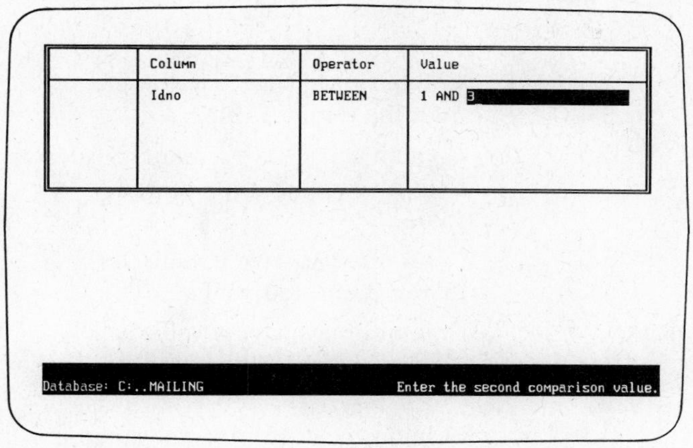

Column	Operator	Value
Idno	BETWEEN	1 AND 3

Database: C:..MAILING   Enter the second comparison value.

Fig. 1.25

A BETWEEN or NOT BETWEEN operator enables you to enter a range of values.

Here are some examples:

Datecolumn BETWEEN 03/01/90, 03/31/90
Idcolumn = 100
Currencycolumn >= $1000
Anycolumn IS NOT NULL

After you select the comparison operator and enter a value, the operator determines the relationship between the column value and the value you enter. Table 1.2 lists all the comparison operators available in the condition builder.

Tip: | The condition builder provides the most frequently used comparison operators. The WHERE clause, used with a command, has additional operators that provide more possibilities. See Appendix C for information on the WHERE clause.

You have completed the definition of a single condition. Now you can add one or more (up to 10 total) conditions to modify the first condition.

Table 1.2
Comparison Operators

Operator	Definition
= EQUAL	Column and value must be equal.
<> NOT EQUAL	Column and value must not be equal.
> GREATER THAN	Column must have a value greater than the entered value.
>= GREATER THAN OR EQUAL	Column must have a value greater than or equal to the entered value.
< LESS THAN	Column must have a value less than the entered value.
<= LESS THAN OR EQUAL	Column must have a value less than or equal to the entered value.
BETWEEN	Column must be in listed range of values.
NOT BETWEEN	Column must not be in listed range of values.
CONTAINS	Column has specified value somewhere in it. For example, *ed* is contained in *Editor* and *Fred*.
NOT CONTAINS	Column does not contain the specified value.
IN	Column should match one of the values in the list.
NOT IN	Column should not match one of the values in the list.
IS NULL	Column should not contain any value (displayed as -0- in R:BASE).
IS NOT NULL	Column contains any value.
LIKE	Column value is equal to the entered value.
NOT LIKE	Column value is not equal to the entered value.

R:BASE displays a list of connecting operators used to combine more than one condition (see fig. 1.26).

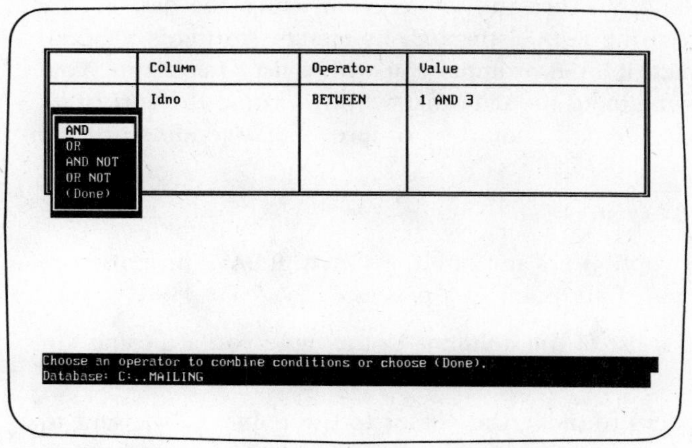

```
        Column       Operator     Value
        Idno         BETWEEN      1 AND 3
  AND
  OR
  AND NOT
  OR NOT
  (Done)
```

```
Choose an operator to combine conditions or choose (Done).
Database: C:..MAILING
```

Fig. 1.26

Use connecting operators to specify several conditions for the comparison of data.

Table 1.3 lists the connecting operators and their functions.

Table 1.3
Connecting Operators

Operator	Definition
AND	Both this and the preceding condition must be met to include the row in the operator.
AND NOT	This condition must not be met if the previous condition is met.
OR	This condition can be met, but is not required to be met, in addition to the preceding condition.
OR NOT	This condition may or may not be met in addition to the previous condition.

To add modifying conditions, follow these steps:

1. Choose a connecting operator and then repeat the preceding set of steps (1 through 3) to define another condition.

2. If no other conditions are needed, highlight Done and press Enter.

Condition building is complete, and R:BASE continues to the next step of the process you are executing.

```
Command: WHERE clause
```

Sorting Data

Sorting is another feature common throughout R:BASE. Sorting is ordering the data in a sequence other than the sequence in which the data is stored. When you are using R:BASE through its menus, sorting is a menu-driven process in which R:BASE prompts you with a list of columns. You choose the column containing the data that will determine the sort order. Then, you choose how the data should be ordered—in ascending order or descending order.

To sort data, follow these steps:

1. Choose the sort option for any process. Often, R:BASE prompts you for a sort order at some point in a process.

   R:BASE displays a list of the columns in the table you are using for the process.

2. Use the arrow keys to move the cursor to the column you want to sort by.

3. Press Enter to place a check mark (✔) next to the column name.

   R:BASE displays a menu with the two sorting orders, Ascending and Descending (see fig. 1.27).

Fig. 1.27

Choosing ascending or descending order.

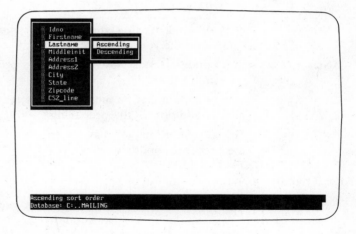

4. Highlight the sort order you want to use and press Enter.

   R:BASE returns to the Column list and places an A (for Ascending) or D (for Descending) next to the column name. In addition, the Column list shows a number. This number indicates the position in the Sort list for this column. If the number is 1 (the first selected column), the data in that column is sorted first and any subsequent sort columns are sorted second, third, and so on (see fig. 1.28).

Fig. 1.28

R:BASE uses numbers to show which columns are sorted first, second, third, and so on.

5. After you ask for sort columns, press F2 to continue to the next part of the process.

Some examples of sort orders follow:

The original data is stored like this:

Column1	Column2	Column3	Column4
3	A	Harry	Brown
1	B	Mary	Stuart
2	B	James	Henry
4	A	Cassandra	Brown

Sort Columns: Column1, ascending :

Column1	Column2	Column3	Column4
1	B	Mary	Stuart
2	B	James	Henry
3	A	Harry	Brown
4	A	Cassandra	Brown

Sort Columns: Column2, ascending, Column1, descending :

Column1	Column2	Column3	Column4
4	A	Cassandra	Brown
3	A	Harry	Brown
2	B	James	Henry
1	B	Mary	Stuart

Sort Columns: Column4, ascending, Column 3, descending :

Column1	Column2	Column3	Column4
3	A	Harry	Brown
4	A	Cassandra	Brown
2	B	James	Henry
1	B	Mary	Stuart

```
Command: ORDER BY
```

Exiting R:BASE

The way you leave R:BASE depends on where you are when you want to exit. As mentioned previously, you can start R:BASE at the main menu, at Prompt By Example, or in Command mode (the R> prompt):

- To leave R:BASE from the main menu, choose Exit and then choose Leave R:BASE.

- To leave R:BASE from Prompt By Example, choose Exit from R:BASE.

- To leave R:BASE from Command mode, type *exit* and press Enter.

Summary

In this chapter, you got an idea of the great power of R:BASE. You learned that R:BASE has a complete set of menu-driven modules that provide nearly every function you need to design and use a database. In addition, you learned that R:BASE has a full set of commands you can use in Command mode or in R:BASE programs.

You learned how to use the R:BASE menu system, the command builder Prompt By Example, and Command mode. You also learned how to use the R:BASE help screens.

These procedures are the R:BASE basics. From here, you can learn how to create and use your own databases.

2

Designing a Database

This chapter describes the basics of relational database design. Before you start building your own database structure, you should first understand how your database works. What do you want your database to hold? How should the parts fit together? This chapter helps you answer these questions so that you can design a database that works efficiently and properly.

Defining a Relational Database

A *relational database* accesses groups of related data that are stored separately in a file or table. A relational database is similar to a file cabinet because it stores sets of similar information in separate files. Each set of files comprises a single database topic, which may relate to other topics. A file containing basic customer data (name and address), for example, may relate to a file containing records of sales for the same customer.

A relational database stores the data separately, as you do in a file cabinet, but it enables you to bring together the related information quickly for viewing, manipulating, or editing. A relational database is a repository for all the facts related to a single topic; therefore, the structure of the database is an outline of the data you want to store. The topic for a database can be quite far-ranging.

A database for an order entry and inventory system, for example, would contain all the information you have about your customers: their addresses, the items they purchase, and the dates they make their purchases. Each part of a database forms a single, cohesive piece of the table where you store the data. The database in this example would have separate tables for customers, products, and purchases.

The database used as an example in the first few chapters contains three tables that hold all the necessary data for tracking information that you send to a list of people. The information mailed could be sales promotions, requests for donations from a not-for-profit organization, or greeting cards for various holidays. The ultimate purpose makes no difference because the database design can handle any of these activities.

The concepts illustrated by this database are intrinsic to a good database design. Starting from this design (and the design of the more complex example used in later chapters), you can design your own database.

First, however, you need to be familiar with the terminology that is defined in Table 2.1.

Table 2.1
Database Terms

Term	Definition
Table	A group of related data within a database. Contains the discrete pieces of data for each item within the subtopic. A customer address table, for example, contains customer names, addresses, and phone numbers. An inventory table contains product names, costs, selling prices, locations, and quantities on-hand.
Column	A title for each piece of information contained in a table. Columns divide the information into separate parts that you can view or update easily. If you store each customer's address separately from his or her name, for example, you can view the names and the addresses separately.
Row	A line of data divided into the column groupings for a single entity. One row, for example, may contain all the information on one person.

Table 2.1 illustrates a two-column table. The first column contains only the word to be defined and the second column contains the definition. Each row in this table contains two pieces of information: the word being defined and the definition.

All tables in a database have this same structure. The only difference is that a database table usually contains more than two columns.

The example database in this chapter contains three tables. At first glance, you may think that all the data in the database could be contained in a single table. This chapter explains why three tables are used and helps you make decisions about your own data requirements for designing a database.

Mapping Out Table Design

Before entering the design in R:BASE, you should sketch your design on paper. The preliminary sketch can reveal design flaws before you do the work on the computer.

Ask yourself the following questions:

1. What data do I want to store?

2. How should I divide the data into tables?

3. How should each table look?

4. What are the relationships between the tables?

With a good design, you can retrieve and correlate your data in a variety of ways. If the structure is correct, data retrieval will flow naturally from the design.

Defining Tables

First, make a detailed list of all the pieces of data you want to store. For the example database, the list may be as follows:

Name
Address
What item was mailed to this person
When you mailed the item

Using this information in a single-table design, the following columns could be defined for the table:

Name
Address
What Mailed
When Mailed

One row of data for this structure would appear as follows:

```
John Doe  1 East Street, Chicago, IL  60602  Solicit Letter  5/23/90
```

Here you have all the data you need. Suppose, however, that you send John another letter:

```
John Doe  1 E. Street, Chicago, IL  60602  Response Letter  6/14/90
```

Notice that a problem arises here. You have entered John Doe's address twice, but the two addresses do not match exactly. They are close enough that you know they are the same address, but which one is really correct?

This design presents another problem when you print mailing labels; you will have two address labels for John Doe—each with different information.

In general, you should not duplicate data in a database; the design shown here is problematic because it requires you to enter the same information more than once. In addition, you have no way of making sure that the data matches.

The solution to this problem is to divide the data into two tables. The first table holds only the information about John Doe that you do not want to duplicate: name and address. The second table holds the information about the item and the date mailed:

Name Table

Name	Address
John Doe	1 East Street, Chicago, IL 60602

Mailing Table

Name	What Mailed	When Mailed
John Doe	Solicit Letter	5/23/90
John Doe	Response Letter	6/14/90

Relating Tables to Each Other

Notice that the name is repeated in each table in order to form a relationship between the two tables. When you want to look at both tables, you use the Name column to link the tables together.

You now can enter as many mailing items as you want without repeating the address. In addition, when you are mailing letters, you can print a single label for John Doe. In this way, you can be sure that the address you have is correct and that you have to change it in only one place if John Doe moves.

To improve this design further, look at the What Mailed column. Having a code for this column for use in the Mailing table would be much easier. Therefore, you can add a third table to the design to describe the code:

Code Table

What Mailed	Description
LT1	Initial solicitation letter
LT2	Follow-up letter

The Mailing table contains only the code—not the description—to ensure that similar mailings sent to different people end up in the same category. All mailings assigned the code LT1 always will have the same description.

You now have three tables with links to each other, as figure 2.1 illustrates.

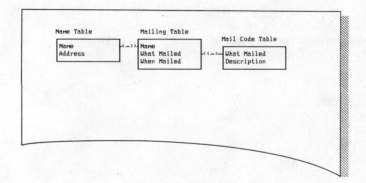

Fig. 2.1

Linking tables by repeating a column in each table.

Determining Table Relationships

Another important database concept involves the type of relationship between tables: one-to-many, many-to-one, many-to-many, and one-to-one relationships are possible. However, a good database design has only one-to-many and many-to-one relationships.

In figure 2.1, the lines among the tables show how they are linked to each other. If the line has a < or > character (indicating *one*), a link exists to only one row in the table. If the line has « or » characters (indicating *many*), multiple rows in the table are pointed to. Thus, figure 2.1 shows the following relationships:

- The Name table has a one-to-many relationship to the Mailing table.

- The Mailing table has a many-to-one relationship to the Name table and to the Mail Code table.

- The Mail Code table has a one-to-many relationship to the Mailing table.

A *one-to-many relationship* occurs when a single row in one table is related to multiple rows in another table, as in the relation of the Name table (one-side) to the Mailing table (many-side).

A *many-to-one relationship* always occurs with a one-to-many relationship; it is the relationship between the multiple-entry table and the single-entry table, as illustrated by the relationship between the Mailing table (many-side) and the Mail Code table (one-side).

Many-to-many relationships occur when each table has multiple entries relating to the other table. Although this may seem to be the only possible way to design a database, in some cases, you should add a table that relates to both tables in the preferred one-to-many or many-to-one configuration.

Consider the following example of two tables with a many-to-many relationship for a simple inventory system. Part names identify the item; component names identify a part contained in the product. The location indicates where the product is stored in the warehouse.

Table 1	Table 2
Product ID	Product ID
Component	Location (product data)

Data in Table 1		Data in Table 2	
Television	Picture Tube	Television	Warehouse A
Television	Chassis	Television	Warehouse B
Stereo	Receiver	Stereo	Warehouse A
Stereo	Speakers	Stereo	Warehouse C

As you can see, both tables contain multiple occurrences of the product name. To handle these relationships properly, you can set up an intermediary table:

Table 1	Table 2	Table 3
Product ID	Product ID	Product ID
Component ID	(product data)	Location

You enter the data as follows:

Table 1

Television	Picture Tube
Television	Chassis
Stereo	Receiver
Stereo	Speaker

Table 2

Television	(product data)
Stereo	(product data)

Table 3

Television	Warehouse A
Television	Warehouse B
Stereo	Warehouse C

You now have a many-to-one relationship between Table 1 and Table 2, and a one-to-many relationship between Table 2 and Table 3. A many-to-many relationship still exists between Table 1 and Table 3, but Table 2 is to be used as the relating table. Notice that the concern here is that the only possible way to relate two tables should not be many-to-many. By adding the third table, you define another way to relate the tables.

One-to-one relationships occur when you have a single entry in one table relating to a single entry in another table. In this case, you usually can combine the columns from the two tables into a single table. Be careful not to confuse a one-to-one relationship with a one-to-many relationship for which the many-side has only a single entry. The question is, can more than one entry occur on the many-side, or does the design restrict the entry to a single row?

Improving Table Design

The three-table design solves most of the problems that existed in the two-table design. In the three-table design,

- Redundant data entry is kept to a minimum.

- Each table contains only necessary data.

- Each table has a single subject.

- Relationships between tables are one-to-many or many-to-one.

- Each table is linked to another table through a common column.

You can improve the Mailing database design further by subdividing the data in each column into multiple columns so that you can sort your data in as many ways as possible. To be able to print a report of the people in the Name table, sorting by last name and first name, you should subdivide the Name column into First Name and Last Name, and possibly Middle Name or Initial as well. Similarly, you should divide the Address column into Street Address, City, State, and ZIP Code so that you can group your data using these categories.

In addition to enabling you to sort and limit the data (to a list of only the people who live in Minneapolis, for example), subdividing the data in this way follows a basic rule of good database design: each column should contain only one type of information. You should never put two or more types of information under a single column heading.

Identifying Rows Uniquely

If you subdivide data, the relationships between tables are more likely to become confused. If you subdivide the Name table into two or three columns, for example, its relationship to the Mailing and Category tables is no longer clear. If the relation is by last name only and you have more than one Doe in the Name table, for example, you may not know which Doe was sent a letter.

You can use more than one common column as the link between tables to solve this problem. If you use Last Name and First Name, for example, the problem is solved unless you have more than one John Doe.

Instead of using multiple columns to link tables, a better solution is to use a unique value to identify each row in the master table and then use this unique column to link the rows to the related tables. Thus, the design for the tables is as follows:

Name Table

ID Number	First	Last	Address	City	State	ZIP Code
100	John	Doe	1 East Street	Chicago	IL	60602
101	Fred	Roe	2 West Street	Ida	OK	70449

Mailing Table

ID Number	What Mailed	When Mailed
100	LT1	5/23/90
100	LT2	6/14/90
101	LT1	5/24/90

The design already used the concept of unique identification when the What Mailed column was coded.

The ID Number column becomes the key that links the tables. You can ensure that a key column is unique by defining a data entry rule that requires uniqueness. R:BASE also can number the column for you, so that you can be sure that the value is unique and sequential.

Figure 2.2 shows the final sketch for the Mailing database.

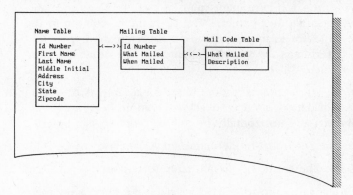

Fig. 2.2

The final sketch for the Mailing database design, with data categories subdivided into tables.

When you enter this design into R:BASE, you need to make some additional choices. You can name the database anything, as long as it is descriptive to you and R:BASE enables you to use the name (that is, it is not a reserved word, such as a command name, and it is within the maximum length requirements explained in Chapter 3). Data types are determined by the type of data that is stored; data entry rules are a result of your data requirements.

When you design your database, be sure to define the following:

- Names of tables

- Names of columns in tables

- Type of data held in each column (text, numeric, date, time, and so on).

- Data entry rules you need to ensure proper entry

Many other relational database concepts and rules exist that have little practical importance. Generally speaking, you probably do not need to know about determinants, tuples, attributes, or relations. As a person with a job to get done, you probably are interested more in how to apply the features of your database system so that it works for you.

Note: The terminology used in the preceding paragraph is used by database theorists when writing about relational database models. A *model* is a theoretical design. R:BASE uses the more easily understood terms: links, rows, columns, and tables. Other term definitions follow:

- *Determinant:* A determinant value in a column can provide the value in another column. The ID Number column in the Name table, for example, contains a determinant value—its value determines the values contained in the other columns in the table.

- *Relation:* The relational model name for a table. A relation consists of data divided vertically by column headings (attributes) and horizontally by one or more rows (tuples).

- *Tuple:* The relational model name for a database row.

- *Attribute:* The relational model name for a column.

Nevertheless, if you want to learn more about database theory, a number of good books are available. In particular, any work on databases by E.F. Codd or C.J. Date provides complete coverage: *The Relational Model for Database Management*, by E.F. Codd or *Guide to the SQL Standard* and *An Introduction to Database Systems*, by C.J. Date. (*SQL* is language that is designed specifically for use with relational databases and is used in R:BASE.) The design of R:BASE is based on the relational model defined by Dr. Codd, with some exceptions to allow for practical, day-to-day use.

Normalizing Your Database

Normalization, in database terms, means analyzing your design to determine whether any of the following is true:

- When you add data, do you need to add more data than you really need?

- When you modify data, do you need to change it in more than one table?

- When you delete data, do you lose essential data?

These three questions point to the three types of data-modification flaws most commonly found in database designs.

Data-Insertion Flaws

When you add a piece of data to a database, you should add it to only one table. You should not, for example, need to add a name to more than one table. If you do, then you have data redundancy that should be eliminated. The only exception is the addition of the linking column data to each table that shares the column.

The easiest way to eliminate redundancy is to make sure that no column other than a linking column appears in more than one table in your database.

Data-Modification Flaws

You should design each table so that when you modify data in one table, you need not modify the same data in any other table. In other words, the data should not be redundant from table to table. The only column that should be changed in more than one table is the linking column. That is, if you change the identification number for a row in the Name table, you also need to change the identification number in any related table. However, you should not change any other column in the Name table; that data should not be duplicated elsewhere in the database.

Data-Deletion Flaws

You should design each table so that you do not lose essential information if you delete a row from a table. A common error database designers make is to create a table that holds two categories of information. Then, when they delete one category of information, the second category also is lost. Suppose that you have a table with the following design and data:

Sales Table

CustName	Address	City	State	ZIP	Product	Price
Jones Co.	11 S Street	Oki	WI	88888	Lamp	$29.95
Smith Co.	22 N Street	Ely	NV	77777	Desk	$150.00
Smith Co.	22 N Street	Ely	NV	77777	Chair	$32.75

Besides having the obvious data-insertion and modification flaws, this table also has the data-deletion flaw. If this is the only table containing customer names and addresses, and you delete the sale of the lamp to Jones Co., you lose more than just the sales information. In this case, two categories of information are held in a single table: name and address information and sales information.

Avoiding Common Mistakes in Database Design

Remember while you design your database to never enter data as a column name and to avoid the spreadsheet configuration. For example, some people design a table as follows:

Mailing Table

ID Number	LT1	LT2	LT3
100	05/24/90	06/20/90	07/14/90

The problem here is that if you add another letter for mailing, you have to add a column—LT4, for example. This type of design is unwieldy and does not allow for growth. Suppose that you complete the LT1 mailing and add an LT4 mailing. You not only have to add a column, but all the new rows would leave a blank under the LT1 column because it is no longer needed. This problem would continue as you add new mailings and drop old ones.

Remember that a database is not a spreadsheet. Spreadsheets generally are formatted in columns, whereas databases are formatted in rows. The following tables illustrate the way a spreadsheet and a database handle the same data:

Spreadsheet

	January	February	March	...
Region 1	100.00	200.00	150.00	...
Region 2	150.00	175.00	200.00	...

Database

Area	Month	Sales Amount
Region 1	January	100.00
Region 2	January	150.00
Region 1	February	200.00
Region 2	February	175.00
Region 1	March	150.00
Region 2	March	200.00

The order of the rows in the database does not matter because you can group or sort the data in any way you want. The basic problem with the spreadsheet design is that you cannot sort the data if you use the data as a column name (in this case, the name of the month).

Summary

R:BASE enables you to design your database in any way you want; this chapter suggests the best methods to use. When you create the actual design, R:BASE provides you with the tools that you need.

Remember to keep the following points in mind when designing your database:

- Group the data you want to store in logical sets. These are your tables.

- Determine the relationships between the groups. Make the relating data a column that is common to all tables in the relationship.

- Avoid repeating data in more than one table when possible. This guards against data-insertion, deletion, and modification flaws.

- Choose database, table, and column names that are meaningful to you.

- Determine what type of data is to be stored in each column and make the data type for the column appropriate for the data.

If you read Quick Start 1, you already have experienced creating a database structure. That quick start led you through the steps of creating the Mailing database used as an example in this chapter. Chapter 3 describes each of these steps in more detail.

3

Using the Database
Definition Module

This chapter describes how to use the Database Definition module
to create a database—the tables, rules, passwords, and column structures.

In the first part of this chapter, "Creating Database Structures," you learn
to do the following:

- Create a database structure that suits the data you want to store.

- Define the types of data stored in the database.

- Have R:BASE assign sequential numbers for you.

- Ensure that the data entered is what you want.

- Define relationships between the tables in your database.

- Protect your data from unauthorized use.

In the second part of this chapter, "Modifying Existing Databases," you
learn to do the following:

- Modify an existing database structure—its tables and the types of
  data that it holds.

- Change the rules that ensure correct data entry.

- Remove, rename, and copy tables within the database.

- Redefine how automatic, sequential numbering works.

- Modify passwords and access rights.

You learn how to delete, rename, and copy an existing database in the
third part of this chapter, "Managing Database Files."

73

Creating Database Structures

Before you can add data to a database, you must create a structure, or outline, describing the data for R:BASE to follow when storing your data. The main component of this storage structure is a table. You can break down a table into separate partitions, or *columns*, where you store individual data items.

You begin to define the database structure by creating the first table in a database. After you define a single table, all subsequent table definitions are modifications to the database structure.

This section describes how to define the first table in your database. The methods for adding more tables are the same as for the first table.

Tip: Map out the structure of all the tables you want in your database before you start defining tables so that you can identify the relationships you want to form between tables.

You can start the Database Definition module in any of three ways:

- Choose Create/Modify from the Databases pull-down menu on the R:BASE main menu.

- Use the RBDEFINE command in Prompt By Example.

- Type *rbdefine* at the R> prompt and press Enter.

When you start the Database Definition module, R:BASE displays the Database Definition main menu. You use the Create option to create a new database (see fig. 3.1). The other options follow:

- *Modify:* Modifies an existing database structure.

- *Delete:* Removes a database.

- *Rename:* Changes the name of a database.

- *Copy:* Makes a copy of a database.

- *Exit:* Leaves the Database Definition module.

For information on these options, see "Modifying Existing Databases," later in this chapter.

```
Command: RBDEFINE
```

To create the new database, highlight Create and then press Enter to choose New Database. R:BASE prompts you for the name of the new database (see fig. 3.2). Type the name and press Enter.

Fig. 3.1
**The Database
Definition
main menu.**

R:BASE stores a database on the current drive and directory as a set of three DOS files. All the files start with the database name you entered and are numbered 1, 2, and 3, respectively; therefore, following the DOS rules for naming files, the name you give the database can have no more than seven characters. The DOS files contain the following information:

- *File 1:* The structure definition of the database
- *File 2:* The data
- *File 3:* The indexing instructions

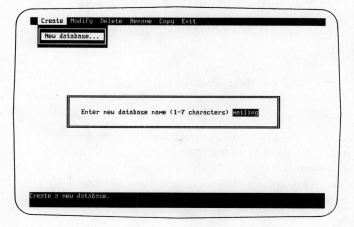

Fig. 3.2
**Entering the
name of a
new database.**

Tip: DOS file names can contain no more than eight alphanumeric characters. You may use the following punctuation:

$ % − @ { } ! # , _

In general, avoid using punctuation for database names. In addition, do not use any names that DOS already uses: AUX, CLOCK$, COM, CON, LPT, NUL, or PRN.

The database files are given the extension RBF. If you name your database MYDATAB, for example, the DOS files for this database follow:

- MYDATAB1.RBF
- MYDATAB2.RBF
- MYDATAB3.RBF

Never delete or rename any of these files, or your database will not be usable. You learn more about the structure and indexing later in this chapter.

Note: You can attach a dBASE III, III PLUS, or IV database file to an R:BASE database and then treat the dBASE file just as if it were an R:BASE table. R:BASE refers to dBASE files as *file-tables*. After you attach your d:BASE file to an R:BASE database, you can modify the data in the file, but there are restrictions on modifying the structure (you can change the column names and data types, but you cannot reorder, add, or delete columns). Refer to the R:BASE 3.1 documentation and "ATTACH" and "DETACH" in Appendix C of this book for further details on using dBASE files in R:BASE.

Creating Tables

The table structure is the basic building block of a database; a database does not exist unless it has at least one table. You cannot define another database object (form, report, or view) until at least one table exists.

After you choose Create or Modify from the Database Definition main menu, R:BASE responds with another menu (the Database Building menu) or with a series of selections, lists, or dialog boxes. Figure 3.3 shows the Database Building menu with the Tables pull-down menu displayed.

Use the options on the Tables menu to define the tables that comprise the structure of your database. The options follow:

- *Tables:* Defines the basic table structure and the column structure within a table and assigns indexing to a column (discussed in this section).

- *Autonumber:* Defines an existing column in a table to be numbered automatically by the system when new rows are added (see "Defining Autonumber Columns," later in the chapter).

- *Rules:* Defines rules for data entry to ensure accuracy (see "Creating Data Entry Rules," later in the chapter).

- *Access Rights:* Defines passwords to protect access to tables in your database (see "Assigning Database Passwords," later in the chapter).

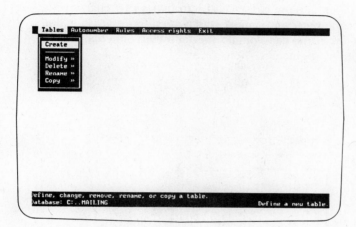

Fig. 3.3
The Database Building menu.

To define a new table, highlight the Tables option on the Database Building menu. R:BASE displays these choices:

- *Create:* Defines a new table (see the rest of the information in this section).

- *Modify:* Modifies the structure of an existing table (see "Modifying a Table," later in the chapter).

- *Delete:* Removes an existing table (see "Deleting a Table").

- *Rename:* Changes the name of an existing table (see "Renaming a Table," later in the chapter).

- *Copy:* Makes a new table with a structure identical to an existing table (see "Copying a Table," later in the chapter).

Commands: CREATE SCHEMA, CREATE TABLE

To create a new table, highlight Create and press Enter.

Entering Table Names and Descriptions

When you begin to define a table, R:BASE displays an empty Table Definition screen, which is laid out in much the same way a table is structured. You first must provide R:BASE with the name of the table and, if you want, an optional table description. R:BASE does not use the description for processing, but whenever you highlight the table on a menu, the table description appears at the bottom of the screen.

Type the name of the table in the box at the top of the screen (see fig. 3.4) and press Enter. A table name can be from 1 to 18 characters long; it can include numbers, but it must start with a letter (case is not significant). Finally, the name can contain the following punctuation: #, $, _, or %. The following names, then, are valid:

- sales_amounts
- employee#
- purchase$

Fig. 3.4

Naming a table and providing a table description.

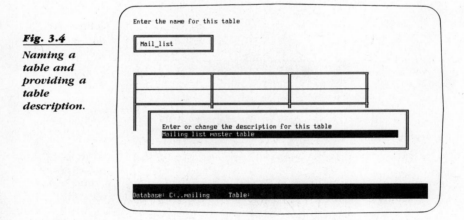

The first eight characters of the table name must be unique among the tables or views in the database. If you already have a table with the same first eight characters, R:BASE cannot differentiate between the two names because it only reads the first eight characters for some operations. If you enter a name that duplicates the name of an existing table, R:BASE does not accept the name.

Tip: Make your table name informative so that you always know what its purpose is. Table names such as TABLE1 and TABLE2 are not very helpful in reminding you of the contents of the table. Adding a description also can help you remember the purpose of the table.

After you type the table name, R:BASE asks for a description of the contents of the table. Type a description—up to 50 characters—and press Enter. Give each table a description that is significant to you. Even an 18-character name can be confusing, so the description gives you the opportunity to identify a table's use clearly.

Entering Column Names and Descriptions

Tables are divided into columns, which define how the table separates the data contained in it. Each column should contain only one piece of information. That is, you should not define a single column for the address and then expect it to hold the street address, city, state, and ZIP code. Define a separate column for each piece of information.

After you enter the table name and description, you can define the columns that make up the table. R:BASE positions the cursor in the first column name box on the left side of the screen (see fig. 3.5). Enter the first column name and its description; for example, type *Idno* and press Enter.

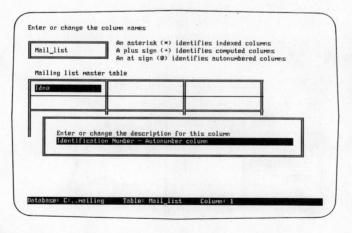

Fig. 3.5

Naming a column and providing a column description.

A column name must follow the same rules as for table names: it can contain from 1 to 18 characters; it can include numbers, but it must start with a letter (case is not significant). As with table names, column names can contain the following punctuation: #, $, _, or %. Thus, the following column names are valid:

    sales%
    customer_name
    sales_$

The first eight characters must be unique among the other column names in the database. If you already have a column with the same first eight characters, R:BASE cannot differentiate between the two names because it only reads the first eight characters for some operations.

After you type a column name, R:BASE prompts you for an optional column description. Type a description of up to 35 characters that identifies the use of the column and press Enter. Whenever you highlight the column name on a menu, the description appears at the bottom of the screen.

Choosing Column Data Types

R:BASE requires that you assign each column a data type that matches the kind of data you want to hold in that column. If you want to store a date in one column, for example, giving the column a Date data type ensures that only dates are entered into that column.

After you name a column, R:BASE prompts you for the data type with a list of data types under the column name (see fig. 3.6). Notice that the ↓ at the lower right of this menu indicates that more options are available. Use the down-arrow key or press PgDn to move past the last displayed entry to view the additional options. Table 3.1 describes the data types you can assign to a column.

Fig. 3.6

A list of data types.

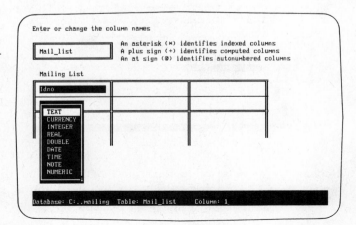

Table 3.1
R:BASE Data Types

Data Type	Specifies
Currency	Monetary amounts. Because R:BASE currency values can be defined for other than American currency, the displayed value depends on the currency definition. You can enter values of up to 99999999999999.99, and the displayed format can be up to 23 characters long. The default American display format is $999,999,999,999,999.99.
Date	Dates. Internally, dates are stored as an integer number of days since January 1, 3999 B.C. The way a date is displayed depends on the way you define the date format. The default American display format is MM/DD/YY.
Double	Double-precision decimal numbers. This data type can hold values in the range $\pm 10^{\pm 308}$. If you are using the Command mode, you can use the alternate name FLOAT.
Integer	Whole numbers in the range ± 999999999. If you are using the Command mode, you can use the alternate names INT or SMALLINT.
Note	Variable-length text of up to 4,092 characters less the length taken by other columns in the table. The actual length of the column is determined by the longest Note entry.
Numeric	Double-precision decimal numbers with a definable precision and scale. The range is the same as Double. The default precision and scale are 9 and 0, respectively. The precision can be from 1 to 15 and the scale can be from 0 up to the defined precision. If you are using the Command mode, you can use the alternate names DEC and DECIMAL.
Real	Decimal numbers in the range $\pm 10^{\pm 38}$ with six-digit accuracy. Real numbers with more than six digits are displayed in scientific notation.
Text	Text strings containing up to 1,500 characters. You define the maximum string length with the data type.

Table 3.1—*continued*

Data Type	Specifies
Time	Times. Internally, times are stored as an integer number of seconds since midnight. The way a time is displayed depends on the way you define the time format. The default American display format is HH:MM:SS.
Computed	Not a true data type. This indicates that the value of the column is calculated from an expression you enter. The parts of the expression determine the data type of the column. You can use other columns, system variables (#DATE, #TIME, #PI), and values as part of the expression.

The data type you assign depends on the kind of data you plan to store under each column name. If you are storing a name, for example, you should make the column a Text data type. If you are storing a dollar value, assign the column a Currency type. Examine the data to be stored and then decide the most appropriate data type for it. If you choose the wrong data type for a column, you easily can change it later by modifying the table structure (see "Modifying a Table," later in this chapter).

Defining Computed Columns

The value found in a computed column is the result of a calculation based on the values in other columns. Computed columns are a useful tool for displaying calculated data without having to store the calculated value or refigure the calculation each time you want to see it. Computed values ensure that a calculated value is accurate according to the data used in the calculation, and they enable you to store a calculated value without taking up space in the table. Only the formula is stored—not all of the calculated values.

How you use a computed column depends on the type of data you are storing, the type of data you want R:BASE to provide, and the way you have designed your database. The following examples suggest some uses for computed columns; the potential uses are limited only by your data needs and imagination.

Suppose that you have a table with Item_price and Quantity columns. Instead of calculating and entering the total price (item price × the quantity sold), you can define a computed column that always holds the correct total even when the value of either of the columns changes. The expression for the computed column is as follows:

(item_price * quantity)

A *computed column* is a method of combining data from other columns in a table. To combine data, you first must create an expression that tells R:BASE how to do the combining. An *expression* is an arithmetic, mathematical, or string manipulation formula that uses operators such as + or − to combine data. The valid R:BASE expression operators follow:

Operator	Definition
+	Addition, unary plus, or linking text without a space
−	Subtraction or unary minus
*	Multiplication
/	Division
**	Exponentiation
&	Linking text with a space
Functions	Any of the R:BASE SuperMath functions listed in Appendix C

Expressions in R:BASE can contain up to 160 characters and must be enclosed in parentheses. If any of the values in an expression are a constant (for example, 100, John Brown, or 5/24/90), enclose the constant value in single quotation marks. Examples of constant values follow:

('100' - columnvalue)
('John Brown' & 'Mary Doe')
(column1 / column 2)

Whenever you look at the data, the value of the computed column accurately reflects the values in the columns used in the expression.

You also can use computed columns for date manipulation. Dates indicate when something happened—for example, the day a letter was mailed. If you want to determine how many letters were sent in a month, you can define a computed column to determine the number from a full date using the following expression:

(IMON(datesent))

The IMON function extracts the number of the month (1-12) from a date. If a letter was sent on January 15th, for example, then the value of this computed column is 1.

Tip: Functions are built-in expressions that R:BASE has predefined for you. By applying your data to a function, R:BASE performs one or more calculations to find a result based on your data. For more information on functions, see the "Functions" section in Appendix C.

At times, you may want to set date and time stamps for a table. You may include a date stamp computed column, for example, so that you will always know on what date a row is added or changed. If you add or change a row, R:BASE recalculates the computed columns for that row, thereby updating the date stamp to the current date. A time stamp is similar, except that the time the row was added or changed is calculated, rather than the date. You can use expressions like these with a computed column:

(#DATE)
(#TIME)

These expressions use R:BASE system variables. R:BASE system variables include the current date and time as shown here, the value of π (#PI), and the current page for reports only (#PAGE). You can use only system variables in an expression for a computed column; you cannot use a global variable that you have defined yourself. (*Global variables* are temporary storage areas for data. They have a variety of uses in forms, reports, and programming. Chapters 5, 7, and 8 provide more information about global variables.)

#DATE always holds the current date and #TIME always holds the current time. Dates and times are derived from the DOS level date and time, so if your computer does not have an internal clock, the date and time used are the ones you enter when you start your computer.

Tip: If you define a date or time stamp column, be aware that the date or time value changes each time you modify the data in the row. Rows that are not changed keep their previous date or time values.

Figure 3.7 shows the screen for defining a computed column.

To define the computed columnn shown in figure 3.7, follow these steps:

1. Define the column name and description as described earlier (note that the computed column must follow the definition of any columns contained in the computed column's expression).

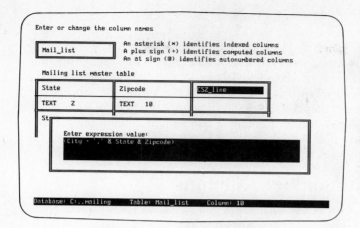

```
Enter or change the column names
                          An asterisk (*) identifies indexed columns
  Mail_list               A plus sign (+) identifies computed columns
                          An at sign (@) identifies autonumbered columns
  Mailing list master table

  State                Zipcode              CSZ_line

  TEXT    2            TEXT    10

  St
    ┌──────────────────────────────────────────────────────────┐
    │  Enter expression value:                                  │
    │ (City + ',' & State & Zipcode)                            │
    │                                                           │
    │                                                           │
    └──────────────────────────────────────────────────────────┘

  Database: C:..mailing    Table: Mail_list    Column: 10
```

Fig. 3.7

Defining a computed column.

2. For the data type, move the cursor past the bottom of the list until you see COMPUTED. Choose Computed for the column type.

   R:BASE displays a dialog box, where you type the expression for the computed column.

3. Type *(City + ';' & State & ZIPcode)* in the dialog box and press Enter.

   R:BASE knows that this expression will be text because you have mentioned three columns that already were defined as Text columns.

4. Type *30* and press Enter when R:BASE asks for the length. This is the total length of the three columns used in the expression plus two characters for spaces and one character for a comma.

Defining Column Indexes

Indexing a column changes the way in which R:BASE searches for data. An *index file* is a quick reference to the data contained in a column—similar to the card catalog used in libraries. The index entry contains a pointer to the row in the table where the data is located. If a column is indexed, R:BASE does not look directly at the data in a table when sorting. Instead, it looks at the index, finds the pointer to the row, and then gets the data. This may seem more complicated, but internally, an index operates much faster than a sequential search through the table data.

After you define the data type for a column, R:BASE asks whether this column is to be indexed. Press Y to answer Yes and then press Enter to assign indexing to a column.

```
Command: CREATE INDEX
```

You should apply indexing only to those columns you will use for sorting.
In general, the data type for an indexed column should be numeric. A Text
column can be indexed, but it is not a good choice unless the entries
contain less than four characters (R:BASE uses only the first four characters
to index Text columns). Indexed columns also should contain unique data,
such as identification numbers.

Defining Autonumber Columns

To ensure unique rows in your database, you should define an identifying
number to hold a unique number or designation. You can have R:BASE
assign these unique numbers for you by indicating that you want an
autonumber column. *Autonumbering* is the process by which R:BASE
supplies sequential numbers for you whenever you add a new row to a
table. In this sample database, the Idno column in the Mail_list table is
defined as an autonumbering column.

```
Command: AUTONUM
```

You can define any text or numeric column for autonumbering. With text
values, part of the column must be a number, which increases by the
increment value each time you add a row. The rest of the column format
consists of a text string that you enter when you define autonumbering.

To define an autonumber column in the Database Definition module,
highlight the Autonumber option on the Database Building menu. R:BASE
displays the options: Create, Modify, and Delete. Press Enter to choose
Create. R:BASE displays a list of the tables in the database. Choose the table
containing the column you want to autonumber. R:BASE then displays a list
of the columns. Choose the column you want to autonumber.

Finally, R:BASE displays a dialog box where you enter the starting numeric
value and the amount to add each time a column is numbered
automatically. Figure 3.8 shows all of these steps on-screen.

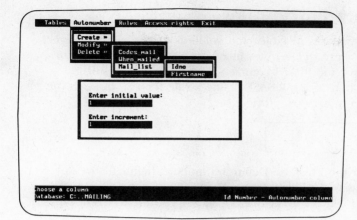

Fig. 3.8

Defining an autonumber column.

If the column you are autonumbering has a Text data type, R:BASE asks for the format. Enter the text string enclosed in square brackets and the position for the number with one or more zeros. The following are some examples:

Format	Initial Value	Stored Value
[PART]00	1	PART01
[AA-]0000	100	AA-0100
000[-B]	100	100-B

If the table already has data in it, R:BASE asks whether you want to renumber the existing values. Choose Yes to renumber the column values in the existing rows. The renumbering is sequential through the rows as they are stored in the table.

If the column is used as a link with other tables already containing that number, renumbering is not a good idea. If a column has the number 100, for example, and another table, using the same column name, already has 100 to identify it as linked to the first table, then renumbering the first table breaks the link between the two tables. For a column link to work, both tables must have the same identifying value in the common column.

If you want to define an autonumbering column for a table containing rows—renumbering in a different order than the stored order—you can use the AUTONUM command at the R> prompt (Command mode) or from within an application to sort the data before renumbering. (See the "AUTONUM" command section in Appendix C for information on this command and Chapter 8 for information on applications.) You cannot sort when using the Autonumber option in the Database Definition module.

Creating Data Entry Rules

You apply data entry rules to tables and columns to ensure that correct data is entered. You can define rules in two ways: using the Database Definition module or the RULES command. Both methods result in the same product, but having R:BASE define a rule for you through the Database Definition module is a little easier.

```
Commands: LIST RULES, RULES
```

To define a rule in the Database Definition module, highlight the Rules option on the Database Building menu. Then highlight the Create option on the Rules pull-down menu. Figure 3.9 shows you the different types of rules you can define.

Fig. 3.9

The Rules pull-down menu.

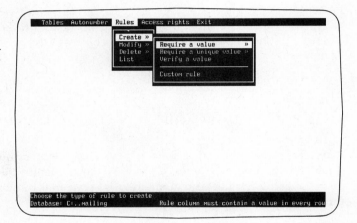

You have the following rule-definition options in the Database Definition module. These are the most common types of data entry rules used in R:BASE databases. If you define rules using the RULES command, you have more options; however, these standard rule types probably are the only rules you need for your database:

- *Require a Value:* This rule enforces an entry into a column, preventing null values from being left in the column. Usually, you should require a value in the key column of a table.

- *Require a Unique Value:* This rule enforces entry in the same way as the Require a Value rule, but it also requires that the value entered in the column be unique in the table. If you enter the value 100 in a column with this rule, for example, no other row in the table can have the value 100.

- *Verify a Value:* This rule requires that the value being entered in the column already exists elsewhere in the database in a defined location. R:BASE uses this rule to confirm that you made a master table entry before a subsidiary table entry. In the Mailing database, for example, you must enter the name of the person in the Mail List table (the master table containing the names and addresses) before you can make an entry for that customer in the When_mailed table.

- *Custom Rule:* This rule option enables you to enter a free-form rule definition.

The first three rules are standard rules that R:BASE creates for you if you select the tables and columns to which the rule should apply. The fourth rule enables you to define any condition or set of conditions that ensures proper entry of data into a column.

The syntax of a rule is as follows:

```
'message displayed if the rule is violated' FOR tablename SUCCEEDS/
FAILS WHERE conditions that must be met.
```

The message displayed when the rule is broken must be clear enough for a data entry operator to understand what is wrong. The FOR phrase specifies which table is to be checked for the rule violation. SUCCEEDS indicates that the conditions entered in the WHERE clause must be true to satisfy the rule. FAILS indicates that the conditions in the WHERE clause must be false to violate the rule (you select SUCCEEDS or FAILS, but not both). Finally, the WHERE clause specifies the conditions that must succeed or fail for the rule to be satisfied or violated.

Requiring Values

The Require a Value rule ensures that when you add a row to the table, any column with this rule assigned to it always will have a value entered. To define a required value rule, follow these steps:

1. Choose Rules from the Database Building menu.

2. Select Create from the Rules pull-down menu.

3. Choose Require a Value from the list of rules displayed.

   R:BASE displays a list of the tables.

4. Choose the table that holds the column the rule is to be assigned to. (In the sample database, you may want to require a last name to be entered, so you would select the Mail_list table, which contains the Lastname column.)

   R:BASE displays a list of the columns.

5. Choose the column for which you want to assign the rule.

Figure 3.10 shows the screen for defining a rule that requires a value entry in the Lastname column of the Mail_list table.

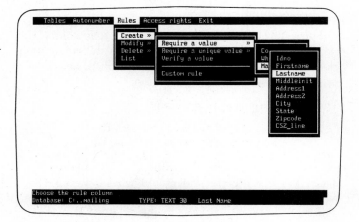

Fig. 3.10

Defining a rule that requires data entry in a specified column.

R:BASE writes the rule to the database structure. Any data entry to the table now requires that you enter a value for the column.

When defined, the rule is as follows:

```
MESSAGE : 'Value for Lastname cannot be null.'
TABLE : Mail_list   Row is added or changed if condition SUCCEEDS
WHERE : Lastname IS NOT NULL
```

Broken down, this rule means *The message* Value for Lastname cannot be null. *is displayed if, when entering data in the Mail_list table, you attempt to leave the row before entering a value into the Lastname column.* The word SUCCEEDS indicates that if the condition "Lastname IS NOT NULL" (has a value) fails, then the message is displayed and the operator cannot store the row in the database until the correction is made.

Requiring Unique Values

The second type of standard rule, which requires a unique value, is much like the first. The only difference is that you must enter data not only in the column—the data also must be unique in the table. To define a Require a Unique Value rule, follow these steps:

1. Choose Rules from the Database Building menu.

2. Choose Create from the Rules pull-down menu.

3. Choose Require a Unique Value from the list of rules displayed.

4. Choose the table that holds the column that the rule is to be assigned to. (In the sample database, you may want to require a unique value for the identification number, so you would select the Mail_list table, which contains the Idno column.)

5. Choose the column for which you want to assign the rule.

Figure 3.11 shows the screen for defining a rule that requires a unique value in the Idno column of the Mail_list table.

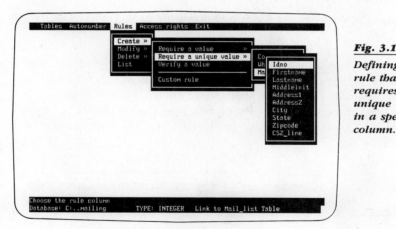

Fig. 3.11

Defining a rule that requires a unique value in a specified column.

R:BASE writes the rule to the database structure. Any data entry to the table now requires that a unique value be entered for the column. Of course, if you defined a column as an autonumber column, you do not need to assign this rule to the column because autonumbering ensures unique values.

When you want a unique required value, two data entry rules are created. The first is the same as for the required value. The second ensures a unique value:

```
MESSAGE : 'Value for Idno must be unique.'
TABLE : Mail_list   Row is added or changed if condition SUCCEEDS
WHERE : Idno NOT IN ( SELECT Idno FROM Mail_list)
```

This condition uses an R:BASE sub-SELECT clause to view the data in the existing rows in the Idno column. This condition says *Look at all the existing entries in the Idno column and make sure that the value does not exist. If it does, you violate the rule.*

Verifying Values

The third standard rule, which verifies a value, requires that an entry exist elsewhere in the database first. That is, when you attempt to enter a value in a column to which this rule has been assigned, R:BASE looks at another (or the same) table first to ensure that the value already exists. You can use this type of rule to ensure that a row exists in a master table (such as Mail_list) before adding a row in a detail table (such as When_mailed).

To define a Verify a Value rule, follow these steps:

1. Choose Rules from the Database Building menu.

2. Choose Create from the Rules pull-down menu.

3. Choose Verify a Value from the Rules list.

   R:BASE displays a dialog box, where you enter the rest of the rule parameters. For each entry field in the dialog box, R:BASE displays a list of tables or columns as appropriate for what needs to be entered. This type of menu within a dialog box operation is shown in figure 3.12 by the column list displayed under the Verification Column field.

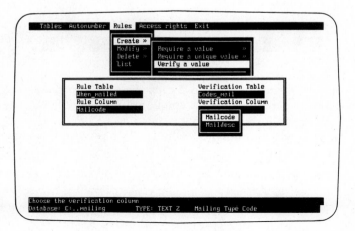

Fig. 3.12

The dialog box for assigning a Verify a Value rule.

4. For the Rule Table field, choose the table where the rule is to be assigned (in the sample database, this is the When_mailed table).

5. For the Rule Column field, choose the column to which the rule is to be assigned (in the sample database, you would choose the Mailcode column to verify that the code already exists in the Codes_mail table).

6. For the Verification Table field, choose the table to be checked to confirm that the entered value already exists (in the sample database, codes and their descriptions are stored in the Codes_mail table).

7. For the Verification Column field, choose the specific column in the verification table that already should hold the value being entered (in the sample database, this is the Mailcode column).

8. Press Enter or F2 after you select the last column.

R:BASE writes the rule to the database. Now you cannot enter a code in the When_mailed table unless you already have entered that code in the Codes_mail table.

The rule is written to the database as follows:

```
'Value for Mailcode must exist in Mailcode in Codes_mail' FOR
When_mailed SUCCEEDS WHERE Mailcode IN (SELECT Mailcode FROM
Codes_mail)
```

When this rule is applied, R:BASE views all the entries in the Mailcode column of the Codes_mail table. If the Mailcode value being entered in the When_mailed table already exists in the Codes_mail table, then the rule is not violated.

Defining Custom Rules

The syntax for defining a custom rule follows the same pattern as for the three standard data entry rules. The custom rule defined here for the sample database ensures that the identification number does not consist of more than four digits.

To define a custom rule, follow these steps:

1. Choose Rules from the Database Building menu.

2. Choose Create from the Rules pull-down menu.

3. Choose Custom Rule from the Rules list.

    R:BASE displays a dialog box where you enter the custom rule parameters (see fig. 3.13).

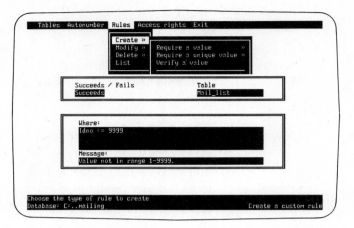

Fig. 3.13

The dialog box for entering customized rule parameters.

4. Choose Succeeds or Fails. If you choose Succeeds, R:BASE requires that the rule expression (entered in the Where field) must succeed for the rule to be met. For this example, choose Succeeds.

   To decide whether you want to use Succeeds or Fails, first write your rule as an English sentence. This will help you decide which option is more appropriate. If you want a rule violation message if something else is true, choose Succeeds. If you want a rule violation message if something else is false, choose Fails.

5. Choose the table to hold the rule. For the example, you choose Mail_list because it contains the Idno column.

6. In the Where field (WHERE clause), enter a comparison of a column, called a *condition*, which is a specification telling R:BASE what to look for when examining the data for a rule.

   If you chose Succeeds in Step 4, this condition must be true; if you chose Fails, it must be untrue. For the example, you do not want identification numbers greater than 9999. Because you have specified Succeeds, you must enter the condition as a statement you want to be true: Idno is less than or equal to 9999 (*Idno <= 9999*). If you chose Fails, you would enter the opposite condition (*Idno >= 9999*).

7. In the Message field, enter the message you want to display if the rule is violated. This message can contain up to 80 characters.

With a custom rule, R:BASE prompts you for part of the rule parameters (tables, columns, whether the rule is to succeed or fail), and you enter the conditions and the message to be displayed.

Be careful that your rules do not make data entry impossible. If you define a rule requiring that the data in a Firstname column be unique, for example, you will have a problem if you need to enter more than one "Fred."

Also, be careful that rules do not conflict with one another. R:BASE checks rules sequentially through the rules list for a table. If your data breaks the first rule and you change the data to obey the rule, but the change breaks a subsequent rule, you can be stuck in the Data Entry mode with no way to leave the table.

When you test your database, you can discover if you have any conflicting rules. Before adding real data to a database structure, you always should enter test data that covers as many possibilities as you can think of. If your test data is sufficiently varied, you can test thoroughly the validity of your data entry rules.

```
Command: RULES
```

Listing Rules

You can look at the rules you defined from the Database Definition module or by using the LIST RULES command. In the Database Definition module, highlight the Rules option and choose List from the Rules pull-down menu. Figure 3.14 shows a listing of rules defined for the Mailing database.

```
( RULES    ) ON  Check data validation RULES
MESSAGE :  Value for Lastname cannot be null.
  TABLE :  Mail_list    Row is added or changed if condition SUCCEEDS
  WHERE :  Lastname IS NOT NULL

MESSAGE :  Value for Idno must be unique.
  TABLE :  Mail_list    Row is added or changed if condition SUCCEEDS
  WHERE :  Idno NOT IN ( SELECT Idno FROM Mail_list )

MESSAGE :  Value for Mailcode must exist in Mailcode in Codes
  TABLE :  When_mailed   Row is added or changed if condition SUCCEEDS
  WHERE :  Mailcode IN ( SELECT Mailcode FROM Codes_mail )

MESSAGE :  Value not in range 1-9999.
  TABLE :  Mail_list    Row is added or changed if condition SUCCEEDS
  WHERE :  Idno <= 9999

Press any key to continue
```

Fig. 3.14

A list of rules defined for the Mailing database.

The first item on the rules list indicates whether the rules are being checked. When the default rule value is ON, the rules are checked during data entry. If you want to enter data that you know breaks a rule you defined, you can change this condition to OFF by using the Settings menu available from the Tools option on the R:BASE main menu. Alternatively, you can enter the command SET in Command mode.

Assigning Database Passwords

You can assign passwords to the database (owner password) and to tables and forms. Table passwords restrict access to tables by users based on the access privileges assigned to the users.

Passwords usually are necessary only if other people have access to your database and you want to restrict use of the database. Typically, passwords are assigned for multi-user systems (local area networks) in which a database is shared among several users.

Before you can assign passwords for tables, you first must define an owner password for the database. Only the database owner can define table passwords.

To define an owner password, follow these steps:

1. Highlight the Access Rights option on the Database Building menu in the Database Definition module.

2. Choose the Change Owner option.

3. Type the owner password in the dialog box provided (see fig. 3.15).

Fig. 3.15

Assigning an owner password.

The owner password, as well as the table passwords, can contain from one to eight characters and should start with an alphabetic character; the password can contain numbers and the punctuation _, %, #, (, or). Be sure to write down this password somewhere so that you will not forget it.

After you enter the owner password, you must enter it whenever you attempt to perform operations that are restricted to the owner (such as modifying the database structure). When you assign an owner password, R:BASE assumes that you are the owner (because you just defined the owner password). However, after you leave R:BASE and then return, R:BASE prompts you for the owner password when it is needed.

If you want to change the owner password, you follow the same steps as for defining the password if you are using the Database Definition module. If you are in Command mode, you can use the RENAME OWNER command.

```
Command: RENAME OWNER
```

After your database has an owner password, you can assign table passwords. If a table does not have access rights assigned to it, anyone who opens the database can use the table. The default password is "public," indicating that anyone can use it.

You can assign the following access rights to a table:

- *Select:* Permission to display the data in the table but not to modify it. Because this access right enables the user only to view data, you may want to assign it to users who use the database only for inquiry.

- *Update:* Permission to modify the table by changing existing rows. Update includes Select privileges.

- *Insert:* Permission to modify the table by adding new rows. Insert includes Select and Update privileges.

- *Delete:* Permission to modify the table by deleting existing rows. Delete includes Select and Update privileges.

- *All Privileges:* Permission for all access rights.

```
Commands: GRANT, LIST ACCESS, REVOKE
```

If you use the GRANT command to assign passwords, you can limit not only the table that a user has access to, but also access to certain columns.

In the Database Definition module, you can grant or revoke table passwords using the Access Rights option on the Tables menu as follows:

1. Highlight Access Rights on the Tables menu.

2. Press Enter to choose the Grant option. (The Revoke option removes access rights previously granted to a user.)

3. Select the access rights you want to grant. Highlight the access right and press Enter to put a check mark next to it (see fig. 3.16). To grant all rights, press Shift-F6 to place check marks beside the entire Rights list.

Fig. 3.16

Granting access rights to a table.

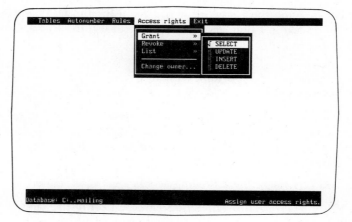

4. Press F2.

   R:BASE displays a list of tables.

5. Choose the table to which the passwords and access rights will be assigned.

   R:BASE displays a dialog box for the user passwords.

6. Enter one or more user passwords. (They may be cryptic codes or simply the user names in a less restrictive system.) Figure 3.17 shows how the screen would appear if you were assigning access rights to the Mail_list table for users whose passwords are Joan, Mary, and Tom.

7. After you enter the list of user passwords, R:BASE asks you to confirm that you want to grant the listed privileges. Highlight Yes and press Enter for confirmation.

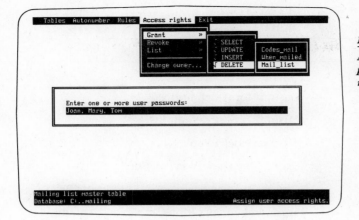

Fig. 3.17

Assigning passwords to multiple users.

Creating Additional Tables

You use the same techniques to create additional tables as you used to create the first table in a database. Here are a few guidelines to follow:

1. If you want to link a new table to an existing table, include a common column in both tables.

2. New tables can have the same column names as columns already defined in earlier tables. However, make the names the same only if you intend to have the columns hold the same data (as a common column). If you need different address columns in two different tables, give the columns different names. A client address column, for example, should have a different name than an employee address column.

3. Be sure that the first eight characters of table names are unique. R:BASE looks at only the first eight characters for many processes and may not locate the correct table if these eight characters are not unique. If you name two tables Customer_data and Customer_sales, for example, the first eight characters are not unique. Instead, name the tables Customer_data and Sales_custs.

4. A database can have up to 400 tables. However, R:BASE creates some special tables that add to the table total. If you define a data entry rule, for example, R:BASE creates a table named SYSRULE to hold the rule definitions. Table 3.2 lists the possible system-defined tables.

Table 3.2
R:BASE System Tables

Table Name	Use
SYSRULE	Rule definitions
SYSFORM	Custom form definitions
SYSREP	Custom report definitions
SYSLABEL	Custom label templates
SYSVIEWS	User-defined query (view) definitions
SYSPASS	Owner and user passwords (hidden table)
SYSINFO	Autonumber definitions, table, and column descriptions
SYSCOMP	Computed column definitions

You should not use these system-defined table names when defining your own table names. Note that the columns in these tables all begin with SYS; thus, you should avoid beginning any of your column names with SYS (or any upper- or lowercase variation).

Some processes create temporary tables; therefore, as a rule of thumb, define no more than 390 tables in one database.

5. A database can have up to 800 columns. Again, the system tables use up some of this total. If you defined all possible database objects (forms, rules, reports, and so on), R:BASE would take 36 of the possible 800 column names. You should define no more than 750 columns in one database.

6. The number of rows you can store in a database is limited only by the physical space you have available on your computer or network drive that contains the database. However, you should always leave free at least as much space as your three database files use (remember that R:BASE creates three DOS files for each database). That is, if your database takes a total of 400,000 bytes of storage, leave an additional 400,000 bytes free.

Modifying Existing Databases

You use the same techniques to modify existing databases as to create new ones. To modify an existing database, choose Modify from the Database

Definition main menu. R:BASE displays a list of databases on the current drive and directory. If the database you want to modify is not on the list, it may be in a different directory.

To change directories, you must exit from the Database Definition module by doing the following:

1. Highlight Databases on the R:BASE main menu.

2. Select Change directory from the pull-down menu.

3. Enter the directory path in the dialog box that R:BASE provides. To change to a directory named \RBFILES\DATABASE on drive C, for example, type *c:\rbfiles\database* and press Enter.

When you are in the correct directory, you can open the database by choosing it from the Databases pull-down menu. If you have assigned passwords, R:BASE asks you to enter a password for access. Because you want to modify the database structure, enter the owner password.

Start the Database Definition module by choosing Create/Modify from the Databases pull-down menu.

Using Function Keys in Database Definition

In addition to the standard function keys available (see Chapter 1), you can use several other function keys when modifying tables in the Database Definition module. Table 3.3 lists these modification function keys.

Table 3.3
Modification Function Keys

Key	Effect
F5	Restores a table or column name to its original state (modifying a table only).
Shift-F5	Restores a table definition to its original state (modifying a table only).
F9	Deletes the column at the cursor.
F10	Inserts a blank column at the cursor, ready for definition.

Modifying Tables

After you choose the database you want to modify, R:BASE displays the Database Building menu. Highlight the Tables option and choose Modify to change the structure of an existing table. When you choose to modify an existing table, R:BASE displays a list of the tables already defined in the database. Choose the table you want to modify (see fig. 3.18).

Fig. 3.18

Modifying a table.

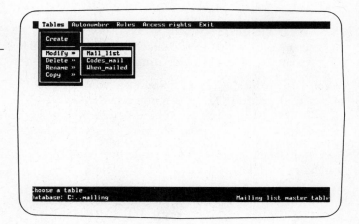

```
  Tables  Autonumber  Rules  Access rights  Exit
 ┌─────────┐
 │ Create  │
 ├─────────┤┌─────────────┐
 │ Modify »││ Mail_list   │
 │ Delete »││ Codes_mail  │
 │ Rename »││ When_mailed │
 │ Copy    »└─────────────┘
 └─────────┘




 Choose a table
 Database: C:..mailing                        Mailing list master table
```

```
Commands: ALTER TABLE, REDEFINE
```

R:BASE displays the Table Definition screen. The only difference between this display and the display when you create a new table is that the definition already is on-screen. Figure 3.19 shows a completed Table Definition screen.

Press Enter to move around the Definition screen. At each entry point—column name, description, data type, or indexing—you can change the definition or continue by pressing Enter. If you want to make a change, enter the new information as if you were defining a new table. The following sections provide specific information on each part of a column definition.

If you want to move to a specific column without going through the definition prompts for each column, press Tab until you highlight the column you want to change. Then make the changes to that column.

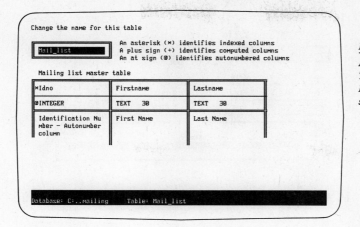

```
Change the name for this table

                          An asterisk (*) identifies indexed columns
 Mail_list                A plus sign (+) identifies computed columns
                          An at sign (@) identifies autonumbered columns

 Mailing list master table

 *Idno                 Firstname            Lastname

 @INTEGER              TEXT    30           TEXT    30

 Identification Nu     First Name           Last Name
 mber — Autonumber
 column



 Database: C:..mailing      Table: Mail_list
```

Fig. 3.19

A completed Table Definition screen.

When you make a change, you can use the left- and right-arrow keys to move backward or forward. Press Del to delete characters; press Ins to toggle between the Overwrite and Insert modes. In the Insert mode, you can add characters at the cursor; in the Overwrite mode, you type over the characters at the cursor.

Changing Table Names

When the Table Definition screen is displayed, the cursor is positioned in the Table Name box. To change the name, type over the existing name. When you change a table name, the same rules apply: the table name must be unique through the first eight characters and can have up to 18 alphanumeric characters; however, the name must begin with a letter.

If you make changes in the table name and then decide that you do not want to modify it, press F5 before you leave the Table Name box to restore the name to its original value.

After you change the table name or choose not to change the table name, press Enter to continue.

Changing Table Descriptions

After you leave the Table Name box, R:BASE displays the Table Description dialog box (see fig. 3.20). Type a new name or edit the original name. When you finish, or if you choose not to change the description, press Enter to continue.

Fig. 3.20

The Table Description dialog box.

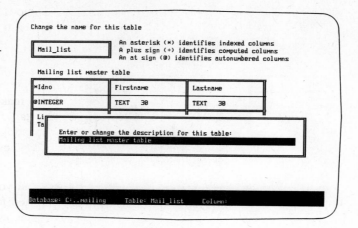

Changing Column Names

To change a column name, highlight the name by pressing Tab until you reach the column name you want to change. Type a new name or edit the original name. The new column name must follow the rules for column names: the first eight characters must be unique, it can contain up to 18 alphanumeric characters, and it must start with a letter.

If the column you are changing is a common column (it exists in more than one table to link the tables together), be sure to change the column name in all tables unless you want to remove the common column link.

If, after making changes, you decide that you want to leave the column name as is, press F5 before leaving the Column Name box to restore the name to its original value.

If you used the column in a view definition (see Chapter 5, "Using Query By Example"), you cannot change the column name unless you first remove the view.

After you change a column name, you can press Tab to move to another column or press Enter to change other parts of the column definition.

Changing Column Descriptions

If you press Enter at a column name, R:BASE displays a dialog box containing the column description. You can change an existing column description by typing over it (be sure to press Ins if you are not already in Overwrite mode), or you can edit what is displayed.

After you change the column description, or if you choose not to change it, press Enter to continue to the next part of the column definition.

Changing Column Data Types

Changing the data type of a column can affect the data stored in a table if you already have added data. Simple changes, such as making a Text data type column longer or shorter, do not change the data (data will be truncated if you make the length shorter than the existing data). More drastic changes can modify the way the data appears or even eliminate existing data.

If a column contains Currency values, for example, and you change the data type to Integer, the data remains, but in a modified form: $100.10 is changed to 100. If you change to a data type that is incompatible with the existing data—for example, changing a Currency data type to a Date data type—the column values are removed so that the column becomes null. Other incompatible data types follow:

Existing Data Type	*Incompatible Data Type Change*
Date	Currency
	Double
	Integer
	Numeric
	Real
Double	Date
Integer	Time
Numeric	
Real	
Time	Currency
	Date
	Double
	Integer
	Numeric
	Real

Changing any data type to a computed column also destroys existing data.

Keeping these dangers in mind, change the data type of a column by highlighting the column and pressing Enter (or changing the column name and pressing Enter). R:BASE displays the data type list under the column name.

Select the new data type. If you are changing to a Text data type, R:BASE prompts you for the length. If you are changing to a Numeric data type, R:BASE prompts you for the precision and scale for the numeric value. See Table 3.1 for a complete list and description of data types.

If you choose Computed for the data type, R:BASE prompts you for the computed column expression. See "Defining Computed Columns," earlier in this chapter for information on defining a computed column.

After you change a data type, R:BASE asks you for the column's index status.

Changing Column Index Status

At this point, you can add index status or remove a previously assigned index from a column. If a column is indexed, an asterisk (*) appears next to the column name. R:BASE prompts you with the question

    Do you want this column to be an indexed column?

Highlight Yes or No and press Enter to change the status. If the column already was an indexed column, Yes is highlighted; if the column was not an indexed column, No is highlighted. To keep the same status, press Enter to select the highlighted response.

After you respond to this question, R:BASE highlights the next column in the table. You can continue to change the existing column definitions, or you can further modify the table definition by adding or removing columns.

```
Commands: CREATE INDEX, DROP INDEX
```

Changing the index status of a column has no effect on data that the column already contains.

Refer to "Defining Column Indexes," earlier in this chapter, for additional information on column indexing.

Inserting Columns

To insert a new column, press F10. R:BASE inserts the new column before the currently highlighted column. You can add a column at the end by pressing Tab until the next blank column name box is highlighted. Then add the new column information just as if you were defining a new table.

If data already exists in the table, the values for the new column are null for every row currently in the table. You can add the data to the new column by using R:BASE tabular edit (see Chapter 4) or a custom form (see Chapter 6).

Removing Columns

To remove a column, press F9. R:BASE deletes the currently highlighted column. If data already exists in the table, the data as well as the column is removed. If you used the column in a view definition, you cannot remove it until you remove the view (see Chapter 5).

```
Command: REMOVE COLUMN
```

Deleting Tables

You can create duplicate tables or tables for temporary use only. You may want to combine data from several tables, for example, to export to another system; after the export is complete, you no longer need the table. If you want to remove a table for any reason, you can do so through the Database Definition module, following these steps:

1. From the Database Definition main menu, highlight Modify.
   If you have not opened a database, R:BASE prompts you for the database and the owner password, if you have assigned one.

2. Highlight Delete on the Tables pull-down menu.

3. Choose the table you want to delete from the list of tables in the database that R:BASE displays.

4. Select Yes to delete the table.

```
Command: REMOVE TABLE
```

If you used the table in the definition of a view (see Chapter 6), you cannot delete the table until you redefine or remove the view.

Renaming Tables

When you create your database and the tables in it, you choose the best possible names. Later, you may add additional tables and find that you should assign to a new table the first eight characters that you assigned to an earlier table. You can rename the older table to keep the first eight characters of all table names unique.

To rename a table, follow these steps:

1. From the Database Definition main menu, highlight Modify.
   If you have not opened a database, R:BASE prompts you for the database and the owner password, if you have assigned one.

2. Highlight Rename on the Tables pull-down menu.

3. Choose the table you want to rename.

4. When prompted, enter the new name for the table, following the rules for table names: the first eight characters must be unique to table names, you can use up to 18 alphanumeric characters, and the first character must be a letter.

> Command: RENAME TABLE

R:BASE renames the table. If you used the table in the definition of a view (see Chapter 6), you cannot rename the table until you redefine or remove the view.

Copying Tables

The Copy option in the Database Definition module copies the structure and the data in a table, so that entire columns and rows are copied to the new table. For whatever reasons you need to copy a table (you may want to copy a table to create a history table, for example), the Copy option is quick and easy to use.

To copy a table, follow these steps:

1. From the Database Definition main menu, highlight Modify.
   If you have not opened a database, R:BASE prompts you for the database and the owner password, if you have assigned one.

2. Highlight Copy on the Tables pull-down menu.

3. Choose the table you want to copy.

4. Enter the name for the new table, following the rules for table names: the first eight characters must be unique to table names, you can use up to 18 alphanumeric characters, and the first character must be a letter.

R:BASE copies the structure and data of the first table under the new table name. Copying a table does not affect the structure or data of the original table.

Several other methods for creating a new table from one or more existing tables are available. Refer to Chapter 9, "Using Relational Commands," for information on these other methods.

Changing Autonumbering

You can redefine an autonumber definition for a column in the same way that you originally defined the definition. Choose Autonumber from the Database Building menu, choose the table containing the autonumber column, and then choose the column containing the autonumber definition you want to change.

You need to renumber when you remove one or more rows from a table and you want the numbers to remain sequential. You also need to renumber when you add rows that you want to include in a specific number sequence. To renumber a table, perform the following steps:

1. From the Database Definition main menu, highlight Modify.
   If you have not opened a database, R:BASE prompts you for the database and the owner password, if you have assigned one.

2. Highlight Autonumber on the Database Building menu.

3. Choose Modify from the Autonumber menu.

4. Choose the table containing the column you want to number or renumber.

5. Choose the column you want to number or renumber.

   R:BASE prompts you with a dialog box containing the existing autonumber starting number and increment.

6. Change the starting number and increment as needed.

   R:BASE displays the current autonumber format.

7. Edit or type over the numbers with the change you want to make. Figure 3.21 shows the screen for changing an autonumber format for a Text data type column.

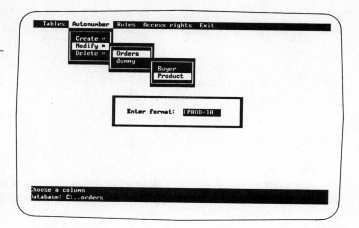

Fig. 3.21

Changing the autonumber format.

Command: AUTONUM

If you renumber a column that provides a link to another table, you lose the link established through the common column because the other table's common column values will no longer match the first table. You also need to edit the second table to change the common column values (see Chapters 4 and 6).

Changing Rules

You can add new rules, change the definition of existing rules, or delete existing rules. To do so, highlight Rules on the Database Building menu. To modify an existing rule, choose Modify. To create a new rule, choose Create.

Commands: DROP RULE, LIST ACCESS, RULES

The procedure to modify a rule is the same procedure used to define a custom rule, regardless of whether you defined a standard rule originally. See "Creating Data Entry Rules," earlier in this chapter, for information on rule formats.

To modify a rule, perform the following steps:

1. From the Database Definition main menu, highlight Modify. If you have not opened a database, R:BASE prompts you for the database and the owner password, if you have assigned one.

2. Highlight Rules on the Database Building menu.

    R:BASE displays a list of messages for the existing rules.

3. Choose the rule you want to change.

R:BASE steps through the definition process for custom rules, displaying the table and column already defined for the rule. You can choose a new table or column or press Enter to keep the existing table or column. The dialog box containing the rule message and condition shows the existing message and definition.

To keep the displayed values, simply press Enter to bypass the Dialog Box field. If you want to change the message, you can edit it by typing over what is displayed or by inserting or deleting information. To type over, be sure that you are in Overwrite mode (the cursor appears as an underscore). To insert, be sure that you are in Insert mode (the cursor appears as a block). Press Del to delete from the cursor position to the right. Press Backspace to delete from the character to the left of the cursor.

If you want to delete the rule completely, choose Delete from the Rules pull-down menu. R:BASE displays a list of rule messages. Choose the rule you want to delete and press Enter. R:BASE asks you to confirm that you want to delete the rule. You may need to delete rules if you find that a rule conflicts with another rule. Refer to "Creating Data Entry Rules," earlier in this chapter, for details.

Changing Passwords

Two types of passwords exist: the password for the database owner and passwords assigned to tables. Before you can change either type, you must enter the owner password to show that you have the authority to reassign password protection for the database. You may need to change or remove a password if a person leaves the company or his or her duties change.

Before you can assign any table passwords, you must have assigned an owner password. You change an existing owner password or enter a new owner password by using the Change Owner option on the Access Rights pull-down menu.

```
Command: RENAME OWNER
```

After you attach an owner password to a database, you can grant or revoke access rights for tables. Grant access rights by using the Grant option on the Access Rights pull-down menu. Remove previously granted rights by using the Revoke option on the Access Rights pull-down menu.

    Commands: GRANT, REVOKE

To view the assigned rights to be sure of what you want to change, use the List option on the Access Rights pull-down menu. You can view all assigned rights, only the rights for a specific user, or all users for a specific table. Figure 3.22 shows a Password list when all rights are requested.

Fig. 3.22

A list of passwords for users who have all access rights to a table.

User Password	Table	Access	Column
Joan	Mail_list	×SELECT	
Joan	Mail_list	×UPDATE	
Joan	Mail_list	×INSERT	
Joan	Mail_list	×DELETE	
Mary	Mail_list	×SELECT	
Mary	Mail_list	×UPDATE	
Mary	Mail_list	×INSERT	
Mary	Mail_list	×DELETE	
Tom	Mail_list	×SELECT	
Tom	Mail_list	×UPDATE	
Tom	Mail_list	×INSERT	
Tom	Mail_list	×DELETE	

Press any key to continue

    Command: LIST ACCESS

Managing Database Files

In addition to creating and modifying a database structure, the Database Definition module provides options for deleting, renaming, and copying a database.

Deleting Databases

If you no longer need a database, you can delete it to free more disk space. Remember that a database consists of a set of three DOS files, each beginning with the name of the database followed by a number 1, 2, or 3 and ending with the DOS file extension RBF. You can delete a database at the DOS prompt by using the DOS ERASE command, from within R:BASE by using the R:BASE version of the ERASE command, or in the Database Definition module by using the Delete option. This last method is the safest because R:BASE handles the deletion for you, ensuring that only the database files are removed.

To delete a database, follow these steps:

1. Start the Database Definition module.

2. Highlight Delete on the Database Definition main menu.

   R:BASE displays a list of the databases on the current drive and directory. If the database you want to delete is not on the list, you may be on the wrong drive or directory. In this case, exit from the module and change to the correct drive and directory using the Change Directory option on the Databases pull-down menu.

3. Choose the database you want to remove. R:BASE asks for confirmation.

4. Choose Yes to delete the database.

A deleted database is not recoverable unless you have some type of file recovery utility (for example, Norton Utilities). Be absolutely sure that you want to delete a database before doing so. You may want to make a backup copy of the database on a floppy disk before deleting in case you want to recover it later. Refer to Chapter 11, "Managing Your Database," for information on backing up a database.

```
Command: ERASE
```

Renaming Databases

You may want to rename a database if the database name conflicts with other files stored on the same drive and directory. Or, you may have a database with a name such as TEMP that you are practicing with in order to learn R:BASE; if you decide that you want to keep the database, you should change the database name to be more descriptive.

To rename a database, follow these steps:

1. Start the Database Definition module.

2. Highlight Rename on the Database Definition main menu.

   R:BASE displays a list of the databases on the current drive and directory. If the database you want to rename is not on the list, you may be on the wrong drive or directory. In this case, exit from the module and change to the correct drive and directory by using the Change Directory option on the Databases pull-down menu.

3. Choose the database you want to rename.

4. Enter the new database name following the rules for naming databases—you should have no more than seven alphanumeric characters.

R:BASE renames all three original database files with the new name. Renaming a database has no effect on the tables or the data contained in them.

```
Command: RENAME
```

Copying Databases

Copying a database is a simple way to make a backup copy. For other methods, refer to Chapter 11, "Managing Your Database." To copy a database, follow these steps:

1. Start the Database Definition module.

2. Highlight Copy on the Database Definition main menu.

   R:BASE displays a list of the databases on the current drive and directory. If the database you want to copy is not on the list, you may be on the wrong drive or directory. In this case, exit from the module and change to the correct drive and directory by using the Change Directory option on the Databases pull-down menu.

3. Choose the database you want to copy.

4. Enter the new database name following the rules for naming databases—you may include no more than seven alphanumeric characters.

R:BASE copies all three original database files to the new name. You now have a duplicate of the database. Copying a database has no effect on the tables or data contained in it.

```
Command: COPY
```

Summary

In this chapter, you learned to create a database, defining the structures that make up a database. You also learned how to define a column to be numbered automatically, and how to define data entry rules and passwords. You linked columns and indexed data, redefined and modified the original database structure, and managed database files.

You learned that the Database Definition module, reached from the Databases option on the R:BASE main menu, is a menu-driven system that leads you through the steps required to define a basic database structure.

Part II
Using Data Entry and Viewing Functions

Includes

Using Tabular Edit

Entering and Editing Data

Using Query By Example

Quick Start 2
Using Tabular Edit

This quick start covers the most common data entry and viewing functions in R:BASE. Two methods exist for modifying data in your database: the tabular edit screen and a custom data entry form. To report data, you can display data selected by using Query By Example, using R:BASE's calculation options, or printing a custom report.

Starting R:BASE

To start R:BASE, follow these steps:

1. Make current the directory containing the sample MAILING database. Type *chdir \samples* and press Enter.

2. Type *rbase* and press Enter.

   R:BASE displays its main menu. In this example, use the MAILING database that you created in Quick Start 1.

3. Highlight MAILING on the Databases pull-down menu and press Enter. When a database is open, its name appears at the bottom of the screen.

If you assigned an owner password or table passwords to the database, R:BASE prompts you to enter a password. Press Enter to display the dialog box for entering a password and then type the password. R:BASE displays the main menu.

Using Tabular Edit

You can enter or edit data by using R:BASE's default tabular edit format. The data you want to modify is restricted to a single table. To enter data in the tabular format, follow these steps:

1. Highlight the Info option.

R:BASE displays a list of tables in the MAILING database.

2. Choose Mail_list.

Because no data exists in this table yet, R:BASE asks whether you want to add rows.

3. Press Y and then press Enter to answer Yes.

R:BASE displays the columns for the Mail_list table on the Tabular Edit form (see fig. QS2.1). Notice that the new row already has a 1 in the Idno column. When you defined the Mail_list table in Quick Start 1, you made the Idno column an autonumber column. The rest of the columns have -0- in them—the symbol for a null value. When you enter values in each column, remove the null value symbol. Type over the symbol if your cursor is an underscore, or press Del three times to delete the symbol.

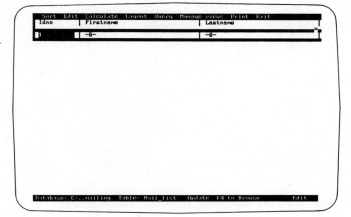

Fig. QS2.1

Adding a new row.

4. Press Tab and type *John* for the Firstname column. Do not press Enter at the end of each entry because pressing Enter simply moves the cursor back to the first column in the table.

5. Press Tab to move to the Lastname column. (You use the Tab key to move from column to column across the table.)

6. Enter the following information in the rest of the columns:

Column Name	Data
Lastname	Doe
Middleinit	A.
Address1	1105 Kentucky Ave.
Address2	Apt. 2
City	Chicago
State	IL
Zipcode	50606

7. Press Tab after you enter the ZIP code. The CSZ_line column is automatically filled with the city, state, and ZIP code. This result occurs because CSZ_line is a computed column with an expression that says to combine the values of the City, State, and Zipcode columns.

8. To add more rows to the table, press Alt-E. Highlight Insert Row, as shown in figure QS2.2. Press Enter.

   R:BASE adds another row with the Idno column filled in with the next number.

Fig. QS2.2

Inserting new rows in a table.

9. Add two more rows to the table in the same way you added the data in the first row:

Column Name	Row 2 Data	Row 3 Data
Firstname	Fred	Mary
Lastname	Roe	Brown
Middleinit	B.	
Address1	999 Ventnor	434 Pacific
Address2		#404
City	Indianapolis	Fort Wayne
State	IN	IN
Zipcode	46204	40322-9033

In columns where you do not enter data (such as the Middleinit column for Mary Brown), just press Tab to skip the column. You can leave the null symbol, which means that the column does not contain a value. If you make a mistake and need to go back to a column, press Shift-Tab to go backward. You can edit the data by typing over the data, inserting characters (press Ins to switch between Overtype and Insert modes), or deleting characters (press Del).

Because you inserted new rows at the top of the table, the rows are ordered 3, 2, 1 by Idno. You can sort them to appear in 1, 2, 3 order.

To sort the columns, follow these steps:

1. Highlight the Idno column in any row. (You press Shift-Tab to move backward or press Enter to move to the first column in a row.)

2. Press Alt-S to choose a sort order. Highlight Single Column to sort the rows by the values in a single column. Press Enter.

    You must choose to sort in ascending or descending order, as shown in figure QS2.3.

Fig. QS2.3

Sorting in ascending order.

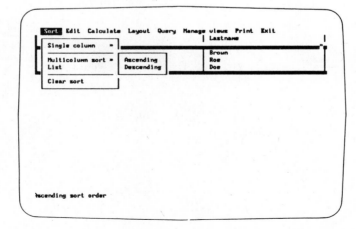

3. Press Enter to select Ascending.

R:BASE sorts the rows by Idno in ascending order, as shown in figure QS2.4.

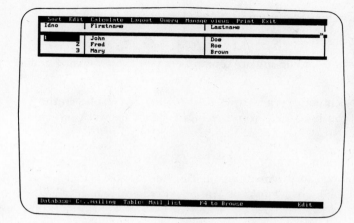

Fig. QS2.4

The Idno column when sorted in ascending order.

You also can move the columns to make the display more readable. Suppose that you want to put the middle initial between the first name and last name. To move a column, follow these steps:

1. Press Tab until the Lastname column is highlighted.

2. Press Alt-L to change the display layout. Highlight Move Column and press Enter (see fig. QS2.5).

    R:BASE displays a list of the columns.

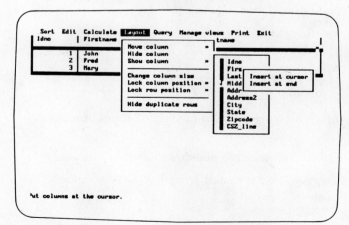

Fig. QS2.5

Moving the columns without affecting the data.

3. Highlight Middleinit and press Enter.

The program puts a check mark (✔) next to the column name.

4. Press F2.

R:BASE asks whether you want to insert the column at the cursor.

5. Press Enter to insert at the cursor.

R:BASE moves the middle initial column between the Firstname and Lastname columns.

Now use the same technique to add rows to the other two tables in the database. To begin, you must exit from the Info (or Edit/Browse) screen. Follow these steps:

1. Press Esc to highlight Exit and press Enter.

R:BASE returns you to the main menu. The Info option is still highlighted. R:BASE always returns you to where you started a module.

2. Highlight Codes_mail and press Enter.

3. Press Y to answer yes to the Add Rows question.

4. Enter the data for each column heading:

Column Name	Data
Mailcode	L1
Maildesc	Initial mailing

5. Press Alt-E to display the Edit pull-down menu.

6. Highlight Insert and press Enter to select it.

7. Enter the data for the next row:

Column Name	Data
Mailcode	L2
Maildesc	First response letter

8. After you add these rows, press Esc to highlight Exit and then press Enter.

9. Highlight When_mailed on the Info pull-down menu and press Enter.

R:BASE asks whether you want to add a row because the table does not contain any data.

10. Press Enter to choose Yes to add a row to the table.

11. Enter the data for the When_mailed table in the same way you added data to the other two tables. Enter the first row. When you are ready to add the next row, press Alt-E to highlight the Edit pull-down menu and choose Insert Row.

Column Name	Row 1 Data	Row 2 Data	Row 3 Data	Row 4 Data	Row 5 Data
Idno	1	2	2	1	3
What_mailed	L1	L1	L2	L2	L2
When_mailed	03/24/90	03/24/90	04/14/90	04/14/90	04/14/90

Press Del to remove the rest of the null symbols from the Idno column, or press the space bar if you are in Overwrite mode (the cursor is an underscore).

12. Press Esc and then Enter to exit from the Info screen.

R:BASE returns you to the main menu.

Refining Your Data with Views

Query By Example enables you to examine and edit data in your database. Query By Example is most useful when you need to display data from more than one table at a time. You can look at the When_mailed table to see the mailing codes, for example, but you need to link the Codes_mail table to see the full descriptions for the mailings.

Note: | When you look at data from more than one table, you are restricted to querying—you cannot change the data. If you want to modify data in more than one table at the same time, you need to define a multitable form (see Chapter 6).

The following steps lead you through the process of selecting two tables from the database, telling R:BASE how to link the tables, and then displaying the data through the Info screen:

1. Highlight Views on the R:BASE main menu.

2. Press Enter to select Create/Modify.

   R:BASE displays the Views menu with the Query pull-down menu on-screen (see fig. QS2.6). Notice that some of the options on the menu are white rather than black. When you cannot use a pull-down menu option in R:BASE, the option is white. This is called *graying* the options to indicate which ones cannot be used.

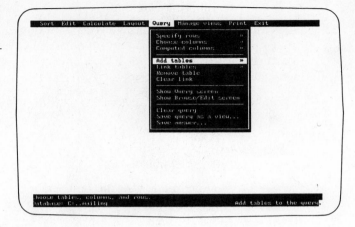

Fig. QS2.6

The Query pull-down menu.

This menu provides most of the options you need to specify the way you view data.

3. Press Enter to select Add Tables.

   R:BASE displays the three tables contained in the database.

4. Choose Mail_list for the first table.

   R:BASE displays the table layout on-screen. Notice that the title of the table is #T1.Mail_list. The #T1 is added to the table name to indicate that it is the first table in the view you are defining.

   You need to tell R:BASE which columns to use in this table. The easiest way is to select all columns. (Later, you can unselect columns you do not want to include.)

5. Press Shift-F6.

   R:BASE marks each column with a check mark. Now you can add the next table.

6. Press Alt-Q. Add Tables is highlighted. Press Enter and choose When_mailed for the second table.

   R:BASE adds the When_mailed table to the screen.

7. Select all columns from When_mailed by pressing Shift-F6.

   Figure QS2.7 shows what the screen should look like now.

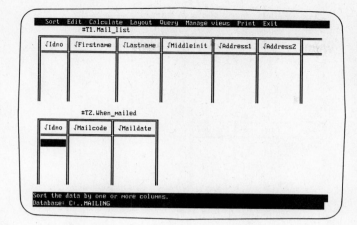

So far, you have told R:BASE that you want to look at the data from two tables. When you defined these tables, you made sure they were related by giving them a common column (Idno). Now you should tell R:BASE that Idno is the column to use to link the tables. Follow these steps:

1. Press Shift-F7 to move the cursor to the Idno column in the Mail_list table.

2. Press Alt-Q and choose Link Tables.

   R:BASE asks what kind of link you want.

3. Press Enter to choose = EQUAL.

   This procedure tells R:BASE that you want all rows from the Mail_list table where the value of Idno is equal to the value of a column in the second table. R:BASE displays = ‹link1› under the Idno column in the Mail_list table.

4. Press Shift-F8 to highlight the Idno column in the When_mailed table. Press Enter to establish this column as the other side of the link.

   R:BASE displays ‹link1› under the Idno column in the When_mailed table (see fig. QS2.8).

You have completed a simple view definition. You should save this view because you use it to create a report in Quick Start 3. Views gather data before reports are processed, so this method of printing a report is quicker than using the report lookup features. To save the view, follow these steps:

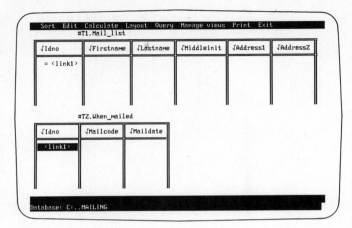

Fig. QS2.8

Linking tables.

1. Press Alt-Q, highlight Save Query as a View, and press Enter.

   R:BASE asks for a name to give the saved view.

2. Type *Q_mail*. The screen looks like figure QS2.9.

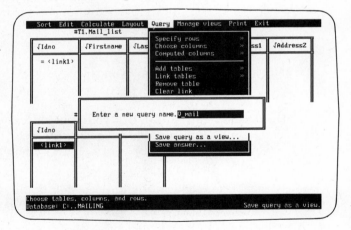

Fig. QS2.9

*Saving the
view
definition for
later use.*

3. Press Enter to save the view.

Now you can look at the combined data on the Info screen. You can go directly to the Info screen from the Views screen. To view the data, follow these steps:

1. Press Alt-Q, highlight Show Browse/Edit Screen, and press Enter.

   R:BASE displays the first three columns in the combined view (see fig. QS2.10).

```
 Sort  Edit   Calculate  Layout  Query  Manage views  Print  Exit
#T1.Idno     #T1.Firstname              #T1.Lastname

1            John                       Doe
        1    John                       Doe
        2    Fred                       Roe
        2    Fred                       Roe
        3    Mary                       Brown




Database: C:..mailing     Read                         Browse
```

Fig. QS2.10

Looking at the combined data on the Edit screen.

This screen is slightly different from the one you saw when you were adding new rows to the Mail_list table. The words Query Browse appear at the bottom of the screen. The columns have the table identifier as a prefix (#T1 in the case of the Mail_list table). The Idno column appears to contain duplicate values.

This last difference is a result of combining the data from two tables. When you entered data in the When_mailed table, you added two rows for Idno 1, two rows for Idno 2, and one row for Idno 3. Because you asked to link the two tables where Idno was equal, the only rows that appear in the view are the rows where the same value exists in both tables. Also, because two occurrences of Idno 2 and Idno 3 exist in the second table, the data from the first table (Mail_list) appears twice for each.

2. Press Tab until you reach the second Idno column.

   The table identifier is #T2, indicating that the data you see here is drawn from the second table.

3. Browse through the View data. When you are ready to continue, press Esc and then Enter to exit to the R:BASE main menu.

   Notice that the View Q_mail is now on the list on the Views pull-down menu.

Using the Calculation Options

You can perform a variety of calculations on the data in a table or combination of tables. Calculation options from the Views or Info menus include the following:

- *Compute:* Provides the sum, average, minimum, maximum, or count of a column. You can, for example, display the total of all the currency values in a column, find the earliest date, and count the number of rows containing a value.

- *Tally:* Counts the number of occurrences of each value in a column. You can find out, for example, how many letters of each type have been sent by tallying the Mailcode column.

- *Group:* Displays data grouped by value. You can, for example, display all letters for each person grouped by Idno.

- *Crosstab:* Displays a tabular display of data by comparing one column value to another.

After you see the type of display that Crosstab can provide, you will think of many uses for Crosstab in your database applications. To use the Crosstab option, follow these steps:

1. Highlight Views and press Enter to select Q_mail.

   You created this view earlier in this quick start. This view combines data from the Mail_list and When_mailed tables. R:BASE displays the data defined by the view.

2. Press Alt-C to highlight Calculate.

3. Highlight Crosstab and press Enter.

   R:BASE displays the cross-table form and asks for the column containing the values that are to appear across the top.

4. Move the cursor down in the list until you get to Mailcode. Press Enter to select Mailcode for the values to appear across the top of the screen.

   R:BASE then asks for the column containing the values to be displayed on the left side of the table format (see fig. QS2.11).

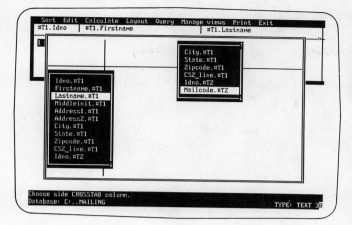

Fig. QS2.11

Building a cross-tabulation.

5. Choose the Lastname column for the left side of the table.

   R:BASE asks for the column containing the values to be calculated in the center of the table and how you want to calculate. For a numeric column, you can display a sum or average. Because you are using a text column, you realistically can count only the number of occurrences.

6. Choose Count.

7. Move down the column list and choose Mailcode.

   Figure QS2.12 shows you how the screen should look.

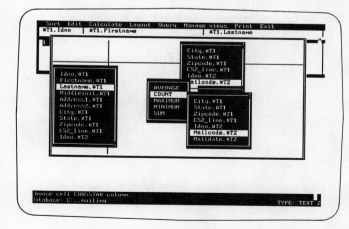

Fig. QS2.12

The last step in building a cross-tabulation.

8. Press F2 to present the cross-tabulation.

   Figure QS2.13 shows the result of the cross-tabulation. As you can see, Crosstab presents a summary of the data stored in the table. Crosstab takes the data stored in database format and presents the data in a spreadsheet format. One piece of the data becomes the heading (the mailing code), another piece shows how the data is broken down (by last name), and the center of the table provides the calculated result of comparing the top and side values (counting the number of mailing codes for each person).

Fig. QS2.13

Cross-tabulation summarizes your data in a tabular format.

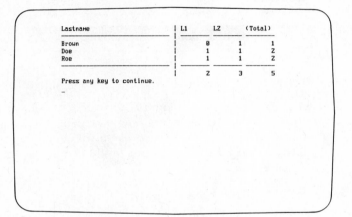

```
Lastname                     | L1     LZ      (Total)
                             |
Brown                        | 8      1       1
Doe                          | 1      1       Z
Roe                          | 1      1       Z
                             |
                             | Z      3       5
Press any key to continue.
_
```

9. Press any letter or number key to remove the cross-tabular display.

10. Press Esc to highlight Exit and then press Enter.

Summary

In this quick start, you learned how to use the Tabular Edit method for entering and editing data. You learned how to refine a request for data on a tabular browse by using R:BASE's Query By Example module. Finally, you learned how to use one of the tabular editor's calculation options — Crosstab.

You now know how to enter and edit data by using R:BASE's Tabular Edit feature (the Info option) and how to display data from more than one table by using Query By Example (the Views option). Chapters 4 and 5 cover each of these topics in detail.

4

Entering and Editing Data

From the R:BASE main menu, the Info and Views options display the same menu. These two options provide the capability to work with tables in two ways:

- Defining tables, columns, and data you want to browse or edit.

- Browsing or editing data from tables.

Chapter 5 explains how to use the first feature (Definition), which is called Views or Query By Example. This chapter tells you how to use the second feature (Browsing and Editing).

R:BASE has two main menu options to reach a single menu for the following reasons:

- The options together provide a single, seamless unit. You can toggle between the two functions by pressing Ctrl-F3.

- When you are editing or browsing data, you can switch quickly to the definition side of the function to refine the way that R:BASE presents the data. After selecting the tables, columns, and rows that you want to look at, you just as easily can toggle to the Browse/Edit function.

First, look at what happens if you choose each of these options from the R:BASE main menu.

If you highlight Info, R:BASE displays a pull-down menu with a list of the tables in your database and a Create/Modify option. If you choose a table from the list, R:BASE displays the Info/Views menu and the data from the table you selected. If you choose Create/Modify, R:BASE sends you to the Database Definition module so that you can define a table structure. See

Chapter 3 for information on using the Database Definition module to create table structures.

If you highlight Views, R:BASE displays a pull-down menu with a list of views in your database (see Chapter 5) and a Create/Modify option. If you choose a view, R:BASE displays the Info/Views menu and the data from the view you selected. At this point, the screen is just the same as if you had chosen Info, but the data displayed is from a view structure rather than a table. If you choose Create/Modify, R:BASE displays the Info/Views menu, but the screen is blank—ready for you to select tables, columns, and data that you want to browse through or edit.

Because this chapter discusses the Edit/Browse feature, you will be using the Info option to select a table for editing. Chapter 5 shows you how to use Info's alter ego, Views, to refine your data query.

Using the Info Menu

Keeping in mind that you are working with the Edit/Browse features, you should think of the menu you reach from the Info option on the R:BASE main menu as the Info menu. When you reach the same menu from the Views option, you can call that menu the Views menu. In this chapter, you learn how to use the options for editing and browsing data only; in Chapter 5, you learn how to use the options when defining a view.

After you highlight Info on the R:BASE main menu and select a table from it, R:BASE displays the menu shown in figure 4.1.

Fig. 4.1

The Info menu.

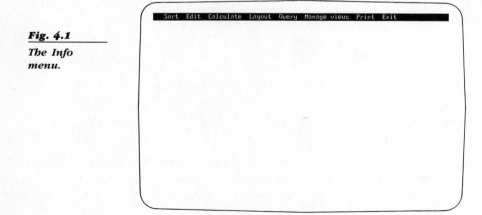

The information that appears below the menu and the options available from the pull-down menus depend on which module you are executing. If an option is not available for the module you are executing, the pull-down options are displayed in gray rather than black characters. You cannot select an option displayed in gray.

The menu options shown in figure 4.1, used with Info, provide the following functions:

Option	Mode	Function
Sort	Edit/Browse	Sorts the order of the rows on display.
Edit	Edit	Provides insert, modify, delete, and global replace options.
Calculate	Edit/Browse	Provides four methods of making calculations on the displayed data.
Layout	Edit/Browse	Enables you to reorder the columns, change their display width, hide columns, or lock column or row positions.
Query	Views	Enables you to choose the tables and links between tables for a query definition. This menu also has a single option available in Info: Show Query. You can use this option to display the Views screen.
Manage Views	Edit/Browse or Views	Saves, modifies, deletes, renames, or copies a view.
Print	Edit/Browse or Query	Provides options for printing the displayed data or saving the data in an ASCII file.

Inserting and Adding Rows

Adding new rows to a table is a simple exercise of typing data into the space provided for each column defined for the table. You can add new rows to the end of a table or you can insert rows within existing data. You should keep the following in mind when adding or editing data:

- Enter data for each column that is appropriate to the column's data type definition. Do not, for example, add dates to numeric columns. If you do attempt to add inappropriate data to a column, R:BASE displays a message telling you that you cannot enter that data. R:BASE then keeps the cursor in the column's entry field until the data is right for the column. R:BASE checks the correctness of data as soon as you attempt to move the cursor out of the field.

- If you defined data entry rules, be sure that the data you are adding does not violate a rule. If a rule requires that a column must contain unique data, for example, do not add data that duplicates an existing row's data. R:BASE checks data entry rules when you attempt to exit from the Info module by choosing the Exit option or by toggling to the Views module. If you violate a rule, R:BASE displays the rule's message and does not enable you to exit from the Info module until you follow the rule.

- After you enter data in a column's field, you can edit it before you leave the field or you can return to the field and edit it later. See "Editing the Data," later in this chapter, for information on edit keys and procedures.

- If you add or insert a row and then decide that you do not want to add it, you can remove the row by using the Delete Row option on the Edit pull-down menu. See "Editing the Data" for information.

Essentially, entering data is no different than editing data because of the way R:BASE operates when you add or insert a row. When you ask to add or insert, R:BASE creates a row for you with all of the columns filled in with a null value (shown as -0- on-screen). These null values indicate that you now can edit data. You will be changing the null value symbol -0- for the actual data you want in the row. Be sure to remove the null symbol from the field as you type the new data. The easiest way to do this is to press Ins to toggle to Overwrite mode (the cursor will be an underscore) and then type over the null symbol with your real data. Alternatively, you can delete the null symbol by pressing Del before you begin typing the new data. See Table 4.1 for a complete list of editing keys.

When you start the Info module by selecting a table from the Info pull-down menu on the R:BASE main menu, R:BASE displays the first screen of data already in the table. If no data exists in the table, R:BASE asks whether you want to add a row to the table (see fig. 4.2). Answer Yes to add a row. Then type the data for each column, pressing Tab to move from column to column.

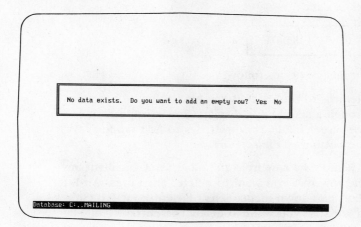

Fig. 4.2

R:BASE asks you if you want to add data when no rows exist.

After you add the first row to a table, you need to ask R:BASE to add any additional rows to the table. To add rows to a table, use the Edit option. Press Alt-E to display the Edit pull-down menu and then choose Insert Row (see fig. 4.3). You can insert the new row as the row before the currently highlighted row, or you can add the new row to the end of the table. Because row order has no importance to R:BASE, choose either place that you want.

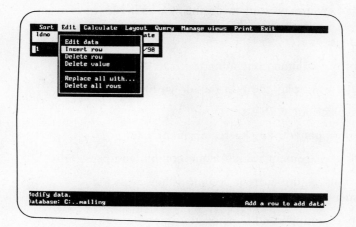

Fig. 4.3

The Insert a Row option on the Edit pull-down menu.

Editing Data

You edit data by typing over existing data, clearing the column and entering new data, or clearing the column and leaving it with a null value (if data entry rules allow). You also can replace the value of a column in one or more rows by using a pull-down menu option. Finally, you can remove entire rows of data.

> Commands: EDIT, DELETE, UPDATE

The Edit pull-down menu options follow:

- *Edit Data:* Returns to the data display for editing. If you were browsing through a single-table display (Browse appears at the bottom of the screen), Edit Data switches to Edit mode (Edit appears at the bottom of the screen).

- *Delete Row:* Removes a row from the table. First, highlight any column in the row that you want to delete. Then press Alt-E to display the Edit pull-down menu. Select Delete Row. R:BASE asks whether you are sure you want to delete the currently highlighted row. Press Y and Enter to delete the row.

- *Delete Value:* Erases the value from the currently highlighted column. This is easier sometimes than inserting and deleting individual characters. After you delete what you want, you can type the data you want. Highlight the column containing the data to be deleted. Press Alt-E to display the Edit pull-down menu. Then select Delete Value.

- *Replace All With:* Changes the value of a column to a new value in all rows selected. You may want to do this, for example, to change the ID number for all rows in a detail table. To use Replace All With, follow these steps:

    1. Highlight the column containing the data to be replaced.

    2. Press Alt-E to display the Edit pull-down menu.

    3. Select Replace All With.

        R:BASE prompts you for the replacement value.

    4. Enter the replacement value for the column and press Enter.

        R:BASE replaces the current column values with the replacement values.

        Remember: Setting conditions on the query may limit the rows included in the query.

- *Delete All Rows:* Removes all rows selected for editing. You may want to do this to remove all detail references for a specific ID number, for example. To use Delete All Rows, follow these steps:

  1. Highlight the column containing the data that you want to delete.

  2. Press Alt-E to display the Edit pull-down menu.

  3. Highlight Delete All Rows.

     R:BASE asks for confirmation.

  4. Press Y and then Enter to delete the rows from the table.

R:BASE removes all rows. At this point, you will have to exit or use the Insert Row option to add more rows to the table.

Some menu options have corresponding function keys that you can use to perform the same task. Press Shift-F1 to see a list of available function keys and their uses. Table 4.1 lists the editing function keys not duplicated by a menu option.

Table 4.1
Editing Function Keys

Key	Effect
Ctrl-F3	Toggles between Info and Views.
F4	Toggles between Edit and Browse.
Shift-F4	Enlarges (zooms) a long Text or Note column so that all the data contained in the column appears in a large window in the center of the screen.
F5	Resets a field to its original value.
F6	Marks the beginning and ending points of data that you want to copy to another column or row.
F7	Returns to the preceding row.
Ctrl-F7	Copies the marked data to the current column.
F8	Goes to the next row.
Ctrl-F8	Removes the highlighted column from the display.
F9	Deletes the current row.
Shift-F9	Clears the highlighted column.
Ctrl-F9	Clears from the cursor position to the end of the highlighted column.
F10	Inserts a row below the current row.

Marking and Copying Data

Marking and copying is a useful feature that enables you to duplicate data from one row to another or from column to column. Marking and copying in R:BASE is similar to cutting and pasting in a word processor. When you edit data, you mark the beginning and end positions of the data that you want to copy, move the cursor to the location where you want to place the copied data, and then place the data. You can copy data only when you are in Edit mode (the word Edit appears in the bottom right corner of the screen).

To mark and copy data, follow these steps:

1. Move the cursor to the first character of the data you want to copy.

2. Press F6 to mark the start of the data that you want to copy.

3. Move the cursor with the arrow keys to highlight the area of data that you want to copy. Press F6 again.

4. Move the cursor to the location where you want to place the copied data.

5. Press Ctrl-F7 to insert the copied data.

The data is saved until you exit from Info/Views or until you mark another area of data for copying.

The data that you copy must be contained within a single column. You can mark all or any portion of the data in the column. You can copy the data to a single column in the same row or in another row. Also, the data type of the column to receive the data must have a compatible data type—for example, you cannot copy a Text name to an Integer column.

Sorting Data

When the data is displayed on the Info screen, the rows are in the order in which they were stored in the database. If you want to change that order, you can do so by using the Sort option.

Press Alt-S to highlight Sort. You can sort by a single column or multiple columns. The pull-down menu also provides options for listing any currently defined sort order or for clearing the defined sort order. For a complete description of sorting, see Chapter 1.

The method for sorting is similar for single- and multicolumn sorting. The only difference is that with a single-column sort, you just choose one column from the list and the sort order (ascending or descending).

With a multicolumn sort, you can continue to choose columns and the sort order for each until you press F2 to tell R:BASE that you are finished. Figure 4.4 shows the screen displayed while you are asking for a multicolumn sort.

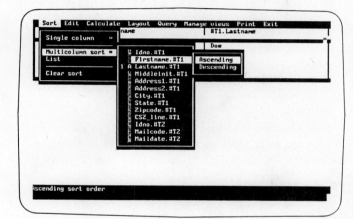

Fig. 4.4
Sorting the data on-screen.

If you are not sure which sorting you have defined, you can list the sort columns, as shown in figure 4.5. This screen shows you how to enter the sort clause in a command line. The table identifier prefixes each column name. ASC follows the column if you choose Ascending; DESC follows the column if you choose Descending.

Because the sample data shows only five rows, the following additional example illustrates the effect of a multicolumn sort. Notice that the following data is in no particular order. The Column 1 ID numbers are even out of order. This makes no difference to R:BASE:

Column 1	Column 2	Column 3
100	Fred	Jones
109	Charles	Denwich
103	Mary	Brown

111	Harry	James
101	Terri	Smith
102	Harry	Brown
104	Letitia	Jones

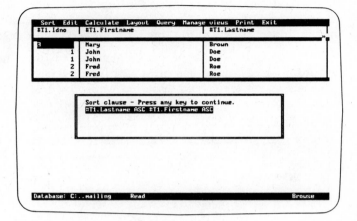

Fig. 4.5

Viewing the sort order that you selected for the table.

Notice that by sorting on Column 2, the first names are now in ascending order, alphabetically. However, note that the original order of the table is kept when two first names are the same (Harry James and Harry Brown):

Column 1	Column 2	Column 3
109	Charles	Denwich
100	Fred	Jones
111	Harry	James
102	Harry	Brown
103	Mary	Brown
104	Letitia	Jones
101	Terri	Smith

The two-column sort puts the names in the correct alphabetical order: last names are sorted first (this groups the Browns, for example), and then first name are sorted (this puts Harry Brown before Mary Brown):

Column 1	Column 2	Column 3
102	Harry	Brown
103	Mary	Brown
109	Charles	Denwich
111	Harry	James
100	Fred	Jones
104	Letitia	Jones
101	Terri	Smith

Tip: You will find that sorting works fastest if you sort on a column that is defined as an indexed column. If you find that you are constantly sorting by a specific column, you probably should index that column. Use the Database Definition module to modify your table. Highlight the column you want to index. Step through the column's definition parts by pressing Enter until R:BASE asks whether you want to define an index for this column. Answer Yes.

Modifying the Information Layout

The sequence of the columns and the width on the Info display are by default the sequence and width assigned when you defined the table. You can change the column sequence by using the Layout options. You may want to change the sequence if you are editing only a few columns of data but want to have available the columns that you are not editing. In this case, you would find it more convenient to group the columns to be edited on one side of the table, and the columns for reference on the other side.

The layout you define will be saved so that the next time you edit the table, it will have the same look. See Appendix C for more information.

You may want to change the width of long columns to make them take up less space on-screen. By making a long column narrower, you can fit more columns on-screen.

Press Alt-L to highlight Layout. The Layout pull-down menu has several options for dealing with the display format (see fig. 4.6). The next sections describe how to use each of the Layout options.

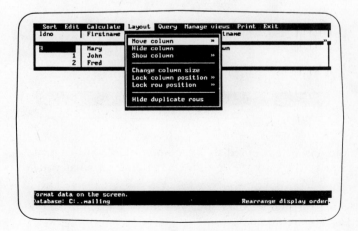

Fig. 4.6

Working with the column display format on the Layout menu.

Moving Columns

Use Move Column to change the location of a column. Follow these steps to move a column:

1. Highlight the position of the column where you want to move another column.

2. Press Alt-L and press Enter to select Move Column.

   R:BASE displays a list of columns.

3. Select the column that you want to move to the column cursor position.

   R:BASE places a check mark (✔) next to the column. Select as many columns as you want to move to the new position.

4. Press F2.

   R:BASE asks whether you want to insert at the cursor or at the end of the table.

5. Highlight Insert at Cursor to move the columns to the highlighted column position. Alternatively, highlight Insert at End to move the columns to the far right side of the table (see fig. 4.7).

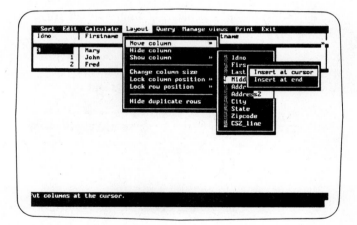

Fig. 4.7

Moving the columns around to group data.

R:BASE moves the columns you selected to the column position that you highlighted in Step 1 or to the end of the table, depending on what you chose in Step 5.

Figure 4.8 shows the screen as it appears after you move the Middleinit column before the Lastname column.

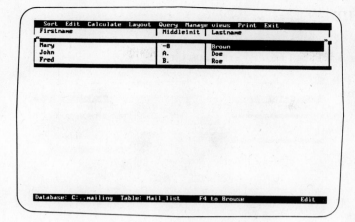

Fig. 4.8

Viewing data after moving a column.

Hiding Columns

Use the Hide Column option on the Layout menu to make a column and its data disappear from the screen. If you include a computed column (defined in the table or created on-the-fly), you must include any columns used in the computed column's expression. This means that you will have duplicate data (for example, with the CSZ_line column that contains the city, state, and ZIP code) unless you hide the unneeded columns. Because it may be confusing to see duplicate information, it is usually a good idea to hide the columns that you do not need to look at, but which are necessary for use with another column, such as a computed column.

To hide a column, follow these steps:

1. Highlight the column you want to hide.

2. Press Alt-L to display the Layout pull-down menu.

3. Select Hide Column.

The column and its data immediately disappear from the screen.

Showing Hidden Columns

Use the Show Column option on the Layout menu to redisplay a column that was previously hidden. You also can use this option to add another column to the display that was not selected on the Views screen. Follow these steps:

1. Press Alt-L to display the Layout pull-down menu.

2. Select Show Column.

   R:BASE displays a list of hidden columns (see fig. 4.9).

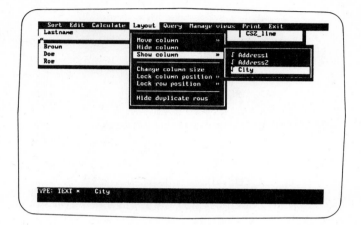

Fig. 4.9

Showing a previously hidden column.

3. Highlight the column you want to reappear and press Enter to place a check mark next to it. Select as many columns as you want in the same way.

4. Press F2.

   R:BASE asks if you want to insert the columns at the cursor or at the end.

5. Select Insert At Cursor or Insert At End.

The columns reappear in their previous positions if they were hidden, or at the end of the table if you did not previously select the columns on the Views screen.

Changing Column Sizes

Use the Change Column Size option on the layout menu to change the display width of a column. Text columns often contain fewer characters than the default width allows, for example. You can "shrink" columns to take up less space, thereby allowing more columns to be displayed on-screen at the same time. Follow these steps:

1. Highlight the column with the size you want to change.

2. Press Alt-L to display the Layout pull-down menu.

3. Highlight Change Column Size.

   R:BASE highlights the data cell.

4. Use the arrow keys to shrink or expand the column width.

5. Press Enter when you are satisfied with the size.

If you shrink a column smaller than the width of the column's name, the name is shortened to fit the new width. This may make some columns appear to have the same name. If all of the data is not displayed for a column because you made the width smaller, highlight the column and press Shift-F4. This expands the column size to enable you to see all of the data. The zoom screen can expand to full screen size, if needed. If more information is available (such as with a long Note column), you can scroll the screen by pressing the down-arrow key on the last data line. Figure 4.10 shows what the Edit screen looks like after you use the Zoom function key (Shift-F4) to zoom the CSZ_line column.

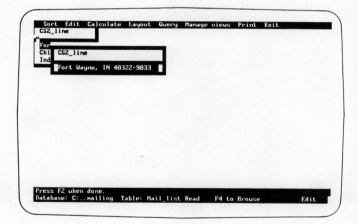

Fig. 4.10
Zooming a column size to view all of the data.

Press F2 to return to the normal display.

Locking Column Positions

Use the Lock Column Position option on the Layout menu to set a specific place for the column to appear even when scrolling from left to right or vice versa. You may want to lock the position of the row identifier, for example—Idno for the Mail_list table—so that it is always on-screen. Follow these steps to lock a column position:

1. Highlight the first column you want to lock into position.

2. Press Alt-L to display the Layout pull-down menu.

3. Highlight Lock Column Position.

   R:BASE displays a pop-up menu with the position options: Left Margin, Right Margin, and Clear.

4. Choose Left Margin or Right Margin to lock the columns in either of these positions.

   R:BASE highlights the column you started on.

5. Use the arrow keys to highlight all columns that are in the position you want locked. When you finish, press Enter.

R:BASE places a "fence" to delineate the locked column or columns, as shown in figure 4.11. In this case, Idno is locked on the left margin of the screen.

Fig. 4.11

Locking columns.

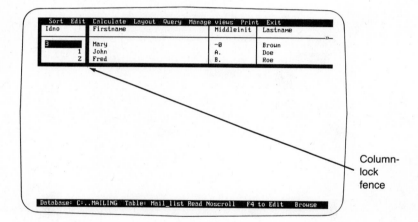

Column-lock fence

To move between the locked and unlocked columns, press Ctrl and the left- or right-arrow key, depending on which direction you are moving.

Choose Clear if you want to clear a previously locked column. To clear a previously locked column, highlight the locked column, choose Lock Column Position, and then choose Clear.

Locking Row Positions

You use the Lock Row Position option on the Layout menu to lock a row into place. R:BASE always displays the row—even while you scroll up or down through the data. You may want to lock a row into place to keep a base row on-screen, regardless of how many rows are available for viewing. When you move up or down through the rows, R:BASE scrolls rows off the screen. Locking a row or rows keeps those rows on-screen, no matter how many rows the table contains. You may want to lock a row, for example, so that you can copy data from one row to another row.

To lock a row's position, follow these steps:

1. Highlight the first row that you want to lock into position.

2. Press Alt-L to display the Layout pull-down menu.

3. Choose Lock Row Position.

   R:BASE displays a pop-up menu with the row locking options: Top, Bottom, and Clear.

4. Choose Top to lock the row as the top row on-screen. Choose Bottom to lock the row as the bottom row on-screen.

   R:BASE highlights the current row.

5. Use the arrow keys to "paint" the rows that you want to lock. Press Enter.

R:BASE places a "fence" on-screen to mark the locked rows (see fig. 4.12).

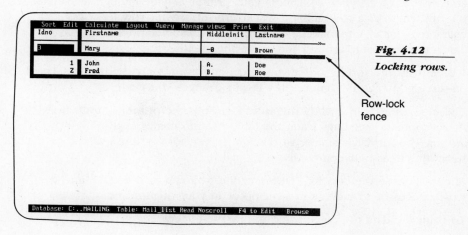

Fig. 4.12
Locking rows.

Row-lock
fence

To move between the locked and unlocked rows, press Ctrl and the PgUp or PgDn key, depending on which direction you are moving.

Choose Clear from the Lock Row Position pop-up menu to clear a previously locked row. Highlight the first locked row, choose Lock Row Position from the Layout menu, and then choose Clear.

Hiding Duplicate Rows

Use the Hide Duplicate Rows option from the Layout menu to hide duplicated data from view. Duplicate rows sometimes occur when you combine data from two or more tables by using the Views options (see Chapter 5). Viewing the same data more than once can be confusing, so you may want to hide duplicate rows to simplify the screen display. Hiding duplicate rows also enables you to see more unique data on-screen at one time.

Follow these steps to hide duplicate rows:

1. Press Alt-L to display the Layout pull-down menu.

2. Choose Hide Duplicate Rows.

R:BASE immediately hides duplicate rows from view.

Printing Data

The Info menu provides two print options: Print and Create Text File. In both cases, R:BASE sends all of the data to the requested output device (the printer or a DOS file). Unless your printer is wide enough to handle the full length of a row, R:BASE will overprint. If your row length is 120 characters, for example, and you have an 80-character printer, the last 40 characters will wrap around and overprint the line.

R:BASE uses the sorting order you select and prints only the data displayed on-screen, but R:BASE ignores any layout changes you made.

The file output is in exactly the same format as the printer output. Both formats include headings using the table column names as displayed on-screen. The format is similar to the Info screen format, but without separating lines between columns.

After you store the data in a DOS text file, you can load the file into a word processor to include in a memo or in your documentation.

To print the data to your printer, follow these steps:

1. Press Alt-P to display the Print pull-down menu.

2. Highlight Print (see fig. 4.13).

R:BASE prints the data to the default printer.

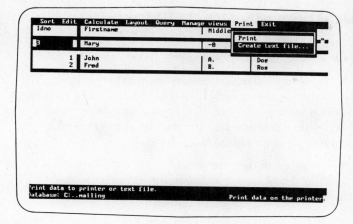

Fig. 4.13

Sending data to the default printer, the screen, or a DOS file.

To print the data to a DOS file, follow these steps:

1. Press Alt-P to display the Print pull-down menu.

2. Select Create Text File.

   R:BASE displays a dialog box for you to enter the file name.

3. Type the file name. Include a drive and directory path if you want the file stored somewhere other than the current drive or directory. Follow DOS file-naming conventions. Include an extension if you want (see fig. 4.14).

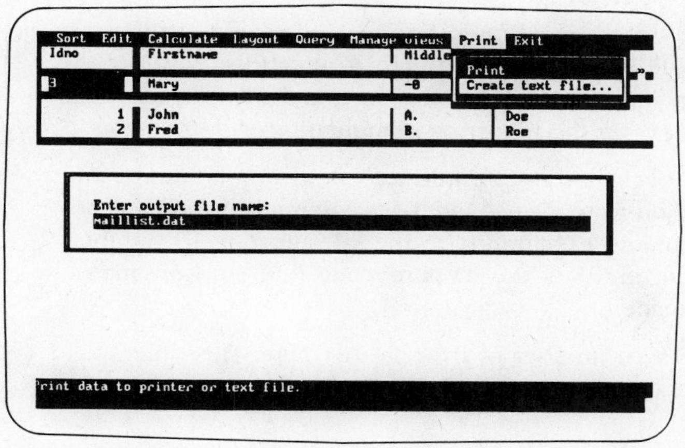

Fig. 4.14

Creating a DOS file to store information.

Making Calculations on Your Data

You can use the Calculate option when you are displaying data. If you highlight the Calculate option, the pull-down menu shows four possibilities:

- *Compute:* Provides the sum, average, minimum, maximum, count, standard deviation, or variance (these last two are statistical analysis functions) of a column. For example, you can display the total of all the currency values in a column, find the earliest date (minimum), or count the number of rows containing a value.

- *Tally:* Counts the number of occurrences of each value in a column. You can use Tally on the Mailcode column, for example, to find out how many letters of each type have been sent.

- *Group:* Displays data grouped by value. You can display all letters for each person grouped by Idno, for example.

- *Crosstab:* Shows a tabular display of data by comparing one column value to another. "Displaying Data in a Cross-Tabulation," later in this chapter, guides you through the Crosstab process to illustrate its use. After you see the type of display that Crosstab can provide, you will think of many uses for it in your own database applications.

Each of these options represent functions that perform some type of calculation on your data, as explained in the next four sections.

Computing Values

You use the Compute option most often on numeric values—columns with an Integer, Real, Double, or Decimal data type. You can use some of the functions described in this section on Date, Time, and Text values, however. Compute provides the following computations:

Count: Counts the occurrences of duplicate values in a column (you can use Count also on Date, Time, and Text columns). Suppose that your sales table contains a column with the salesperson's ID number. You can count occurrences of the ID number to find out how many sales each person made.

Rows: Displays the total number of rows in the table. This differs from Count in that all rows are counted, rather than just those with a matching value.

Minimum: Displays the lowest value in a specified column (you can use Minimum on Date, Time, and Text columns also). Suppose that you have a date column indicating when a sale is made. You can find out the earliest sales date by using the minimum computation.

Maximum: Displays the highest value in a specified column (you can use Maximum also on Date, Time, and Text columns). Suppose that you have an invoice amount column. By using the maximum computation, you can find out the largest invoice amount.

Sum: Displays the total of all values in a specified column. Suppose that you have a column containing an invoice amount. You can compute quickly the sum for all the rows to get a grand total of all sales.

Average: Calculates and displays the average value of a specified column (you can use Average on Date and Time columns also). Suppose that you have an invoice amount column and you want to compute the average sale. The average computation provides the average value of all sales.

Std Dev (Standard Deviation): Calculates and displays the standard deviation between the values contained in a column.

Variance: Calculates and displays the variance between values contained in a column.

```
Command: COMPUTE
```

To view these calculations, follow these steps:

1. Press Alt-C to highlight Calculate.

2. Select Compute.

   R:BASE displays a list of the columns that are currently available.

3. Choose the column containing the values you want to use in the calculation. For this example, choose Idno from the Compute menu to calculate on a date value (see fig. 4.15).

R:BASE displays the computed values for all of Compute's functions. In figure 4.16, R:BASE shows the number of unique values in the Idno column (Count); the number of total rows in the table column (Rows); the lowest Idno value (Minimum); the highest Idno value (Maximum); the total of the Idno column values (Sum); the average of the Idno column values (Average); and the meaningless, in this example, standard deviation (Std Dev) and variance (Variance) on the Idno column values. If you use the COMPUTE command in Command mode, you can ask for any one of these functions or all of them. If you use the COMPUTE command from the Calculate menu, you always get the result of all functions.

Fig. 4.15

Computing on a column.

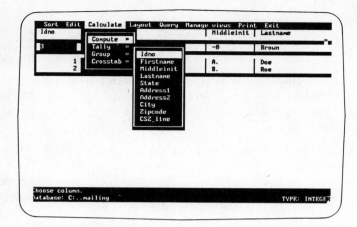

Fig. 4.16

Several computations on a single column's data.

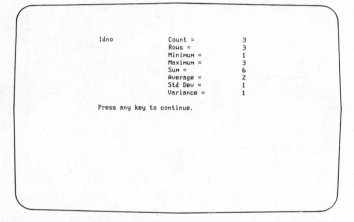

A few examples using numeric columns may help you better understand these calculations. Because the MAILING database does not contain any numeric columns, use the data in table 4.2. You may define this table in a new database (or add the table to MAILING, although it will not be related to any other table) and try out all of the functions on the numeric columns.

Table 4.2
Orders

Buyer	Product	Quantity	Listprice	Sellprice
100	PROD-1	100	$159.95	$138.72
100	PROD-2	125	$49.95	$43.52
101	PROD-3	110	$219.50	$195.17

Suppose that you want to find the number of products sold. Choose the Quantity column to get the display shown in figure 4.17.

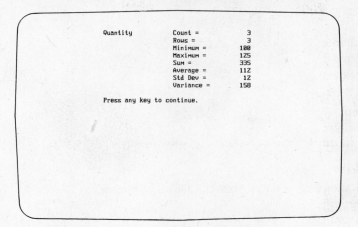

Fig. 4.17

Computing on a numeric column.

Suppose that you want to find the average selling price of all products. Choose the Sellprice column to get the display shown in figure 4.18.

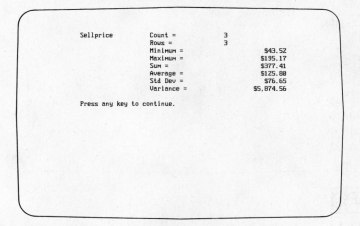

Fig. 4.18

Computing a currency column.

Counting Occurrences

You can count the specific number of times that values appear for a column by using the Compute Count function. Tally also counts occurrences, but it looks for the occurrences of all values in a column and gives you individual counts for each time a value occurs.

```
Command: TALLY
```

Look at a tally of the Mailcode column in the When_mailed table. You should have the following rows in When_mailed:

Idno	Mailcode	Maildate
1	L1	03/24/90
2	L1	03/24/90
2	L2	04/14/90
1	L2	04/14/90
3	L2	04/14/90

To tally the data, follow these steps:

1. Press Alt-C to display the Calculate pull-down menu.

2. Select Tally.

3. Choose the Mailcode column from the list of columns.

Figure 4.19 shows the Tally display.

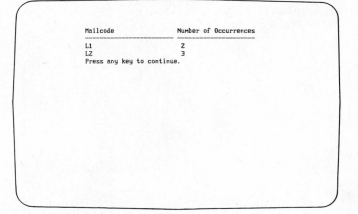

Fig. 4.19

Using Tally to count the number of values in a column.

```
Mailcode                Number of Occurrences
--------------------    ---------------------
L1                      2
L2                      3
Press any key to continue.
```

Grouping Data

When you group data by using the Group option, R:BASE displays one row for each value in the table. That is, if you have two occurrences of L1 (as you do in the When_mailed table), only one row is displayed for L1 data. If you include a numeric value in the table, the total of the values for both rows is displayed, assuming that you select the numeric column for grouping.

```
Command: SELECT
```

When you use the Group function, you are telling R:BASE to combine data based on the value of a column. You also tell R:BASE which calculation you want to perform and on which column, as well as which columns you want to display.

To use the Group function, for example, look at the Orders table in the "Computing Values" section. Follow these steps:

1. Press Alt-C to display the Calculate pull-down menu.

2. Select Group.

3. Select the columns to display by highlighting each column that you want and pressing Enter to place a check mark beside the column. Then press F2 to execute the Group function.

Figure 4.20 shows the grouping being defined, and figure 4.21 shows the result of the grouping.

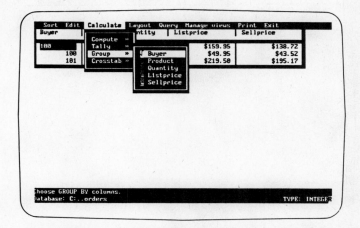

Fig. 4.20

Grouping data.

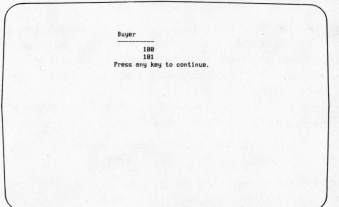

Fig. 4.21

Grouping condenses many rows of data.

Displaying Data in a Cross-Tabulation

The last function, Crosstab, formats a table display of the data, making some calculations on one of the columns and showing the relationship between two other columns in a table. Crosstab is useful for providing a summary of activity—comparing two columns. If you keep track of time spent on projects (a timelog), for example, Crosstab is a good way to quickly give you total hours spent on different projects by day.

```
Command: CROSSTAB
```

Cross-tabulation creates a spreadsheet format; it calculates the sum, average, minimum, maximum, or counted values for a column as it relates to one or two other columns in the table. To learn how cross-tabulation works, look at figure 4.22.

Fig. 4.22

Cross-tabulation creates an array of data cross-referenced by two columns.

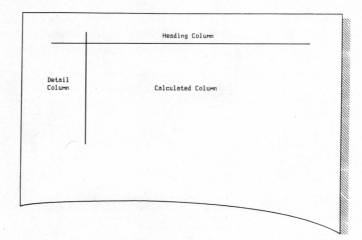

Heading Column

Detail Column

Calculated Column

The Heading Column supplies the column headings for the cross-tabular display. Generally, you can switch the positions of the Heading and Detail columns with the same cross-tabulation results, except that the data is oriented differently (the Heading becomes the Detail and vice versa). Choose the column with the fewest unique values so that more data can be displayed across the screen. You cannot scroll a cross-tabular display, so you want as much data as possible to appear on-screen.

The Detail column supplies the detailed unique values related to the Heading Column.

The Calculated column forms a cell on the cross-tabular format, containing a calculated amount (count, sum, average, and so on), showing the calculated relationship between the Heading column and the Detail column.

After you select a column for the Heading column, R:BASE sorts the data contained in all rows of the table and uses only unique values as headings. If the Heading column has two rows containing the value L1, for example, then only a single L1 heading is displayed.

When you select a column for the Detail column, R:BASE sorts and groups the data just like the Heading column. The values for this column appear on the left side of the table.

When you select the Calculated column, you also tell R:BASE the function to perform the calculation: Average, Sum, Count, Minimum, or Maximum. R:BASE makes the calculation on each Calculated column value as it relates to the Heading column and the Detail column.

A simple cross-tabulation follows. First, you see the table from which R:BASE derives the data; then you see how R:BASE identifies each column for cross-tabulation. Figure 4.23 shows what the cross-tabulation request will look like, and figure 4.24 shows the cross-tabulation result.

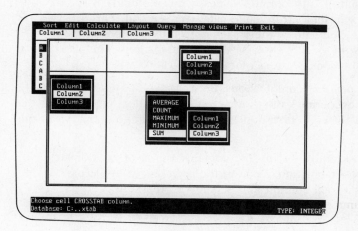

Fig. 4.23

Defining a cross-tabulation.

Column1	Column2	Column3
A	10	25
B	10	250
C	10	75
A	10	100
B	20	200
C	10	300

Heading Column: Column1
Detail Column: Column2
Function: Sum
Calculated Column: Column3

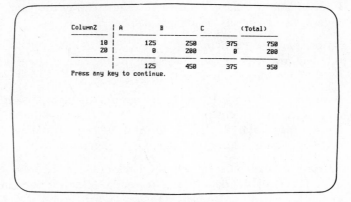

Fig. 4.24

A completed cross-tabulation.

Look at the upper-left cell containing the calculated values. This number should contain a sum of all Column3 values where Column1 is A and Column2 is 10. If you look at the table data, you see that there are two A/10 combinations. The sum of the values in Column3 opposite the A/10 combinations adds up to 125. Look for A/20 combinations. This time there are no A/20 combinations, so the Column3 result is 0.

Look at the other possible combinations: B/10, B/20, C/10, and C/20. To find the sum of the Column3 values for each combination, look in the cross-tabulation in the cell corresponding to the proper combination of the Heading and Detail columns.

Now look at the bottom line. This line contains a total of each of the columns in the cross-tabulation. Also, on the right side of the cross-tabulation there is a total column for each row in the table.

Study the preceding example until you are sure that you understand the relationships between the columns.

Now look at an example taken from the Orders table described in the "Computing Values" section:

1. Press Alt-C to highlight Calculate.

2. Choose Crosstab from the pull-down menu.

   R:BASE displays the Crosstab screen, with a format that looks similar to the final appearance of the cross-tabulation. The column lists appear in the area where their values will be used.

3. Choose the column containing the data that will make up the heading.

   For this example, choose Buyer for the column headings.

4. Choose the column containing the data that will make up the left side of the cross-tabulation.

   For this example, choose Product as the detail column.

5. Choose the column containing the data that you want to be computed by a Crosstab function.

   For this example, choose Sellprice for the calculated cell value.

6. Choose the function to compute the cell values.

   For this example, choose Sum to provide a total.

Figure 4.25 shows the screen where you enter the cross-tabulation parameters. Figure 4.26 shows the completed cross-tabulation.

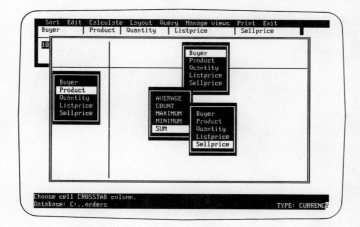

Fig. 4.25

R:BASE displays lists of columns for each position of the cross-tabulated table.

In figure 4.26, you see that each Buyer ID number becomes a heading on the display. Although Buyer 100 has two rows in the table, the ID number is presented only once on the display. The selling price is broken down by product, as shown on the left side of the display. This means that R:BASE uses each product's individual selling price, as provided for each buyer, in the calculation for the cell data. The sum of the Sellprice column is given in the cell matrix. Notice that if a given buyer did not purchase a given product, the cell for the relationship is $0.00. Finally, the totals at the right show you, for example, that all PROD-1 products sold to all buyers have a total selling price of $138.72. The totals at the bottom tell you how much each buyer purchased, regardless of product.

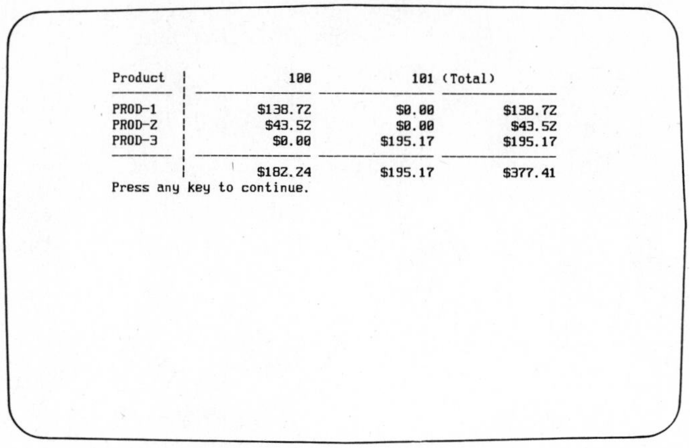

Fig. 4.26

Cross-tabulating sales data by customer.

```
Product  |           100           101  (Total)
---------|------------------------------------------
PROD-1   |        $138.72         $0.00      $138.72
PROD-2   |         $43.52         $0.00       $43.52
PROD-3   |          $0.00       $195.17      $195.17
         |------------------------------------------
         |        $182.24       $195.17      $377.41
Press any key to continue.
```

Summary

This chapter showed you how to enter and edit data by using the Info module. You also learned how to manipulate the screen layout to make the edit format easier to read and use.

Finally, you learned how to use the Calculate function on the displayed data to derive specific, calculated values from the data.

5

Using Query By Example

This chapter shows you how to use the Views option, which you access from the R:BASE main menu. This option is closely related to Info (the option appearing next to Views on the main menu) in that you can move quickly between the Info and Views modules without having to return to the main menu.

The Info module enables you to enter and edit data, by using a default tabular format. Unlike a customized form in which you can enter data for multiple tables, the Info module restricts you to entering data in a single table. The Views module, on the other hand, enables you to combine data from multiple tables for display only. You can save a view definition and then use that view in a report or with any data display command.

The combination of the two modules is called Query By Example. With this feature, you can manipulate how you want data displayed (the Query) and then you can look immediately at the data (the Example) to determine whether your view definition is correct. You can use either option as a stand-alone module—Info to enter or edit, and Views to create a view to be used for some other option, such as a report's driving table (see Chapter 7).

All the options available for the Info screen are discussed in Chapter 4. In this chapter, you learn how to use the Views option to define and modify a view definition and how to save the view permanently.

Understanding the Two Types of Views

In Chapter 2, you learned how to design a database with a set of tables related to each other by a common column—a column that appears in

163

each table and includes the same name and type of data. A *view* combines the data from as many as five related tables into a single set of data that you can use for query or as the driving table for a report. This type of view is called a *multi-table view*. In the MAILING database, for example, you can combine all three tables into one view to provide simultaneous access to all data from all tables.

You also can create a *single-table view* when you want to access data in one table, but only certain columns or rows in that table. With a single-table view, you can edit the data in the table by using the view as the window to the table. You might want to create such a view of a payroll table, for example, in which you want someone to be able to edit the employee's general information (address, marital status, and so on) but not be able to look at the employee's salary.

Keep in mind that views do not contain data, but only the means of extracting the data from the tables defined in the view.

Starting the Views Module

R:BASE offers two ways to define views: through the Views module and by using the CREATE VIEW command. The second method always creates a saved view; the first method creates the view definition only in memory. You must save the view if you want to retain it for later use.

You can get to the Views module in one of two ways:

- Choose the Views option from the R:BASE main menu. You then can display the data defined by a previously saved view or create a new view definition.

- Use the QUERY command in Command mode or from Prompt By Example. Depending on how much data you supply on the command line, you can just start the menu-driven Views module, completely define the view, or call an existing view definition for data display.

```
Commands: CREATE VIEW, QUERY
```

Note: If you want to edit or enter data, use the Info option to go directly to a single table. You do not need to define a view to edit all columns in one table. When you are in the Info module, you can modify how the data appears on-screen when you are editing. See Chapter 4 for information on using Info to enter and edit data.

Using the Views Menu

Because the Info and Views modules can be used together, their menus are identical (see fig. 5.1).

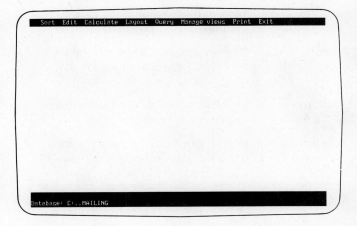

Sort Edit Calculate Layout Query Manage views Print Exit

Database: C:..MAILING

Fig. 5.1
The Views menu.

You can toggle between the Info or Views module by pressing Ctrl-F3 or by selecting a Query pull-down menu option.

The data that appears below the menu and the options available on the pull-down menus accessed from the menu depend on which module you are executing. If an option is not available for the current module, that option is in white rather than black characters (*grayed out*). You cannot select a grayed-out option.

Table 5.1 gives brief descriptions of the menu options.

Table 5.1
Using the Info and Views Menus

Option	Mode	Function
Sort	Edit/Browse	Sorts the order of the rows on display
Edit	Edit	Provides insert, modify, and delete capabilities
Calculate	Edit/Browse	Provides four methods of performing calculations on the displayed data

Table 5.1—*continued*

Option	Mode	Function
Layout	Edit/Browse	Enables you to reorder the columns, change their display widths, hide columns, or lock column or row positions
Query	Views	Enables you to choose the tables and links between tables for a query definition
Manage Views	Edit/Browse or Views	Enables you to save, modify, delete, or rename a view
Print	Edit/Browse or Views	Provides options for printing the displayed data or saving the data in a new table

Creating Views

The Views module provides definition options for the following:

- Choosing a table for the view. (required)

- Selecting the columns to include in the view. (required)

- Refining the data by selecting additional tables and establishing links between them. You do this to create a multi-table view—a window to more than one table in the database. (optional)

- Removing columns from the tables (the columns are not deleted from the database but are simply removed from the display). You do this to limit the data that can be accessed from the view. (optional)

- Setting conditions to limit the rows displayed from the tables. You do this when you want to look at only some of the rows of data, for only certain dates or people, for example. (optional)

Most of the options available in the Views module are accessed from pull-down menus. A few functions, however are accessible only through function keys. Table 5.2 lists the Views function keys not duplicated by a menu option. You can press Shift-F1 at any time to display a list of the available function keys and their uses.

Table 5.2
Function Keys in the Views Module

Key	Function
Shift-F3	Shows the current view's definition as a command line.
Ctrl-F3	Shows the current view's data.
Shift-F6	Selects/unselects all columns in a list.
Shift-F7	Moves to the previous table.
Shift-F8	Moves to the next table.

Adding Tables and Selecting Columns

The first thing you need to do when defining the data you want to look at is to tell R:BASE which table or tables you want to use. If you recall from Chapter 2, all the tables in your database should be linked, if not directly to each other, then through interim tables. If you use more than one table in a view, you will have to define how the tables are linked. You choose the tables you want to include in a view by using the Query option's pull-down menu. Follow these steps:

1. Press Alt-Q to display the Query pull-down menu, if it is not displayed already.

2. Select Add Tables.

3. From the list of displayed tables, choose a table to be the first table in your view.

R:BASE then displays a table format containing all the columns from the table you selected. The program also assigns a prefix to identify the table's position in the table list. The first table in the view is given the prefix #T1; the second, #T2, and so on. Figure 5.2 shows what the screen looks like if you first choose the Mail_list table from the sample MAILING database.

Next, you need to tell R:BASE which columns you want to include in the view. To choose the columns, follow these steps:

1. Press Alt-Q to display the Query pull-down menu.

2. Highlight Choose Columns.

   R:BASE displays a pop-up menu with two options: Select/Unselect and Select/Unselect All.

Fig. 5.2

Adding a table.

```
    Sort  Edit  Calculate  Layout  Query  Manage views  Print  Exit
            #T1.Mail_list

      Idno   Firstname   Lastname   Middleinit   Address1   Address2




Database: C:..MAILING
                   Query/Info Main Menu — adding a table.
```

3. Press Enter to choose Select/Unselect and thus select columns individually.

4. From the list of columns, select the columns you want for the view by highlighting each column name and pressing Enter. A check mark then appears beside the column name. After you select all the columns you want, press F2 to leave the column list.

Tip: A quick way to select columns is to use the Select/Unselect All option first and then unselect those columns you don't want. To unselect columns, follow the steps for selecting columns. When you press Enter next to a column with a check mark, the check mark disappears and the column is unselected.

Defining Computed Columns

Not only can you select columns already defined in the table, but you also can create on-the-fly columns similar to the computed column already contained in the Mail_list table. A computed column provides a value that is calculated from an expression you enter. The Mail_list table, for example, already contains the CSZ_line computed column that combines the city, state, and ZIP code into a single value. You can define a similar computed column that combines the first name, middle initial, and last name.

Because you cannot edit data in a view comprised of more than one table, combining as many columns as possible into a single, computed column is useful for making the display easier to read. Also, if, after saving the view definition, you use it in a report, the data looks better if multiple columns are combined when possible. Column combining with a computed column works only with text data. If you combine numeric columns, arithmetic calculations are performed instead (you can add, subtract, multiply, divide, or do whatever arithmetic calculation you want to perform).

Tip: When using a computed column, whether defined in the table or on-the-fly, the columns used to calculate the computed column's value must be included in the view's column list. You can hide columns when on the Info screen, however, so that repetitive data is not displayed to simplify the display.

A computed column you define in a view is exactly the same as a computed column you define with the table structure (see Chapter 3). The same rules apply. The expression can contain column names, arithmetic operators (+ , − , /, *), system variables (#DATE, #TIME, #PI), and literal values (text or numeric). Basically, the expression must be a viable arithmetic or text expression that R:BASE can calculate.

To define a computed column, follow these steps:

1. Press Alt-Q to display the Query pull-down menu.

2. Select Computed Columns.

3. Select Add.

4. Type the expression in the dialog box field and press Enter to add it to the view.

R:BASE prompts you for the expression, as shown in figure 5.3. The expression in this example combines the first name, middle initial, and last name columns. Note the "&" and spaces used to combine text values. The expression becomes the column name for the purposes of the view on which you are working. A computed column is added as the last column in the table and is selected automatically for the table.

You can modify or delete a computed column. To modify an existing computed column, follow these steps:

1. Highlight the computed column you want to modify.

2. Press Alt-Q to display the Query pull-down menu.

3. Select Computed Columns.

4. Select Modify.

   R:BASE displays a dialog box containing the computed column's expression.

5. Edit the expression just as you would edit data anywhere in R:BASE.

6. Press Enter or F2 when you have finished modifying the expression.

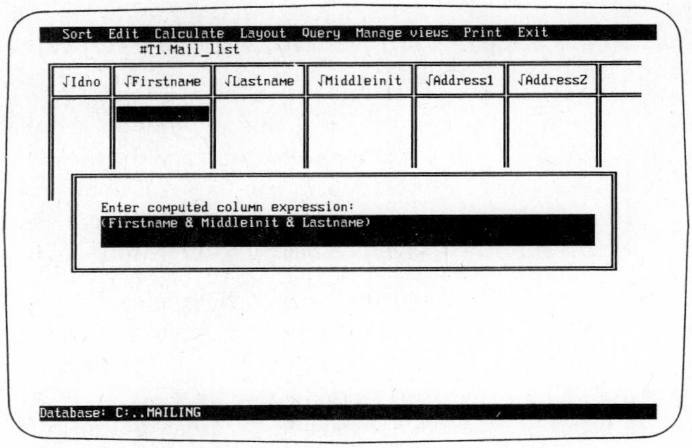

Fig. 5.3

Defining an "on-the-fly" computed column.

To delete a computed column, follow these steps:

1. Highlight the computed column you want to delete.

2. Press Alt-Q to display the Query pull-down menu.

3. Select Computed Columns.

4. Select Delete.

R:BASE immediately removes the last computed column from the table.

Establishing Links between Tables

Figure 5.4 shows the screen after a second table has been added to the view (in this case, the When_mailed table from the MAILING database).

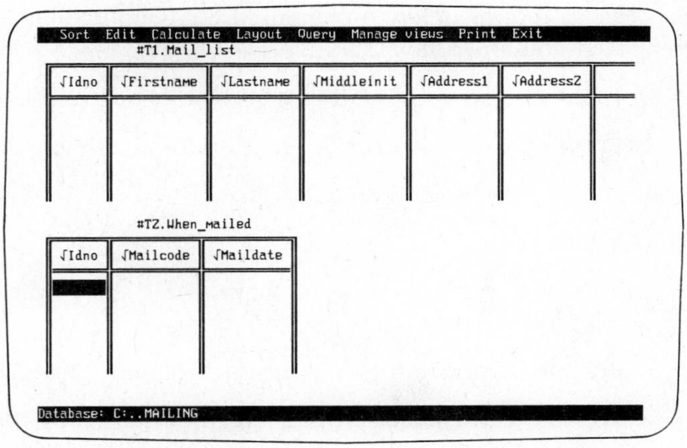

Fig. 5.4

A view with two tables.

When you add a second or subsequent table to a view, you need to tell R:BASE how to relate the new table to another one in the view. Usually, you use the column that has the same name in both tables—the common column. You can, however, link tables by using columns with different names or establish more than one link between tables. The linking process is the same whether the columns have the same name or not. The only requirement is that the data types of the two columns be the same. You cannot link a date column to a currency column, for example.

Linking date columns is an example of a noncommon link. Suppose that you have two tables, one for sales and one for advertising contacts. Each would probably have a date column indicating when a sale was made or an advertisement mailed. By linking the two columns, you can find out whether a customer bought an item and was sent an advertisement on the same day.

To define a link, follow these steps:

1. Move the cursor to the column in the first table that should define the link. To do so, press Shift-F7 (Previous Table) or Shift-F8 (Next Table) to move to the table; then press Tab to move to the appropriate column.

2. Press Alt-Q to display the Query pull-down menu.

3. Choose Link Tables.

   R:BASE marks the column as the table's linking column and displays a list of ways that the linking columns can be compared (see fig. 5.5). These operators should look familiar; they are a subset of the comparison operators used in the condition builder to compare a column to a value. In this case, the comparison is between column values, not a column value and a literal value. The most common link is to link rows where the column values are equal.

4. Choose the linking method you want to use.

5. Move to the second table by pressing Shift-F7 or Shift-F8.

6. Press Tab to highlight the column for the other side of the link.

7. Press Enter to select the second linking column.

You can remove links in a similar way. If you want to establish a different linking criteria or have simply linked the wrong columns, highlight the first linking column and then choose Clear Link from the Query pull-down menu.

The links between tables don't have to be sequential—table 1 to table 2, table 2 to table 3, and so on. You can establish a link between the first and

Fig. 5.5

Telling R:BASE how to link the tables in the view.

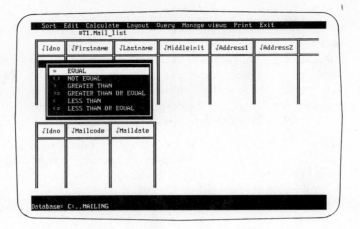

fifth tables, second and fourth, or even sixth to first. The positioning doesn't matter as long as every table is linked to at least one other table in the view.

Initially, choose the tables and links that you think will work and then take a look at the data to see whether you got what you expected. If the tables, columns, or links aren't quite right, you can always return to the Views screen from the Info screen to make adjustments. (See the section on "Modifying Views" in this chapter for more information.)

In addition to adjusting tables, columns, and links, you also can adjust the data you want to view by setting conditions.

Using the Condition Builder

The R:BASE condition builder is used in the same way throughout R:BASE. With the condition builder, you tell R:BASE the requirements you want each row to meet before it is included in the data. You set conditions to limit or specify the rows on which you want commands or options to act. A *condition* can be a simple comparison of a column's data to a value, or if can contain multiple comparisons of several columns.

In Query By Example, conditions are used to limit the data that is edited or displayed on the Info screen. Suppose, for example, that you want to find out information about a specific person. For this task, you need to set a condition specifying that person's ID number. If you want to see only data about a certain date or date range, you set conditions on the Date column.

```
Command: WHERE Clause
```

You need to know these basic concepts of condition building:

- All conditions are based on comparing a column to a value you enter or to the value of another column. You use a comparison operator to make the comparison (see table 5.3).

- Multiple conditions are connected by a connecting operator: AND or OR. R:BASE assumes an AND condition when you simply add a condition to a second or subsequent column. You can add an OR condition only to a column already containing a condition. (See the section on "Adding an Either-Or Condition" for an explanation of the difference between AND conditions and Either-Or conditions in the Views module.)

Table 5.3 lists the comparison operators you use to set a condition. Figure 5.6 shows an example of how to connect multiple conditions with AND and OR conditions.

Table 5.3
Comparison Operators

Operator	Meaning
=	Equal
< >	Not equal
>	Greater than
> =	Greater than or equal to
<	Less than
< =	Less than or equal to
BETWEEN	The column value must be in the listed range of values. This condition, for example, selects only rows in which the date value is a day in March: Datecolumn BETWEEN 03/01/90, 03/31/90.
NOT BETWEEN	The column value must not be in the listed range of values. This condition, for example, selects all rows except those having a date value in March: Datecolumn NOT BETWEEN 03/01/90, 03/31/90.

Table 5.3—*continued*

Operator	Meaning
CONTAINS	The column has the specified value somewhere in it. The letters "ed" are contained, for example, in both "Editor" and "Fred".
NOT CONTAINS	The column does not contain the specified value.
IN	The column value should match one of the values in the list. This condition, for example, selects all rows having an ID number of 1, 2, or 5: Idnumber IN (1, 2, 5).
NOT IN	The column value should not match one of the values in the list.
IS NULL	The column does not contain a value (displayed as -0- in R:BASE).
IS NOT NULL	The column contains any value.
LIKE	The column value is similar to the entered value. This condition, for example, selects rows in which a last name is similar to Brown: Lastname LIKE 'Brown'.
NOT LIKE	The column value is not similar to the entered value.

The condition list for this figure reads this way:

condition1 AND condition2 AND (condition3 OR condition4)

The parentheses are added by R:BASE. The tests for condition3 and condition4 are performed first. Then R:BASE checks condition1 and condition2 and adds the answer to the result of the condition3/condition4 comparison.

Chapter 1 provides a complete explanation of the R:BASE condition builder. But for a reminder, take a look at a specific example. The conditions include the following:

Condition 1: ID number must be in the range 1 to 3.
Condition 2: State must be IN (for Indiana).
Condition 3: Mailcode must be LT1.
Condition 4: OR Mailcode must be LT2.

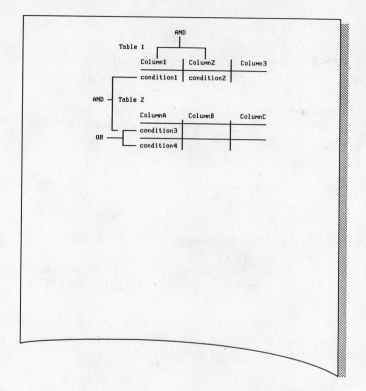

Fig. 5.6

Using the AND and OR connectors.

Suppose that this data is contained in the first table:

ID number	State
1	IN
2	MI
3	IN
4	IL
5	IN

This data is in the second table:

ID number	Mailcode
1	LT1
1	LT2
2	LT1
3	LT2
4	LT3

Condition 1 tells R:BASE to look only for ID numbers 1, 2, and 3.
Condition 2 tells R:BASE (in addition to condition 1) to look only for
rows in which the state is IN, but only in the subset of rows that meet

condition 1. Thus ID number 2 is eliminated and ID number 5 isn't added back to the rows; it already failed the first condition.

Condition 3 tells R:BASE that in addition to condition 1 and condition 2, only rows with letter codes LT1 should be included. This condition eliminates ID numbers 3 and 4 because they do not have an LT1 code. Condition 4 provides an alternative to condition 3. LT2 also is permitted, which adds back the possible rows for ID number 3, even though it failed condition 3.

The final result, when the data from the two tables is combined, follows:

ID number	State	Mailcode
1	IN	LT1
3	IN	LT2

Tip: The condition builder functions much like the R:BASE WHERE clause. A WHERE clause is added to many commands to limit the rows acted on, just as the condition builder does in Views. When typed in Command mode, however, a WHERE clause has many more features.

Now that you know the basic building blocks, a couple of examples should clarify any questions you have. The following examples use the Q_mail view defined in Quick Start 2.

Suppose that you want to limit the data you see to data pertaining to people residing in Indiana:

    Column to compare: State
    Comparison operator: =
    Value to compare: IN (state abbreviation for Indiana)

Figure 5.7 shows what the screen looks like if you specify the preceding condition parameters.

Suppose that you want to see the people in Indiana again, but this time, you want to see only those who got the L2 mailing:

    First column to compare: State
    Comparison operator: =
    Value to compare: IN
    Second column to compare: Mailcode
    Comparison operator: =
    Value to compare: L2

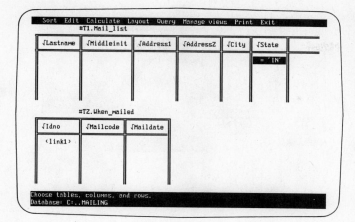

Fig. 5.7

Using a simple condition to limit rows.

Figure 5.8 shows what the screen looks like if you enter the second condition for Mailcode.

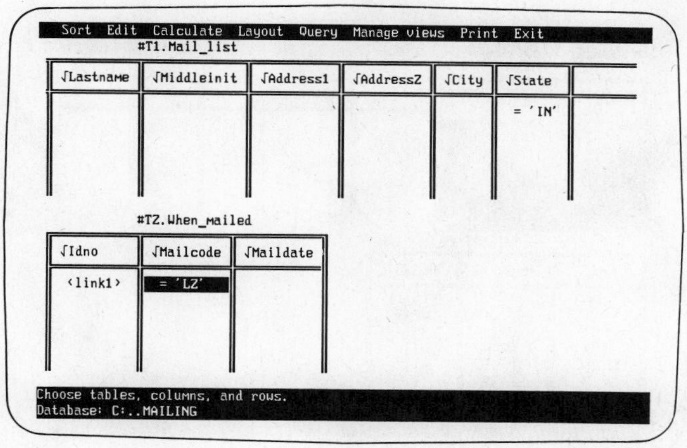

Fig. 5.8

Combining AND conditions to limit rows.

Adding Conditions

To add a condition to a column, follow these steps:

1. Press Tab to highlight the column.

2. Press Alt-Q to display the Query pull-down menu.

3. Select Specify Rows.

    The condition options are displayed in a pop-up menu, as shown in figure 5.9.

Fig. 5.9

Setting conditions.

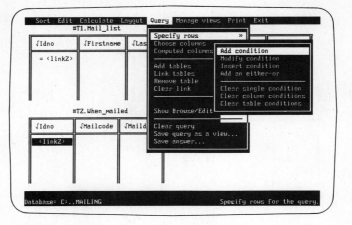

4. Select Add Condition from the pop-up menu.

5. Select a comparison operator (see fig. 5.10).

Fig. 5.10

Comparison operators.

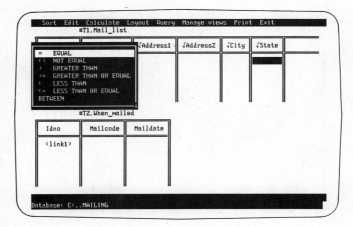

6. Enter a comparison value and press Enter to add it (see fig. 5.11).

When you enter a comparison value, you need to enclose the value in single quotation marks; otherwise, R:BASE mistakes the value for a column name. If your condition is State = IN, for example, R:BASE displays a message saying that it cannot find a column named IN. This is because you can compare the values of two columns by using a column name on the right side of the comparison operator (=, in this case). While you are still learning, the conditions that you define should be as simple as possible.

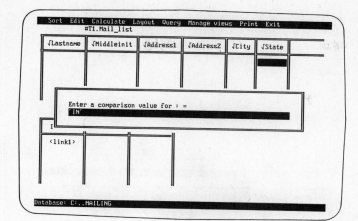

Fig. 5.11
Entering a comparison value.

Establishing a link between tables creates a two-column condition. Note that when you added a link, you chose a comparison operator. You were setting a condition that required the values of the data in the columns of the first table to compare in some way (as indicated by the comparison operator) to the values of the data in the columns of the second table. You will learn more about how to define these types of linking conditions in Chapter 9. It is sufficient at this point to understand the theory of conditions—not all of the fine details that R:BASE offers.

Modifying Conditions

You may want to modify an existing condition if you change your mind or if you made an error when entering the original comparison value. Suppose that you typed *ID* rather than *IN* for a state comparison value. You can change the *ID* to *IN* by using the Modify Condition option.

To modify a condition, follow these steps:

1. Press Tab to highlight the column, and use the arrow keys to highlight the condition you want to modify.

2. Press Alt-Q to display the Query pull-down menu.

3. Select Specify Rows.

4. Select Modify Condition from the pop-up menu.

5. Redefine the condition just as if you were defining a new condition.

An alternative to this method is to edit the condition in a dialog box. Follow these steps:

1. Press Tab to highlight the column, and use the arrow keys to highlight the condition.

2. Press Enter.

   R:BASE displays a dialog box with the condition displayed as a line (see fig. 5.12).

Fig. 5.12

Editing defined conditions.

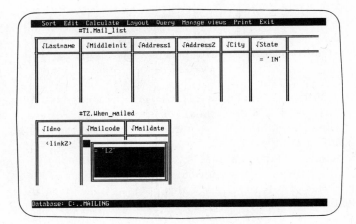

3. Edit the condition in the dialog box.

When editing conditions, you can use the same techniques you used to edit column data. Press Ins to toggle between Overwrite and Insert mode. (Watch the shape of the cursor: an underline signifies Overwrite mode, and a block indicates Insert mode.) Use the Del key to remove characters at the cursor.

Inserting Conditions

Inserting a condition is different from adding a condition in that you can place the new condition before or in the middle of an existing set of conditions. To insert a condition, follow these steps:

1. Press Tab to highlight the column, and use the arrow keys to highlight the condition before which you want to insert the new condition.

2. Press Alt-Q to display the Query pull-down menu.

3. Select Specify Rows.

4. Select Insert Condition.

5. Choose the comparison operator and then enter the value for the new condition.

Clearing Conditions

If you find that one or more of the conditions you have defined are incorrect or unneeded, you can clear conditions selectively by using the Clear options. Use the Clear Single Condition option to clear a single highlighted condition. Use Clear Column Conditions to clear all conditions defined for the highlighted column. Use the Clear Table Conditions option to clear all conditions defined for the current table (the current table has a highlighted column).

To clear one or more conditions, follow these steps:

1. Press Tab to highlight the column. (If you want to remove a single condition, use the arrow keys to highlight that condition.)

2. Press Alt-Q to display the Query pull-down menu.

3. Select Specify Rows.

4. Highlight one of the three Clear options, depending on which conditions you want to remove.

Adding Either-Or Conditions

The last condition-setting option is Add an Either-Or. Use the Either-Or condition only if you have defined at least one condition for a column. If you add a second condition to a column, it must be an Either-Or. R:BASE will enable you to add an AND condition, but you will probably defeat the purpose of the first condition set for the column, as the example that follows shows:

```
State = 'IN'
      = 'CA'
```

Assuming that you added the second condition as an AND (Add a Condition option), you are telling R:BASE to give you only those rows where the State column contains *both* IN and CA. Obviously, the column cannot contain both IN and CA, so you will not get any rows. However, if you add the second condition as an Either-Or, you tell R:BASE to give you rows where the State column contains *either* IN or CA, which is entirely possible. R:BASE will not prevent you from adding an AND condition when it does not make sense; you find out only when you switch to the Info module and you do not see any data.

To add an Either-Or condition, follow these steps:

1. Press Tab to highlight the column to which you want to add an Either-Or condition.

2. Press Alt-Q to display the Query pull-down menu.

3. Select Specify Rows.

4. Select Add an Either-Or from the pop-up menu.

5. Define the Either-Or condition in the same way you define a new condition. Choose the companion operator and enter the comparison value.

R:BASE places the Either-Or condition below the existing condition with a line between the two. Condition sets displayed without a line are AND conditions. Condition sets displayed with a line are OR conditions.

Storing Views

After you define a view, you can save it so that you can use it later without having to redefine it in the Views module. You then can recall the view, make changes, restore it with the modifications, use it in a report, and specify it in a number of R:BASE commands.

To save a view definition, follow these steps:

1. Press Alt-Q to display the Query pull-down menu.

2. Select Save Query as a View.

3. When prompted for the name of the view, enter a 1- to 18-character name (see fig. 5.13). The first 8 characters must be unique to view names in the database, and the first character must be a letter. The rest of the characters can be letters, numbers, or the following punctuation symbols: #, _, %, or $. If you have used a name for another view, R:BASE warns you and asks whether you want to overwrite the existing view. Answer Yes to copy the new view definition over the existing view. Select No to cancel the request.

To use the stored view, highlight the Views option on the R:BASE main menu. The view name appears on the Views pull-down menu. When you choose a view from this menu, the data appears on the Info screen. You can make modifications to the view definition by moving to the Views screen (use the Query pull-down menu's Show Query Screen option).

You also have the option of saving the data defined by the view in a table. You may want to take this step if you need to use the view in a command

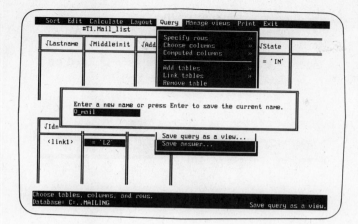

Fig. 5.13
Naming a view to save it.

that requires a table. Or perhaps you want to define a new view that uses the tables already defined in the first view, but you need more than five tables.

To save the view as a table, follow these steps:

1. From the Views screen, press Alt-Q to display the Query pull-down menu.

2. Select Save Answer.

   R:BASE displays the Info screen and a dialog box prompting you for the new table name.

3. Enter a new, unique table name, following the naming conventions described for naming tables.

R:BASE checks the view information while creating the new table. In some cases, you receive warning messages, most of which involve duplicate column names. If your view has used the same column name twice, for example, R:BASE warns you to rename one of the columns before using the table. You can use the new table in any way you would use a table that you defined yourself. You also can modify the new table's structure in the Database Definition module (see Chapter 3).

Displaying Data

After you define the tables, columns, and conditions for the view, you can switch to the Info screen to look at the data. Follow these steps:

1. Press Alt-Q to display the Query pull-down menu.

2. Select Show Browse/Edit Screen.

R:BASE gathers the data meeting the requirements you have defined on the Views screen and displays the data, as shown in figure 5.14.

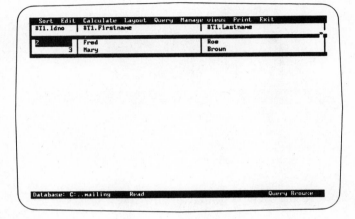

Fig. 5.14

Displaying or editing the extracted data.

When you are displaying the data, you can edit only if the data is extracted from a single table. You can tell whether you can edit the data by looking at the bottom of the screen. If it displays the message Query Browse, you only can look at the data (or print it from the Views screen). If the screen says Read, you can edit the displayed data.

Even if you are only browsing data, you can use several of the main menu options. Choose Sort to sort the data in any order by one or more columns. Choose Layout to move columns around, make them larger or smaller, lock columns in place, or lock rows in place. Choose Calculate if you want to perform calculations on the data.

If you can edit the data, you also can use the Edit option to insert, modify, or delete rows. The next few sections explain each of these options and how to use them.

Chapter 4 describes the entry and edit features of Info. If you have not already done so, read Chapter 4 and work through Quick Start 2 to learn more about entering and editing data by using the R:BASE tabular format.

Managing Views

The options on the Manage Views pull-down menu, which you access from the Views menu, enable you to modify a view, remove an existing view if it was previously saved, rename an existing view, or make a copy of an existing view. The Manage Views pull-down menu is shown in figure 5.15.

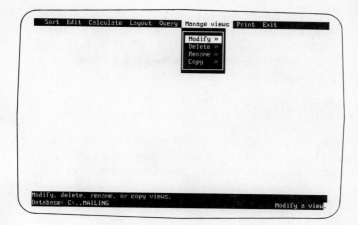

Fig. 5.15

The Manage Views menu.

Modifying Views

Modifying a view that you previously saved is similar to the process you used to define the view in the first place. To modify an existing view, you can select it from the list of views displayed on the Views pull-down menu, which you access from the R:BASE main menu. This approach takes you to the Views screen with the view definition already displayed.

To switch to a different defined view after you are at the Views screen, follow these steps:

1. From the Views screen, press Alt-M to display the Manage Views pull-down menu.

2. Choose Modify.

   R:BASE displays a list of the views in the database.

3. Select the new view that you want to change.

   The view definition appears on-screen.

To modify the tables used in the view, use these options from the Query pull-down menu (see the "Adding Tables and Selecting Columns" and

"Establishing Links between Tables" sections in this chapter for more information):

Option	Effect
Add Tables	Adds another table to the view definition.
Link Tables	Establishes the link between the existing and new tables.
Remove Table	Removes the current table (the one with a highlighted column). Press Shift-F7 or Shift-F8 to move from table to table. Removing a table also removes its link to other tables.
Clear Link	Removes a defined link between tables. If you keep the table, you need to define another link.

To modify the selected columns used in a table, use these options from the Query pull-down menu (see the "Adding Tables and Selecting Columns" and "Defining Computed Columns" sections in this chapter for more information):

Option	Effect
Choose Columns	Selects and unselects the columns specified for the current table.
Computed Columns	Defines a new computed column to add to the table. Computed columns are automatically selected for the table.

To modify conditions you have set, use the Specify Rows option (see "Using the Condition Builder," earlier in this chapter for more information). The condition-setting options follow:

Option	Effect
Add Condition	Adds another condition to the currently highlighted column.
Modify Condition	Enables you to redefine the currently highlighted condition. (You also can highlight the condition and press Enter to edit the condition in a dialog box.)
Insert Condition	Adds a new condition before the currently highlighted condition.
Add an Either-Or	Adds an OR condition to the currently highlighted column.

Option	Effect
Clear Single Condition	Removes the currently highlighted condition.
Clear Column Conditions	Removes all conditions from the currently highlighted column.
Clear Table Conditions	Removes all conditions from the current table (the one with a highlighted column).

To start over and completely redefine a view definition, choose Clear Query from the Query pull-down menu. This option leaves you on a blank screen, ready to redefine the view from scratch.

Deleting Views

If you want to remove a table or columns that are used in a stored view definition, you need to modify the view to remove the table or columns, or delete the view completely, before you can remove the table or columns (see Chapter 3).

To delete a view, follow these steps:

1. Press Alt-M to display the Manage Views pull-down menu.

2. Select Delete.

3. Select the view you want to delete.

4. When R:BASE prompts you to confirm the deletion, choose Yes.

Renaming Views

As with tables, you occasionally may want to rename a view. Suppose, for example, that you have created a view named TEMP and then want to keep the view definition permanently and rename it accordingly. Follow these steps to rename a view:

1. Press Alt-M to display the Manage Views pull-down menu.

2. Select Rename.

3. Select the view you want to rename.

4. Enter the new name. Remember that the first eight characters must be unique to view names in the database, and the first character must be a letter. The rest of the characters can be letters, numbers, or the following punctuation symbols: #, _, %, or $. R:BASE warns you if you already have used this name for another view.

Copying Views

You may want to copy a view if you have a particularly complex definition (more than two tables, multiple conditions, or several computed columns, for example) and want a similar view for a different use. After you copy the view, you can modify its definition to customize it.

Tip: You may want to copy a view to test modifications to the view before saving it permanently. Making a copy ensures that your original view definition is not changed until you want it to be.

To copy a view, follow these steps:

1. Press Alt-M to display the Manage Views pull-down menu.

2. Select Copy.

3. Select the view you want to copy.

4. Enter the new name for the copy, following the rules for naming views.

Printing Views

Printing a view on the Views screen is the same as printing data from the Info screen. The menu options are identical, and the same effect is produced. See Chapter 4 for information on printing data.

Summary

In this chapter, you learned how to define a view to incorporate only the tables, columns, and rows you want to see. You learned how to set conditions to limit the rows included in the view definition and how to define an on-the-fly computed column for the view.

You also learned how to save a view permanently, recall the view for modification, and create a new table containing all the data defined for the view.

To learn more about using the Info options on your view data, return to Chapter 4. Continue to Part III to learn how to design and create customized data-entry forms and reports.

Part III

Producing Forms and Reports

Includes

Creating Forms and Reports

Building and Using Customized Forms

Building and Using Customized Reports

Quick Start 3
Creating Forms and Reports

In this quick start, you learn how to design and create customized forms and reports. R:BASE makes this procedure easy by providing a Quick Form and a Quick Report option for each module. You first will learn to use the Quick options to create a form and a report. Then you will customize those forms and reports by using some of the module features.

The examples in this quick start were not selected to amaze you with the power of each module's capabilities. Instead, they show you how easy the modules are to use. As your knowledge increases, you can move beyond the simple forms and reports shown in this quick start. For a description of the full power of the Forms and Reports modules, see Chapters 6 and 7.

Creating and Using Quick Forms

Although the Info option's tabular edit provides a quick and easy way to enter and edit data (see Chapter 4), often you will want to create a data entry form to customize data entry. In this quick start, you make a simple data entry form—a single screen serving a single table. To learn how to make a form with multiple pages, see Chapter 6.

The form you create in this quick start shows you how R:BASE quickly and easily creates a basic form definition. A Quick form is a good method for getting the basic information on a form. Later, you can enhance the information by using the custom form features. To create the Quick form, follow these steps:

1. Start R:BASE if you have not done so already. Make current the directory containing the sample MAILING database by typing *cd \samples* and pressing Enter.

2. Type *rbase* and press Enter.

3. Open a database. In this example, you use the MAILING database you created in Quick Start 1. Select MAILING from the Databases pull-down menu.

4. Select Forms from the R:BASE main menu.

   Because no forms exist yet in the MAILING database, only the Create/Modify option is shown on the Forms pull-down menu. This option leads to the Forms module, where you can create or modify data entry forms.

5. Press Enter to choose Create/Modify.

R:BASE displays the Forms Module menu (see fig. QS3.1).

Fig. QS3.1

Creating a form.

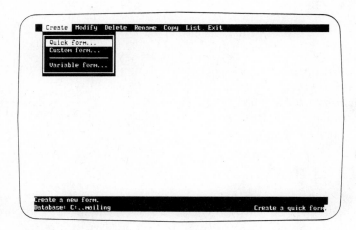

The Create pull-down menu shows three options that you can use to create a new form: Quick Form, Custom Form, and Variable Form. You use Quick Form and Custom Form to create forms for entering data into tables, and you use Variable Form to enter or edit variables. See Chapter 6 for information on forms. To create a Quick form from the Create menu, follow these steps:

1. Select Quick Form from the Create pull-down menu.

   R:BASE asks for the form name and a description of the form.

2. Type *Codeform* for the form name and press Enter.

   R:BASE prompts you for a description of this form.

3. Type *Entry/Edit Form for Mailing Codes* and press Enter (see fig. QS3.2).

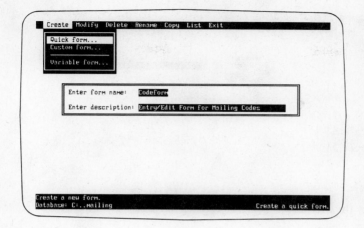

Fig. QS3.2

Describing the form for later identification.

R:BASE displays a list of the tables in the database.

4. Choose Codes_mail.

R:BASE displays a list of the columns in the Codes_mail table.

5. You want to enter data in both columns, so press Shift-F6 to select all columns.

R:BASE puts a check mark next to the column names (see fig. QS3.3).

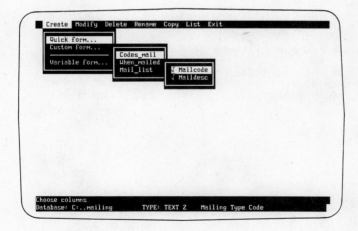

Fig. QS3.3

Choosing a table and the columns you want to include.

6. Press F2 to tell R:BASE that you are finished selecting columns.

R:BASE displays the Form Layout screen with the columns used as the field titles and the fields already entered on the form (see fig. QS3.4).

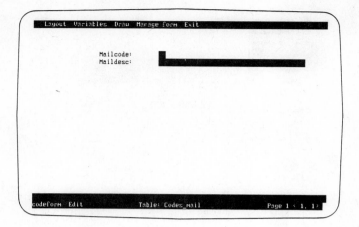

Fig. QS3.4

*Customizing
the form
layout.*

Modifying Quick Forms

The form is already in pretty good shape, but you can make adjustments.
For this quick start, change the labels that identify the entry fields. Follow
these steps:

1. Move the cursor to the title Mailcode.

2. Change to Overwrite mode (if you are not in it). The cursor appears
    as an underscore in Overwrite mode. Press Ins to toggle between
    Overwrite and Insert mode.

3. Type *Mailing Code:* over the old title (Mailcode:).

4. Move the cursor to the title Codedesc and type *Description:*.

5. Move the cursor to Line 2, Column 30.

    The line and column indicator is in the bottom right corner of the
    screen.

6. Type *Mailing Code Form*.

Figure QS3.5 shows the revised screen.

Saving Forms

Now you can use the form to enter new mailing codes or to edit existing
mailing codes. Follow these steps:

1. Press Esc to highlight Exit and press Enter.

    R:BASE asks whether you want to save the changes.

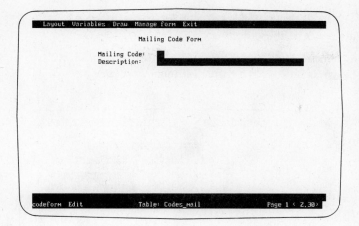

```
Layout  Variables  Draw  Manage form  Exit
                        Mailing Code Form

         Mailing Code:
         Description:
```
```
codeform  Edit              Table: Codes_mail          Page 1 < 2,30>
```

Fig. QS3.5

A simple data entry form.

2. Press Enter to choose Yes.

   R:BASE saves the form and returns to the Forms Module main menu.

3. Press Esc and then press Enter to exit from the Forms module.

R:BASE returns to the main menu.

Using Forms

The Forms option enables you to use the forms you created. You can start a form in Entry or Edit mode. In Edit mode, existing data appears on-screen, depending on the sort order and conditions you specify when you start the form. You can add data to a table even if you are using the form in Edit mode. Similarly, you can edit data in a form if you start the form in Entry mode. Chapter 6 explains many other features of forms.

Follow these steps to use the form:

1. Select Codeform from the Forms pull-down menu.

2. Choose Edit Data.

   R:BASE presents three options: Quick Sort, Quick Select, and Enter WHERE Clause. Quick Sort establishes the order in which you want to use the data. Quick Select uses the condition builder to select specific rows to edit by choosing from lists. Enter WHERE Clause enables you to enter a set of conditions instead of using the condition builder.

3. Press Enter to choose Quick Sort.

   R:BASE displays a list of the columns.

4. Press Enter to choose Mailcode. Then press Enter to choose Ascending, shown as an A next to the column name (see fig. QS3.6).

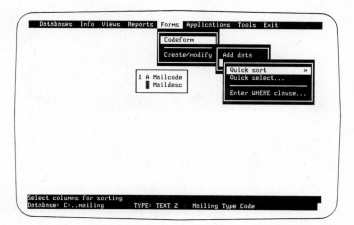

Fig. QS3.6

Sorting the data.

5. Press F2 to tell R:BASE that you are finished sorting.

6. Press F2 again to start using the form.

   Figure QS3.7 shows you what the form should look like.

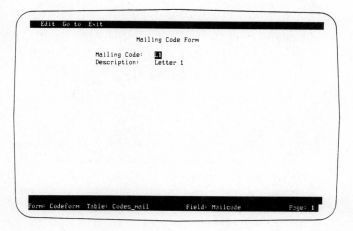

Fig. QS3.7

The highlighted first field, ready for editing.

You can change the information in either field. Suppose that you want to know which codes are stored in the table. Continue following these steps.

7. Press Shift-F3.

   R:BASE displays a dialog box for you to enter a condition, enabling you to limit the codes that R:BASE displays. The dialog box is not particularly useful for limiting the codes for this form, because the list is short. In Chapter 6, you learn more about limiting the number of codes displayed.

8. Press Enter to select all codes.

   R:BASE displays a pop-up menu with all codes already in the table. In this example, only two codes exist: L1 and L2. You can look at the data for any field representing a column in an R:BASE form. In Chapter 6, you learn how to make custom pop-up menus for form fields.

9. Press Esc to leave the pop-up menu.

10. Press Tab to move to the Description field.

11. Type *Initial mailing for funding* and press Enter.

    You have completed the changes. Now you want to save the changes in the table.

12. Press Alt-E to highlight Edit. Select Save Changes (see fig. QS3.8).

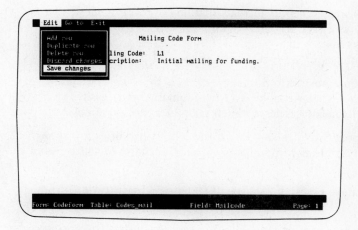

Fig. QS3.8

Saving the data in the table.

R:BASE returns you to the form, with the next row already displayed.

Adding Rows

You can add a row of data to a table even if you started the form in Edit mode. Follow these steps:

1. Press Alt-E to display the Edit menu.

2. Choose Add Row.

   R:BASE clears the fields on the form and places the cursor in the Mailcode field.

3. Type *L3* and press Enter.

4. In the Description field, type *Follow-up to Mailing 1* and press Enter.

   R:BASE adds the row and displays the Edit pull-down menu. You can add another row or press Alt to return to the form to edit the new available row in the table.

5. When you finish editing the form, press Esc and then press Enter to exit.

R:BASE returns you to the main menu. Now that you have data in your database, you can get reports on the data. In the next section, you learn how to create a Quick report.

Creating and Using Quick Reports

You can define customized report formats that, like a form or view, you can use over and over again. A Quick report has several features that make a report a better alternative than simply printing data in a Query By Example. The advantages of a Quick report follow:

- You can divide a custom report into sections by using breakpoint grouping. This division enables you to summarize data easily. You can get grand totals for sales by each customer, for example.

- A custom report provides superior formatting capabilities for your data; you can define field templates (display formats) for all types of data.

- The Draw feature gives you sharper looking reports with lines and boxes.

- You can highlight data or text with any type style that your printer is capable of producing (bold, underline, italic, and expanded).

In this section, you create a Quick report. You then modify the look of the report by changing field text and deleting some fields. Finally, you learn how to print the report. To create a Quick report, follow these steps:

1. Highlight Reports on the R:BASE main menu.

   The Reports pull-down menu has two options: Labels and Create/ Modify. The Labels option uses the Reports module in a special way, creating label formats for your data (see Chapter 7). Right now, you want to define a standard report format.

2. Select Create/Modify.

   R:BASE displays the Reports Module main menu. The Create option is highlighted (see fig. QS3.9). You can define Quick or Custom reports. For Quick reports, R:BASE designs the basic report format for you. For Custom reports, you start with a blank report screen and do everything yourself. Defining a Quick report and then modifying it is a fast method to get a report format started.

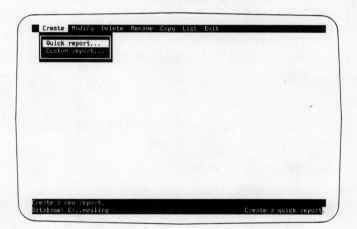

Fig. QS3.9
Creating a report.

3. Press Enter to choose Quick Report.

   R:BASE now will step through the process of choosing the items for the Quick report. This process is similar to the steps you went through to define a Quick form.

4. Type *Mailrep* for the report name and press Enter.

5. Type *Mailing List Report* for the report description and press Enter (see fig. QS3.10).

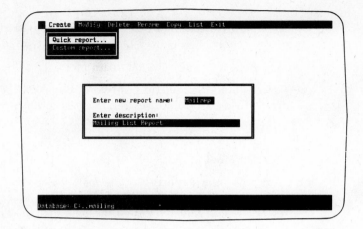

Fig. QS3.10

Entering the description for the Mailrep report.

R:BASE displays a list of the tables and views defined in the database. You can use a view to extract data for the report (see Chapter 5). This enables you to preselect data from multiple tables for your report.

6. Highlight Q_mail (the view you defined earlier in Quick Start 2).

   R:BASE displays the columns defined in the view.

7. Press Shift-F6 to choose all the columns.

8. Move the cursor to the second occurrence of the Idno column and press Enter to unselect it. The check mark disappears.

9. Press F2 to finish working with the column list.

   R:BASE asks whether you want a column-wise or row-wise report.

10. Highlight Row-wise.

    You will have too many columns appearing on-screen if you spread the columns across the top of the report (column-wise). You can ask to orient the columns down the report (row-wise) Figure QS3.11 shows you the screen so far.

11. Press F2 to display the report layout.

Modifying Reports

As shown in figure QS3.12, the column names are used for the field titles and the fields are defined next to the titles. You can improve the look of

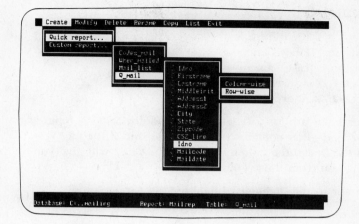

Fig. QS3.11

Orienting the report row-wise.

this report by making a few changes. In this exercise, you will change the titles for some of the fields and delete other fields. See Chapter 7 for more information on enhancing reports.

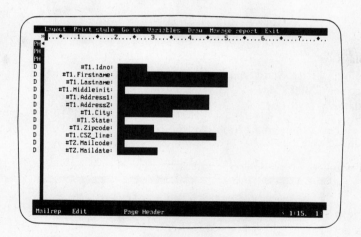

Fig. QS3.12

Customizing the report layout.

Follow these steps to improve your report:

1. Add a report heading on Line 2, starting in Column 30. Type *Mailing List Report*.

2. Be sure that you are in Overwrite mode. The cursor should appear as an underscore. If the cursor is not an underscore, press Ins.

3. Change these field titles:

Original Title	*Change to:*
#T1.Idno:	Identification:
#T1.Firstname:	First Name:
#T1.Lastname:	Last Name:
#T1.Address1:	Address 1:
#T1.Address2:	Address 2:

The next four fields are for City, State, ZIP code, and the computed column—CSZ_line—that contains the city, state, and ZIP code. You do not need the first three columns because CSZ_line will give you all the information from those columns.

4. Move the cursor to the highlighted field for the City column.

5. Press Shift-F9 to delete the highlighted field.

6. Press F9 to delete the line.

   You now have removed the City title and field from the report.

7. Remove the fields and titles for the state and ZIP code in the same way.

8. Complete the title changes:

Original Title	*Change to:*
#T1.CSZ_line:	City, State, Zip:
#T2.Mailcode:	Mail Code:
#T2.Maildate:	Mail Date:

Your report screen now should look like figure QS3.13.

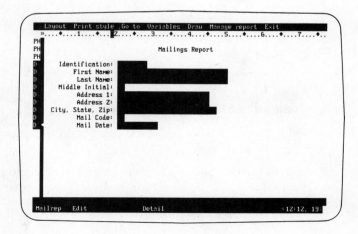

Fig. QS3.13

The report after a few modifications.

9. Press Esc and then Enter to exit the Reports module.

   R:BASE asks whether you want to save your report.

10. Press Enter to choose Yes.

   R:BASE returns you to the Reports Module main menu.

11. Press Esc and Enter to exit.

R:BASE returns you to the main menu. You now are ready to print the report.

Printing Reports

After you define a report, R:BASE saves the report so that you can use it again. This section shows you how to print your report from the R:BASE main menu.

To print your report, follow these steps:

1. Highlight Reports and press Enter to choose Mailrep—the report you just defined.

   R:BASE asks whether you want to use any of three options: Quick Sort, Quick Select, or Enter WHERE Clause.

2. Press Enter to choose Quick Sort.

   R:BASE displays a list of the columns that define the report in the view.

3. Choose Lastname and then choose Ascending to sort the report alphabetically by the last name in ascending order (see fig. QS3.14).

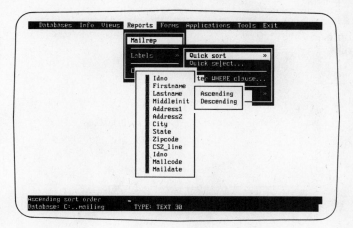

Fig. QS3.14

Sorting the data.

4. Press F2 to finish sorting.

5. Select Print To.

   R:BASE displays destinations for the report: screen, file, or printer (see fig QS3.15). As with all report options and functions, printing options are covered in Chapter 7.

Fig. QS3.15

Choosing the destination for the report.

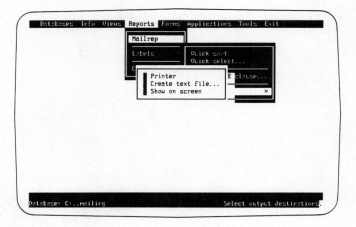

6. Choose Show On Screen and press F2 twice to print the report to the screen.

   R:BASE displays the first report page (see figure QS3.16).

Fig. QS3.16

The report when printed to the screen.

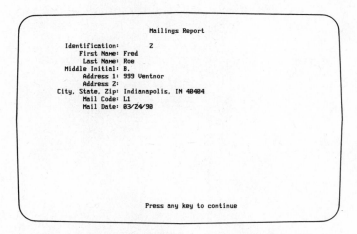

7. Press any letter or number to return to the main menu.

R:BASE returns to the main menu with the Reports option still highlighted. You now can exit R:BASE by following these steps:

1. Press Alt-E to highlight the Exit option.

2. Press Enter to select Leave R:BASE.

Summary

In this quick start, you learned how to create and use a data entry form and how to create and use a custom report. The rest of Part III—Chapters 6 and 7—deals with the advanced features of forms and reports.

6

Building and Using
Customized Forms

Data-entry forms provide an organized way to enter data into your database structure. The Forms module provides all the tools you need to create custom-designed forms. You can create simple single-page, single-table forms with the Quick Form option, or design complex multi-page, multi-table forms with the custom Form option.

Developing forms is especially helpful when you are designing an application for other users. A form enables you to present data on-screen in a more attractive and easier-to-use format than the tabular edit described in Chapter 4. You can include only the columns you want the user to see, make some columns display only, put logical groups of data together, and even execute small programs called *triggers* while a form is executing.

The multi-table entry feature is perhaps the most useful. In a tabular edit, you are limited to entering or editing data in a single table. In a multi-table form, you can manipulate related data on a single screen or set of screens. In the sample database MAILING, for example, the Mail_list and When_mailed tables placed together in one form enable you to edit a person's basic data—name and address—and also either edit or add mailing references. You learn how to create such a form in this chapter.

This chapter has two parts. The first part describes how to use the Forms module to create a customized data-entry form. The second part tells you how to use a form for data entry and editing.

207

The concepts you learn in this chapter follow:

- Designing useful and attractive data-entry forms
- Using a form to enter or edit data in multiple tables
- Using expressions and variables in the form format
- Executing command files from a form
- Using customized forms for data entry and editing

```
Command: FORMS
```

Understanding the Types of Forms

The default tabular method for entering and editing data may satisfactorily meet your data-entry needs. A custom data-entry form, however, gives you more options for presenting your data and enables you to enter data into more than one table on a single form—a feature that is extremely convenient in a complex database design.

With custom forms, you can display data from a table other than the one being edited. Alternatively, you can edit up to five tables in a single form. Suppose that you want to delete a reference in all tables where the reference exists. By using a custom form, you can delete from one table and automatically delete any related table's reference at the same time.

Also, appearance can be a factor. If you are designing a database for someone else to use, you want to make sure that the purpose of the data is understood easily. With a custom form, you can make sure that sufficient text is on-screen to explain each piece of data.

A *custom form* is a form you design yourself, starting from a blank screen. A *Quick form* is a custom form that R:BASE creates after you name the table and the columns to be included in the form layout. You can modify a Quick form, adding any of the custom form features you want.

If you think of custom forms in the following hierarchy, you see that a Quick form is merely the simplest type of custom form:

1. *Quick form:* Single-screen, single-table, direct entry into each requested column once each time the form is displayed.

2. *Multi-row form:* Single-screen, single-table, entry into each requested column for as many rows as you want to add or edit.

3. *Multi-table form:* One or more screens, up to five tables, entry into each requested column each time the form is displayed.

4. *Multi-table, multi-row form:* One or more screens, up to five tables, entry into each requested column for as many rows as you want to add or edit.

Figures 6.1, 6.2, and 6.3 illustrate each of the custom form types that serve tables: single-table forms, multi-row forms, and multi-table forms.

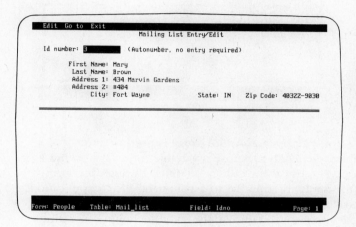

Fig. 6.1

Creating a single-table form in R:BASE.

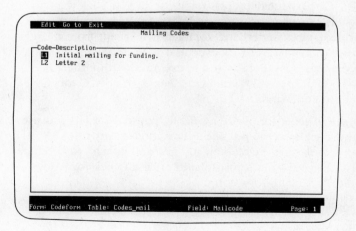

Fig. 6.2

A multi-row form.

Fig. 6.3

A multi-table form.

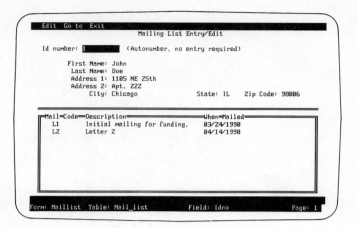

A different type of form entirely, a *variable form*, is used to enter or edit global variables. Generally, you use a variable form only within a programming context, because the variables modified through the form generally are used to supply information to a command file or application. This chapter concerns itself with *table forms*, which you can use separately or from an application. You use the same technique to define a variable form, however, as you do to define a table form. The only difference is that you do not deal with either tables or columns on the form—only variables. Of particular interest for those of you who want to define variable forms is this chapter's section "Working with Expressions." Using a variable form requires underlying commands different from those used in a regular form. A regular form is executed with either the EDIT USING or ENTER command; a variable form is executed with either the EDIT VARIABLE or ENTER VARIABLE command. See Appendix C for more information about these commands.

Although several types of table forms are available, you do not have to use a different method to create each type. The Forms module provides a set of basic form-building tools that enable you to "mix-and-match" to produce exactly the type of form you want. You can start with a Quick form and modify it into a multi-table, multi-row form.

These basic steps apply to the creation of all forms:

1. Determine the characteristics of the form.

    • Specify colors
    • Choose menu options
    • Decide whether to use the form for entry, edit, or both
    • Assign a password to the form

- Clear the screen before or after using the form
- Display a status line

2. Determine the data-entry requirements of each table used by the form.

   - Whether you can add, modify, or delete from the table
   - Whether multiple rows are displayed
   - Whether to add colors for the table area if multiple rows are displayed

3. Determine the data-entry requirements of each field placed on the form. (A *field* in the context of a form or report is a window in which the value of a column or variable is entered or modified.)

   - Whether you can edit a field
   - Whether you use field colors or a blinking display
   - Whether to display a default value in the field
   - What help text to display for the field
   - Where to look up values for a pop-up menu for the field

Starting the Forms Module

You can start the Forms module in one of two ways:

- Choose Forms from the R:BASE main menu, and then choose Create/Modify from the Forms pull-down menu.

- Enter FORMS in Command mode (at the R> prompt) or from Prompt By Example.

Whichever way you start the Forms module, the module's main menu appears on-screen, as shown in figure 6.4. Choose the Create option when you want to create new custom forms or Quick forms. The other main menu options are discussed in "Modifying Forms" and "Managing Forms with the Forms Module's Main Menu," later in this chapter.

Naming the Form and the Driving Table

After you start the Forms module and choose Create, R:BASE leads you through the required steps: naming the form and choosing the driving table for the form.

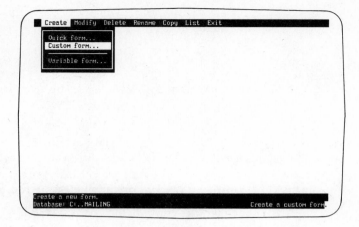

Fig. 6.4

The Forms module's main menu.

To begin creating a custom form, choose Custom Form from the Create pull-down menu. R:BASE displays a dialog box and prompts you for the name of the form. Type a one- to eight-character form name and press Enter. Then enter a description, using as many as 40 characters (see fig. 6.5). The description is optional but is useful for helping you later identify a particular form among the many forms you probably will create for your database. The description is displayed on R:BASE menus when you highlight the form name.

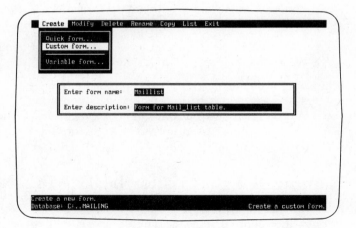

Fig. 6.5

Entering a form name and description.

Finally, R:BASE displays a list of the tables in the database, as shown in figure 6.6. From the list, choose the driving table for the form. The *driving table* is the main table served by the form. Any additional tables used in the form must have a relationship to the first table you choose.

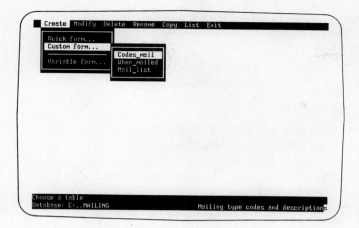

Fig. 6.6

Choosing the first table for the new form.

Using the Form Building Menu and Function Keys

When you create or modify a form, the Form Building menu appears, as shown in figure 6.7. This chapter provides a loose sequence of actions you can take, but you can use the options in any order. You can enter the text for the form and then place the fields, for example. Or place the fields first, draw lines, and then enter text on-screen. Also, you do not have to complete any one action before using another. You can alternate text entry and field placement.

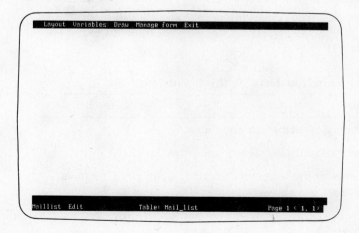

Fig. 6.7

The Form Building menu.

Each of the Form Building menu options displays a pull-down menu with options for handling some part of the form-building process. Table 6.1 describes the Form Building menu options.

Table 6.1
Using the Form Building Menu Options

Option	Function
Layout	Places, clears, and defines field characteristics. Shows and changes field order. Selects and defines table characteristics. Removes, changes, and reorders tables. Defines form characteristics (see "Manipulating Fields").
Variables	Defines, deletes, and changes the data type. Reorders and lists variables (see "Working with Expressions," later in this chapter).
Draw	Draws single or double lines (see "Drawing Lines and Boxes").
Manage Form	Executes the form and saves the form definition (see "Saving Completed Forms").

This chapter describes how to use all these options to create a custom form. Modifying a form uses the same set of options; you simply replace existing definition attributes with new ones.

Although you handle most form development and modification tasks with the menu options on the Form Building menu, some form functions are available only with a function key. Table 6.2 lists the function keys that have uses not available from the menus.

Table 6.2
Using Function Keys in the Forms Module

Key	Effect
Shift-F1	Displays available function keys.
Ctrl-F4	Expands and contracts a multi-row region.
F5	Resets to the original values any field, table, or form settings.
Ctrl-F6	Toggles repeat character on and off or raises and lowers the pen, if drawing lines.
Shift-F7	Moves to the previous table in a multi-table form.

Key	Effect
Shift-F8	Moves to the next table in a multi-table form.
F9	Deletes the current line.
Shift-F9	Deletes a field.
F10	Inserts a line above the current line.
Shift-F10	Duplicates or unduplicates rows in a multi-row region.

Specifying Form Settings

After naming the form and specifying its driving table, you may want to look at the form characteristics. R:BASE provides default characteristics that often are all you need, but you can modify them if necessary. The Form Settings screen lists the form characteristics and the default values already set (see fig. 6.8).

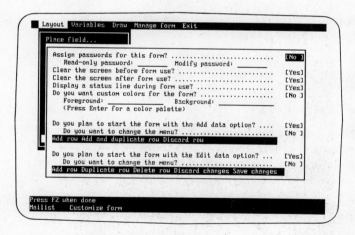

Fig. 6.8

Form settings describe the overall use of a form.

To display the Form Settings screen, press Alt-L to choose Layout from the Form Building menu. Then choose Form Settings from the Layout pull-down menu.

Setting Passwords

Forms can have their own passwords that are separate from table passwords. A form password overrides any table passwords set for the form's tables. By default, a form has no password, in which case, any table passwords you have assigned are in effect.

To create a form password, follow these steps:

1. From the Form Settings screen, press Y in the first field and then press Enter.

   R:BASE places the cursor in the Read-only Password field. The default password NONE appears.

2. If you want to use this form for query only, enter a password in the Read-only Password field. Otherwise, skip to Step 3.

3. Press Enter or Tab to move the cursor to Modify Password, and enter a password for using the form to enter or edit data.

Clearing the Screen

You can choose to leave the form displayed on-screen after you use the form for data entry. Alternatively, you can choose to leave whatever was on-screen before you started the form. The default is to clear the screen before and after use, but you may not want to clear if you want other data displayed at the same time as the form. A form writes over the screen, usually starting on Line 1. You can display a form starting on any screen line if you start the form from Command mode.

To change either of the clearing options on the Form Settings screen, press N or Y with the cursor in the appropriate field.

Displaying the Status Line

The *status line* shows such items as the form name, current table, and current field. By default, the status line displays, but you can choose to omit it from the form display. Just press N with the cursor in the appropriate field of the Form Settings screen.

Setting Custom Colors

You can use the Form Settings screen to set the foreground and background colors for the form. If you leave the Foreground and Background fields blank, the form displays in the current system foreground and background colors (white on blue is the default).

To change the form colors, press Y in response to the question

   Do you want custom colors for the form?

R:BASE moves the cursor to the Foreground field, where you can enter a specific color name (red, blue, black, and so on) or press Enter to use the color palette to select colors. The available colors are in the standard

IBM 16-color palette—16 foreground colors and 8 background colors. See Appendix A for a list of the standard colors.

Changing Menu Options

On the bottom half of the Form Settings screen, you can choose which menu options will be available for data entry and edit on a particular form, or you can omit either mode entirely.

The available Add Data menu options include the following:

Add Row	Enables the form user to add rows manually. You can set the table characteristics for automatic add, so this option is not always needed.
Add and Duplicate Row	Enables the form user to duplicate the last entered row. This option is particularly useful if you are entering many rows with the same values. Remember that your data entry rules must allow duplicate values. (See Chapter 3 for information on data-entry rules.)
Discard Row	Enables the form user to remove the last entered row.
Add Row and Exit	Enables the user to add the current row and exit immediately.

The available Edit Data menu options include the following:

Add Row	Enables the form user to add a row when using the form for editing.
Duplicate Row	Enables the form user to add a row by duplicating the last entered row.
Delete Row	Enables the form user to delete the currently displayed row.
Discard Changes	Enables the form user to reset the data to its original state.
Save Changes	Enables the form user to save changes manually. You can set the table characteristics for automatic storage of changed rows, so this option is not always needed.

Figure 6.9 shows the pop-up menu that appears when you indicate that you want to change the Add Data menu. Press Enter at each menu option you want to retain. The order in which you check off the options is the order in which the options will be displayed on the form when it is used. Press F2 to tell R:BASE when you are finished selecting options for the menu. The process is the same for either menu.

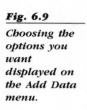

Fig. 6.9

Choosing the options you want displayed on the Add Data menu.

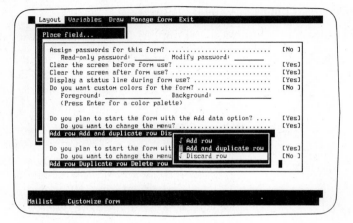

Exiting the Form Settings Screen

After you change the form characteristics as needed, press F2 to return to the Form Building screen.

Entering and Editing Text

The text areas of a form describe what is to be entered into the fields. You can have as much descriptive text as you want, but remember to leave enough room for the fields themselves. A table's fields can be spread across more than one screen (page)—up to five pages—if you are defining a single-row form. For a multi-row form, each table's fields must be entered only on a single form page.

To enter the text on a form, move the cursor to where you want the text and type it on the form. If you want to change text already on the form, you can type over existing text (be sure that the cursor is an underscore to show that you are in Overwrite mode). You can delete text by pressing Del with the cursor on the text character you want to remove.

If you want to delete a whole line of text, move the cursor to the line you want to delete and press F9. You can remove a line only if no fields are placed on the line.

You can enter all the text for a form at one time (field names, instructions, or lines and boxes), or you can alternate between entering the text and then placing the field to go with the text. Figure 6.10 shows a single-table, single-page form with the text entered on the layout.

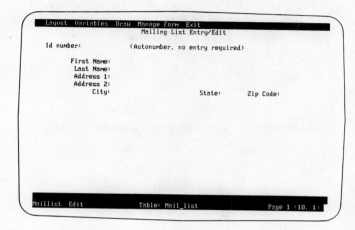

Fig. 6.10

Text on the form tells you what kind of data to enter in each field.

Drawing Lines and Boxes

Sometimes you may want to draw lines or boxes on a form. You may want to use them to make some area of the form stand out from other areas, for example. Lines and boxes are merely an aesthetic choice.

With the Draw option on the Form Building menu, you can draw with single- or double-line characters. Press Alt-D to highlight Draw. R:BASE displays the Draw pull-down menu with three options: Single Lines, Double Lines, and Erase Lines (see fig. 6.11).

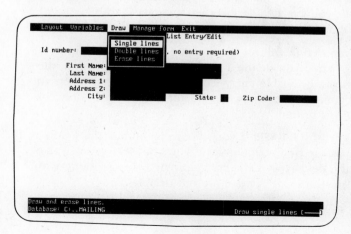

Fig. 6.11

Using the Draw menu options.

Choose one of the first two options to begin drawing a line. When you start, the "pen" is up. To draw lines, you must press Ctrl-F6 to lower the pen (see the message at the bottom of the screen). Then, when you move the cursor by using the arrow keys, a line is drawn on-screen. You can form boxes by turning 90 degree angles. If you are drawing a line from left to right and want a corner, for example, press the down- or up-arrow key to change direction. R:BASE draws the appropriate corner for the line type you are using.

When you finish drawing, press Esc to leave Draw mode. Figure 6.12 shows a double line drawn on the form.

Fig. 6.12

A drawn double line.

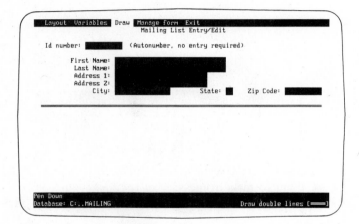

Manipulating Fields

Fields are windows you specify that are used to display column or variable data. For most fields, you can decide whether the data is to be entered, edited, deleted, or only displayed.

Most of the fields you define will be for entering or editing column data from the table. When you define a field for a standard column, the default field characteristics enable entry, editing, and deleting. When you define a field for a computed column, the default is for display only, and you cannot change this setting.

Field types are handled by R:BASE. If you choose a column, the field has the same data type as the original column. If you choose a variable that you have defined, the field type is the variable type (see "Working with Expressions," later in this chapter, for more on variables).

Variable fields can be either Entry/Edit or Display-Only fields. The exceptions are *Lookup fields*, which are explained in the "Working with Expressions" section in this chapter.

Placing Fields

To define a field, you first need to place it on the form. Use the Layout pull-down menu, accessed from the Form Building menu, to place or remove fields, following these steps:

1. Press Alt-L to display the Layout pull-down menu.

2. Choose Place Field.

   R:BASE displays a dialog box in which you can name the field, as shown in figure 6.13.

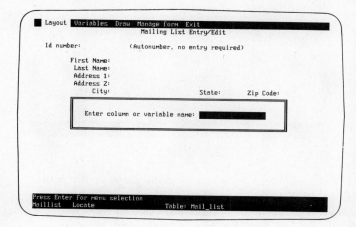

Fig. 6.13

Entering a column or variable name in a dialog box.

You can define a field for a column in the table or a variable. The dialog box enables you to enter a column or variable name directly. Alternatively, you can press Enter at the dialog box prompt and select the table or defined variables from a list of column names. If you enter a name in the dialog box, R:BASE checks to see if it is a column, and then it checks the variable list. If the name is not a column or a previously defined variable, R:BASE assumes you are creating a new variable.

A field for a column must have the same name as the column so that R:BASE will know where to add or modify the data in the table.

You usually do not enter data into fields for variables (although you can); you normally use variables to calculate data or to look up data for display. See "Working with Expressions," later in this chapter, for detailed information on defining and using variables in a form.

3. Type the name for the field or press Enter to display a list. You can display columns or variables, as shown in figure 6.14. To choose a column, highlight the column name and press Enter (the column list already will be displayed). To choose a variable, press Alt-V to display the variable list and then choose a variable.

Fig. 6.14

R:BASE displays a list to help you select columns to place.

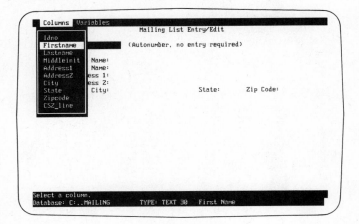

4. After you select the column or variable, R:BASE displays the prompt shown in figure 6.15. The program gives you the opportunity to convert a standard column into a computed column by defining an expression for the column directly in the form. See Chapter 3 for information on computed columns and "Working with Expressions," later in this chapter, for examples of how and why you can define an expression for a column.

5. The next prompt asks

   Do you want to customize field settings?

If you press Y in response to this prompt, R:BASE displays a series of Field Settings screens on which you can specify the field settings for your form. If you press Enter to select No, you then place the field on the form layout. See "Painting Field Locations," later in this chapter, for more information.

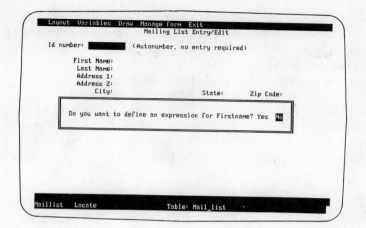

```
 Layout  Variables  Draw  Manage form  Exit
                  Mailing List Entry/Edit
  Id number: ▆▆▆▆▆▆    (Autonumber, no entry required)

        First Name:
        Last Name:
        Address 1:
        Address 2:
           City:              State:       Zip Code:

      ┌──────────────────────────────────────────────────┐
      │ Do you want to define an expression for Firstname? Yes  No │
      └──────────────────────────────────────────────────┘




 Maillist   Locate                  Table: Mail_list
```

Fig. 6.15

Defining an expression for a variable field.

Modifying Field Settings

Field settings are the characteristics of a field: whether the data can be entered and modified, whether the field should be displayed with colors other than the form colors, and other general features of the field. Figure 6.16 shows the first Field Settings screen.

```
 Layout  Variables  Draw  Manage form  Exit
                  Mailing List Entry/Edit
 I┌─────────────────────────────────────────────────────┐
  │ Will new data be entered in the field? ................... [Yes] │
  │                                                          │
  │ Can the user change the data displayed in the field? ....... [Yes] │
  │   Restrict changes to the current table? .................. [Yes] │
  │                                                          │
  │ Do you want to display a default value in the field? ....... [No ] │
  │   Enter default value or #DUP to use the previous row value │
  │   ─────────────────                                      │
  │                                                          │
  │ Do you want custom colors for the field? ................. [No ] │
  │   Foreground: _____  Background: _____             │
  │   (Press Enter for a color palette)                      │
  │                                                          │
  │ Do you want this field to blink when displayed? ........... [No ] │
  │                                                          │
  │         Press PgDn to continue field settings            │
  └─────────────────────────────────────────────────────┘
 Press FZ when done
 Column   Firstname          TEXT      Table: Mail_list
```

Fig. 6.16

The first Field Settings screen.

When you are defining a field for a column, you usually want to leave the default values for entry and edit as they are shown in figure 6.16. Following is a brief description of the settings for entry and edit.

• Will new data be entered in the field?

A Yes answer enables a form user to enter new data in the field. Data entry is not permitted if the field contains a value looked up in another table or if the field is defined for a computed column (see "Defining Lookup Data" in this chapter). If you answer No to this question, you are telling R:BASE to prevent new entries for the field, which means that you only can edit the field. You may want to restrict data entry, for example, if you want a display-only field or do not want the form user to change an existing value. Keep this feature in mind when you modify settings for the form and table (see this chapter's sections on "Specifying Form Settings" and "Changing Table Settings").

- Can the user change the data displayed in the field?

A Yes answer enables the form user to edit displayed data. Again, no editing is permitted for lookup or computed column fields. You may want to restrict edit for fields such as an ID number in a master file (Mail_list, for example) if you want to ensure that the ID number is not changed when the data is edited.

- Do you want to display a default value in the field?

You can assign a default value to display in a field if no data is available from the table, or if the form user bypasses entry in the field. You may, for example, want a date column to display the current date. To provide a default value, press Y in the field and then type the value. Enter #DUP as the default value to duplicate the entry from the last row.

- Do you want custom colors for the field?

and

Do you want this field to blink when displayed?

You can define different colors for each field and choose to have the field blink. If a field is for a key column, such as Idno for the Mail_list table, you may want to change the field's foreground and background colors or make the field blink to draw attention to it. You can use the standard IBM 16-color palette. When you are specifying the colors, you can type in a color name (*red* or *blue*, for example) or press Enter in the Foreground field to use the color palette. If you use the palette to select colors, R:BASE fills in the color names for the foreground and background. If you want to type in the color names, you must press the down-arrow key to move the cursor to the next field setting.

When you have changed the field characteristics as needed, press PgDn (or Enter at the last field) to display the second page of field settings.

On the second Field Settings screen, you can provide help messages and pop-up menus for the fields. These features are useful for data-entry operators not familiar with the data requirements. On this screen, you also can execute a set of commands stored in a file.

Adding Field Help Messages

On the second Field Settings screen, the first setting enables you to enter a message line for the field you are placing on the form. If the form is being used for entry and edit, you may want a special message to appear whenever the cursor is positioned in a field. Field messages can help the data-entry operator enter data correctly.

To add field help messages, follow these steps:

1. Answer Yes to the prompt

       Do you want a help line displayed for this field?

   R:BASE places the cursor on the line under the prompt.

2. Type a help message line, using up to 70 characters.

Creating Pop-up Menus for Fields

Sometimes, the data entered in a column must already be listed in another or the same table. Duplicate entries, however, may sometimes be forbidden. You can define data-entry rules covering both of these situations. A pop-up menu for a field displays data stored in the database, so it is particularly useful if existing data is required for input.

Suppose that you are creating a form for entering mailing information (the When_mailed table in the MAILING database). For a field defined for the Mailcode column, displaying a list of the valid codes stored in the Codes_mail table would be useful. The pop-up menu definition for displaying the appropriate codes is shown in figure 6.17. This definition says "display the codes in the mailing codes table with the upper left corner of the menu starting on Line 3 in screen Column 15."

To create a pop-up menu for a field, follow these steps:

1. Answer Yes to the prompt

       Do you want a pop-up menu for this field?

2. Enter the name of the table containing the data you want displayed on the pop-up menu.

Fig. 6.17

Defining a pop-up menu.

```
 Layout  Variables  Draw  Manage form  Exit

   Do you want a help line displayed for this field? ......... [Yes]
   Enter a valid mailing code - Press Shift-F3 for existing.

   Do you want a pop-up menu for this field? ................. [Yes]
     Table name:Codes_mail          Column name:Mailcode
     Title:Already Used
     Upper left corner: Row 3     Column 15
     WHERE clause (optional):


   Entry/Exit procedures for the field:
      Run _____ IN _____ On entry into field
      Run _____ IN _____ On exit from field

                    Press PgUp to return to the previous screen



 Press FZ when done
 Column   Mailcode          TEXT       Table: Codes_mail
```

3. Enter the name of the column in the table that contains the specific data to display.

4. Enter a brief title for the pop-up menu. The title determines the width of the pop-up menu, and can contain up to 53 characters.

5. Enter a screen row and column coordinate at which the upper left corner of the pop-up menu should be positioned on-screen. Place the pop-up menu close to the entry field.

6. In the Forms module, you enter the WHERE clause by typing it instead of using the condition builder that you learned about in Chapter 1. An example WHERE clause for a pop-up menu may look like this:

   Codemail <> 'L1'

   This clause tells R:BASE to omit the L1 code from the list. You may want to use this WHERE clause, for example, if the L1 code no longer is being used for mailings.

Now, whenever the form user presses Shift-F3 with the cursor in the field, the customized pop-up menu appears. If you have not defined a pop-up menu for the field, R:BASE steps through a process in which the pop-up menu can be defined directly in the form (see "Starting Forms," later in this chapter, for more information).

R:BASE always omits duplicate entries from a pop-up menu and sorts the values in ascending order.

Creating Triggers

The last prompt on the second Field Settings screen requires that you write an R:BASE program (called a *command file* or *procedure file*). You have two options. You can execute the command file just before the cursor moves into the field or after the cursor leaves the field. The term *trigger* is used to describe this command file because entry or exit from a field "triggers" execution of the command file. These procedures are also called entry/exit procedures or pre- and post-exit triggers.

You may use a trigger file, for example, to skip one or more fields when the entry in a field is a certain value. Or, you may use such a command file to calculate on the current data and return a value. This approach is especially useful if a calculation cannot be performed with a single expression.

You create trigger files outside the Forms module by using any ASCII text editor. The R:BASE editor is ideal for this task. The following procedure shows an example of using SKIP in a simple trigger file:

1. Start the R:BASE editor by typing *rbedit* at the R> prompt (Command mode).

2. Type the program. For example, you could enter the following command file as a trigger file:

   ```
   IF field1 IS NULL THEN
       SKIP TO field3
   ENDIF
   RETURN
   ```

   This trigger file says *If no data was entered in field1 then skip to field3*. If field2 exists, then the program skips it in the form if no entry is made in field1.

3. Press Esc and choose Exit.

4. When R:BASE prompts you for it, enter a name for the file—for example, *fldtrig.cmd*.

5. Start the Forms module (type *forms* at the R> prompt).

6. On the Field Settings screen, name this trigger file as an exit trigger for the field named field1. Type *fldtrig.cmd* in the first blank after Run in the On Exit From field under the Entry/Exit procedures for the field heading.

In Chapter 8, you learn more about writing trigger command files.

Painting Field Locations

After you modify the field's settings, you need to paint the data-entry area for the field. On the message line at the bottom of the screen, R:BASE tells you what to do:

1. Move the cursor to the position on-screen where you want the first character in the field. Press S.

2. Use the arrow keys to move the cursor to the ending position for the field, and press E.

R:BASE shows a highlighted area for the field. Figure 6.18, for example, shows the fields painted for the ID number and First Name fields.

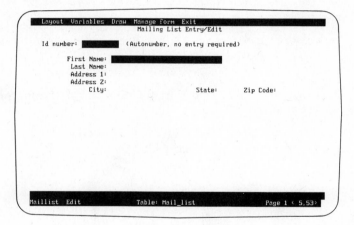

Fig. 6.18

Defining a field location by "painting" it on-screen.

For fields that will contain numeric, date, or time values, R:BASE paints the maximum entry area for the field. For Text or Note fields, you have to paint the entire field area. On Text fields, you cannot make the field size any larger than the defined column size. If the field is for a variable rather than a column, you can make the field as large as you want. You cannot split a field across pages, however.

If the field contains a Text column or variable or a Note column, you can paint the field area across multiple lines. Use the down-arrow key to create more lines for the field. A multiple-line field acts as a scrolling window for text entry longer than the size of the field. When you enter data into the field, R:BASE automatically wraps the entry at the end of each line. If you have more data to enter than will fit in the field, R:BASE scrolls the top line of data up, providing additional space up to the maximum length of the field (1,500 characters for Text, and 4,050 characters for Note).

Changing Field Locations

If you have placed a field incorrectly or need to move it or change its size to make room for other fields, use the following steps to change the position:

1. Move the cursor to the field.

2. Press F6.

   R:BASE asks Do you want to customize field settings?

3. Press Y for Yes if you want to change any of the field settings. See "Modifying Field Settings" for details.

4. When asked Do you want to relocate the field?, answer Yes to change the location or size of the field.

   R:BASE removes the highlight from the data-entry area.

5. Move the cursor to the new beginning position, and press S to start the field location.

6. Move the cursor to the new ending position and press E (or W to wrap a multi-line field).

Removing Fields

If you want to remove a previously placed field, you can use one of two methods. Follow these steps:

1. Place the cursor in the field you want to remove.

2. Press Alt-L to display the Layout pull-down menu. Then select Clear Field.

   or

   Press Shift-F9.

Changing Field Order

As you place fields, enter text, and modify various settings, you may find that you placed a field in the wrong order for entry. The data-entry order of fields follows the same order in which you place them on the form. You can review field order from the Layout pull-down menu. Press Alt-L to display the menu, and choose Show Field Order. R:BASE then steps through the fields in the order in which you placed them. Press Enter to move from field to field.

To change the field order, you use the Change Field Order option. For example, suppose that you placed the Last Name field before you placed the First Name field on the form. These fields are field numbers 2 and 3 (assuming that ID Number is field 1). To switch the order of these fields, follow these steps:

1. Press Alt-L to display the Layout pull-down menu.

2. Select Change Field Order.

   R:BASE displays a list of the field names in their current order.

3. Select Firstname.

   R:BASE prompts you for the new field position.

4. Press 2 to change the Firstname position from 3 to 2 (see fig. 6.19).

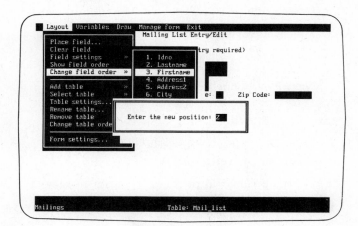

Fig. 6.19

Changing a field's data entry order.

The other fields move to make room for the new field's position.

5. Make any additional field order changes in the same way. Press F2 when you are finished reordering fields.

Figure 6.20 shows the completed single-table, single-page form. The text titles for the fields are entered, the fields are placed, and a line is drawn across the screen.

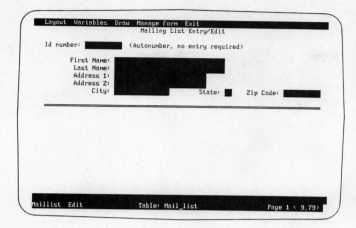

Fig. 6.20

*A complete
Form
Definition
screen.*

Adding Tables to Forms

One form can serve up to five related tables. Suppose that you want to enter mailing data at the same time you enter a person on the mailing list. When you add a table to a form, the table must have a column common with at least one other table in the form. You do not have to place the secondary table's common column on the form. R:BASE assumes that the values in the common columns must match.

Look again at figure 6.20. You can modify this form to serve two tables by adding a second table to the bottom of the screen. In the quick starts in this book, for example, you add the When_mailed table to this form. The When_mailed table holds the specific information about what was mailed to whom and when.

To add a table, press Alt-L to display the Layout pull-down menu. Then choose Add Table. R:BASE displays a list of available tables, as shown in figure 6.21. Select the table you want to add to the form.

Changing Table Settings

As with other characteristics already described, you can modify a table's settings. *Table settings* describe how the table data is used on the form. To modify table settings, press Alt-L to display the Layout pull-down menu, and choose Table Settings. R:BASE displays the Table Settings screen shown in figure 6.22. As on all Settings screens, you modify the default values by pressing Y or N in the Yes/No field.

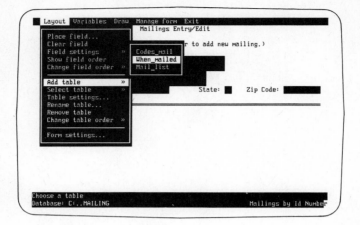

Fig. 6.21

*Adding
another table
to a form.*

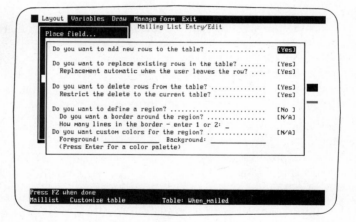

Fig. 6.22

*Using table
settings.*

Specifying Data-Modification Rules

The next Field Settings screen asks three questions:

- Do you want to add new rows to the table?

  Answer Yes (the default) to allow the form user to add rows to a
  table. You may want to answer No if you want to use the form only
  for editing existing data.

- Do you want to replace existing rows in the table?

  Answer Yes (the default) to enable the form user to edit the data in
  the table. You may answer No if you want to use the form for new
  entry or inquiry only.

- Do you want to delete rows from the table?

  Answer Yes (the default) to allow the form user to delete rows from the table. You may answer No if you want to use the form for inquiry only, or if you want to ensure that rows are deleted only when certain other criteria are met (in which case, they may be deleted under a command file's control or manually in Command mode).

With these three options, you can control how the data is handled for a specific table. You may, for example, want to include a table on the form for display only. If you answer No to each of the data-modification questions, the table can be only viewed—not changed.

The last group of questions on the Table Settings screen provides a method for entering, editing, or displaying multiple rows on-screen in a multi-row region.

Defining Multi-Row Regions

To allow multiple rows in a form on-screen, you need to define a region for the table. A *region* defines the borders of the data-entry area for a table. You can define a region any time after you add the table to the form. You do not need to place the fields or enter text first, but you can if you prefer.

To define a region, answer Yes to the question

    Do you want to define a region?

on the Table Settings screen. (If you are not already on the Table Settings screen for the table, make the table current by pressing Shift-F7 or Shift-F8 until the table name is displayed at the bottom of the screen.) Press Alt-L and choose Table Settings from the Layout pull-down menu. On the Table Settings screen, press Enter until the cursor is at the prompt:

    Do you want to define a region?

Press Y to answer Yes. R:BASE immediately returns you to the Form Definition screen and prompts you through the process of building a region. You follow these steps:

1. Use the arrow keys to place the cursor at the upper left corner of where you want the region. Then press Enter.

2. Use the arrow keys to paint the region's area. When the cursor is positioned at the lower right corner, press Enter again.

R:BASE draws a double-line border around the region area and asks you to press any key to continue (see fig. 6.23). You can change this border after you return to the Table Settings screen; it is shown for reference only.

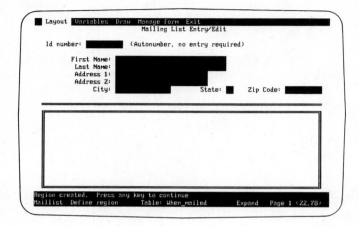

Fig. 6.23

*Defining a
multi-row
region.*

3. Press any alphanumeric key to continue.

    R:BASE returns you to the Table Settings screen.

4. Make any necessary changes to the rest of the region definition questions:

    • Do you want a border around the region?

    Answer Yes (the default) to outline the region with a border. Answer No if you do not want a border.

    • How many lines in the border?

    If you asked for a border, enter 1 or 2 to indicate the type of border—single- or double-line.

    • Do you want custom colors for the region?

    Press Y to specify different foreground and background colors for the region. Enter the color names in the Foreground and Background fields or press Enter at the Foreground field to use the color palette.

When you finish changing table settings, press F2 to return to the Form Building screen. If you have defined a region, you can enter text and place fields as if you were defining the area for a single row. All the fields must be contained within the region area. Often, however, you want the text outside the region area because you do not want to duplicate the text repeatedly for each row. You thus can enter the text on the upper border of the region.

After you enter the text and fields, you are ready to duplicate the rows (called *tiers* in R:BASE because they are like the tiers in a stadium).

To duplicate tiers, follow these steps:

1. Press Shift-F10.

   R:BASE asks you to place the cursor at the upper left corner of the area to be duplicated.

2. When the cursor is in position, press Enter.

3. Use the arrow keys to paint the entire area to be duplicated. Usually, you paint over the fields. You must paint over all fields contained in the region.

4. Press Enter again.

R:BASE duplicates the fields to fill the region. Figure 6.24 shows how the form looks when you have duplicated the rows in the region.

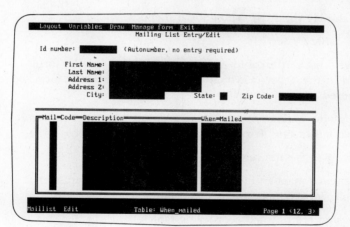

Fig. 6.24

Duplicating a single set of entry fields to provide for multi-row entry and edit.

If you need to make any changes to the fields inside the region, you need to remove the duplicated rows, make the changes, and then reduplicate the rows. To remove duplicated rows, press Shift-F10 when the region table is the current table.

Manipulating Tables

In addition to adding tables to a form, you may decide to change the order in which the tables are used in the form, to substitute a table you have already added to the form for another table, or to remove a table from the form. All these options are available from the Layout pull-down menu.

Reordering Tables

You may want to reorder tables if you started the form with one table and then find that another table would be more appropriate as the first table. This situation is especially common if you have chosen a many-to-one table as the first table and a one-to-many table as the second table. The order should always be one-to-many (see Chapter 2 for an explanation of one-to-many and many-to-one table relationships). Suppose that on the example form, you first choose the When_mailed table, which has a many-to-one relationship to the Mail_list table. Then you decide that you also want to edit the Mail_list data, so you add the Mail_list table. The tables are in the wrong order.

To switch the order of tables, follow these steps:

1. Press Alt-L to display the Layout pull-down menu.

2. Select Change Table Order.

   R:BASE displays a list of the tables associated with the current form. They are listed in the order in which they were added to the form and are numbered.

3. Select the table you want to move. If you are switching two tables, you can choose either one. For this example, select When_mailed.

   R:BASE prompts you for the new position for this table.

4. Enter the new position as an integer number. To make When_mailed the second table, for example, press 2 and Enter.

5. Press F2 when you are finished reordering tables.

Reordering tables does not change the layout of the form. All the text and fields stay where you placed them. What does change is the data-entry order of the tables when the form is used.

Renaming Tables

Renaming a table does not change the table's name in the database; renaming merely changes a table you have added already to the form to a different table. Suppose that when you are defining the form, you add

Codes_mail to the form and then realize that you wanted When_mailed. Press Alt-L and choose Rename Table to change Codes_mail to When_mailed.

To rename a table, follow these steps:

1. Make current the table you want to change. Press Shift-F7 or Shift-F8 to move to the correct table, or use the Layout menu's Select Table option to tell R:BASE which table you want to make current. The table name is shown on the bottom line of the screen.

2. Press Alt-L to display the Layout pull-down menu.

3. Select Rename Table.

   R:BASE asks you to confirm that you want to change the current table to a different table.

4. Press Y and Enter to make the change.

   R:BASE prompts you with a list of tables contained in the database.

5. Select the table that should replace the current table.

If the columns for the new table do not match the columns already placed in fields for the old table, the fields are removed from the form. Any variable fields stay in place, and you may need to modify their expressions. See "Working with Expressions" for more information.

Removing Tables

If you have added a table to the form and then discover that you do not want the table in the form, you can remove the unneeded table. To do so, follow these steps:

1. Make current the table you want to remove. Press Shift-F7 or Shift-F8 to move to the correct table, or use the Layout menu's Select Table option to tell R:BASE which table you want to make current. The table name is shown on the bottom line of the screen.

2. Press Alt-L to display the Layout pull-down menu.

3. Select Remove Table.

4. Press Y and Enter to remove the table. Press Enter to accept No and retain the table.

R:BASE removes the table, any text, and all fields for the table.

Working with Expressions

Expressions have three basic uses in a form:

- To calculate a value for display on the form (see "Defining Computed Values").

- To look up data from the current table, enabling you to edit data with a form when using the form to enter new rows (see "Defining Lookup Data").

- To look up data from other tables in order to provide additional display-only information (see "Defining Lookup Data").

You define all expressions as you place the field or by using the Define option on the Variables menu; the only difference is the exact expression entered for each.

When you place a field, whether it represents a column or a variable, R:BASE asks whether you want to define an expression for it. To define an expression, answer Yes to the prompt. R:BASE then displays a dialog box in which you enter the expression.

You also can define expressions for columns or variables at any time by using the Define option on the Variables menu. Follow these steps:

1. Press Alt-V to display the Variables pull-down menu (see fig. 6.25).

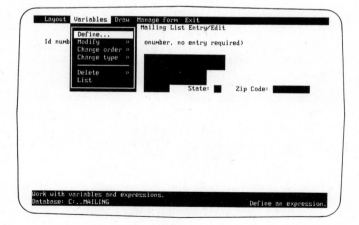

Fig. 6.25

The Variables pull-down menu.

2. Press Enter to select Define.

3. In the Define Expression dialog box, enter the expression for the field.

The next few sections provide specific information on the types of expressions you can define.

Defining Computed Values

Computed values are similar to computed columns and the on-the-fly expressions you used in Chapters 4 and 5. You can compute a value for either a column or a variable.

If you compute a column value, R:BASE adds the value to the table unless you modify it in the form. Computing a value for a column is an easy way to enter data without having to figure out values yourself when using a form.

Use variables on forms whenever you want to see a computed value on-screen but do not necessarily want to add the value to the table.

Computed column values are not calculated until a row is added to the table. If you want to see a computed column's value before adding the row to the table, you can use a variable to emulate a computed column's calculation. Suppose that you have an order-entry system with a table that looks like this:

Orders Table

Buyer	Product	Quantity	Listprice	Sellprice	Totalprice
100	PROD-1	100	$159.95	$138.72	(Computed Value)
100	PROD-2	125	$49.95	$43.52	(Computed Value)
101	PROD-3	110	$219.50	$195.17	(Computed Value)

The Totalprice column is a computed column that uses the expression (Quantity * Sellprice).

If you add or change a row in this table, you do not see the value of Totalprice until you leave the row, which stores it in the table. You can recall the row to see the calculated value, but viewing it as soon as you enter the values for Quantity and Sellprice is more convenient. The solution is to define a variable to use in place of the Totalprice column and then place that variable on the form. For example,

  vtotal = (Quantity * Sellprice)

Notice that this expression is the same one used to define the computed column. Now, when you place the vtotal variable on the form, the calculated total price appears as soon as you enter the two values used in the expression. When the row is saved, the computed column's value is calculated.

An *autonumber* column is similar to a computed column in that the autonumber value is not assigned until you save the row. See Chapter 3 for information on autonumber columns. To display the value of an autonumber column on a form when you are entering a new row, use the Next function, as shown in figure 6.26.

Fig. 6.26

Using the Next function in a variable's expression to display an autonumber column value.

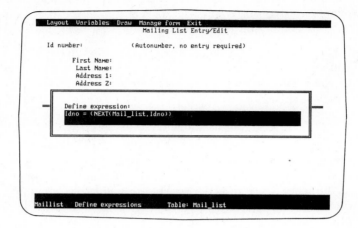

This expression tells R:BASE to show the next available number for the Idno column as it is defined for the Mail_list table. The Idno column automatically receives the correct value when the row is saved because it is defined as an autonumber column.

Defining Lookup Data

You can look up and display data from the current table (same-table lookup) or from another table (other-table lookup) by using a special type of expression called a *lookup expression*. You define lookup expressions in the same way you define calculation expressions. You enter the lookup expression in the expression dialog box when placing the field or by using the Define option on the Variables menu.

In a *same-table lookup*, also called a *master lookup*, you define a special expression for the first column placed on the form following the key column. When you are using the form in Enter mode, R:BASE looks at existing table values to see whether you enter an existing value for the key column. If you do, the existing data is displayed on the form and you are switched to Edit mode.

On the Maillist form, for example, you should define a same-table lookup for the column following Idno. That way, when you enter an identification number, the name and address data is displayed if that number already exists in the Mail_list table. Figure 6.27 shows a lookup expression for extracting data from the Mail_list table.

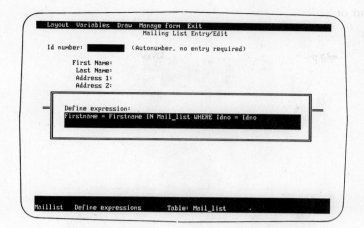

Mailing List Entry/Edit
Id number: ▓▓▓▓▓▓ (Autonumber, no entry required)

    First Name:
    Last Name:
    Address 1:
    Address 2:

Define expression:
Firstname = Firstname IN Mail_list WHERE Idno = Idno

Maillist   Define expressions   Table: Mail_list

Fig. 6.27

Using a same-table lookup.

The general format of a same-table lookup is

column2 = column2 IN same-table WHERE column1 = value

This syntax means *Find and display the row in the table where column2's value is the same as the value just entered on the form.* The value can be the name of the key column in the table, or you can enter a specific value or use a previously defined variable. Idno includes an expression to display autonumbering, and was defined earlier in the form. See "Defining Computed Values" for an explanation of why this expression was defined for the column.

You use *other-table lookups* to display data from another table when you do not want to enter or edit data in the table but just want to look at it. On the Maillist form, for example, the second table is used to enter mailing codes. You can use an other-table lookup to get the description for a mailing code from the Codes_mail table.

Tip: When you want to define an other-table lookup, press F3 to display the Database Information menu. On this menu, you can find the names of the tables and columns in the database. You even can select a table or column name from a list and have R:BASE copy the name to the work area.

Figure 6.28 shows a lookup expression for extracting data from the Codes_mail table. The *vdesc* variable is placed in a field in the region defined for the When_mailed table. The expression says, *Find the value of the Maildesc column in the Codes_mail table, where the Mailcode value is the same as the Mailcode value displayed on-screen. Place the value in the vdesc variable.*

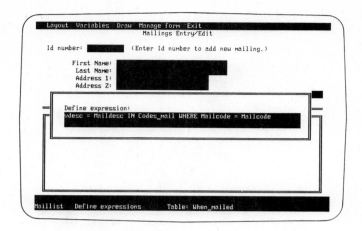

Fig. 6.28

Using an other-table lookup.

The general format of an other-table lookup is

variable = column IN other-table WHERE column = value

After you define either type of lookup, R:BASE asks whether you want to modify the lookup settings. If you answer Yes, the Lookup Settings dialog box appears (see fig. 6.29).

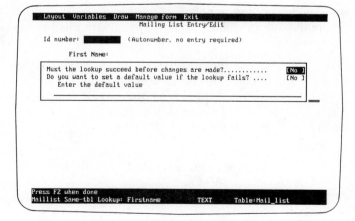

Fig. 6.29

Lookup settings.

Your answer to the first question determines whether the lookup *must* be found. To require that a value be found in the lookup table before changes can be made (a new row entered or an existing row changed), press Y at the first prompt.

The second question enables you to show a default value if the lookup value is not found. If you answer Yes to this question, you also need to enter the default value to display. You may want to enter something like *** *No value in table* *** for a Text column lookup, or *0* for numeric values. Press F2 when you finish. You then are returned to the Form Building screen.

Redefining Expressions

If your expression is not working as you thought it would, and you need to make changes, you can redefine it regardless of whether the field has been placed on the form. To redefine an expression, follow these steps:

1. Press Alt-V to display the Variables pull-down menu.

2. Select Modify.

   R:BASE displays a list of columns and variables that have expressions already defined.

3. Select the column or variable containing the expression you want to change.

   R:BASE displays a dialog box just as it did when you first defined the expression. This time, the existing expression is displayed already.

4. Edit the expression just as you edit all data in R:BASE. You can type over the displayed data, insert characters, or delete characters as needed to modify the expression.

5. Change another expression's order or press Enter when you are finished editing the expression.

Reordering Expressions

The order of expressions can sometimes have an effect on the final result. The expressions in a form are processed one after another. If an expression uses the result of another expression in the form, you need to be sure that the expressions are in the proper order. For example, consider this series of expressions:

```
var1 = (expression)
var2 = (expression containing var1)
```

These expressions are in the correct order because var2 needs to have var1 already processed in order for var2's expression to be evaluated. If you discover that your expressions are not in the correct order, you can reorder them by following these steps:

1. Press Alt-V to display the Variables pull-down menu.

2. Select Change Order.

   R:BASE displays a numbered list of the defined expressions, showing each expression's order.

3. Select the expression you want to move.

4. Enter the new position for the expression.

   R:BASE reorders the expressions.

5. Change another expression's order or press F2 when you finish reordering expressions.

Changing Data Types for Expressions

You can change the data type of an expression only if the expression is defined for a calculation variable. Lookup variables and column expression data types are determined by the data type of the column.

When you define an expression, R:BASE attempts to assign the appropriate data type to it. If you have a currency value in the expression, for example, R:BASE probably will make the expression data type Currency. Sometimes, however, R:BASE can guess incorrectly, and you need to change the data type to one most appropriate for the data derived from the expression calculation.

Note: If you are not sure which data type is assigned for a variable, use the List option on the Variables menu to see the expressions and data types. The section "Listing Expressions" provides more information.

To change a variable expression data type, follow these steps:

1. Press Alt-V to display the Variables pull-down menu.

2. Select Change Type.

3. Choose the variable with the data type to be changed.

   R:BASE displays a list of data types. The currently assigned data type is highlighted. These are the same data types you can assign to columns when you define the table, with two exceptions: no Note or Computed data types are available for variables.

4. Choose the new data type for the variable and press Enter.

Deleting Expressions

If you have defined an expression that you no longer need, you can delete it easily, regardless of whether the field has been placed on the form. Follow these steps:

1. Press Alt-V to display the Variables pull-down menu.

2. Select Delete.

3. Select the expression you want to remove.

R:BASE immediately removes the expression.

Listing Expressions

You can display full names (column or variable), expressions, and data types. Follow these steps:

1. Press Alt-V to display the Variables pull-down menu.

2. Select List.

   R:BASE displays a list of the defined expressions.

3. Press Esc to return to the Form Building screen.

Creating Multi-Page Forms

Creating a multi-page form is no different than building a single-page form. When you want to add a page to a form, press PgDn on the Form Building screen. A new, blank page is displayed. You must follow a few rules when creating a multi-page form:

- You can split fields for a table across pages only if single-row edit-entry is used for the table. In other words, you cannot split a multi-row region across pages.

- You cannot split a field between two pages on the form. The entire data-entry area for a field must be on one page.

- A page must have at least one field placed on it. If no fields are placed (even if you have text), the page is removed when you save the form.

- You can have up to five pages in one form.

Saving Completed Forms

To exit from a form you are creating or modifying, press Esc to highlight the Exit option. Then press Enter. Figure 6.30 shows how R:BASE responds when you ask to exit. Press Enter to select Yes, saving the form with your changes.

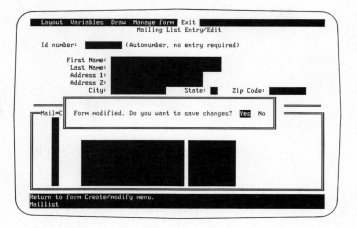

Fig. 6.30

Fig. 6.30

R:BASE asks whether you want to save your changes before you exit a form.

Modifying Forms

Modifying a form that you previously defined and saved is similar to the process you used to create the form. To modify an existing form, follow these steps:

1. Choose Forms from the R:BASE main menu.

2. Choose Create/Modify from the Forms pull-down menu.

   The Forms module's main menu appears.

3. Choose Modify.

4. Choose the form from the pull-down list that appears.

   R:BASE displays the Form Building screen.

To modify form settings—the basic definition of the overall form—use the Form Settings option from the Layout pull-down menu. See "Specifying Form Settings."

To modify the tables used in the form, use the appropriate options from the Layout pull-down menu. See "Adding Tables to Forms," "Changing Table Settings," and "Manipulating Tables."

To modify the field placement and definition, use the appropriate options from the Layout pull-down menu. See "Manipulating Fields."

To modify expressions you have defined for the form, use the appropriate options from the Variables pull-down menu. See "Working with Expressions."

To modify drawn lines and boxes, use the appropriate options from the Draw pull-down menu. See "Drawing Lines and Boxes."

Managing Forms

Two menus in the Forms module offer various options for managing forms: the Manage Form menu (see fig. 6.31), and the Forms module's main menu.

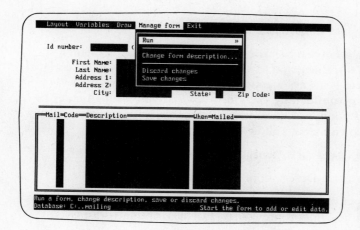

Fig. 6.31

The Manage Form menu.

Using the Manage Form Menu

The options on the Manage Form pull-down menu (from the Form Building menu) enable you to enter or edit data with a form from within the Forms module, change the form description, and discard or save modifications to the form.

Running Forms

When you first define a form, you usually want to test it right away to see whether everything is working properly. You can execute a form from the Form Building screen and avoid having R:BASE ask you for sorting or conditions. (See this chapter's section on "Entering and Editing Data with a Form" for information on how to execute a form with sorting and conditions.)

To execute a form from the Form Building screen, follow these steps:

1. Press Alt-M to display the Manage Form pull-down menu.

2. Press Enter to select Run.

   R:BASE prompts you with a pop-up menu that contains two options: Add Data and Edit Data.

3. Choose Add Data to test data entry with the form, or choose Edit Data to test data editing with the form.

R:BASE first saves the form definition and then executes the form in the mode (Entry or Edit) you requested. When you exit the form, R:BASE returns you to the Form Building screen.

Changing Form Descriptions

Often, people are in a hurry when they start creating forms. Sometimes they do not enter a form description when R:BASE asks for one. Entering a description for a form is always a good idea, however, because the descriptions can help you identify each form later. If you want to enter or change a form description, use the Change Form Description option on the Manage Form pull-down menu. Follow these steps:

1. Press Alt-M to display the Manage Form pull-down menu.

2. Select Change Form Description.

   R:BASE prompts you with a dialog box for the form description. If you entered a description previously, that description is displayed.

3. Enter a new description if none is displayed, or edit the existing description.

4. When you are satisfied with the description, press Enter.

R:BASE returns you to the Form Building screen.

Saving and Discarding Changes

When you exit from a Form Building session (press Esc to highlight Exit and then press Enter), R:BASE asks whether you want to save your changes. If you want to save your changes and *remain* in the form, however, use the Save Changes option on the Manage Form pull-down menu. R:BASE then saves the form to disk and returns you to the Form Building screen.

If you have made changes to a form that you do not want to keep, you can reset the form definition to the state it was in when you started modifications (or when you last saved the form definition). To reset the form definition, choose the Discard Changes option from the Manage Form pull-down menu.

Managing Forms with the Form Module's Main Menu

From the Forms module's main menu, you can work with all the forms in your database. You can remove unneeded forms, change the name of a form, create a new form by copying an existing form, and list the forms in the database with their descriptions.

Deleting Forms

As with any database item (tables, columns, views, reports, and so on), when you no longer need a form you should remove it. Before deleting any database item, however, make a backup of the entire database or at least the part of the database you are going to remove. See Chapter 11 for information on backing up a database.

To delete a form, the Forms module's main menu must be on-screen. Then follow these steps:

1. Press Alt-D to highlight the Delete option.

2. Select the form you want to delete.

3. Press Y and then Enter to delete the form.

Renaming Forms

If you are not satisfied with a name you have given a form (quite often users start naming their forms FORM1, FORM2, and so on), you may want to change the name so that it is more descriptive of the form's use. To rename a form, with the Forms module's main menu on-screen, follow these steps:

1. Press Alt-R to highlight the Rename option.

2. Select the form you want to rename.

3. Enter the new name for the form. If you attempt to give the form the name of an existing form, R:BASE does not rename the form and displays a message to that effect.

Remember that a form name must start with a letter and can contain one to eight alphanumeric characters.

Copying Forms

Quite often you may want more than one form that uses the same tables and columns, but with slight variations. You may, for example, want to make one form an entry-only form, and a duplicate of the form an edit-only form. The fastest way to handle this need is to define one form, copy it, and then make modifications to the copy.

To copy a form, you need to have the Forms module's main menu displayed. Then follow these steps:

1. Press Alt-C to highlight the Copy option.

2. Select the form you want to copy.

3. Enter a valid form name for the copy. If you attempt to give the new form the name of an existing form, R:BASE does not make the copy and displays a message to that effect.

Remember that a form name must start with a letter and can contain one to eight alphanumeric characters.

Listing Forms

Although your form names may be informative enough to let you know which one you want to deal with, sometimes you may need to make sure by displaying the forms list. This list includes the descriptions you entered for each form.

To display the Form list, with the Forms module's main menu on-screen, press Alt-L to highlight the List option. R:BASE displays the list of forms and descriptions.

Entering and Editing Data with Forms

Use a custom or Quick form for editing or entering data. You start a form in one of two modes: Enter or Edit. You can use any form in Enter or Edit mode, unless the form settings specifically do not allow one mode or the other. At least one of the modes must be enabled for a form.

Choose the mode that best serves your primary need for the form. If you plan to edit existing data, choose Edit mode. If you plan to add data, choose Enter mode. Neither mode is restrictive. That is, you can edit data when in Enter mode, and add new data when in Edit mode. The choice of modes merely makes the process you want to perform easier.

```
Commands: EDIT USING, ENTER
```

Enter mode has the following capabilities:

- You can edit an existing row if a same-table lookup field is defined. If you enter a value in a lookup field, and the table already contains a row with a matching value in the column, then the other data in the row is displayed, and you are editing the row instead of entering new data. When you leave the row, you return to Enter mode.

- You can move to the next form section (table or region) by using the Next Section option from the Go To pull-down menu.

- You can duplicate the data in a new row by using the Add Row and Duplicate Row option.

Edit mode has these capabilities (if you did not disenable it in the Form Settings or Table Settings screens when you defined the form):

- The rows displayed are preselected, and you move through them sequentially in the sorting order specified when the form is started.

- You can add a new row to the data by using the Add Row or Duplicate Row menu options.

- You can delete a row from the driving table and any matching rows in secondary tables by using the Delete Row menu option.

- You can move to the next or to a previous row by using the Go To pull-down menu options or the F7 and F8 function keys.

Starting Forms

You can start a form in any of these ways:

- Highlight Forms on the R:BASE main menu, and then choose the form you want to use. Press F2 to start the form in Edit mode, displaying the first row in the form's driving table first. Press Enter to choose Edit (Edit Data) or Enter (Add Data) mode. If you choose Edit mode by pressing Enter and then selecting Edit Data, you also can choose a sort order for the rows (the order in which they will appear in the form) and set conditions to limit the rows that will appear in the form.

- If you are already in the Forms module, you can press Alt-M to display the Manage Form pull-down menu and then choose Run to execute a form. You can choose between Edit and Enter mode, but you cannot sort or set conditions.

- In Command mode (R> prompt), use the EDIT USING command to start a form in Edit mode. Use the ENTER command to start a form in Enter mode. See Appendix C for the complete syntax of these commands.

- In Prompt By Example, use the EDIT command, asking for Form Edit, or the ENTER command.

Using the Function Keys

Form operation is more dependent on function keys than are the other R:BASE modules. Table 6.3 lists all the function keys and other keystroke commands available when you are using a form for editing or new entry. To display the function keys on-screen, press Shift-F1.

Table 6.3
Using Function Keys in Form Edit or Entry

Key	Function
F1	Displays on-line help. If the cursor is in a data-entry field, the help screen shows the editing keys. If the cursor is on a menu option, the help screen shows the use of the menu.
Shift-F1	Displays the available function keys.
F2	Finishes entry or edit and saves the row.
F3	Displays the Database Information menu.
Shift-F3	Displays a pop-up menu for the field. If no custom pop-up menu was defined, R:BASE asks you to supply conditions to limit the items displayed in the pop-up menu. The items displayed are extracted from the column defined for the field. If the field is defined for a variable, Shift-F3 has no effect.
F5	Resets the field to its original value.

Key	Function
F7	Displays the previous row, or moves to the previous row if in a multi-row region.
F8	Displays the next row, or moves to the next row if in a multi-row region.
Shift-F8	Moves to the next table or region on the form. From the last table or region, moves to the first table or region.
Shift-F9	Erases the field.
Ctrl-F9	Erases from the cursor position to the end of the field.
Ctrl-F10	Refreshes the data by displaying any changes made by other users to the same row (multi-user application only).
Enter	Moves to the next column. If leaving the last column in a table, moves to the first column of the next table. If only one table exists, adds the row or makes the changes and continues to the next row.
PgUp	Moves to the previous page.
PgDn	Moves to the next page.
Home	Moves to the beginning of the current field.
End	Moves to the end of the current field.
Tab	Moves to the next field.
Shift-Tab	Moves to the previous field.
Arrow keys	Moves in the arrow direction within a field.

Using the Enter Menu Options

After you start the form in Enter mode, a menu similar to the one in figure 6.32 appears at the top of the form. Because you can select menu options to use with a form, your menu may contain any or all of the options shown in the figure. See "Changing Menu Options" for more information.

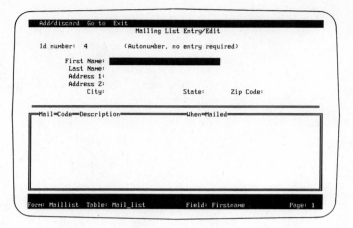

Fig. 6.32

When you display a form in Enter mode, all entry fields except the Autonumber Column fields are blank.

To use the Add/Discard pull-down menu options, press Alt-A. Select the option you want. The Add/Discard menu options are described in table 6.4.

Table 6.4
Using the Add/Discard Menu Options

Option	Function
Add Row	Adds rows manually. You can set the table characteristics for automatic add, so this option is not always needed.
Add and Duplicate Row	Duplicates the last entered row. This option is useful only if your data-entry rules enable duplicate entry for all the columns used on the form (see Chapter 3 for information on data-entry rules).
Discard Row	Removes the last entered row.
Add Row and Exit	Adds the current row and exits from the form.

To use the Go To pull-down menu option, press Alt-G. Press Enter to move to the next section, if any.

Entering Data

If you choose Enter mode, R:BASE displays the form with the entry
fields blank and the cursor in the first entry field. If you have defined an
autonumber expression for a column (as described in "Defining Computed
Values"), the next available number is displayed in that field, as shown
in figure 6.33. Notice that the First Name field displays in inverse video.
This highlighting shows which field you are currently entering.

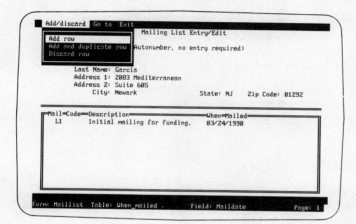

Fig. 6.33

*The Enter
mode menu
options.*

All the keys you can use to move around on a form are listed in table 6.3.
To enter data, just type the information in the highlighted field. Within
the field, you can use the Backspace key to move the cursor left, erasing
as you back up. You can insert and delete characters in the same way you
can edit all data in R:BASE. Toggle between Insert and Overwrite mode
by pressing the Ins key. (Remember that the cursor is a block if you are in
Insert mode, and an underscore if in Overwrite mode.) Move to the next
field by pressing Enter or Tab. Move to a previous field by pressing
Shift-Tab.

Tip: If you change the Autoskip setting from the default Off to On, the
cursor automatically moves to the next entry field if you fill the
current entry field with data. To change the Autoskip setting, use the
Settings menu, as described in Appendix B.

Move to the next table by pressing Shift-F8 or using the Next Section
option on the Go To pull-down menu. If you want to return to a previous
table, press Shift-F7.

If you are working on a multi-page form, move to the next page by pressing PgDn. If the next page contains data for the next table on the form, press Shift-F8 or choose Next Section from the Go To pull-down menu.

Keep in mind that the data you enter in each field must match the data type defined for the field. In a Date field, for example, you must enter a valid date. R:BASE displays a message and does not enable you to leave a field unless the data is valid.

When you leave a row (by moving to the next table or completing your entry), R:BASE checks the row against any rules defined for the table. If you have violated a data-entry rule, the rule message appears. You must correct the data before you can leave the row.

When you finish entering the data, press Alt-A to display the Add/Duplicate pull-down menu. Choose Add Row to add the row to the table and to display a blank form for additional entry.

Using Edit Mode

If you run a form from the R:BASE main menu and choose Edit Data for the Form mode, R:BASE displays a pop-up menu with three editing options, as shown in figure 6.34.

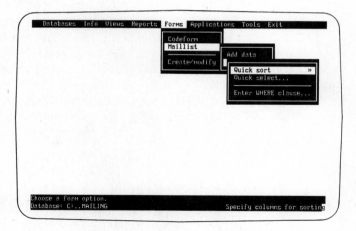

Fig. 6.34

Selecting options to edit data in a form.

You use the first option, Quick Sort, to sort the data by one or more column values. You then can edit the rows in an order other than the way the rows are stored in the table. Using the Sort menu is described in Chapter 1.

The Quick Select option enables you to set conditions to limit the rows you will edit. This option uses the R:BASE standard condition-building menus you learned about in Chapter 1.

You also can set conditions with the Enter WHERE Clause option. It is similar to the Quick Select option, but you enter the condition list in a dialog box rather than working through the condition-building menus.

Sorting Data for Edit Mode

In Edit mode, you can sort the data for a form so that each row appears sequentially according to your preferred sort order. To sort the data, choose Quick Sort from the Edit Data pop-up menu. R:BASE displays a list of the columns contained in the driving table for the form. You can sort on up to 10 columns. The first column you choose determines the initial sort sequence, with subsequent sort columns ordering the data within this sequence.

```
Command: ORDER BY Clause
```

Figure 6.35, for example, shows how the screen looks when data in the Maillist form has been defined for sorting. The first sort column, Lastname, is defined to be sorted in ascending order. The second sort column, Firstname, sorts by first name after sorting by last name. Suppose that you have Don Black, John Brown, and Fred Brown in the table. Don Black's data will appear first because Black comes before Brown in the alphabet. Fred Brown's data will appear before John Brown's because Fred comes before John in the alphabet.

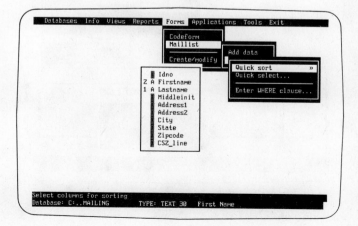

Fig. 6.35

Selecting the sort order for editing.

Setting Conditions for Edit Mode

If you have a large number of rows in the driving table for a form, you probably want to look at only a few of the rows when you are editing. You can limit the rows you view by setting conditions.

You have two ways to set conditions when starting a form from the R:BASE main menu: setting quick conditions or entering a WHERE clause. The quick condition method uses the R:BASE condition-building menus to enable you to choose columns, comparison operators, and comparison values. The WHERE clause method is a command entry method that requires you to know the syntax and use of the R:BASE WHERE clause. The latter method provides more flexibility and power than the condition builder but is a little more difficult to use.

```
Command: WHERE Clause
```

When you choose Quick Select from the Edit Data pop-up menu, R:BASE displays a list of the columns contained in the form's driving table and then leads you through the condition-building procedure. Follow these steps to set conditions:

1. Choose the column containing the values you want to use to limit the rows.

2. Choose the comparison operator with which you want to compare the values contained in the columns (see fig. 6.36).

Fig. 6.36

Using the Quick Select option.

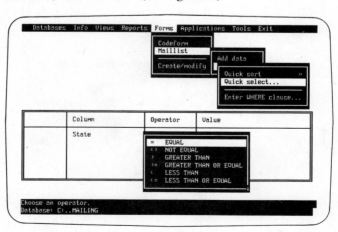

3. Enter the comparison value. Figure 6.37 shows one possible comparison that you could use for the Maillist form.

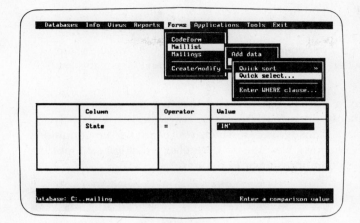

Fig. 6.37

Only rows meeting the specific condition appear on the form.

4. R:BASE displays a list of condition connecting operators: AND, OR, AND NOT, and OR NOT, as shown in figure 6.38.

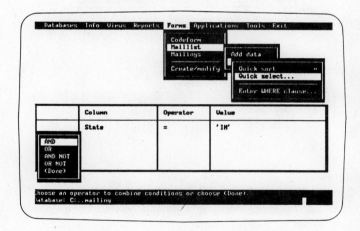

Fig. 6.38

Adding additional conditions by using a connecting operator.

If you want to set additional conditions you connect them to the first condition (and each subsequent condition) by using one of these connecting operators:

AND	The first and second conditions must both be met.
OR	Either the first or the second condition must be met.
AND NOT	The first condition must be met, and the second condition must not be met.

OR NOT   The first condition must be met, or the
second condition must not be met.

5. If you choose a connecting operator, you go back through Steps 1
through 4. When you are finished, choose (Done) from the list
of connecting operators.

If you want to enter a WHERE clause rather than use the condition
builder, and you choose Enter WHERE Clause from the Edit Data pop-up
menu, R:BASE displays a dialog box in which you can type the conditions
you want. Figure 6.39 shows how the WHERE clause dialog box looks if
you define the same condition shown in figure 6.38.

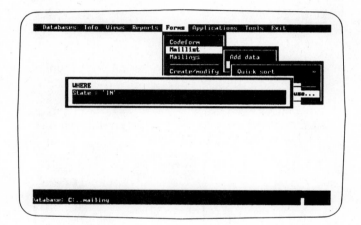

Fig. 6.39

Entering a
WHERE clause
in a dialog
box.

Editing Data

Editing a form in Edit mode is much the same as entering data in Enter
mode. The only difference is that the data already is displayed on-screen.
The data displayed depends on the sorting options and condition settings
you selected when you asked to use the form.

To edit a field, you can type over (be sure your cursor is an underscore
signifying Overwrite mode), insert (the cursor should be a block), or
delete data (with the Del key). See "Using the Function Keys" in this
chapter for a complete list of editing and movement keys. See Table 6.5
for descriptions of all available Edit menu options.

When you have completed editing a row, press F2 to save the row and
display the next row, or use the Edit menu's Save Changes option. You are
returned to the first field in the form with the next row's data displayed.

Keep in mind that the data you enter in each field must match the data type defined for the field. In a Date field, for example, you must enter a valid date. R:BASE displays a message and does not enable you to leave a field if the data is not valid.

When you leave a row (by moving to the next table or completing an entry), R:BASE checks the row against any rules defined for the table. If you have violated a data-entry rule, the rule message appears. You must correct the data before you can leave the row.

Using the Edit Menu Options

If your form uses all the Edit menu options, the menu appears as shown in figure 6.40. Because you can choose menu options for a form, your menu may contain any or all of these options. See "Changing Menu Options" for more information.

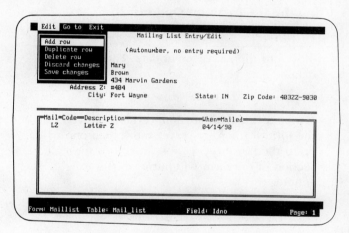

Fig. 6.40

The Edit mode menu options.

To use the Edit menu options, press Alt-E to display the Edit menu. Select the option you want. The Edit menu options are described in table 6.5. The Go To menu options are described in table 6.6.

Table 6.5
Using the Edit Menu

Option	Function
Add Row	Adds a row.
Duplicate Row	Adds a row by duplicating the last entered row.
Delete Row	Deletes the currently displayed row.
Discard Changes	Resets the data to its original state.
Save Changes	Saves changes manually. You can set the table characteristics for automatic storage of changed rows, so this option is not always needed.

Table 6.6
Using the Go To Menu Options

Option	Function
Next Row	Moves to the next row of data. The next row's data is displayed.
Previous Row	Returns you to the last row you edited.
Next Section	Moves to the next section, or table, served by the form if the form serves more than one table. From the last form section, moves to the first section of the form without changing to another row.

Summary

In this chapter, you learned the fundamentals of creating a customized data-entry form. You learned how to modify the default characteristics of a form and its tables and fields, and how to create multi-table forms, multi-page forms, and multi-row entry regions. The chapter also explained how to use a custom data-entry form in Enter and Edit modes.

7

Building and Using
Customized Reports

Reports are an organized way to display or print the data in your database. The Reports module provides the tools you need to create custom-designed reports. In addition, a special Reports module variation, Labels, enables you to create label formats for your data.

R:BASE provides many ways to display and print data in an organized, attractive format. Custom reports enable you to define exactly the way you want to present your information. You can report data from one or more tables in your database, or you can use a stored view to provide the data for a report.

This chapter describes how to use the Reports module to create customized reports and the Labels module to produce a set of labels. The last section of the chapter explains how to print reports and labels. In this chapter, you will learn how to

- Design a useful, attractive report.
- Use a report to correlate data from multiple tables.
- Use expressions and variables in the report format.
- Create labels quickly from your data.

Understanding the Types of Reports

In the quick start to Part III, you used the Quick Report option to create a simple, quick report. *Quick reports* are reports that R:BASE creates for you after you name the table and the columns to be included on the report layout.

263

A *custom report* is a report you design yourself, starting from a blank screen. You can modify a Quick report, adding any custom report features that you want. If you think of customized reports in the following hierarchy, you see that a Quick report is merely the simplest type of custom report:

- *Quick report:* Reports each row without summary sections.

- *Summary report:* Reports only summary information on groups of data.

- *Multisection report:* Groups data, reporting each row and providing summary data for each group.

Figures 7.1 through 7.3 show each of these report types.

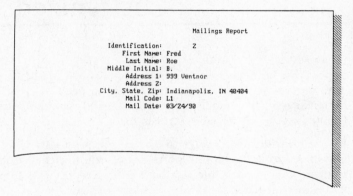

Fig. 7.1

A Quick report.

```
                              Mailings Report

           Identification:     Z
              First Name: Fred
               Last Name: Roe
          Middle Initial: B.
               Address 1: 999 Ventnor
               Address 2:
       City, State, Zip: Indianapolis, IN 40404
               Mail Code: L1
               Mail Date: 03/24/90
```

Fig. 7.2

A Summary report.

```
                    PRODUCT ORDERS              04/04/90
                       SUMMARY          Page:      1

       Buyer   Total Sales Dollars
           100       $13,872.00
           101       $21,468.70
```

```
                            PRODUCT ORDERS                 04/04/90
                                                      Page:    1

        Buyer    Product Quantity  List Price    Selling Price  Total Price

             100
                   PROD-1     100    $159.95        $138.72      $13,872.00
                   PROD-2     125     $49.95         $43.52       $5,440.00

                                                  Total Sold     $19,312.00
             101
                   PROD-3     110    $219.50        $195.17      $21,468.70

                                                  Total Sold     $21,468.70
```

Fig. 7.3

A Multisection report.

Although you can create several different types of reports, you do not have to use different methods to create each type. The Reports module provides a set of report-building tools that enable you to "mix-and-match" to produce exactly the type of report you want. You can start with a Quick report, for example, and modify it into a Multisection report.

You need to make the following basic decisions for any type of report:

- The characteristics of the report: the page length and instructions for including form feeds.

- The way the data is to be grouped: report and page headers and footers, breakpoint sections, detail sections, and variables to supply summary data.

- The print style of the report.

Starting the Reports Module

A custom report can be a new report that you define from scratch using the Custom Report option, or it can be a modification of a Quick report (see Quick Start 3 for information on how to create a Quick report). For a custom report, you first should sketch your report on paper so that when you start defining the format, you know which fields you want to include and where the information is to be placed on the report.

You can start the Reports module in one of two ways:

1. Choose Create/Modify from the Reports pull-down menu on the R:BASE main menu.

2. Enter REPORTS in Command mode (at the R> prompt) or choose the command from the Prompt By Example menus.

No matter how you start the Reports module, the main menu for the module appears on-screen (see fig. 7.4).

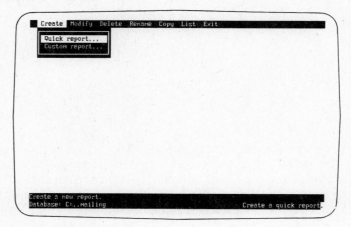

Fig. 7.4

The Reports main menu.

Commands: RBLABELS, REPORTS

Use the Create option to create custom reports or Quick reports. The other options are as follows:

- *Modify:* Makes changes to an existing report (see "Modifying Reports," later in this chapter).

- *Delete:* Removes a report (see "Deleting Reports").

- *Rename:* Renames the report (see "Renaming Reports").

- *Copy:* Copies a report definition to a new report (see "Copying Reports").

- *List:* Displays a list of report names and descriptions (see "Listing Reports").

- *Exit:* Returns to where you started the Reports module.

To begin creating a custom report, choose Custom Report from the Create pull-down menu. R:BASE leads you through the required steps for creating a report, naming it, and choosing the driving table or view.

Naming the Report and the Driving Table

R:BASE displays a dialog box and prompts you for the name of the report (see fig. 7.5). Type a report name (up to eight characters) and press Enter. Then type a description (up to 40 characters) and press Enter. The description is optional, but it can be useful for identifying the different reports you create for your database. As with all database items (tables, forms, rules, and so on), a report is stored in the database, not as a separate file. The report description appears at the bottom of the screen when you highlight the report name on a menu or when you list reports.

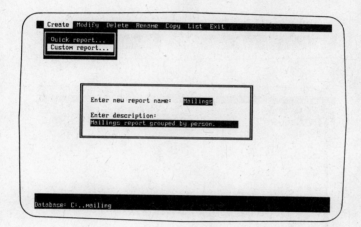

Fig. 7.5

Entering the report name and description.

R:BASE then displays a list of the tables and views in the database, as shown in figure 7.6. From the list, choose the table or view that is to provide most of the data for the report. Because of the way R:BASE handles data, using a view is faster than using a table and extracting data from other tables. Therefore, if you want a report that shows data from two or more tables, you should define a view with all the columns you plan to use in the report. (Chapter 5 provides information on defining a view.)

Using the Report Building Menu and Function Keys

After you have completed these required steps, R:BASE displays the Report Building menu shown in figure 7.7, and you must decide what to do next. You can use the options in any order. You can enter the text of the report and then place the fields, for example, or you can place the fields first, define report sections, and then enter text on-screen. You also can alternate between actions.

Fig. 7.6

Choosing a table or view.

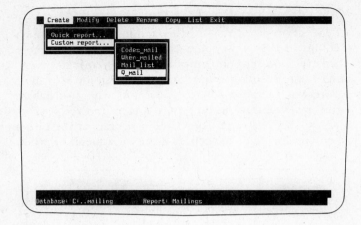

Fig. 7.7

The Report Building menu.

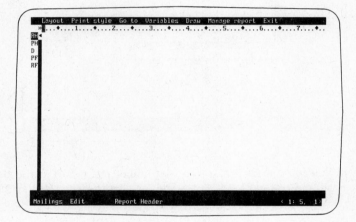

Each option on the Report Building menu displays a pull-down menu with options for the building process, as shown in table 7.1.

This chapter provides a loose order of actions you can take. However, you can perform the tasks necessary to build a report in any order.

When you create a new report or change an existing report, you use the menu options on the Report Building menu. However, some report functions are available only with a function key. Table 7.2 lists the function keys and uses for options not available from the menus.

Table 7.1
Using the Report Building Menu

Option	Effect
Layout	Places columns or variables, assigns page numbering, assigns time and date stamps, and creates report breakpoints (see "Manipulating Fields," "Using Sections in the Report," and "Defining Report Variables").
Print Style	Provides printer control codes for customizing the print style on your report (see "Specifying Printer Fonts").
Go To	Enables you to create or move quickly to any report section (see "Working with Sections in a Report").
Variables	Defines, modifies, reorders, retypes, deletes, and lists variables (see "Defining Report Variables").
Manage Report	Previews the report, changes the report description, and saves the report definition (see "Saving Reports," "Previewing Reports," and "Managing Reports").

Table 7.2
Using Report Function Keys

Key	Description
Shift-F1	Displays all available function keys.
Shift-F3	Displays the format of the current field.
Ctrl-F3	Toggles display of the placed printer control codes.
F6	Locates or relocates a placed field.
Ctrl-F6	Toggles on and off character repeat or, when drawing, lowers and raises the pen.
F7	Moves to the preceding report section.
F8	Moves to the next report section.
F9	Deletes the current line (any placed fields must first be removed).

Table 7.2—*continued*

Key	Description
Shift-F9	Deletes a placed field.
F10	Inserts a line above the cursor position. Adds a line to the current section.
Shift-F10	Inserts a line below the cursor position. Adds a line to the current section.

Working with Sections in a Report

Reports can be a simple listing of the data in a table, or they can provide a complex breakdown of the data into groups that report summary data. Before you design a report, you need to understand how a report can be divided into the following sections:

- *Detail:* Provides a report line for each row in the table (as selected when setting conditions for printing).

- *Report Header and Footer:* Print once for each report—the header at the beginning and the footer at the end of the report.

- *Page Header and Footer:* Print once for each page of the report—the header at the top and footer at the bottom of the page.

- *Breakpoint Header and Footer:* Appears once for each grouping of data.

The report sections create an outline of the report, with the most general data on the report level, more specific data on the page level, summarized data on the breakpoint level, and individual row data on the detail level. These sections are explained more fully in the following sections. Figure 7.8 illustrates the relationships among the report sections.

As you can see from the figure, the report sections are nested, level by level. The lines show how each header section relates to its footer counterpart. Notice, in particular, that the breakpoint footers are in the reverse order of the breakpoint headers, so that you see the data for breakpoint 2 before you see the data for breakpoint 1.

Although you can wait to define the report sections until you have placed fields and entered text on the report, defining the sections first often is easier. If you define the sections first, you do not have to go back and change the default detail lines to the type of section you want to have.

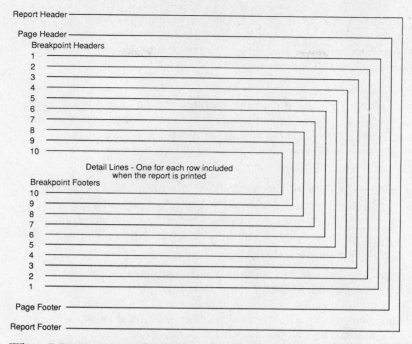

Fig. 7.8
Report sections are nested within each other.

When R:BASE displays the Report Building screen, it provides one line for each of the basic report sections. The codes in the far left column of the screen identify each section (see fig. 7.9). The codes are as follows:

RH – Report Header
PH – Page Header
D – Detail
PF – Page Footer
RF – Report Footer

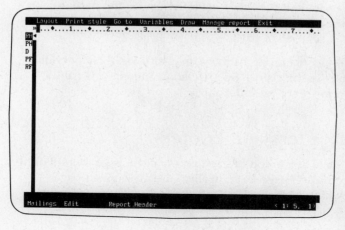

Fig. 7.9
The Report Building screen.

When you are working in a report, the text and fields you deal with are confined to the section your cursor is in. To move to a different section of a report, you need to move the cursor to that section by using the function keys or the Go To menu.

Pressing F7 moves the cursor to the previous section; pressing F8 moves it to the next section. To use the Go To menu, press Alt-G to display the Go To pull-down menu. Then highlight the report section that you want to move to and press Enter. The advantage of using the Go To menu is that if you have deleted a report section, choosing the section name from the menu recreates the section on the report.

You may not want to use all the sections for a report. Many detail reports, for example, do not need a report header and footer. If you want to remove a section, place the cursor on the section line and press F9 to delete the line. You can delete a section line with text already on it if you have not placed a field.

Often a single line for a report section is not enough room for the text and data for that section. To add lines to a section, move the cursor to the section by using the Go To pull-down menu option for that section. Press Enter or Shift-F10 to add a line below the line the cursor is on, or press F10 to add a line above the line the cursor is on.

Using Report Headers and Footers

The report header and footer sections are printed once for each report—the header at the beginning and the footer at the end. Report headers usually contain text, date stamps, and time stamps. If you are creating a report to gather data for your company's annual report, for example, you can reserve an entire page for the header and then center the company name, date, and the title for the report on the page. At the end of the report, the totals for the entire report should appear. These, too, can be placed on a separate page.

Report footers usually contain one or more summary variables providing totals for the columns in the report. See "Defining Summary Variables," later in this chapter, for more information.

Using Page Headers and Footers

Page headers print once at the top of each report page; page footers print once at the bottom of each page. Page headers usually contain page numbers and text, which often consists of column headers for the detail lines of the report.

Page footers usually contain one or more summary variables providing totals for the columns on the page. You may, for example, want to see totals for each page. You can define a summary variable to provide page totals. "Defining Summary Variables," later in this chapter, provides more information.

Using Detail Lines

Detail lines print once for each row in the report's driving table or view, depending on the conditions specified to limit rows when the report is printed. Detail lines usually contain the exact values extracted from the report's table or view. Values are entered on detail lines by placing columns in fields on the line.

If you omit detail lines to define a summary report, the values in the columns are read by R:BASE even if the detail data does not appear on the report.

Defining and Using Breakpoints

The only sections not automatically provided by R:BASE are breakpoint header and footer sections. Breakpoints enable you to group information together into one place on a report. If you tell R:BASE to group all the information for one person in a table by specifying a breakpoint on an identification number, for example, all the rows in the table with the same number are grouped in the same breakpoint section.

You also can subgroup data within a breakpoint. In fact, you can have up to 10 breakpoint groupings. After specifying a breakpoint by identification number, for example, you can specify a secondary breakpoint by mailing code.

Multiple-level breakpoints are most useful when you have several columns that categorize the information in a row. The sample MAILING database is relatively simple, with only a few columns used to categorize data (Idno and Mailcode). The following personnel roster helps to illustrate:

Idnumber	Firstname	Lastname	Department	Region	Company
100	John	Brown	Development	South	1
101	Mary	Stone	Accounting	North	2
102	Charles	Jones	Development	South	1
103	Larry	Smith	Development	South	1
104	Dan	Perkins	Accounting	South	1
105	Adam	Brady	Development	South	2

Here, you have several ways to group the data: by department, region, or company. If you create the primary breakpoint on Company, a secondary breakpoint on Region, and a tertiary breakpoint on Department, the data is grouped as follows:

Company	Region	Department	Idnumber	Firstname	Lastname
1	North	Accounting	104	Dan	Perkins
	South	Accounting	100	John	Brown
			102	Charles	Jones
			103	Larry	Smith
2	North	Accounting	101	Mary	Stone
	South	Development	105	Adam	Brady

When you define a breakpoint, all the data with the same value in the breakpoint column is grouped as it is under the company numbers in the example. Secondary breakpoint values sort and group data for a second column, but only if the first breakpoint column keeps the data in the first breakpoint group. Thus, in the example, all rows are grouped according to Company and then further sorted and grouped by the secondary and tertiary breakpoint columns, Region and Department.

You define breakpoints by using the Create Breakpoints option on the Layout pull-down menu. R:BASE displays the Customize Breakpoints screen shown in figure 7.10. On this screen, you can specify up to 10 breakpoint columns, instruct R:BASE to reset summary variables to zero, and decide whether to force a new page (form feed) at any given breakpoint.

Fig. 7.10

The Customize Breakpoints screen.

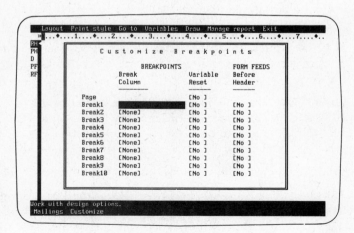

To specify a breakpoint at any level, you enter the column name in the Break Column field next to the level indicator. If you do not remember the column names, press Enter with the cursor positioned in the Break Column field to display a menu from which to choose the column you want. For this example, you would enter Company for Break1, Region for Break2, and Department for Break3.

You can define the breakpoints first and then create the summary variables, returning to the Customize Breakpoints screen later to reset the summary variables as needed (see "Defining Summary Variables," later in this chapter, for information on how to define these variables).

When you put a variable on the Reset list for a breakpoint, you are telling R:BASE to reset the value of the variable to zero each time a new breakpoint group is started. By default, R:BASE resets the values for any summary variables on the Reset list for all higher numbered breakpoints. The following example illustrates how this works:

Break Level 1	Reset Variable vlevel1, vlevel2, and vlevel3
Break Level 2	Reset Variable vlevel2 and vlevel3
Break Level 3	Reset Variable vlevel3

Specifying the breakpoint columns on this screen automatically adds the appropriate breakpoint sections to the report format. If you define breakpoint 1 (Break1) as column Idno, for example, you add the breakpoint sections to your report when you return to the Report Definition screen. The breakpoint codes are H and F suffixed by the number of the breakpoint as follows:

H1 through H10 – Breakpoint headers
F1 through F10 – Breakpoint footers

To add a breakpoint header or footer to your report, use the Go To pull-down menu to choose the breakpoint header or footer you want to add. Remember, a breakpoint is not available until you define it on the Customize Breakpoints screen.

When you choose Break Header from the Go To pull-down menu, R:BASE displays a list of any breakpoints you have defined. Choose the break level you want to add as a section, as shown in figure 7.11.

After you add the section, you have to put something on the section line to retain it. You can enter text or place a field to hold the section in the report. Any report section that does not have text or a field in it is removed from the report format.

Breakpoint headers are added above the detail line section and breakpoint footers below, as figure 7.12 shows.

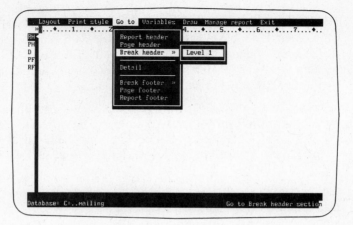

Fig. 7.11

Selecting a breakpoint section to add to a report.

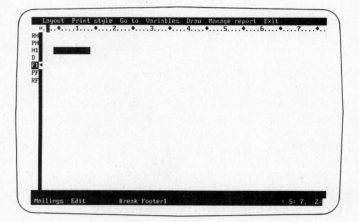

Fig. 7.12

Adding a breakpoint section to the report format.

Entering and Editing Text

The text areas of a report describe the data. You can have as much descriptive text as you want, but remember to leave enough room for the fields themselves. You can spread the text and fields up to 66 lines and across 255 columns for a single report page.

The width of your report is determined by where you enter text and place fields. The report width is as wide as needed to include all the text and fields—up to 255 characters. Many printers have a compressed type font that enables you to print up to 132 characters on an 80-column printer and up to 255 characters on a 132-column printer. You can define compressed font by using the printer control codes listed on the Print

Style pull-down menu. Refer to "Specifying Printer Fonts" for instructions on applying different type styles, and "Printing Reports and Labels" for information on printing. Appendix A, "Installing R:BASE," and Appendix B, "Customizing R:BASE," provide information on selecting printers.

When you enter text or place fields and move the cursor to report column 76 (as shown on the bottom of the screen), the screen flips to display the right side of the page. To return to the right-most part of the report, move the cursor back to Column 76 or less.

To enter text in a report, you move the cursor to where you want the text and type the text. You can repeat a given character by entering the character and pressing Ctrl-F6. You then use the cursor keys to repeat the character in any direction.

The Reports modules also has a draw function that provides single- and double-line drawing capability. You may want to repeat an upper-level ASCII character that you cannot type directly from the keyboard. If you want to draw a fat, dark line on your report, with ASCII 223 (■), for example, you can enter the character once by holding down the Alt key and entering 223 using the 10-key pad numbers. Pressing Ctrl-F6 and moving the cursor in the desired directions repeats the ■ character and creates the line. When you are finished, press any standard alphanumeric key to turn off the Repeat mode.

To edit text already in the report, you simply type over existing text. (Be sure that the cursor is an underscore, indicating that you are in Overwrite mode.) You can delete text by pressing Del with the cursor on the text character you want to delete. If you want to delete an entire line of text, move the cursor to the line you want to delete and press F9. You can remove a line only if no fields are placed on the line (see "Removing Fields" later in this chapter).

You can enter all the text for a report at one time, or you can alternate between entering the text and then placing the field to go with the text. The order in which you perform these actions makes no difference.

The most common place for text in a report is in the report or page headers in order to provide the report title and column headers (see fig. 7.13). However, you can enter text in any report section; the text is repeated each time the section is printed. Text placed on a detail line, for example, appears for every row printed in the report.

Fig. 7.13

Text in a page header.

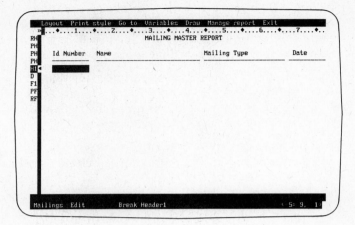

Drawing Lines and Boxes

As an alternative to entering ASCII characters, you can draw single or double lines on the report format by using the Draw option, which provides a "pen" for you to draw with. You may want to draw lines or boxes on a report to emphasize data or simply to make the report more aesthetically pleasing. Follow these steps:

1. Press Alt-D to display the Draw pull-down menu.

   R:BASE displays the three Draw options: Single Lines, Double Lines, and Erase.

2. To draw lines, choose Single Lines or Double Lines. To erase previously drawn lines, choose Erase.

   R:BASE returns to the report format with the "pen" in an up position (you can move around on-screen without drawing lines by using the cursor keys).

3. To draw lines, press Ctrl-F6 to lower the pen and then use the cursor keys to draw the line. Press Ctrl-F6 when you want to raise the pen to move to another part of the report. Then press Ctrl-F6 to lower the pen again.

4. When you are finished drawing, press Esc to leave the Draw mode.

Manipulating Fields

Fields on a report are windows to the data in a table or view. A field also can show the data in a column or a calculated value (called a variable). For many reports containing numeric data, you can create summary variables that total the values in a column. A summary variable is placed in a field on the report, just the same as in a column.

Placing Fields

To define a field, you need to place it on the report. To place column values in fields, follow these steps:

1. Press Alt-L to display the Layout pull-down menu.

2. Choose Data Fields.

   R:BASE displays a list of the columns (see fig. 7.14).

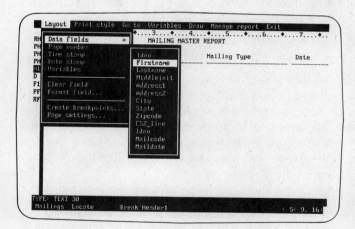

Fig. 7.14

Choosing a column for placement.

An alternate method is to press F6. R:BASE displays a dialog box, where you type in a column or variable name in order to name the field (or press Enter to choose from a column or variable list). Figure 7.15 shows how R:BASE prompts you with a dialog box for a field name.

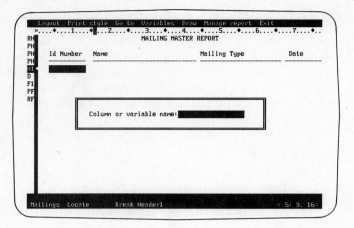

Fig. 7.15

Prompting for a field name with a dialog box.

Fields for columns are given the same name as the column.

3. Place the field by positioning the cursor at the first character position for the field and pressing S.

4. Move the cursor to the last character position for the field and press E. R:BASE shows a highlighted area for the field.

If the column for the field has a Text or Note data type, you can paint the field location across multiple lines. R:BASE recognizes that you are placing a Text or Note column field and asks you to press E to end the field location or W to mark the wrapping location. Pressing E limits the field to one line; pressing W identifies the right margin for the field. When the data is printed, long text fields are printed on as many lines as needed, wrapping to the next line at the W position.

For long Text or Note fields, you also may want to limit the number of lines to be printed in order to shorten the report. When you press W, the next text field placement prompt asks you to press T to truncate the field or Esc to allow the field to have as many lines as needed to show all the data. Pressing T tells R:BASE to truncate the text at the T position. Only as many characters as can fit into the defined area are printed.

Finally, you can indent Text or Note fields. R:BASE prompts you to place the cursor at the indentation point and press I. You can indent anywhere within the defined field location. If you do not want to indent the field, press Esc instead. Figure 7.16 shows how the screen looks when you are placing a wrapped text field.

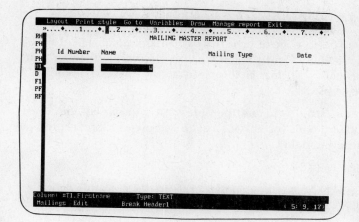

Fig. 7.16
Wrapping
text fields.

After you place the field, R:BASE asks whether you want to define a format for the field. The next section provides details for defining field formats.

You can give variable fields any name that is not a column name in the report's table or view. "Defining Report Variables," later in this chapter, provides information on creating variables. To place a variable value on the report, follow these steps:

1. Press Alt-L to display the Layout pull-down menu (or press F6 and enter a variable name in the dialog box).

2. Choose Variables.

   R:BASE displays a list of variables already defined for the report.

3. Choose the variable you want to place in a field. If the variable has not been defined, R:BASE prompts you with a dialog box for you to enter an expression for the variable (see "Defining Report Variables"). You can define an expression now, or define it later by using the Variables options.

   If you bypass defining an expression, R:BASE prompts you with a list of data types. Choose an appropriate data type for the variable; if you expect the variable to hold currency values, for example, choose Currency.

4. Place the field on the report layout using the S, E, W, and T keys to mark the beginning and ending positions for the field. Then define a field format if needed.

Defining Field Formats

Field formats enable you to control how the data in a particular field will be printed. You can define a format when you are placing the field, or you can do it later by using the Format Field option on the Layout pull-down menu. Follow these steps:

1. Place the cursor in the field and then press Alt-L to display the Layout pull-down menu (or answer Yes to the picture format prompt when you place the field).

2. Choose Format Field.

   R:BASE displays the dialog box shown in figure 7.17. In this figure, a picture format is being defined for a Date field.

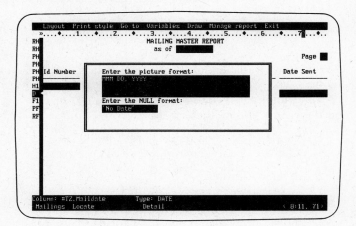

Fig. 7.17

Defining a field format.

3. Enter the format for the field.

   The rest of this section describes how picture formats are defined.

A picture format can be used for Text, Date, Time, or Numeric fields.

All fields can be placed as follows:

[<]   Left-justify
[>]   Right-justify
[^]   Center

Text fields are always left-justified by default and Numeric fields are right-justified by default. Text fields can be in all lowercase, all uppercase, or mixed case. These fields default to the column or variable value as mixed case:

_ or %	Uppercase
I or ?	Lowercase

You specify the format for a Date field by using M for months, D for days, and Y for years, entering separator characters as desired. For months, M or MM display a number, MMM displays the first three characters of the text month, and MMM+ displays the full month name. The following are some examples of date formats and their resulting displays:

Format	Display
MM/DD/YYYY	03/15/1990
MM-DD-YY	03-15-90
MMM DD, YYYY	Mar 15, 1990
MMM+ DD, YYYY	March 03, 1990
[^]MMM+ DD, YYYY	March 03, 1990 is centered in the width of the field.

Time fields are similar to Date fields; you use H for hours, M for minutes, and S for seconds. Enter separator characters as desired. The following are examples:

HH:MM:SS	12:30:25
HH-MM	12-30

Numeric fields (Currency, Decimal, Double, Integer, Real) use the following formatting options:

Option	Definition
[CR]	Credit for positive numbers
[DB]	Debit for negative numbers
[−]	Minus sign for negative numbers
[()]	Enclose negative numbers in parentheses
9	Blank if the number does not fill the format
0	Zero if the number does not fill the format

The following are examples of Numeric field formats:

Format	Display
[CR]0	CR$0.00
[CR]0	CR$100.00
9[DB]	$100.00DB
[()]	($100.00)

Removing Fields

If you want to remove a previously placed field, you can use one of two methods. First, place the cursor in the field you want to remove. Then press Shift-F9, or press Alt-L and select Clear Field.

Changing Field Locations

If you have placed a field incorrectly or need to move it or change its size to make room for other fields, follow these steps to change the position:

1. Move the cursor to the field.

2. Press F6. R:BASE removes the reverse video that marks the field.

3. Move the cursor to the new beginning position and press S to start the field location.

4. Move the cursor to the new ending position and press E (or W to wrap a multiline field).

Defining Report Variables

To define variables for your report, use the Define option on the Variables pull-down menu shown in figure 7.18.

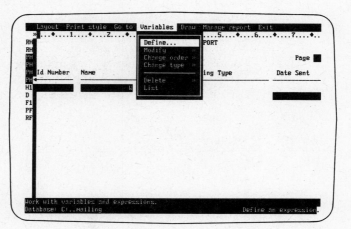

Fig. 7.18

The Variables pull-down menu.

You also have the following options:

- *Modify:* Changes the expression for an existing variable.

- *Change Order:* Changes the order of the defined variables, necessary when the expression for one variable depends on the value of a previous variable. Variables are calculated in order (see "Changing Variable Orders").

- *Change Type:* Changes the data type of a variable (see "Changing Variable Data Types"). You may need to change the data type if R:BASE assigns an unwanted data type to a variable. If an expression results in a decimal number, for example, R:BASE assigns a Double data type (double-precision decimal). If you know that all the numbers only need one or two decimal places, you may want to change the data type to Real (single-precision decimal).

- *Delete:* Removes a variable (see "Deleting Variables").

- *List:* Lists the defined variables (see "Listing Variables").

The procedure for defining any type of variable is as follows:

1. Press Alt-V to display the Variables pull-down menu.

2. Highlight Define and press Enter.

   R:BASE displays a dialog box for you to enter the variable name and expression.

3. Enter the variable name, an equal sign (=), and the expression for the variable (see fig. 7.19).

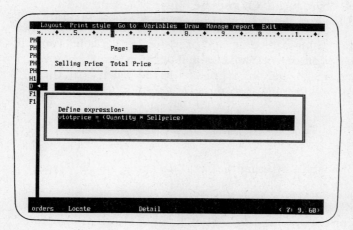

Fig. 7.19

Defining a variable expression.

A variable name can contain up to 18 alphanumeric characters. It must start with a letter and can include the ÷, _, #, or $ characters. The following are valid variable names:

    vfull_name
    Id#
    amount$

When naming your own variables, a useful (but not required) convention is to make the letter "v" the first character of the name in order to identify it as a variable.

Variables have the following uses on a report: adding time and date stamps, page numbering, calculating values, linking text columns, computing totals for summary reporting, and extracting data from tables not included in the report. The next sections describe the major categories of variables you can define.

Tip: You can use any variables that you have previously defined and still exist in R:BASE's variable list to pass information to a report. When defining the report, first define the variable (see the SET VARIABLE command in Appendix C). Then you can use the variable in an expression you define for a report variable. This is most often done when you are printing reports from a command file. Chapter 8 provides information on applications and command files.

Adding Page Numbering, Date, and Time Variables

R:BASE provides date, time, and page numbering values that are available from the Layout pull-down menu. Choose the option you want and then place the field for it in the same way you place a column field.

Alternatively, you can define date, time, and page number variables yourself by using the Define option on the Variables pull-down menu. Enter the variable name, an equal sign, and the expression in the dialog box. The variable definitions should be similar to the following:

    vdate = #DATE
    vtime = #TIME
    vpage = #PAGE

You then place the variables by using the Variables option on the Layout pull-down menu.

The #DATE, #TIME, and #PAGE designations are R:BASE system variables. #DATE holds the current system date, #TIME holds the current system time, and #PAGE initializes to 1 when a report is printed and is incremented for each new report page.

Computing Values

Computed values include any type of calculation that can be put in an expression:

- *Concatenation:* Combines text values into a single text string.

- *Arithmetic calculations:* Add, subtract, multiply, divide, and square.

- *Mathematical calculations:* Use any R:BASE SuperMath function (see "Functions" in Appendix C for a complete list of functions).

Concatenations use the + and & operators. The + combines the text values without a space; & combines the values and adds a space between them. Figure 7.20 shows how to enter a concatenation variable expression for a name. As with all variables, you define the expression by choosing the Define option from the Variables pull-down menu.

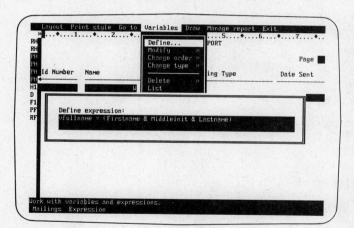

Fig. 7.20

A concatenation variable expression.

You enter arithmetic and mathematical expressions in much the same way. The following examples illustrate the kinds of variable expressions you can define, but they are not comprehensive.

Suppose that you emulate a computed column by including column names in the expression (see Chapter 3 for information on computed columns). Assuming that you have two columns in the table (Quantity and Sellprice), you can perform calculations using column names:

vtotal = (Quantity * Sellprice)

Suppose that you want to find the number of days between two dates. You have a date column, Maildate, and you want to find how many days have passed since the date contained in the column. Notice that you can use the #DATE system variable in the calculation:

    vdiffdate = (#DATE − Maildate)

Suppose that you want to find the average value of three numeric columns. You can mix columns and literal values to come up with an answer:

    vaverage = ((numcol1 + numcol2 + numcol3) / 3)

Another way to find the average is to use the SuperMath LAVG (list average) function:

    vaverage = (LAVG(numcol1,numcol2,numcol3))

Suppose that you want to calculate a percentage. You have two Currency columns, and you want to find the ratio between the two. You can use the following expression format to calculate a percentage:

    vpercent = (100 * (currcol1 − currcol2) / currcol2)

If currcol1 contains a value of $600.00 and currcol2 contains a value of $450.00, calculation of this expression is as follows:

    vpercent = (100 * ($600.00 − $450.00) / $450.00)
    vpercent = (100 * ($150.00) / $450.00)
    vpercent = (100 * .3333..)
    vpercent = 33.3333...

Thus, the value of currcol1 is 33.33 percent greater than the value of currcol2.

Defining Summary Variables

Summary variables, which are defined by using the special report function SUM OF, calculate the total of a column for the rows processed in a report. The variable holds that total value until you reset it to zero.

When you define a summary variable (or any variable with a numeric value), you can reset the variable value to zero at various points in the report, usually at breakpoints or page breaks. If you want to calculate total sales by region, for example, you define a summary variable (vtotal = SUM OF Totalsales) to keep adding the Totalsales column until all sales for a given region are added to it. At the end of the section for the region (usually a breakpoint), the vtotal value is printed and then reset to zero for the next region.

If you have not read the section on defining breakpoints, turn back to "Defining and Using Breakpoints" and review that section. Breakpoints and summary variables work hand-in-hand to provide summary values for groups of rows in the report.

As with all variables, you define a summary variable by pressing Alt-V to display the Variables pull-down menu and then choosing Define. Enter the summary variable name, an equal sign, and the SUM OF expression in the dialog box. Figure 7.21 shows an example of a summary variable definition.

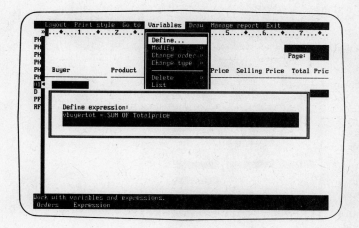

Fig. 7.21

A summary variable definition.

After you define a summary variable, you can add it to the Reset list for the breakpoint (if in a breakpoint footer) or for the page, depending on where you place the total. You do this from the Customize Breakpoints screen (see fig. 7.22).

You get to the Customize Breakpoints screen by pressing Alt-L and then choosing Create Breakpoints from the Layout pull-down menu.

You can place a summary variable in the footer section of a breakpoint, page, or report. (You must define the breakpoint first.) Figure 7.23 shows how a summary variable is placed in a breakpoint footer. In this example, the vbuyertot summary variable is placed next to the text *Total Sold*.

If you have defined a summary variable to appear in the report footer, you do not need to add it to a Reset list because the value appears only once, at the end of the report.

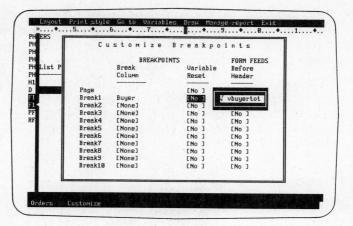

Fig. 7.22

The Customize Breakpoints screen.

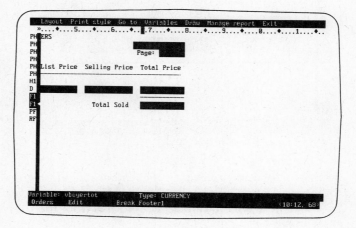

Fig. 7.23

Placing a summary variable.

If you want totals for breakpoints, pages, and at the end of the report, define a separate summary variable for each, as follows:

    vbreaksum = SUM OF colname1
    vpagesum = SUM OF colname1
    vreportsum = SUM OF colname1

All three variables have the same definition (SUM OF colname1) and perform the same function—they keep a running total of the value of colname1. However, you put the variables defined for the breakpoint and the page in their respective Reset lists (vbreaksum in the breakpoint list and vpagesum in the page list). In this way, when the value of the breakpoint column changes, the breakpoint summary variable is printed in the breakpoint footer and its value is reset to zero for the next group of data. In the same manner, the page summary variable keeps a running total until the end of the page is reached. Its value is printed in the page footer and then reset to zero for the next page.

Figure 7.24 shows a sample report using the breakpoint summary variable vbuyertot and data from the following table:

Orders Table

Buyer	Product	Quantity	Listprice	Sellprice	Totalprice
100	PROD-1	100	$159.95	$138.72	Computed Column with expression
100	PROD-2	125	$49.95	$43.52	(Quantity * Sellprice)
101	PROD-3	110	$219.50	$195.17	

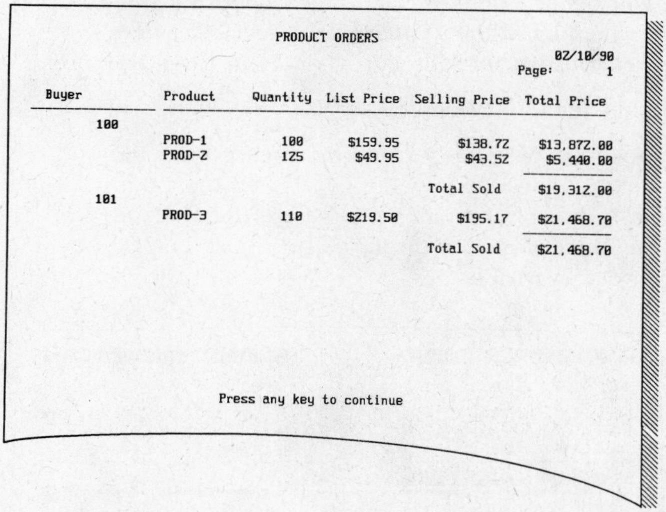

Fig. 7.24
A sample report.

The report in figure 7.24 is designed with one breakpoint using the Buyer column in order to group the sales by buyer. The detail lines show the row data for the Product, Quantity, Listprice, Sellprice, and Totalprice columns.

The breakpoint header contains a single piece of data: the buyer number. The breakpoint footer contains a line to separate each breakpoint total, the text *Total Sold*, and the result of a summary variable defined to total the Totalprice column for the Buyer (vbuyertot). This summary variable is included in the Reset list for the Buyer breakpoint so that its value is reset to 0 before the next buyer group is printed.

Defining Lookup Variables

Lookup variables extract data from tables other than the report's driving table or view. If you use the view Q_mail as the source for the report data, for example, you are provided a mailing code, which resides in another table, Codes_mail, but not the description for the code. If you want to print the mailing code description on the report, you use a lookup variable to extract the description from the other table.

Tip: When you define a lookup variable, press F3 to display the Database Information menu. On this menu you can find the names of the tables and columns in the database. You even can select a table or column name from a list and have R:BASE copy the name to the work area.

As with all variables, you define a lookup variable by choosing Define from the Variables pull-down menu and then entering the variable name, an equal sign, and the special format for a lookup variable in the dialog box:

    variable = column IN table WHERE column = value

Figure 7.25 shows a lookup expression for extracting data from the Codes_mail table. The expression instructs R:BASE to find the value of the Maildesc column in the Codes_mail table, where the Mailcode value is the same as the Mailcode value displayed on the screen, and to place this value in the vdesc variable.

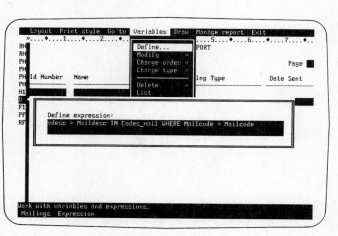

Fig. 7.25

Defining a lookup variable.

The vdesc variable is placed on the report wherever you want to see the mailing code description (see fig. 7.26). In this example, the vdesc variable is placed under the Mailing Type header.

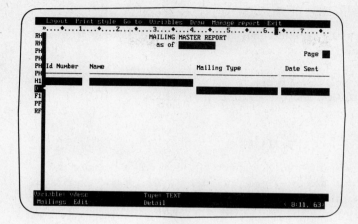

Fig. 7.26

Placing a lookup variable on the report.

Notice that you do not have to place the Mailcode column on the report; you can look up data using a column without actually printing the column value. Figure 7.27 shows how the description appears on the report when it is printed. Notice that the descriptions are truncated when the field is too small for the data.

```
                        MAILING LIST REPORT
                         as of 04/04/90
                                                   Page   1
Id Number  Name                   Mailing Type        Date Sent

        1 John A. Doe
                                  Initial mailing for fundi   Mar 24, 1990
        2 Fred B. Roe
                                  Initial mailing for fundi   Mar 24, 1990
                                  First response letter       Apr 14, 1990



            Press any key to continue
```

Fig. 7.27

A printed report with data extracted by using a lookup variable.

Modifying Variable Expressions

If a variable expression is not working as well as expected and you need to make changes, you can redefine it whether or not the field has been placed on the form. Follow these steps:

1. Press Alt-V to display the Variables pull-down menu.

2. Highlight Modify and press Enter.

3. Highlight the variable containing the expression you want to change and press Enter.

   R:BASE displays a dialog box with the existing expression displayed.

4. Edit the expression and press Enter.

Changing Variable Orders

The order of expressions sometimes affects the final result because the expressions in a report are processed one after another. If one expression uses the result of another expression in the report, you need to be sure that the expressions are in the proper order. Consider this series of expressions:

    var1 = (expression)
    var2 = (expression containing var1)

These expressions are in the correct order because var1 must be processed before var2's expression can be evaluated. Suppose the expressions were in the following order, however:

    var2 = (expression containing var1)
    var1 = (expression)

In this case, var2 would be processed first, but it would not have the correct data because var1's expression would not yet be processed. If your expressions are not in the proper order, you can reorder them:

1. Press Alt-V to display the Variables pull-down menu.

2. Highlight Change Order and press Enter.

   R:BASE displays a list of the defined expressions with a number before each showing the expression's order in the list.

3. Highlight the expression you want to move and press Enter.

4. Enter the new position for the expression. For the example shown earlier (moving var1), enter 1 as the new position.

5. Press F2 when you are finished reordering expressions.

Changing Variable Data Types

You can change the data type of a variable only if the expression is defined for a calculation variable. Lookup variable data types are determined by the data type for the column containing the data being extracted.

When you define a variable, R:BASE attempts to assign the appropriate data type for it. If you have a currency value in the expression, for example, R:BASE will probably assign the Currency data type to the expression. Sometimes, however, R:BASE guesses incorrectly, and you need to change the data type to the type most appropriate for the data derived from the calculation.

If you are not sure what data type is assigned for a variable, use the List option on the Variables menu to view the expressions and data types (see "Listing Variables," later in this section).

To change a variable data type, follow these steps:

1. Press Alt-V to display the Variables pull-down menu.

2. Highlight Change Type and press Enter.

3. Choose the variable containing the data type to be changed.

   R:BASE displays a list of data types with the currently assigned data type highlighted. These are the same data types that you can assign to columns when you define a table, with two exceptions: Note and Computed data types are not available for variables.

4. Choose the new data type for the variable and press Enter.

Deleting Variables

If you have defined an expression that you no longer need, you can delete it easily, whether or not the field has already been placed on the form. Follow these steps:

1. Press Alt-V to display the Variables pull-down menu.

2. Highlight Delete and press Enter.

3. Highlight the variable you want to remove and press Enter.

R:BASE immediately removes the variable and any fields where the variable was located.

Listing Variables

You can display the full variable names, expressions, and data types by using the List option:

1. Press Alt-V to display the Variables pull-down menu.

2. Highlight List and press Enter.

   R:BASE displays all of the defined variables, their expressions, and their data types.

3. Press any key to return to the Report definition screen.

Specifying Printer Fonts

The print fonts available to you depend on the printer table you requested when you installed R:BASE. You also can change the printer table from within R:BASE if you have more than one type of printer attached to your computer or network.

When you install R:BASE, you select one or more printers to use. You then can switch the default printer from within R:BASE by using the Printer option on the Settings menu. For information on the Settings menu, refer to Appendix B, "Customizing R:BASE."

You place a print style in a report in the same way that you place columns or variables. The only difference is that you select the font code from the Print Style pull-down menu. Figure 7.28 shows the print styles available for an Epson FX series printer.

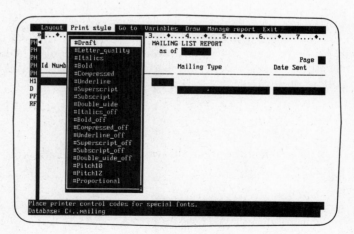

Fig. 7.28

A list of available print styles.

Most printers provide at least the set of print styles shown in figure 7.28. The actual list of fonts provided depends on the printer you are using.

If you want to boldface the report header, follow these steps:

1. Press Alt-P to highlight Print Style. Choose #Bold from the list of fonts.

   R:BASE directs you to place the cursor where you want the print style to start.

2. To boldface the header, place the cursor on Line 1 in Column 1 and press S. This sets the beginning point for bold print. You do not need to mark the end with an E as you did when you placed column or variable fields.

3. To return the font to normal type after the header, press Alt-P and choose #Bold-off from the font list.

4. Move the cursor to the line and column where you want the bold print to stop and press S.

Type style placements are shown on the Report Building screen by a small triangle. If you move the cursor to a font marker, R:BASE displays the type of font at the bottom of the screen. To delete a font marker, place the cursor on the marker and press Shift-F9.

Changing Report Parameters

Each report prints according to a set of parameters, each of which has a default value. To modify the report parameters, press Alt-L and then choose Page settings from the Layout pull-down menu. The Reports setup screen appears (see fig. 7.29).

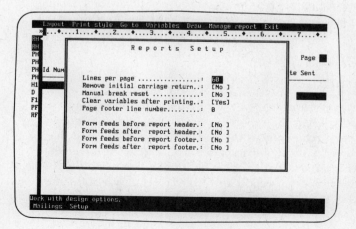

Fig. 7.29

The Reports setup screen.

Setting Lines Per Page

The default setting is 60 lines per page, but you can set up to 999 lines per page. The report detail and breakpoint lines continue to print up to the maximum number of lines specified (assuming that you have not requested a form feed for breakpoint headers). If you set the number of lines to 0, the report has only the page breaks defined for breakpoints.

You may want to change the lines per page to 66 so that every line on a standard 8 1/2- by 11-inch page is used (or to 85 for 8 1/2- by 14-inch, legal-size paper). To change the number of lines per page, type the number you want in the Lines Per Page field (see "Setting Page Footer Lines").

Changing Initial Carriage Returns

By default, R:BASE moves the printer head to the left margin before printing any report lines. If you answer Yes to this parameter, printing begins wherever the printer head currently is placed. You may change this setting if you are printing multiple reports and want the data for the next report to start immediately following the last report. To change the initial carriage return setting from No (the default), press Y in the Remove Initial Carriage Return field.

Resetting Breaks Manually

By default, R:BASE resets to 0 all summary variables defined for higher level breakpoints. Press Y in the Manual Break Reset field to prevent variable reset for higher numbered breakpoint levels. Refer to "Defining and Using Breakpoints" and "Defining Summary Variables," earlier in this chapter, for more information on summary variable resets.

Clearing Variables

When you define report variables, they are by default available only while the report is printing. When the report is finished, the variables are cleared. If you want to retain any of the variable values generated during report printing, answer No to this parameter. You may want to retain variable values if you want to use them in an R:BASE command file or as startup values for another report or form. To retain variables after report printing, press Y in the Clear Variables After Printing field.

Setting Page Footer Lines

You can specify the exact line on which the page footer is to print. This is useful when you are printing on forms where the footer total must be exact. If you leave this parameter as 0, the page footer of the last page may not print at the bottom of the page, because the footer prints immediately following all of the detail or breakpoint data.

The page footer line can range from 0 (if the lines-per-page setting is 0) up to the value you have entered in the Lines Per Page field (the default is 60), minus the number of footer lines. Be sure to leave enough lines for the footer to fit on the page. If your page footer has three lines and the lines per page setting is 60, for example, then the footer line setting cannot exceed 57.

To change the footer line, enter the new footer line number in the Page Footer Line Number field.

Setting Form Feeds

Answer Yes to any of the parameters controlling form feeds to force a printer form feed when the report prints. You can force form feeds before and after the report header (RH) section and before and after the report footer (RF) section. If you have omitted the report header or footer from the report, these settings have no effect.

Saving Reports

When you have completed the report description or are ready to quit, press Esc to highlight the Exit option and press Enter. R:BASE displays a dialog box asking whether you want to save the report. Press Enter to accept Yes to save the report. If you want to discard your report or the modifications you have made, press N and then Enter.

If you want to save or discard your work but remain on the Reports Building screen, press Alt-M to display the Manage Report pull-down menu (see fig. 7.30).

To save your work, highlight Save Changes and press Enter. To discard your work, highlight Discard Changes and press Enter. R:BASE asks whether you are sure you want to discard. Press Y and then Enter to confirm.

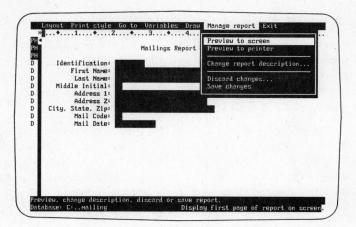

Fig. 7.30

The Manage Report pull-down menu.

Previewing Reports

On the Manage Report pull-down menu, you also have options for printing the report to the screen or to the printer so that you can view the report quickly without leaving the Reports module. To preview the report, choose Preview to Screen or Preview to Printer. R:BASE first saves the report format and then previews the report to the screen or printer.

Changing Report Descriptions

The last option on the Manage Report pull-down menu enables you to enter or modify the report description. A good report description can be helpful to you after you have defined several reports. The description can be long enough (80 characters) to describe the report in greater detail than the eight-character report name provides.

To change or enter the report description, Select Change Report Description on the Manage Report pull-down menu. R:BASE displays the current report description in a dialog box. Enter a new description or edit the existing description.

Modifying Reports

Modifying a report uses the same processes as defining a new report. This section summarizes the ways in which you can modify a report and refers you to the sections in this chapter that contains the relevant information.

- To create or change report sections, see "Working with Sections in a Report."

- To modify fields, see "Manipulating Fields."

- To modify print styles, use the options on the Print Style pull-down menu. See "Specifying Printer Fonts."

- To draw or erase lines and boxes, use the options on the Draw pull-down menu. See "Drawing Lines and Boxes."

- To modify the text on a report, see "Entering and Editing Text."

Managing Reports

You can work with all the reports in your database from the Reports main menu. You can remove unneeded reports, change the name of a report, create a new report by copying an existing report, and list the reports in the database with their descriptions.

Deleting Reports

As with any database item (tables, columns, views, reports, and so on), you should remove a report when you no longer need it. Before deleting a database item, make a backup of all or at least the part of the database you are going to remove (see Chapter 11 for information on backing up a database). To delete a report, you need to be on the Reports main menu. Then follow these steps:

1. Press Alt-D to highlight the Delete option.

2. Highlight the report you want to delete and press Enter.

3. Press Y to confirm and then Enter to delete the report.

Renaming Reports

If you are not satisfied with a name you have given a report, you may want to rename it to give it a more descriptive name. To rename a report, you need to be on the Reports main menu. Then follow these steps:

1. Press Alt-R to highlight the Rename option.

2. Highlight the report you want to rename and press Enter.

3. Enter the new name for the report. If you attempt to give the report the name of an existing report, R:BASE does not accept the name and displays a message.

A report name can contain from one to eight alphanumeric characters and must start with a letter.

Copying Reports

You often may want more than one report that uses the same table or view and columns, but with slight variations. The fastest way to do this is to define one report, copy it, and then make modifications to the copy. To copy a report, you need to be on the Reports main menu. Then follow these steps:

1. Press Alt-C to highlight the Copy option.

2. Highlight the report you want to copy and press Enter.

3. Enter a valid report name for the copy. If you attempt to give the new report the name of an existing report, R:BASE does not make the copy and displays a message. A report name can contain from one to eight alphanumeric characters and must start with a letter.

   R:BASE displays a list of tables and views in the database. At this point, you can choose a different table or view for the copied report. If you choose a different table or view, any fields placed for columns that do not exist in the new table are removed from the report format. You may want to do this if, for example, you have created the original report using a table with several lookups to other tables, and then find that using a view is faster. You create the view and then copy the report, naming the view for the new table. Most of the columns will be intact, so that you only need to replace your lookup variables with column names.

4. Choose a table or view for the report copy.

R:BASE makes a copy of the original report, using the new table if you chose one.

Listing Reports

Although report names can be informative enough to tell you which one you want to deal with, sometimes you may want to make sure by displaying a list of existing reports. This list includes the descriptions you entered for each report.

To display the report list, you must be on the Reports main menu. Press Alt-L to highlight the List option. R:BASE displays the list of reports and descriptions.

Creating Labels

Creating a label template is similar to creating a report format. You use many of the options in the same way as in defining a report. The options that are used in the same way in the Reports and Labels modules include the following:

- Placing and defining field formats for columns and variables
- Defining variables
- Controlling printer fonts
- Placing date and time stamps
- Managing labels (Delete, Rename, Copy, and List)

The options and features that differ in the Labels module include the following:

- Setting label dimensions and the number of labels to print across
- Setting a right margin to limit the data width
- Defining only detail lines

The options in the Reports module that are not available in the Labels module include drawing lines, specifying the report setup, and entering report, page, and breakpoint sections (only detail lines are available for labels).

To define a label template, highlight Reports on the R:BASE main menu and choose Labels from the pull-down menu. R:BASE displays a pop-up menu that lists the names of existing label templates, if any are defined, and the Create/Modify option. Choose Create/Modify to create a new label template or to modify an existing label template. Figure 7.31 shows the R:BASE main menu with options selected for creating a new label template.

R:BASE takes you to the Labels main menu, which has the same options as the Reports main menu. At this point, however, the Labels module begins to look somewhat different from the Reports module. The Create pull-down menu lists the tables and views in the database rather than the Custom Report and Quick Report options (see fig. 7.32).

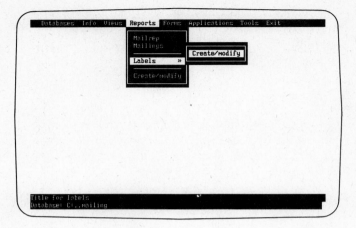

Fig. 7.31

Creating a label template.

Fig. 7.32

Choosing a table or view for labels.

Choose the table from which the label data is to be taken. If you were using the sample MAILING database, you would probably choose the Mail_list table. Next, enter the name for the label template and a description of up to 40 characters (see fig. 7.33). The label description appears at the bottom of the screen when you highlight the label name on a menu or when you list labels.

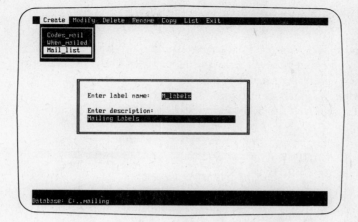

Fig. 7.33

Entering a name and description for a label template.

Defining Label Sizes

R:BASE then displays the Label Layout screen shown in figure 7.34. Notice that detail lines are the only sections available for a label template. R:BASE also displays a right margin strip to show you the label width.

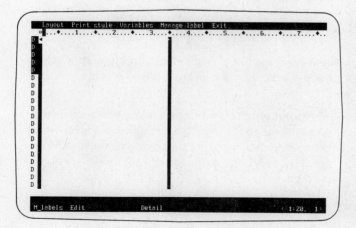

Fig. 7.34

The Label Layout screen.

The default width is set for standard 1-up, 3 1/2-inch labels. If you want to use a different size or number of labels across, you need to change the right margin and the label dimensions.

You can set the label size and format for printing in two ways. The Size Template option provides a list of standard label types from which you can choose. The Dimensions option enables you to customize the dimensions for the labels.

Press Alt-L and choose Size Template to change the label types. Figure 7.35 shows the pop-up menu that appears with the label types you can use. This menu contains nearly every standard label configuration you may need. If you are not sure what your labels are, look at the label box for a description and then find that label configuration on the pop-up menu.

Fig. 7.35

Selecting a predefined label size.

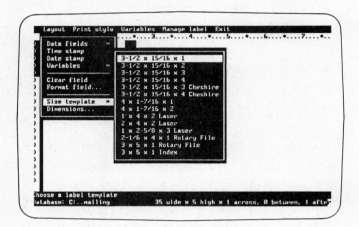

When you select a label type, R:BASE automatically moves the right margin to match the width of the label type you select. However, the screen format only shows a single label even if you choose a multiple-up label format. When you print the labels, they are printed with the correct number of labels across.

If your labels do not correspond with any of the standard sizes provided, press Alt-L and choose Dimensions to change to a custom label size. Figure 7.36 shows the Labels Dimensions screen. To change any of these options, type the new value in the field provided. Note the default values displayed on the right side of the screen.

The following list explains what you can enter in each field:

- *Label Width*: Defaults to 35 characters. Type the new width to match the size of the labels, or make it smaller or larger, depending on the actual width of the labels you are using.

- *Label Height*: Defaults to 5 lines. Type in the number of lines to match the labels you are using.

- *Labels Across*: Defaults to 2 labels. Type in the number of labels across to match your labels.

- *Spaces*: Defaults to 1. Type in the number of spaces between labels to match your labels.

- *Lines After*: Defaults to 1. Type in the number of lines following the label to match your labels.

- *Left Margin*: Defaults to 0. Type in the new left margin to match your labels.

- *Top Margin*: Defaults to 0 (no lines before the first label line). Type in the top margin as needed.

- *Labels Down Page*: Defaults to 0 (no paging). Type in the number of labels that fits down one page. This is used for single-sheet feed for laser printers.

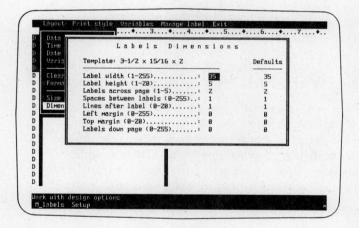

Fig. 7.36

The Labels Dimensions screen.

Press F2 after you set the dimensions.

Placing Label Fields

Label fields can include data fields (data to be printed directly from a column), a time stamp (prints the time when the label is printed), a date stamp (prints the date when the label is printed), and variables (data to be calculated or extracted and printed on the label format).

The procedure for placing these fields is the same as in the Reports module:

1. Press Alt-L to display the Layout pull-down menu.

2. Highlight the field type you want to place and press Enter.

3. Mark the beginning of the field by moving the cursor to the place you want to locate the field and press S.

4. Mark the end of the field by moving the cursor to the ending place and pressing E. In the case of text fields, you can mark the end with a W to wrap the line when it prints. Also, you can mark an indent point with an I.

Remove placed fields by placing the cursor in the field, pressing Alt-L, and selecting Clear Field from the Layout pull-down menu.

Define field formats by placing the cursor in the field, pressing Alt-L, and selecting Format Field from the Layout pull-down menu. R:BASE displays a dialog box for you to enter a format. Refer to "Defining Field Formats" in the Reports section of this chapter for details.

Defining Label Variables

On standard address labels, you usually put the person's first name, middle initial, and last name on a single label line. If you have not defined a computed column that concatenates a name into a single column, you will probably want to define this type of variable in the Labels module. Defining concatenation variables for all your label lines is useful (if the values you are printing on the labels have a Text data type).

To define variables, follow these steps:

1. Press Alt-V to highlight Variables.

2. Choose Define from the pull-down menu.

   R:BASE displays a dialog box for you to enter the variable and its expression. Figure 7.37 shows how to define a label line variable for the full name.

3. Enter the variable name, an equal sign, and the expression for the variable in the dialog box.

You can define any of the report variable types for labels, but summary variables are not very useful because you do not have breakpoints or paging available. Lookup variables can be used, as they are in a report, to extract data from a table other than the driving table. See "Defining Lookup Variables," earlier in this chapter, for information.

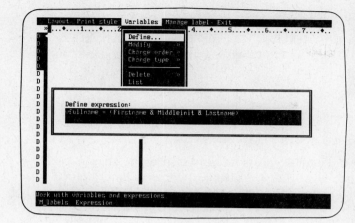

Fig. 7.37

Defining a variable for a label line.

When you have defined all your label line variables, place the columns and variables on the label format. On the Layout pull-down menu, use the Data Fields option to place columns and the Variables option to place variables.

You place fields on a label in the same way that you place them on a report. "Placing a Field" in the Reports section provides details.

The label sizing sets the number of label lines and the number of lines to feed between labels. You need not worry about the extra lines in the detail section. If you do not enter text or place fields on a line, R:BASE omits them from the format.

Figure 7.38 shows the final layout for 25-character wide labels.

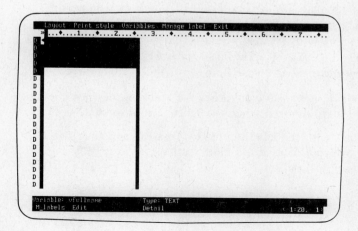

Fig. 7.38

A completed label format.

Saving Label Formats

When you finish the label definition, you can save the format and exit or save the format and remain in the Labels module. To save and exit, follow these steps:

1. Press Esc to highlight Exit and then press Enter.

   R:BASE asks whether you want to save the label format.

2. Press Enter to accept Yes to save the format.

To save and stay in the module, press Alt-M to display the Manage Label pull-down menu. Then highlight Save Changes and press Enter. R:BASE saves the label format and returns to the label screen.

To discard changes, use the save-and-exit procedure, but answer No (press N and Enter) when R:BASE asks whether you want to save the label. Alternatively, you can use the save-and-stay procedure, choosing Discard Changes rather than Save Changes. R:BASE asks you to confirm that you want to discard your changes. Press Y and Enter to confirm.

Previewing Label Formats

Before you leave the Labels module, you may want to preview the appearance of the labels. You can preview your labels using one of the Preview options on the Manage Labels pull-down menu. Press Alt-M to display the Manage Labels pull-down menu and choose Preview to Screen or Preview to the Printer.

R:BASE saves the current label format and then displays or prints the labels as you have configured them. Previews use only 10 rows of data from the driving table so that you are not saddled with a pile of labels with the wrong format. The Preview to Printer option is useful for aligning the label stock on your printer. Figure 7.39 shows a set of labels previewed to the screen. The label dimensions are set to a 3-up label format.

Notice that the labels do not have blank lines if a column does not contain data. Any unused lines are omitted when the labels are printed.

When you are finished with the label template, press Esc and then Enter to exit. Confirm that you want to save the modifications.

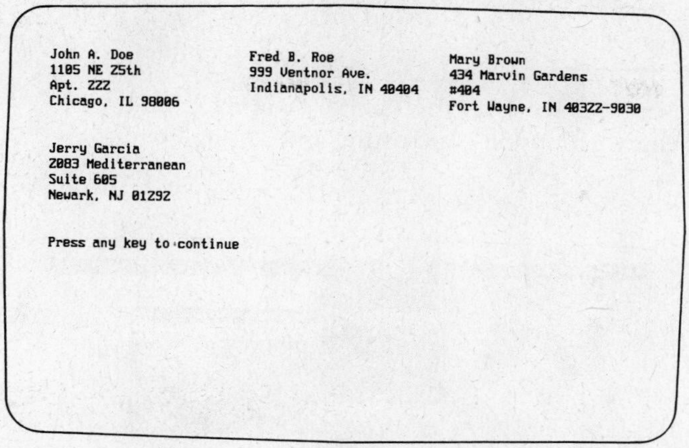

```
John A. Doe           Fred B. Roe           Mary Brown
1105 NE 25th          999 Ventnor Ave.      434 Marvin Gardens
Apt. ZZZ              Indianapolis, IN 40404  #404
Chicago, IL 98006                           Fort Wayne, IN 40322-9030

Jerry Garcia
2083 Mediterranean
Suite 605
Newark, NJ 01292


Press any key to continue
```

Fig. 7.39
A *label format previewed to the screen.*

Printing Reports and Labels

You follow the same steps to print reports or labels from the R:BASE main menu. The only difference lies in the item you choose to be printed. For reports, highlight the Reports option and choose the report name from the pull-down menu. For labels, highlight the Reports option, choose Labels, and then select the label template you want to print from the pop-up menu.

For reports and labels, you can choose to sort the data, set conditions to limit the rows included, and direct the output. The following sections describe how to do these procedures for both reports and labels.

Commands: LBLPRINT, PRINT

Sorting

When you print or display a report or set of labels, you can sort the data so that each row appears sequentially according to the sort order you set. If you have set breakpoints for a report, the sort order is determined already and sorting should not be required.

You may want to sort the data for your report or labels if the sort order you want is for a column other than a breakpoint column. A common sort column is the ZIP code, especially for labels, so that your data is printed in ZIP code order.

```
Command: ORDER BY Clause
```

If you print a report or label set from the R:BASE main menu, R:BASE displays a pop-up menu with options for sorting and setting conditions (see fig. 7.40).

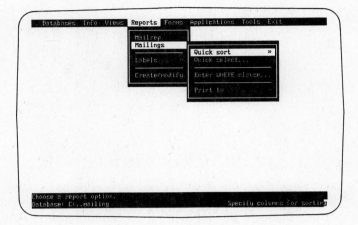

Fig. 7.40

Options for sorting and setting conditions.

If you have gone through the Forms chapter already (Chapter 6), this menu should look familiar. R:BASE uses the same sorting and selecting techniques throughout the system. After you learn how to sort and set conditions in one area of R:BASE, you know how to sort and set conditions for all areas.

To sort the data, choose Quick Sort. R:BASE displays a list of the columns in the table. You can sort on up to 10 columns. The first column chosen determines the initial sort sequence, with subsequent sort columns ordering the data within this sequence. Figure 7.41 shows the screen when you are sorting data to print the report or label set.

The first sort column, Lastname, is defined to be sorted in ascending order. The second sort column, Firstname, sorts by first name after sorting by last name. If you have a John Brown and a Fred Brown in the table, the data for Fred appears before the data for John because John is farther down in the alphabetic sequence.

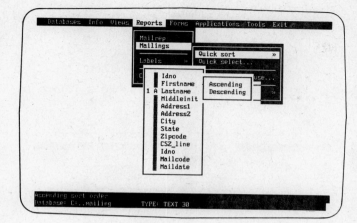

Fig. 7.41
Sorting data.

Setting Conditions

You can print a report or label set from the R:BASE main menu in two ways: by setting quick conditions or by entering a WHERE clause. The quick condition method uses the R:BASE condition-building menus to choose columns, comparison operators, and comparison values (see Chapter 1). The WHERE clause method is a command-entry method that requires you to know the syntax and use of the R:BASE WHERE clause. It provides more flexibility and power than the condition builder, but is a little harder to use.

You often may want to print a report for only part of the data stored in a table or view. You may, for example, want to print a sales report for a specific month. If your table contains all the sales information for the entire year, you can use a condition to limit the data to a specific month. Suppose, for example, that you have a Salesdate column. You define a condition that instructs R:BASE to use only those rows for the report where the Salesdate column is greater than the first day of the month and less than the last day of the month.

```
Command: WHERE Clause
```

When you choose Quick Select, R:BASE leads you through the steps for setting the conditions you want. R:BASE first displays a list of the columns in the driving table or view for the report or label set. You then follow these steps:

1. Choose the column containing the values you want to use to limit the rows.

2. Choose the comparison operator to compare the values contained in the columns, as shown in figure 7.42.

Fig. 7.42

Selecting a comparison operator.

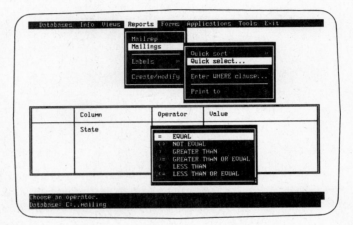

3. Enter the comparison value. Figure 7.43 shows one possible comparison for the Maillist form. This condition limits the data to only those rows where the State column contains IN (Indiana).

Fig. 7.43

Entering a comparison value.

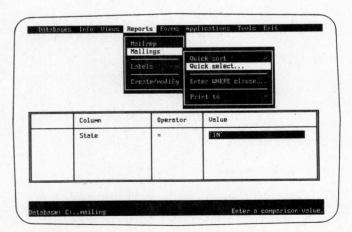

R:BASE displays a list of operators for connecting conditions:
AND, OR, AND NOT, and OR NOT (see fig. 7.44).

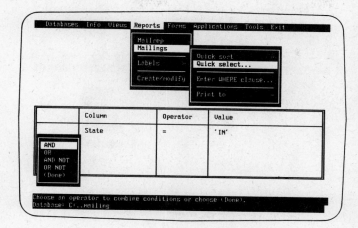

Fig. 7.44

*Combining
conditions
with
connecting
operators.*

4. If you want to set additional conditions, you connect them to
the first condition (and each subsequent condition) by using a
connecting operator. Then repeat Steps 1 through 3.

5. When you are finished defining conditions, select (Done).

If you choose to enter a WHERE clause instead of using the condition
builder, R:BASE displays a dialog box for you to type in the conditions that
you want. Figure 7.45 shows the WHERE clause dialog box with the same
condition defined as the one shown in figure 7.44.

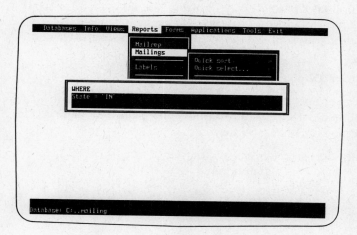

Fig. 7.45

*Entering a
WHERE clause.*

Sending to an Output Device

After you add sorting and conditions for the report or label set, you choose where you want to send the report. R:BASE displays the Output Device menu shown in figure 7.46.

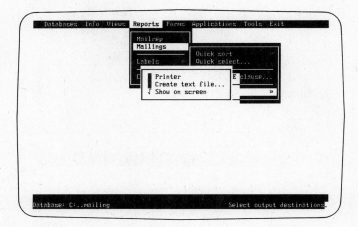

Fig. 7.46

The Output Device menu.

```
Command: OUTPUT
```

You have the following choices for output of your report or labels:

- *Printer:* Prints on the default printer device.

- *Create Text File:* Sends the formatted data to a DOS file. If you choose this option, R:BASE displays a dialog box asking for the name of the file. Enter a valid DOS file name, including a drive and directory path if you want to store the file on a different drive and directory.

- *Show On-Screen:* Displays on-screen.

You can check off one, two, or all three of the options. If you choose Create Text File, R:BASE asks for the drive, directory path, and name of the file to which the report or label is to be sent.

After you select the sorting conditions and output device, press F2 to print the report. Figure 7.47 shows a sample report sent to the screen.

```
                    MAILING LIST REPORT
                    as of 04/04/90
                                                    Page   1
 Id Number  Name                 Mailing Type       Date Sent
       1 John A. Doe
                                 Initial mailing for fundi   Mar 24, 1990
       2 Fred B. Roe
                                 Initial mailing for fundi   Mar 24, 1990
                                 First response letter       Apr 14, 1990




                    Press any key to continue
```

Fig. 7.47

A report printed on-screen.

Summary

In this chapter you learned how to create a custom report and how to set up a label template. You learned that custom reports are made up of several report sections that divide and format your report.

You learned how to define variables to place on the report or label format and how to place fields and text. Finally, you learned how to print the report or label.

Part IV
Using Advanced Features

Includes

Building Applications
Building and Using Applications
Using Relational Commands
Importing and Exporting Data
Managing Your Database

Quick Start 4
Building Applications

The purpose of this quick start and Part IV is to introduce you to one of the more advanced features of R:BASE: Application Building. Quick Start 4 shows you how to create and use an application by using R:BASE's Application-Building module: Application EXPRESS.

An application provides an easy-to-use menu structure specifically designed for your database. You decide what you want to do and then create an application with options specific to your needs. Application EXPRESS makes it easy to define an application without having to understand or write any R:BASE programs; R:BASE creates the program for you.

Not only does R:BASE create the program for you, but it also leads you through the process of creating the menus and options. Each time you choose an action for a menu option (load data, edit, print a report, and so on), R:BASE automatically asks the right questions or displays the correct list of items from which to choose. You do not need to know how to go through the process; R:BASE will do it for you. In this quick start, each action you take is a reaction to R:BASE's prompting. If, for example, you want to print a report, R:BASE automatically asks which table contains the data. After you choose the table, R:BASE shows you a list of the appropriate reports from which to choose, or you can create a new report, just as if you were in the Reports module.

Creating Applications

In this section, you create a simple application with the sample MAILING database, which you in Quick Start 1. If you have not created the MAILING database, you should go back to Quick Start 1. This chapter also uses the forms and reports you created in Quick Start 2. The application you will create will have four main menu options:

Edit: Executes the Mailings form in Edit mode

Reports: Displays a pull-down menu that enables you to print the Mailrep and Mailings reports

Labels: Prints labels using the M_labels label format

Exit: Exits the application

Starting Application Express

Application Express enables you to create a new application or modify an existing application. You cannot, however, modify an application that was not created with Application Express (see Chapter 8). To start Application Express, follow these steps:

1. Make current the directory containing the MAILING database. This directory should be SAMPLE. Type *cd \sample.*

2. Start R:BASE by typing *rbase.*

3. Press Alt-A to highlight Applications.

4. Choose Create/Modify from the Applications pull-down menu.

   R:BASE displays the Application Express main menu as shown in figure QS4.1. The Create menu has a single item: New Application.

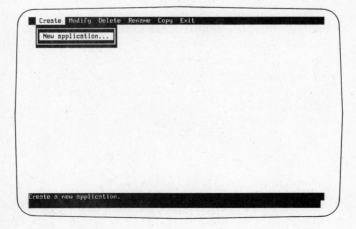

Fig. QS4.1

The Application Express main menu.

5. Press Enter to select New Application.

   R:BASE asks you to open a database.

6. Choose Mailing from the database list. Enter the owner password if necessary.

   R:BASE displays a dialog box asking for the name for this application. This name applies to the three application files that Application EXPRESS creates for you.

7. Type *Mailapp* as the name for the application (see fig. QS4.2).

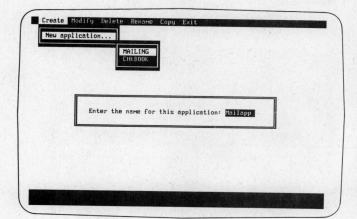

Fig. QS4.2

Naming an application with a valid DOS file name.

Defining the Main Menu

All applications created by Application Express are built around a menu structure and have at least one menu—the application's main menu. R:BASE prompts you for the name of the main menu. Follow these steps to define the Mailapp main menu:

1. Press Enter to accept Main as the application's main menu name.

   You can name menus with any unique alphanumeric name of one to eight characters. (No two menus in the application can have the same name.)

   R:BASE displays a list of menu types, as shown in figure QS4.3. You have a choice of four menu types:

   • *Pull-down menus* appear as a single line of options across the top of the screen. Each option is a pull-down menu.

- *Pop-up menus* list options in an on-screen box.

- *Vertical menus* are numbered like the Prompt By Example main menu.

- *Horizontal menus* have a series of options oriented horizontally like Prompt By Example menus.

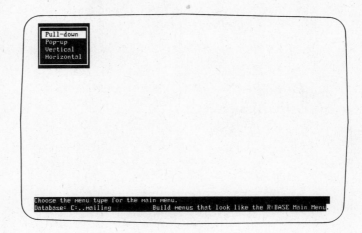

Fig. QS4.3

The menu types available for applications.

2. Choose Pull-down.

   This option defines a menu like the R:BASE main menu—a list of options across the top of the screen, with pull-down menus that appear when you highlight an option on the horizontal menu.

   R:BASE asks whether you want to customize colors for the menu.

3. Answer Yes and choose the foreground and background colors from the 16-color palette. Press F2.

   R:BASE now prompts you for the words (options) that you want on the main menu.

4. Enter the following options, pressing Enter after each one.

   > Edit
   > Reports
   > Labels
   > Exit

   After you enter all the options, the screen should look like figure QS4.4.

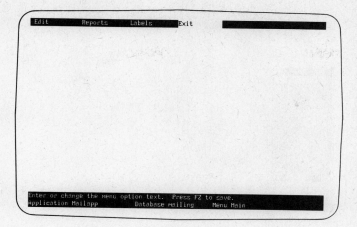

5. Press F2 to tell R:BASE that you are finished entering text.

   After you define the main menu and enter the options for it, R:BASE asks whether you want to designate the Esc key as a way to exit from this menu.

6. Even though you have an Exit option, the Esc key is a convenient alternative way to exit, so answer Yes.

   R:BASE displays another dialog box asking whether you want to define a Help screen for this menu.

7. Answer No. You can define a Help screen later if you want.

You now have specified the first menu's type and the text for the options. Now you tell R:BASE what each option does.

Defining Actions

R:BASE displays a list of actions for the first menu option, Edit, as shown in figure QS4.5. For this application, you will be using the Edit, Print Reports, Print Labels, Menu, and Exit options. You will learn about the other options in Chapter 8. Follow these steps to define actions for the menu items:

1. Choose Edit for the first option's action.

   When you use the application, choosing this option brings up a data entry form in Edit mode. Next, you must choose the table you are going to edit and a form from the list defined for that table.

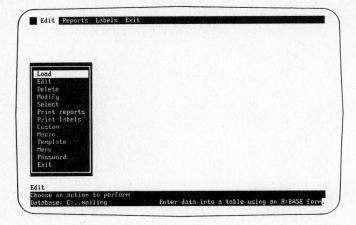

Fig. QS4.5

An option that can affect the database.

2. Choose Mail_list from the table list.

3. Choose Mailings from the Form list (see fig. QS4.6).

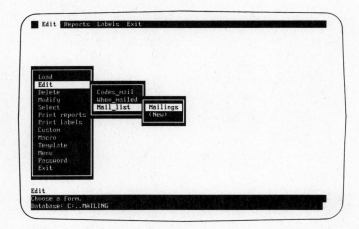

Fig. QS4.6

Using the Mailings form in an application instead of creating a new form.

With the (New) option on this list, you can create a new form in Application Express. This procedure is similar to the Quick Form option procedure in the Forms module (see Chapter 6).

4. When R:BASE asks whether you want to edit the form, answer No.

R:BASE displays a list of the columns in the table. If, when you use the application, you want the data sorted when it is presented, you need to decide the sort order.

5. Press Enter to choose Idno and then press Enter again to sort in ascending order, as shown in figure QS4.7. This procedure displays the rows in ID-number order.

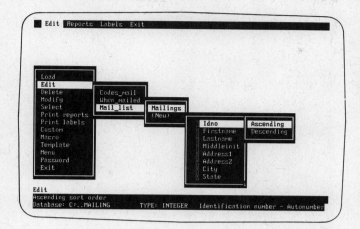

6. Press F2 to finish with the sort order.

   With the Condition Builder, you can limit the rows that can be edited with this form and have the application users fill in the comparison value. The application users, therefore, can ask for the data they want to edit. Because not many rows exist in the table, however, you will bypass condition setting, enabling the users to edit all rows.

7. Press F2 to bypass setting conditions.

8. When R:BASE asks whether you want another action for this option, answer No.

R:BASE goes on to the next main menu option: Reports. This option displays a second-level menu. To define a second-level menu, choose the menu type, set any colors you want, and enter the menu text. Follow these steps:

1. For the Reports option, choose the Menu option.

   You must create a list of items for the pull-down menu for that option. If you had chosen a vertical or horizontal menu type for the main menu, R:BASE also would ask you to define the menu type. Because you chose a pull-down menu, you already have defined the secondary menu type for the main menu—pull-down menus for each option.

2. When R:BASE asks for the name for the pull-down menu, type *Reports*.

   R:BASE displays a blank pop-up menu on the left side of the screen.

3. Enter the option text for the Reports pull-down menu:

   Mailing List
   Mailings Sent

   The screen should look like figure QS4.8.

Fig. QS4.8

*Using a
pull-down
menu in an
application.*

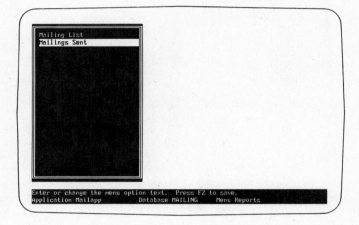

4. Press F2 to indicate that you have finished entering text for the pull-down menu.

Later, you can choose actions for these options.

Now you are ready to define the action for the next main menu option: Labels. You want to define this option to execute a label format. Follow these steps:

1. For the Labels option, choose Print Labels as the action.

2. When R:BASE displays a list of tables, choose Mail_list.

   R:BASE displays a list of the label formats defined for the Mail_list table.

3. Choose M_labels.

4. When R:BASE asks whether you want to edit the label format, answer No.

   R:BASE displays the list of columns for sorting.

5. Move the cursor past the last column to highlight ZIPcode and press Enter.

6. Choose Ascending and then press F2 (see fig. QS4.9).

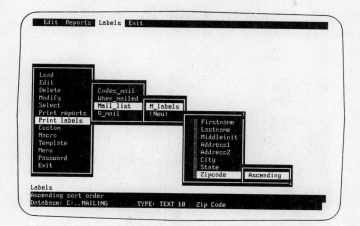

Fig. QS4.9
Sorting labels in ascending order for printing.

R:BASE displays the Condition Builder. Conditions limit the rows included on the labels. Again, you can enter the comparison value after you execute the Labels option. Because few rows exist in the table, you can bypass setting conditions so that every row prints a label.

7. Press F2 to bypass setting conditions.

8. When R:BASE asks whether you want another action for this option, answer No.

The last option provides a way to exit from the application. Although you have already set Esc as an exit method, the user may not know this. A menu option makes the exit method obvious. If an exit is provided from a lower-level menu (such as the Reports menu), control returns to the next higher menu level. From the main menu, you use an Exit option to leave the application. For the Exit option, choose the Exit action.

You now are ready to assign actions to the second-level menu you created for the Reports option. R:BASE displays the pull-down menu you defined for the Reports option.

For the Mailing List option, choose these options:

1. Choose No when asked whether you want a Help screen.

2. Choose Print Reports.

3. Choose Q_mail from the table list.

4. Choose Mailrep for the report.

5. Answer No when asked whether you want to edit the report.

6. Choose Lastname and Ascending for the sort order. The screen should look like figure QS4.10.

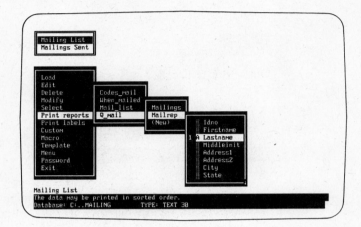

Fig. QS4.10

The options for printing a report.

7. Press F2 to continue.

8. Press F2 again to bypass setting conditions.

9. Answer No when asked whether you want another action.

Next, assign actions for the Mailings Sent option:

1. Choose Print Reports.

2. Choose When_mailed from the Table list.

3. Choose Mailings for the report.

4. Answer No when asked whether you want to edit the report.

5. Press F2 to bypass sorting.

6. Press F2 again to bypass setting conditions.

7. Answer No when asked whether you want another action.

Finishing Applications

Now that you have defined all the actions for the menus, you may change several default settings. These settings establish how the application will look and operate when it executes. These defaults follow:

- Display of standard messages (default: no)
- Display error messages (default: no)
- Colors to display for the application (default: white on blue)
- Bell on errors (default: yes)

To complete the application, you answer two final prompts, as described in the following steps:

1. Answer No to the prompt

   ```
   Do you want to change default settings?
   ```

   so that you do not change any of settings.

   R:BASE displays the commands it has created for you. These commands run quickly down the screen as R:BASE creates the executable application.

   R:BASE asks whether you want to create a start-up file for the application. If you do, every time you start R:BASE from the directory containing the application, the application automatically starts.

2. Answer No to the prompt

   ```
   Do you want to create a startup file?
   ```

   You do not want this application to execute every time you start R:BASE, so you do not want to create a startup file that forces you into the application. R:BASE returns you to the Application Express main menu.

3. Press Esc and then Enter to exit from Application Express.

Using Applications

The rest of this quick start shows you how to use the application you have just created. You will go through the steps for using one of the report's menu options, and then you will try out any or all of the rest of the options, as you want.

Follow these steps to try out your application:

1. Press Alt-A to display the Applications pull-down menu.

2. Choose MAILAPP from the list. MAILAPP is the application you just created.

    R:BASE displays your application's main menu on-screen (see fig. QS4.11). The first option (Edit) is highlighted. If you choose the Edit option, you start the form in Edit mode.

Fig. QS4.11

Selecting options in an application.

3. Press Tab to highlight Reports.

4. Highlight Mailings Sent and press Enter.

    R:BASE displays a pop-up menu with the output options: Printer, Screen, and Both. R:BASE created this menu automatically when you defined the option to print a report.

5. After making sure that your printer is ready, choose Both. If you do not have a printer available, choose Screen.

    R:BASE displays and prints the Mailing List report (see fig. QS4.12).

6. Press any key to return to the application's main menu after the report prints. (You may need to press a key while the report is printing if you have more than one screen of data.)

7. Choose any other option. See what happens when you use each option.

8. When you are finished, highlight Exit and press Enter.

R:BASE returns you to the R:BASE main menu.

```
                    ┌──────────┐
                    │ Printer  │
                    │ Screen   │
                    │ Both     │
                    └──────────┘

                MAILING LIST REPORT
                as of 04/12/90
                                            Page   1
Id Number  Name             Mailing Type      Date Sent
           1 John A. Doe
                            Initial mailing for fundi   Mar 24, 1990
           2 Fred B. Roe
                            Initial mailing for fundi   Mar 24, 1990
                            First response letter       Apr 14, 1990


Press any key to continue.
```

Fig. QS4.12

The printed report displayed on the screen while printing on the printer.

Summary

You now have completed your first application. Chapter 8 explains all the actions you can choose, including how to write Small Command files for inclusion in your application. Chapter 8 also includes information on writing Trigger Command files for use with your custom data entry forms.

8

Building and Using Applications

This chapter describes how to use Application Express, the R:BASE application-creation module, and how to write your own programs for R:BASE. You will be introduced to a new sample database named CHKBOOK. This database is a simple checkbook database used to maintain checkbook entries such as checks written, cash withdrawals, and deposits. This chapter uses CHKBOOK because it shows currency data for numeric calculations, a summary table created using an R:BASE program, and form triggers (see Chapter 6 for information on forms).

The two most important concepts to grasp about programming are 1) not everyone can grasp it, and 2) failing to grasp it is not a character flaw. One person can sit down at the word processor and churn out a 20-page report with hardly a second thought. Another person who is assigned the same task will labor, make false starts, fill the wastebasket with multiple drafts, and produce a barely readable report. Is the second person illiterate or stupid? Not hardly. Programming, like writing, can be learned to some degree, but some people seem to be able to handle it intuitively. The rest of us have to work harder and deal with the frustrations.

Microrim developed Application Express especially for those users who find programming difficult. Application Express leads you step-by-step through the programming process and then writes the code, compiles the application for execution, and presents you with a complete product. At the same time, Application Express provides areas where the more experienced programmer can add bells and whistles. Indeed, many capable programmers use Application Express to develop the application shell; then they edit the application file directly.

If you have written any programs before—using BASIC, another database system, or even functions in a spreadsheet—R:BASE programming will not seem mysterious. If you have never written a program, Application Express can help you learn the concepts so that you can program, or may even provide sufficient programming capability that you never need to write your own R:BASE programs.

If you do need to write your own programs, R:BASE makes the task easy. Microrim provides a separate tool for the programmer: an application encoder. In the beginning, this encoder, CodeLock, was developed only as a part of Application Express. When developers realized that the application encoder would be helpful to users who wanted to develop, edit, and encode their own applications, CodeLock was duplicated outside Application Express, and menus were added to make the encoder easy enough for beginners to use.

CodeLock processes programming files by converting them into a binary format. This conversion has two purposes: it protects the files from inadvertent changes and compiles multiblock procedure files (like those created with Application Express) so that R:BASE can execute them.

In this chapter, you first examine the terminology of programming and learn the details of the application builder. You then learn how to write some of the specialized programs that are used with the application builder and how to use CodeLock to encode applications.

Creating Applications

An *application* is an R:BASE program that displays menus leading to database-modification options. An application consists of one or more R:BASE program files called *command files*. When a series of command files is combined into a single file, it is called a *procedure file*. A procedure file must be processed by R:BASE's CodeLock compiler before it can be used. If you create a procedure file with Application Express, the procedure file is processed for you.

You can write applications yourself by using the R:BASE text editor to enter the program commands into a DOS file. A more convenient method, however, is to let R:BASE build the application shell for you with Application Express. Application Express creates a menu structure and applies commands to each of the options on the menus to perform a variety of functions.

Without writing a single line of code, you can create an application that does the following:

- Uses custom data-entry forms to enter and edit data
- Uses R:BASE's tabular edit format to enter and edit data
- Deletes data from a table
- Prints custom reports or labels
- Displays or prints data, using R:BASE's default report format
- Displays a submenu with additional options
- Provides help screens for every menu in the application

In addition, you can execute your own command files from an application, include your own series of commands, or use a command template to create a series of executable commands.

Although Application Express takes care of writing the R:BASE commands that perform all these functions (except the inclusion of custom commands), you need to be familiar with the terminology and understand what Application Express is doing behind the scenes. Then, you will be able to fine-tune the application files yourself. Table 8.1 describes the parts of an application.

Table 8.1
Understanding Application Terminology

Term	Definition
Command File	A stand-alone DOS file in a readable ASCII format containing a series of R:BASE commands that execute one after another or loop to re-execute commands when required.
Procedure File	An application file processed by CodeLock and contained in a DOS file with a nonreadable binary format.
Application File	A series of command, menu, and screen blocks contained in a DOS file with a readable ASCII format.
Command Block	A series of R:BASE commands similar to a command file but contained in an application file. A command block is not executable until the application file is processed by CodeLock.

Table 8.1—*continued*

Term	Definition
Menu Block	The definition of a menu: the type of menu, title, and option text. A menu block is contained in an application file and is not usable until the application file is processed by CodeLock.
Screen Block	One or more pages of text to be displayed as a help screen or whenever additional text is needed on-screen. A screen block is contained in an application file and is not usable until the application file is processed by CodeLock.
Template	A stand-alone ASCII file similar to a command file, but executable only if included by Application Express as a command block in an application file.
Macro	A stand-alone command file that is merged into an Application Express application file, where the macro command file becomes a command block.
Trigger	A command file or procedure file with the specific purpose of executing from a data-entry form.

Figure 8.1 illustrates how the parts of an application fit together.

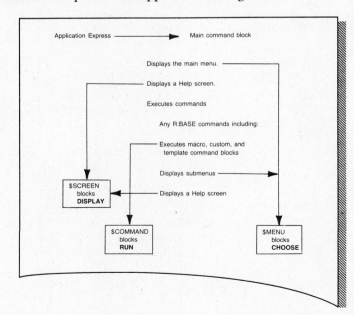

Fig. 8.1

An application consisting of blocks of different types.

Application Express creates a main command block from which all other parts of an application are executed. These other parts can be menu definitions starting with the keyword $MENU, screen displays starting with the keyword $SCREEN, or other sets of commands starting with the keyword $COMMAND. Application Express executes these blocks with the commands CHOOSE, DISPLAY, and RUN, respectively. Any other R:BASE command can be executed from any of the command blocks—the main block or any of the subsidiary command blocks. R:BASE creates these blocks and the commands to execute them as you define an application in Application Express. You do not need to know how to program. When you write your own applications, you use the same programming techniques that Application Express uses.

Starting Application Express

You can start Application Express in one of three ways:

- Highlight Applications on the R:BASE main menu and choose Create/Modify.

- Start the module from Command mode by typing *express*.

- Choose the Express option in Prompt By Example.

```
Command: EXPRESS
```

No matter how you start the Application Express module, its main menu is displayed as shown in figure 8.2. You can choose Create to create a new

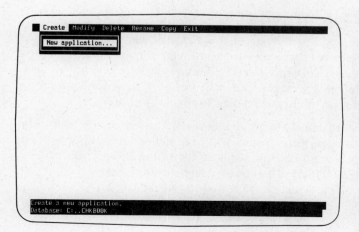

Fig. 8.2

The Application Express main menu.

application, Modify to change an existing application, Delete to remove all files for an existing application, Rename to change the name of an existing application, Copy to make a copy of an application, or Exit to return to wherever you were when you started the application builder.

In addition to menu options, you can use function keys in Application Express to perform some actions. Table 8.2 lists the function keys available in this module.

Table 8.2
Using Function Keys in Application Express

Key	Function
F1	Displays on-line help about the function you are performing
Shift-F1	Displays the usable Function Key list
Shift-F3	Displays the Application Menu tree
Shift-F6	Selects all tables or all columns in a list
F9	Deletes the current option from a menu
F10	Inserts an option on a menu

To begin creating an application from the Applications module, press Enter to select New Application from the Create pull-down menu. R:BASE asks for the database to be used with the application. Choose the appropriate database from the list that appears. The next task is to define the application's main menu.

Defining Menu Structures

An application is simply a set of one or more menus with each menu option performing actions that you want to provide for the user of the application. An Application Express application has at least one menu: the Application main menu. The application also can have submenus leading from the main menu or submenus leading from another submenu.

You can have up to 15 menus in an application. At any time, you can press Shift-F3 to display a map of the menus you have defined. Highlight a menu and press Shift-F3 a second time to display a list of the actions you have defined for that menu. Figure 8.3 shows a map of the MAILAPP application's main menu, which you created in Quick Start 4.

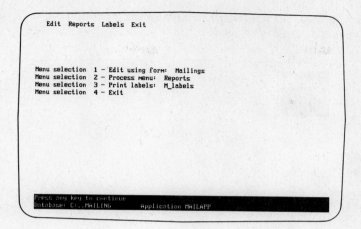

Fig. 8.3

Pressing Shift-F3 to display a "map" of your application.

Defining a menu involves three steps: naming the menu, choosing the type of menu, and entering the menu title and the text for each option. After you define these three aspects of a menu, R:BASE leads you through the steps of defining the actions for each menu option.

Tip: When you define a menu in Application Express, R:BASE creates a menu block and adds it to the application file. In the body of the application's main command block, R:BASE adds a CHOOSE command to display and select options from the menu. See "Encoding Applications" in this chapter and "Programming Commands" in Appendix C for more information on CHOOSE.

Naming Menus

To begin creating an application, define the application's first-level menu. By default, R:BASE assigns the name "Main" to the first menu in an application. When presented with the dialog box asking for the name, you can press Enter to accept "Main" as the menu name, or type some other one- to eight-character alphanumeric menu name.

You can name second- and third-level, as well as first-level menus with any sequence of one to eight alphanumeric characters. Each menu must have a name different from any other menu. You create second- and third-level menus by choosing the menu action for an option.

Choosing Menu Types

When you define any menu, you need to tell R:BASE what type of menu it is. As soon as you name a menu, R:BASE prompts you for the menu type.

Figure 8.4 shows the Menu Type Selection list. Choose the menu type by highlighting it and pressing Enter.

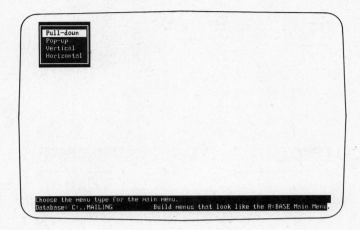

Fig. 8.4

Choosing the type of menus you use in your application.

The menu types follow:

- *Pull-down:* The standard R:BASE menu type. An example is the R:BASE main menu. A pull-down menu can include a maximum of 6 options on the bar, each containing from 1 to 12 characters, and up to 19 options on each pull-down submenu, each containing from 1 to 27 characters.

- *Pop-up:* A boxed menu that appears by itself anywhere on-screen. A pop-up menu can have a maximum of 19 options, each containing from 1 to 60 characters.

- *Vertical:* A numbered, boxed menu with the options displayed in a single, vertical column. A vertical menu can include a maximum of 9 options, each containing from 1 to 60 characters.

- *Horizontal:* A text, boxed menu with the options displayed horizontally. A horizontal menu can include a maximum of 12 options, each containing from 1 to 10 characters.

Tip: If you create your own menu blocks, these menu types are encoded as pull-down, pop-up, column, and row. Pull-down menus can have submenus defined in the same menu block of any other type except another pull-down.

Except for pop-up menus, all menu types are defined the same way, as explained in the following section, "Entering Titles." If you choose a pop-up menu type, R:BASE asks you to paint the area on-screen where you want the menu to appear. (Other menus are displayed in default positions and sizes.) To create a pop-up menu, move the cursor to where you want to place the menu's upper left corner and press Enter. Then move the cursor to the lower right position and press Enter again. Remember that the number of options you can enter for the menu is limited by the size you make the menu area. Allow two extra lines—one each for the top and bottom lines of the menu box. Also, be sure that the menu width is sufficient for the option text. Figure 8.5 shows how a pop-up menu is painted on-screen.

Fig. 8.5

*"Painting"
pop-up menus
on-screen by
moving the
cursor with
the arrow
keys.*

Entering Titles

After you choose a menu type (and, if it is a pop-up menu, paint the menu area), R:BASE prompts you to enter the menu title (see fig. 8.6). A vertical, horizontal, or pop-up menu can have a menu title centered on the top line of the menu box. If your application's main menu needs a title, choosing one of these types for the main menu is a good idea.

Specifying Other Menu Features

When you finish entering the title, you specify three additional menu characteristics:

- Menu colors
- Esc key exit
- On-line help

R:BASE prompts you for these characteristics as you define the menu. The first prompt asks whether you want to change the menu colors. Answer

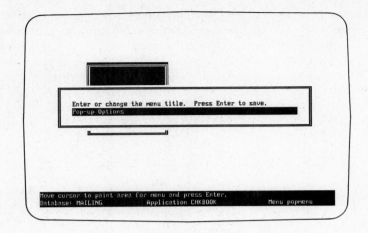

Fig. 8.6

*All menus
except pull-
down menus
can have a
title.*

Yes to display the color palette, from which you can select the foreground
and background colors for the menu. This palette is the same 15-color
palette used throughout R:BASE. The initial character on nonnumbered
menus, however, is red by default (unless you change the initial character
color on the Settings menu, as described in Appendix B). Also, some of the
inverse video colors for certain color combinations may be hard to read.
Experiment with menu colors to find a combination that works for you.
Press F2 when you are satisfied with the colors.

The second prompt asks whether you want to use the Esc key as an exit
key from menus. From lower-level menus, Esc exits to the next higher
menu level. From the main menu, Esc exits the application. If you want to
use Esc to exit menus, answer Yes to the prompt.

The third prompt asks whether you want a help screen for the menu. To
add a help screen, follow these steps:

1. Answer Yes to the prompt.

   R:BASE asks for a name for the help text (this name becomes a
   screen block).

2. Enter a unique block name for the help screen. For example, for the
   main menu, name the help screen *mainhelp*.

   R:BASE takes you to the R:BASE text editor so that you can write as
   much help text as you want.

3. Enter the text you want to display as a help screen. (See "Using the
   R:BASE Text Editor" in this chapter for more information.)

4. Press F2.

When your help text is displayed in the application, R:BASE pauses at the end of each screen to enable the application user to continue (press a key) or exit the help screen (press Esc). The Esc key works even if you did not indicate that Esc should exit menus.

Tip: When you write a help screen, you are adding a screen block to the application file. R:BASE creates a screen block in the application and uses the DISPLAY command in the main command block to display the screen.

Entering Option Text

After the title and menu characteristics are defined, R:BASE prompts you for the option text. The screen format resembles the menu type you have chosen, with the cursor positioned in the first area where you can enter option text.

Type the appropriate text for each option you want to include on the menu. Press Enter at the end of each option to move to the next option area. Figure 8.7 shows what the screen looks like when you are entering option text.

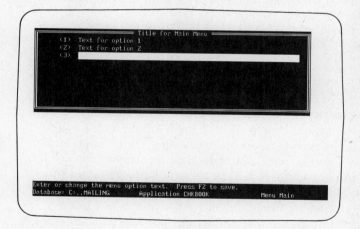

Fig. 8.7

Option text consists of words that describe an option.

Choosing Actions

When you finish entering option text, press F2 to continue to the next step: specifying actions for each menu option. R:BASE highlights the menu's first option and displays the action list, as shown in figure 8.8.

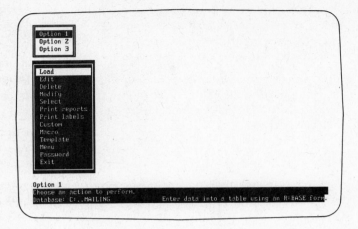

Fig. 8.8

You can assign one or more actions to each option.

These choices provide just about any database action you may want to include in an application. Those actions that are not included as direct actions can be added as a custom or macro command file (see "Writing Program Files for Applications" in this chapter). Table 8.3 describes the available actions. The sections that follow provide more detail about how to use these actions.

Table 8.3
Choosing an Action

Action	Function
Load	Starts a custom form with the ENTER command. If you do not have a form defined, R:BASE enables you to define a Quick form on the spot. You can go into the Forms module later to make any improvements. If you already have a form defined, R:BASE enables you to modify the form on the spot. (For information on creating and using forms, see Chapter 6. For more information on this action, see "Loading Data" in this chapter.)
Edit	Starts a custom form with the EDIT USING command. (For more information, see "Editing Data" in this chapter.)
Delete	Deletes rows from a specific table. This function is useful for removing temporary data. (For information on deleting rows, see Chapter 4. For more information on this action, see "Deleting Data" in this chapter.)

Action	Function
Modify	Starts tabular edit for a specific table. (For information on using tabular edit, see Chapter 4. For more information on this action, see "Modifying Data" in this chapter.)
Select	Executes a SELECT command. (For information on SELECT, see Chapter 9. For more information on this action, see "Displaying Selected Data" in this chapter.)
Print Reports	Prints a custom report. As with Edit and Load, you can define a Quick report in the application builder or modify an existing report. (For information on building and using reports, see Chapter 7. For more information on this action, see "Printing Reports" in this chapter.)
Print Labels	Prints a custom label set. As with Print Reports, you can define a label format in the application builder or modify an existing label format. (For information on building and using labels, see Chapter 7. For more information on this action, see "Printing Labels" in this chapter.)
Custom	Takes you to the R:BASE text editor where you can enter a series of R:BASE commands. (For more information, see "Using the R:BASE Text Editor" and "Using the Custom Action" in this chapter.)
Macro	Installs an existing command file as a command block in the application. To use this action, you must already have a command file in ASCII format. (For more information, see "Using the R:BASE Text Editor" and "Using the Macro Action" in this chapter.)
Template	Uses a template file to create a command block in your application. When completed, the template block operates just like a custom command block. To use this option, you already must have a prepared template file. (For more information, see "Using the Template Action" in this chapter.)

Table 8.3—*continued*

Action	Function
Menu	Defines a submenu that is called from the main menu. (For more information, see "Defining the Menu Structure" in this chapter.)
Password	Sets a user password in the application. This action is most often used in conjunction with another action. (For more information, see "Setting Passwords" in this chapter.)
Exit	Defines an exit from the menu. (For more information, see "Defining an Exit Option" in this chapter.)

Most of these actions act on tables. When you choose the Load, Edit, Delete, Modify, Select, Print Reports, or Print Labels action, R:BASE asks for a table name. When you choose an action that uses a form, report, or label, R:BASE also asks for the name of the form, report, or label. If one does not already exist or you want to define a new one, you can do so right in the application builder. If you choose an existing form, report, or label, R:BASE enables you to modify it.

Some of the actions also ask for sort order and conditions. Any action that enables sorting—including Edit, Modify, Select, Print Reports, and Print Labels—prompts you for a sort order when you assign the action to an option. R:BASE prompts you for sorting by displaying a list of columns. The process for specifying a sort order is the same one used throughout R:BASE. Highlight a column and press Enter to select it. Choose Ascending or Descending for the type of sort, as shown in figure 8.9. When you are finished selecting columns to sort by, press F2.

Condition-building in Application Express is similar to what you have used in R:BASE, with one major difference. Because the application will be used over a period of time, you may want to vary the conditions under which rows are selected. R:BASE therefore enables you to prompt the application user for the comparison value rather than enter it directly on the condition builder.

As it does throughout R:BASE, the first part of the condition calls for a column to compare and the comparison operator. In Application Express, R:BASE then asks whether you want to prompt the user for the comparison value. If you answer No, you enter a specific value for comparison. If you answer Yes, R:BASE displays a dialog box asking for the prompt message

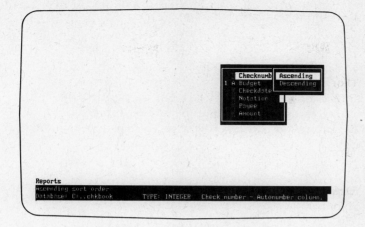

Fig. 8.9
Choosing a sort order.

(see fig. 8.10). When you complete the prompt message and press Enter, you are finished with the condition, and you can continue to the next prompt.

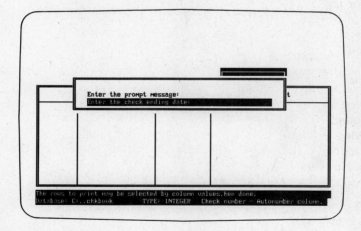

Fig. 8.10
Prompting the application user to enter the comparison value while setting conditions.

Each option can execute more than one action. As you complete the entry for each action (respond to all prompts), R:BASE asks whether you want to assign another action to the option. Press Y and Enter to assign additional actions.

When the application user chooses a multi-action option, each action executes one after the other. A typical series of actions might be as follows:

1. *Password:* Provide the correct password to access a table.

2. *Load:* Enter data into a table, using a form.

3. *Select:* Display the data just entered.

Loading Data

Use the Load action to use a form to add (load) data to the database. You can use a form you have created (see Chapter 6), or you can create a Quick form while in Application Express. Follow these steps to assign the Load action to an option:

1. Select Load.

2. Choose the table into which data is to be loaded.

   R:BASE checks the forms already defined for the database and displays a list of the forms that use this table as the first table in the form. In addition, the program provides a (New) option if you want to create a Quick form (see fig. 8.11).

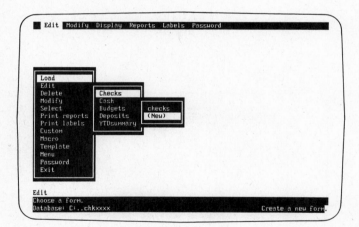

Fig. 8.11

Choosing or creating a new form while using the Load action.

3. Choose an existing form, or choose New to create a Quick form.

   If you choose an existing form, R:BASE asks whether you want to edit the form. Press Y and Enter to edit the form. R:BASE then takes you to the Forms module with the selected form displayed. See Chapter 6 for information on modifying forms.

   If you choose New, R:BASE steps you through the process of creating a Quick form. Because you have chosen a table, R:BASE prompts you only for the columns to include on the form. After you choose the columns, R:BASE sends you to the Forms module, where you can edit the Quick form to suit your preferences.

When you exit the Forms module, R:BASE returns you to Application Express.

R:BASE next asks whether you want to assign another action to this option.

4. Press Y and then Enter to assign another action. Press Enter to select No.

Tip: When you use the Load action, R:BASE puts an ENTER command in the main command block of the application file.

Editing Data

Use the Edit action to use a form to edit data in the database. You can use a form you have created (see Chapter 6), or you can create a Quick form while in Application Express. Follow these steps to assign the Edit action to an option:

1. Select Edit.

2. Choose the table that contains the data to be edited.

   R:BASE checks the forms already defined for the database and displays a list of the forms that use this table as the first table in the form. In addition, the program provides a New option if you want to create a Quick form.

3. Choose an existing form to edit the form or choose New to create a Quick form (see figure 8.12).

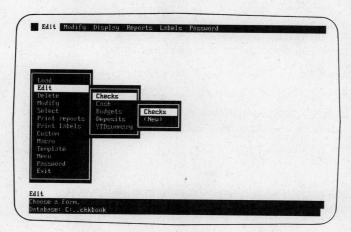

Fig. 8.12

Choosing a form or creating a new form while using the Edit action.

4. When asked whether you want to assign another action to this option, press Y and then Enter to assign another action. Press Enter to select No.

Tip: When you use the Edit action, R:BASE puts an EDIT USING command in the main command block of the application file.

Deleting Data

Use the Delete action to remove rows from a table. If the application user selects an option for which you have specified this action, the rows you specify when building the action are deleted. Follow these steps to assign the Delete action to an option:

1. Select Delete.

2. Choose the table from which rows are to be deleted.

3. When the condition builder is displayed, define the conditions under which the rows should be deleted.

4. When asked whether you want to assign another action to this option, press Y and then Enter to assign another action. Press Enter to select No.

Tip: When you use the Delete action, R:BASE puts a DELETE ROWS command in the main command block of the application.

Modifying Data

Use the Modify action to edit data in a table, using the tabular edit format. (For information on using tabular edit, see Chapter 4.) Follow these steps to assign the Modify action to an option:

1. Select Modify.

2. Choose the table you want the application user to edit.

   R:BASE displays a list of columns from the table.

3. Select up to 10 columns to edit. To select a column, highlight it and press Enter to put a check mark next to it (see fig. 8.13). When you are finished selecting columns, press F2 to continue.

   R:BASE displays the column list again so that you can specify the sort order.

4. Choose the columns to sort by and the direction of the sort— Ascending or Descending—for each column.

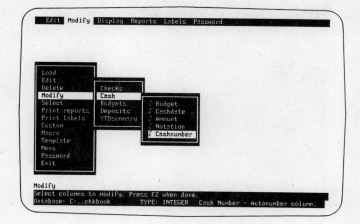

Fig. 8.13
The Modify action uses tabular edit with a limit of 10 columns.

5. Define the conditions that select the rows to edit.

   R:BASE asks whether you want to assign another action to this option.

6. Press Y and then Enter to assign another action. Press Enter to select No.

Tip: When you use the Modify action, R:BASE puts an EDIT command in the main command block of the application.

Displaying Selected Data

Use the Select action to display data from a table or view. (For information on using the SELECT command (the underlying command for this action), see Chapter 9. For information on views, see Chapter 5.) Follow these steps to assign the Select action to an option:

1. Choose Select.

2. Choose the table or view that contains the data you want to display.

3. Select the columns to display. To select a column, highlight it and press Enter to put a check mark next to it (see fig. 8.14). When you are finished selecting columns, press F2 to continue. Keep in mind that if you select more columns than will fit on-screen, the columns that extend past the screen boundaries will not appear after you select the option.

4. Choose the columns to sort by and the direction of the sort—Ascending or Descending—for each column.

Fig. 8.14
Checking off the columns you want to display with the Select action.

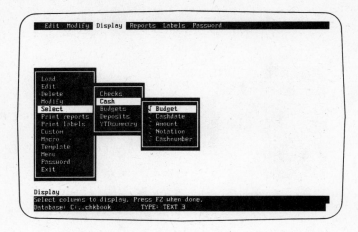

5. Define the conditions that select the rows to display.

6. When asked whether you want to assign another action, press Y and then Enter to assign another action. Press Enter to select No.

Tip: When you use the Select action, R:BASE puts a SELECT command in the main command block of the application.

Printing Reports

Use the Print Reports action to print an existing report. You can use a report you have created (see Chapter 7), or you can create a Quick report while in Application Express. Follow these steps to assign the Print Report action to an option:

1. Select Print Reports.

2. Choose the table for the report.

   R:BASE checks the reports already defined for the database and displays a list of the reports that use this table. In addition, the program provides a (New) option if you want to create a Quick report.

3. Choose an existing report or choose New to create a Quick report, as shown in figure 8.15.

   If you choose an existing report, R:BASE asks whether you want to edit the report. Press Y and Enter to edit the report. This answer takes you to the Reports module with the selected report displayed. (See Chapter 7 for information on modifying reports.)

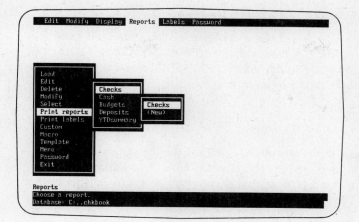

Fig. 8.15
Choosing or creating a new report.

If you choose New, R:BASE steps you through the process of creating a Quick report. Because you have already chosen a table, R:BASE prompts you only for the columns to include on the report. Choose up to 10 columns, and choose the orientation of the report—Row-wise or Column-wise. R:BASE then sends you to the Reports module where you can edit the Quick report to suit your preferences.

When you exit from the Reports module, R:BASE returns you to Application EXPRESS.

R:BASE next displays the column list for specifying the sort order.

4. Choose the columns to sort by and the direction of the sort—Ascending or Descending—for each column.

5. Define the conditions that select the rows to display or print.

6. When asked whether you want to assign another action to this option, press Y and then Enter to assign another action. Press Enter to select No.

Tip: When you use the Print Reports action, R:BASE defines a menu block to provide selection of the output device (printer, screen, or file) and puts the following commands in the main command block of the application file: a CHOOSE command for selection of the output device, an OUTPUT command to direct the output to the device, and a PRINT command to print the report.

Printing Labels

Use the Print Labels action to print mailing labels for a selected table. You can use a label template you have already created (see Chapter 7) or can create a label format while in Application EXPRESS. Follow these steps to assign the Print Labels action to an option:

1. Select Print Labels.

2. Choose the table for the labels.

   R:BASE checks the labels already defined for the database and displays a list of the labels that use this table. In addition, the program provides a New option if you want to create a label format.

3. Choose an existing label format to edit, or choose (New) to create new labels, as shown in figure 8.16.

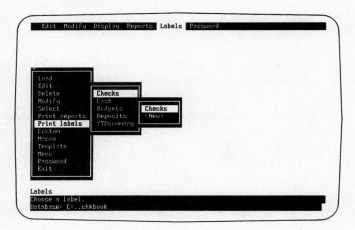

Fig. 8.16

Choosing or creating a label format.

R:BASE displays the column list for specifying the sort order.

4. Choose the columns to sort by and the direction of the sort—Ascending or Descending—for each column.

5. Define the conditions that select the rows to display or print.

6. When asked whether you want to assign another action to this option, press Y and then Enter to assign another action. Press Enter to select No.

> **Tip:** When you use the Print Labels action, R:BASE defines a menu block to provide selection of the output device (printer, screen, or file) and puts the following commands in the main command block of the application file: a CHOOSE command for selection of the output device, an OUTPUT command to direct the output to the device, and a LBLPRINT command to print the labels.

Setting Passwords

If you have defined passwords for your database, you need to give the application user access to the tables. R:BASE gives you two ways to include passwords in your application: the Password action and the Custom action.

The Password action is included in Application Express to ensure that the password is available when the application user attempts to modify the database. If you password-protect your application, this method can be sufficient. If you want to protect tables from within the application, however, you need to use a better method: the Custom action. If you have assigned passwords to protect your data, entering the password in the application by using the Password action defeats the purpose of password protection. (For information on specifying passwords for your database, see Chapter 3.)

Usually, you use the Password action in conjunction with an action that requires a password for access. For example, if you want to use the Load action, and the table to which you want data added has a password assigned to it, you need to use the Password action first and then, when R:BASE asks whether you want to assign another action to the option, you answer Yes and use the Load action.

To assign the Password action to an option, follow these steps:

1. Select Password.

2. Enter the password that accesses the table at the level of access needed for the other action you plan to assign (see fig. 8.17 and table 8.4). All the access levels are explained in Chapter 3. Keep in mind that the Load and Edit actions use forms. If a form password is assigned, it takes precedence over the table-level password.

   R:BASE next asks whether you want to assign another action to this option.

3. Press Y and then Enter to answer Yes.

4. Assign the next action as described in the previous sections.

Fig. 8.17

The Password action enables you to give anyone access to your data.

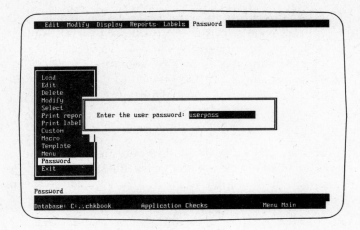

Table 8.4
Access Rights for Actions

Action	Access Level
Load	Insert
Edit	Update
Delete	Delete
Modify	Update
Select	Select
Print Reports	Select
Print Labels	Select

A better method of including a password involves using the Custom action. Follow these steps:

1. Select Custom.

2. When prompted for the name of the block, enter any one- to eight-character name that is unique in this application. (The name must be unique for all blocks—command, menu, or screen.)

   R:BASE sends you to the text editor.

3. Type these command lines, pressing Enter at the end of each line to move to the next line:

   ```
   FILLIN vpassword USING 'Enter the password: '
   USER .vpassword
   RETURN
   ```

These lines prompt the application user for a password, which is stored in the variable vpassword. Then, the USER command specifies the entered password as the one to use right now. If the password is not valid for the next action, the user is not given access. The user can choose the option again to try a different password, but R:BASE does not enable the user to access the option until the password is valid.

4. Press Esc and choose Exit from the Editor menu.

5. Assign the next action as described in the previous sections.

(See "Using the R:BASE Text Editor" in this chapter for detailed instructions on entering and editing commands in the text editor. For more information on the Custom action, see "Using the Custom Action" in this chapter.)

Defining an Exit Option

You can give an application user two methods to use for exiting a menu or the application. You can assign Esc as an exit option, and you can put an Exit option on the menu. Both methods have the same effect. The advantage of an Exit option is that the method for exiting is displayed on the menu, so the application user can see clearly how to exit.

To put an Exit option on the menu, highlight the Exit action. Then press Enter to select it. R:BASE continues to the next option or menu. You are not asked whether you want another action for this option.

Tip: When you use the Exit action in an application, R:BASE puts a GOTO command in the main command block. GOTO specifies the last menu level to return to. From the third-level menu, Esc returns the application user to the second-level menu. From the second level, Esc returns the user to the first level (main). From the main menu, Esc exits the application.

Finishing Applications

Completing an application involves a few more steps, which are described in the following sections.

Setting Environments

When you finish defining menus and actions, R:BASE asks whether you want to modify the environment settings (see fig. 8.18). If you do, press Y and then Enter to display the application environment menu shown in figure 8.19. From this menu, you can modify the environment under which the application operates.

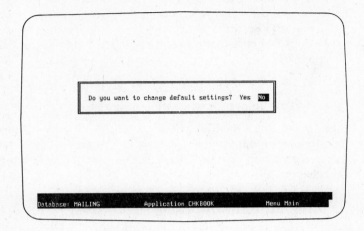

Fig. 8.18

R:BASE asks whether you want to change the operating environment for this application.

Do you want to change default settings? Yes No

Database: MAILING   Application CHKBOOK   Menu Main

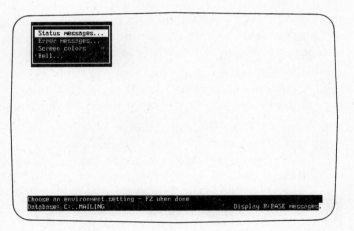

Fig. 8.19

Setting the environment to be used when the application is executed.

Status messages...
Error messages...
Screen colors   »
Bell...

Choose an environment setting – F2 when done
Database: C:..MAILING   Display R:BASE messages

Choose the Status Messages option and select Yes to display status messages, which tell the application user what is happening. If you use the Delete action with messages set to display, for example, the application user sees a message such as

```
15 row(s) have been deleted from table Mail_list
```

These messages can be useful when you are testing your application. The default is to not display messages.

Choose the Error Messages option to display error messages, which indicate when an error occurs. If you use the Load action in an application with messages set to display, for example, and then remove the form used by the option, the application user sees a message such as

```
Form Mailcode is not in the SYSFORM table
```

These types of messages are extremely useful when you are testing your application but may prove disconcerting to an application user. The default is to not display error messages.

Choose the Screen Colors option to select colors for the screen background. The default screen colors are the colors set in R:BASE when the application is started. If you already have selected menu colors, you may want to select some pleasing screen background colors to match. When you choose Screen Colors, R:BASE displays the color palette, from which you can select the colors.

Choose the Bell option and answer Yes to sound the bell when an error occurs. (This setting is the default.) If the error message display is off, a bell sounding may prove disconcerting to a user. If you display error messages, choose Yes for sounding the bell. If you do not display error messages, choose No to suppress the bell.

Writing Application Files

When you return from changing the environment settings (or if you answer No to that prompt), R:BASE starts writing the application files. It creates three DOS files, each bearing the name you gave to the application and one of three different extensions: APP, API, and APX.

The APP file is the ASCII file for the application. You can edit this file to make manual changes to the application and then use CodeLock to re-encode the file to create a new executable file (see "Encoding Applications" in this chapter).

The API file is a binary file used only by Application Express and is *the* application file as far as Application Express is concerned. As long as this file remains intact, you can modify your application through Application Express.

The APX file is the encoded executable file. Files with this extension appear on the Applications pull-down menu accessed from the R:BASE main menu. You execute this file to run an application.

Creating Start-up Files

When R:BASE finishes creating the files, it asks you to press any key to continue and then asks whether you want to create a start-up file (see fig. 8.20). Answer Yes if you want your application to execute automatically when you start R:BASE. An application start-up file is useful when other people will be using your application and you want to make sure that they use only the options provided in your application. The start-up file created by R:BASE is always named RBASE.DAT and includes the following commands:

Fig. 8.20

Start-up files execute an application when R:BASE is started.

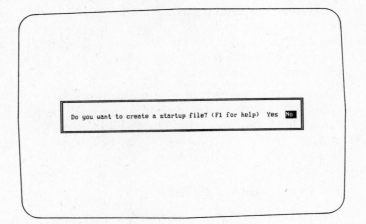

Do you want to create a startup file? (F1 for help)   Yes   No

```
RUN yourapp IN yourapp.apx
EXIT
```

These commands execute the application immediately when R:BASE is started and exit R:BASE when the user exits the application. The file works only if the user starts R:BASE from the directory containing both the RBASE.DAT file and the application that will be executed. Keep this in mind when defining your application. You also should have the database in the same directory.

You can modify the start-up file by using the R:BASE text editor. You may, for example, want to enable the user to stay in R:BASE when exiting the application. In this case, you would remove the EXIT line.

You also can rename the start-up file to any other valid DOS file name so that the process is not automatic. You then can provide a DOS batch file that starts R:BASE and uses the renamed start-up file. Suppose, for example, that you want your application user to use only the application you created, but you want to be able to get into R:BASE without running the application. Rename the start-up file to YOURAPP.CMD (supposing that your application is named YOURAPP). Then create a DOS batch file with this command:

    RBASE YOURAPP.CMD

Give this batch file your application user's name: MARY.BAT. Then tell the user to type *mary* to use the application. The batch file executes, starting R:BASE and telling the program to execute the commands it finds in YOURAPP.CMD. These commands execute the application and then exit R:BASE when the application is exited.

Executing Applications

You have four ways to execute applications:

- From the R:BASE main menu, you press Alt-A to highlight Applications and choose the application name.

- From Command mode, enter a RUN command to execute your application. If your application is named YOURAPP, for example, type this command:

    RUN YOURAPP IN YOURAPP.APX

- From Application Express, choose Manage Application from the Modify Application menu to run your application.

- From DOS, start R:BASE with a start-up file that automatically executes the application.

Regardless of the way you start your application, its main menu appears. You use an application's menu in the same way you use R:BASE menus—by highlighting options and pressing Enter to select them. See Quick Start 4 for practice in designing and using an application.

```
Command: RUN
```

Modifying Applications

After you first create an application and test it, you may find that you want to modify how it works. You may, for example, want to add menu options, add menus, remove options from menus, change the options on the menus, or change the operating environment for the applications.

To modify an existing application, follow these steps:

1. From the R:BASE main menu, press Alt-A to display the Applications pull-down menu, and choose Create/Modify.

   or

   From the R> prompt, type *express*.

   In either case, R:BASE displays the Application Express main menu.

2. Highlight Modify.

3. Select the name of the application you want to modify.

R:BASE displays the Modify menu (see fig. 8.21). The following sections explain how to use each of these menu options.

Fig. 8.21

You can change an application by using the Modify menu.

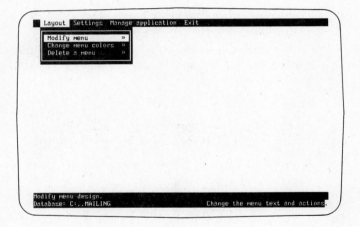

Changing the Application Layout

The Layout option on the Modify Application menu deals with the menus, the options on the menus, the actions assigned to each option, and the menu colors.

Modifying Menus

The methods for modifying an application menu are similar to the methods you use to create the menu. Rather than enter a new title and new option text and assign actions from scratch, you highlight an existing part of the menu and then re-enter or reassign, depending on how you want to change the menu.

To modify a menu, press Alt-L and select Modify Menu from the Layout pull-down menu. R:BASE displays a list of the menus in the application, in order from first level downward. Select the menu you want to change.

If the original menu type is pop-up, R:BASE displays the Pop-up Modify menu (see "Modifying Pop-up Menus" for more information). If the original menu is not a pop-up, R:BASE displays the menu just as it appeared when you defined it. Unless the menu is a pull-down menu, which does not have a title, the menu title is highlighted.

Editing Menu Titles and Options

Edit the menu title by simply typing over the displayed title. Insert characters or delete characters just as you would edit any data in R:BASE. Press Enter to highlight each option in turn and edit the option text as needed.

If you want to add an option, highlight the option that currently is located at the position where you want the new option. Press F10. R:BASE inserts a blank option space. If you want to add an option at the end of the existing options, press End to move to the end and open a new option space by pressing F10. Then enter the text for the option.

If you want to delete an option, highlight the option and press F9. R:BASE asks you to confirm the deletion. Press Y and Enter to remove the option.

Changing Esc and Help Settings

When you are finished modifying the menu text, press F2 to continue to the next step. R:BASE asks

    Do you want to use Esc to exit from the menu? Yes No

The menu's current use of Esc already is highlighted. If you recall, when you defined the application, you determined whether to enable the Esc key to act as an exit option.

R:BASE then asks you

    Do you want to define a help screen for this menu? Yes No

When you defined the application, you had the opportunity to define a help screen for the menu. Choose Yes to enter a new help screen or to modify the existing help screen. If you already have defined a help screen, R:BASE takes you to the text editor with the help text already displayed on-screen. If you are defining a new help screen, R:BASE asks for the name of the help screen block. Enter a one- to eight-character name that is unique to all blocks in the application. You then are sent to the text editor with a blank screen displayed. See "Using the R:BASE Text Editor" for information on how to use the editor.

When you exit from the editor by pressing F2 (or if you answer No to the help screen prompt), R:BASE asks whether you want to modify actions for the menu. Answer Yes to modify the actions. Answer No to return to the Modify menu.

Changing Actions

If you choose to modify actions for a menu, R:BASE asks whether you want to review all the options for the menu (see fig. 8.22). Answer Yes to step through all actions for every option on the menu. When you reach an action you want to modify, you can change it.

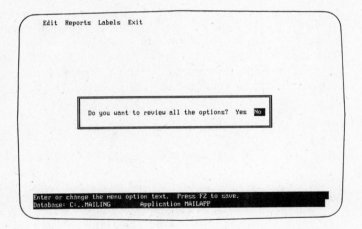

Fig. 8.22

R:BASE enables you to modify parts of your application selectively.

If you want to review the actions for only one or two menu options, answer No to R:BASE's question. Then use the arrow keys to move to the option you want to modify and press Enter. R:BASE displays a list of that option's actions and asks whether you want to add an action before the first one listed.

If you answer Yes, you add an action in the same way you assign an action, as described in the section "Choosing Actions" in this chapter. Choose the action from the menu and answer any questions relevant to the action. Answer No to the Add an Action question if you want to continue to the first assigned action. R:BASE then displays the menu shown in figure 8.23.

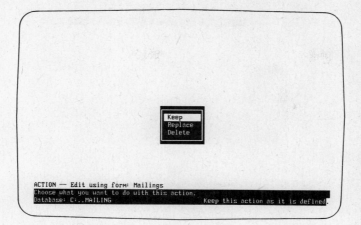

Fig. 8.23
For each option, you can choose to keep, replace, or delete any or all of the assigned actions.

Choose Keep to retain the action as is. R:BASE continues to the next action for the option. Choose Replace to change the action. R:BASE displays the action list, from which you can choose a new action and then answer any questions relevant to it. Choose Delete to remove the action.

When you keep an action that uses a form, report, or label format, R:BASE asks whether you want to modify the database item used by the action. Answer Yes to go to the indicated module so that you can modify the form, report, or label. Answer No if you do not want to change the form, report, or label.

When you have gone through all the actions for an option, R:BASE then asks whether you want to add another action to this option. Answer Yes to add an action. Assign the action in the same way you assigned the first action for the option. Answer No to finish modifying this option's actions.

Highlight the next option you want to modify and press Enter to repeat the process, or press F2 to return to the Modify Application menu.

Modifying Pop-up Menus

The only difference between modifying a pop-up menu and modifying any other type of menu is that the interim Pop-up Modify menu provides options for changing the pop-up menu location and size along with changing the menu's text and actions (see fig. 8.24).

To modify a pop-up menu's text or actions, choose Change Text and Actions from the Pop-up Modify menu. Changing the option text and actions is identical to the way you modify these parts of a menu for any menu type.

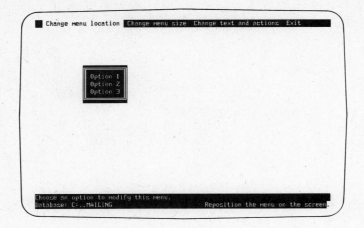

Fig. 8.24

You can change a pop-up menu's options, move the menu, or resize the menu.

To change a pop-up menu's location, follow these steps:

1. Select Change Menu Location on the Pop-up Modify menu.

2. Move the cursor to the new upper left position and press Enter.

To change a pop-up menu's size, follow these steps:

1. Select Change Menu Size on the Pop-up Modify menu.

   R:BASE places the cursor at the menu's upper left corner.

2. Use the down- and right-arrow keys to paint the new menu size. Be sure to allow enough room for all the options and for a line above and below the options.

Changing Menu Colors

You can change the menu's foreground and background colors with the Change Menu Colors option on the Layout pull-down menu. Select the option. Then highlight the menu for which you want to change colors, and press Enter. R:BASE displays the color palette—the same 15-color palette used throughout R:BASE. The initial character on nonnumbered menus is red by default (unless you change the initial character color on the Settings menu, as described in Appendix B). Also, the inverse video colors for some color combinations may be hard to read. Experiment with foreground and background menu colors to find a combination that works for you. When you are satisfied with the colors, press F2 to return to the Layout menu.

Deleting Menus

After creating a menu, you may decide that you prefer not to offer those options, or you may want to consolidate the options on another menu. You can delete an entire menu—all its options and all actions assigned to those options. Follow these steps:

1. Select Delete a Menu from the Layout pull-down menu.

   R:BASE displays a list of all the menus except the main menu. (The main menu always must stay in the application; see "Deleting Applications" in this chapter.)

2. Choose the menu you want to delete.

3. When prompted, answer Yes to delete the menu. If this menu has submenus, the submenus are deleted as well.

Changing Application Settings

Changing an application's environment settings follows the same process you use to control settings when you create a new application (see fig. 8.25 and "Setting the Environment," earlier in this chapter). The only difference is that you choose the setting options from the Settings pull-down menu, which is accessed from the Modify menu.

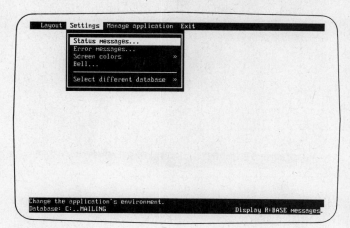

Fig. 8.25

Changing the application's environment settings or database.

Besides displaying the environment options, the Settings pull-down menu does have one additional option. You can change the database used by the application. This option is helpful if you want to use the same application for several similar databases. Follow these steps:

1. Highlight Settings on the Modify menu.

2. Choose Select Different Database from the pull-down menu.

3. Select the database you want to use.

When R:BASE rewrites the application files, it opens the new database rather than the old one. If any option's actions ask for database items that do not exist in the new database, the option does not work.

Testing Applications

When you are developing an application, you probably will modify it more than once, test it, and return to make more changes. Rather than exit Application Express each time you want to test the application, you can run the application by using the Manage Application pull-down menu. Follow these steps:

1. From the Modify menu, press Alt-M to display the Manage Application pull-down menu.

2. Select Run (see fig. 8.26).

Fig. 8.26

The Manage Application menu.

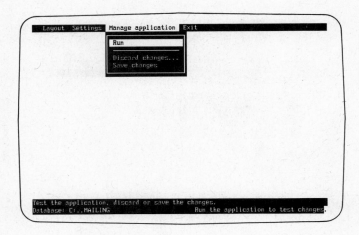

R:BASE saves any changes you have made (it does not ask about a start-up file) and immediately executes the application. When you exit the application, R:BASE returns you to the Modify menu.

Saving and Discarding Applications

When you finish modifying an application, press Esc to exit. R:BASE asks whether you want to save your modifications. Answer Yes to save the changes. R:BASE writes the new application files and asks whether you want to create a start-up file. See "Finishing Applications" in this chapter for more information on start-up and application files.

Another way to save your modifications is to use the Save Changes option on the Manage Application menu. When you choose this option, R:BASE goes through all the same steps you see when you exit and save the application.

In the midst of modifying an application, you may realize that this application is not the one you wanted to change or that the changes you have made are not what you wanted. You have two ways to discard modifications:

- Press Ctrl-Break. All modifications are immediately discarded, and R:BASE returns you to the Application Express main menu.

- Display the Manage Application pull-down menu, and choose Discard Changes. R:BASE asks you to confirm that you want to discard changes. Answer Yes to reset the application to its state before you began modifications and to return to the Modify menu.

In both cases, any changes you made to a form, report, or label format remain. You need to return to the appropriate options to undo any modifications you made to these database items.

Managing Applications

From the Application Express main menu, you can do much more than just create and modify applications. You can work with all the applications on the current directory, removing unneeded applications, changing the names of applications, or creating new applications by copying existing ones.

Deleting Applications

If you no longer need an application, you can remove all its files by using the Delete option. Follow these steps:

1. From the Application Express main menu, press Alt-D to choose the Delete option.

2. Select the application you want to delete.

3. Press Y and then Enter to delete all three application files.

Renaming Applications

If you are not satisfied with a name you have given an application (often users start naming their applications APP1, APP2, and so on), you may want to change its name so that it is more descriptive of the application's use. Follow these steps:

1. At the Application Express main menu, press Alt-R to choose the Rename option.

2. Select the application you want to rename.

3. Type the new name for the application and press Enter. The name must be a valid DOS file name.

R:BASE renames all three application files.

Copying Applications

Often an application can be used by more than one database, but with variations. The fastest way to use an application for multiple databases is to define one application, copy it, and then make modifications to the copy. Follow these steps to copy an application:

1. At the Application Express main menu, press Alt-C to choose the Copy option.

2. Select the application you want to copy.

3. Type a name for the new application and press Enter. The name must be a valid DOS file name.

R:BASE copies all three application files to the new name.

Writing Program Files for Applications

This part of the chapter deals with programming. The intent is not to teach you how to program in R:BASE; programming is something you need to learn by doing. Instead, this section shows you how to use the tools that R:BASE offers to make programming easier. You learn how to use the R:BASE text editor and how to get started in programming by creating custom, macro, and template files to use in your application, and trigger files to use with your forms.

Using the R:BASE Text Editor

You use the R:BASE text editor in Application Express to write custom actions for options and to create help screens for menus. The editor works the same, whether you start it from Application Express or use it outside the module.

To start the editor outside Application Express, use one of these two methods:

- From the R:BASE main menu, choose Tools. Then choose Editor from the Tools pull-down menu.

- Type *rbedit* in Command mode.

```
Command: RBEDIT
```

If you start the editor from command mode, R:BASE displays the Editor main menu, as shown in figure 8.27.

```
┌────────────┐
│ Old file...│
│ New file   │
│ Exit       │
└────────────┘




R:BASE screen editor
Database: C:..MAILING
```

Fig. 8.27

The Editor main menu.

Tip: When you start the editor with the RBEDIT command, you can include the file name on the command line:

RBEDIT *d:\path\filename.ext*

If the file exists, it is displayed on the Edit screen. If it does not exist, a blank Edit screen appears. When you exit, R:BASE asks you to confirm the file name.

To work on an existing file, choose the Old File option and then enter the name of the file in the dialog box. Enter the full file name, including a drive and directory path, if the file is not on the current drive and directory. If you are starting from the R:BASE main menu, R:BASE will display a list of all files from which you can choose. Alternatively, you can choose the Other option to enter a file name in a dialog box.

Choose the New File option to create a new file. Enter the name for the new file and include a drive and directory path if you want to store the file on a drive and directory other than the current one.

Choose the Exit option to leave the editor.

When creating a new file, the Edit screen displays only the current line and column and the message F2 to exit. On the Edit screen, you enter text by typing it and pressing Enter at the end of each line. Lines do not wrap; you must press Enter to move to a new line. You can enter approximately 600 80-character lines. The actual number of lines depends on how much text is on each line. R:BASE reserves an area of memory for the file while you are editing, so you have approximately 64K to include in the text file.

Edit text by typing over, inserting, and deleting, just as you edit any data in R:BASE. Move around on-screen by using the arrow keys and the other cursor-movement keys listed in table 8.5. Note that pressing Enter inserts new lines only at the bottom of a file. If you are in the middle of a file, pressing Enter takes you to the beginning of the next line. Several function keys are also available, as described in table 8.6.

Table 8.5
Using Cursor-Movement Keys in the Text Editor

Key	Function
Tab	Moves right to the next tab position (tab positions are in multiples of 10)
Shift-Tab	Moves left to the preceding tab position
Ctrl-→	Moves to the end of the current line
Ctrl-←	Moves to the start of the current line
Enter	Moves to the start of the next line
Home	Moves to the first page (first 23 lines) of the text file
End	Moves to the last line of the file on the first screen line
PgUp	Moves to the preceding screen page
PgDn	Moves to the next screen page

Table 8.6
Using Function Keys in the Text Editor

Key	Function
F1	Displays on-line help for the editor
Shift-F1	Displays the usable function key list
Ctrl-F6	Turns on or off Alt character repeat and enables entry of special 10-key characters on the ASCII-code numeric keypad
F6	Marks the beginning and end of a text block
F7	Searches and replaces text
Shift-F7	Specifies search/replace text
Ctrl-F7	Copies a marked text block
F8	Searches for text
Shift-F8	Specifies search text
Ctrl-F8	Moves a marked text block
F9	Deletes the current line
Ctrl-F9	Deletes a marked block of text
F10	Inserts a line above the current line

After you enter or edit the file, press F2 to exit. R:BASE displays the editor's Exit menu, as shown in figure 8.28.

The Exit menu contains the following options:

Option	Function
Edit Again	Returns you to the Edit Screen.
Save File	Saves the file as it is and returns you to the Edit screen.
Next File	Saves the current file and prompts you for a new file to edit.
Exit	Asks whether you want to save the current file (if you have changed it) and, if so, asks for a new file name or confirms an old file name.

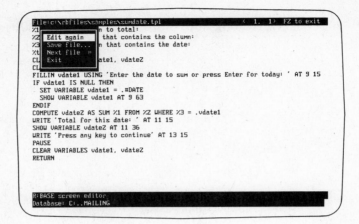

Fig. 8.28

*The editor's
Exit menu.*

```
File:c:\rbfiles\samples\sumdate.tpl                      ( 1, 1)  FZ to exit
%1            n to total:
%2  Edit again     that contains the column:
%3  Save file...   n that contains the date:
%t  Next file  »
CL  Exit           ate1, vdate2
CL
FILLIN vdate1 USING 'Enter the date to sum or press Enter for today: ' AT 9 15
IF vdate1 IS NULL THEN
  SET VARIABLE vdate1 = .#DATE
  SHOW VARIABLE vdate1 AT 9 63
ENDIF
COMPUTE vdate2 AS SUM %1 FROM %2 WHERE %3 = .vdate1
WRITE 'Total for this date: ' AT 11 15
SHOW VARIABLE vdate2 AT 11 36
WRITE 'Press any key to continue' AT 13 15
PAUSE
CLEAR VARIABLES vdate1, vdate2
RETURN



R:BASE screen editor
Database: C:..MAILING
```

Using the Custom Action

The Custom action in Application Express enables you to write a command
block to include in your application file. Usually, custom command blocks
are only a few lines long. To include longer command blocks in your
application, you need to use the Macro action instead.

You saw one example of a custom command block in this chapter's
"Setting Passwords" section. This example illustrates the typical size and
complexity of a custom block, but the only size limit is the 64K limit of
the editor.

The process for including a Custom action is similar to assigning any
action:

1. Select Custom from the Action list.

2. When prompted for a name for the custom command block, enter a
   one- to eight-character name. The name must be unique to
   command, menu, or screen blocks included in the application file.

   R:BASE starts the editor and displays the Edit screen.

3. In the editor's Edit screen, enter the custom block's commands,
   using RETURN as the last line.

4. Press F2 to leave the editor.

R:BASE returns you to Application Express, bypassing the editor Exit menu.

You may want to use a custom command block to execute commands that
are not specifically included in the Application Express list of actions.

Suppose that you want to use the Tally option in the Info module so that you can see a count of data. You could use the Modify action to get to this option in the Info module, but a more convenient method is to include the command in a custom block. You can even write the block so that the application user can pick the table and column on which to tally. The following custom command block handles this task:

```
CHOOSE vtable FROM #TBLVIEW
CHOOSE vcolumn FROM #COLUMNS IN .vtable
TALLY .vcolumn FROM .vtable
RETURN
```

The first CHOOSE command displays a pop-up menu containing the names of the tables and views in the database. The application user can highlight a table or view name and press Enter to select it.

The second CHOOSE command displays a pop-up menu containing all the columns in the table or view chosen with the first CHOOSE command. R:BASE knows which table to use because you use a variable (*vtable*) in place of the table or view name in the command.

Tip: CHOOSE is an extremely powerful and versatile R:BASE command. By using the # options (such as #COLUMNS), you can display any database item on a pop-up menu. In addition to the simple form in the example, CHOOSE has a number of other optional clauses to enable you to control where the menu is displayed on-screen, what colors to use, and whether the menu is to cascade from an already displayed menu. See "Encoding Applications" in this chapter and the discussion of CHOOSE under "Programming Commands" in Appendix C for more information.

The TALLY command then counts the occurrences of unique values in the selected column. The RETURN command tells R:BASE to send control back to the application's main command block at the point where the application called the custom block.

To use the custom block, R:BASE inserts in the main application block a RUN command that executes the custom block. The RUN command looks like this:

```
RUN custblk IN yourapp.apx
```

If you have read this chapter's section on "Creating a Start-up File," this command line should look familiar. By naming the block and the application file that contains the block, the RUN command tells R:BASE exactly what to execute.

Take a look at another example. Suppose that you need more than three levels of menus in your application. You can use a custom block to execute a second application, in effect providing another three menu levels. The custom block looks like this:

```
RUN main IN app2.apx
RETURN
```

This RUN command names the main block of the second application and the name of the executable application file. R:BASE simply leaves the first application and executes the second application. When the user exits the second application, the program returns to the next line following the RUN command in the custom block. In this case, the command is RETURN, which tells R:BASE to return to the main block in the first application. What you see here is called *nesting*. You can nest applications and stand-alone command files. As you execute through the programs, R:BASE keeps track of where you came from as well as where you are going. When you exit the inner programs, R:BASE can return you to the next level up.

As you practice writing R:BASE programs, you will discover many ways you can use custom blocks to include any type of R:BASE operation in an application.

If you need to change a custom block, use the techniques described in "Changing Actions," later in this chapter. When prompted with the Keep/ Replace/Delete menu, choose Keep. R:BASE asks whether you want to edit the custom block. Answer Yes to modify the custom block, using the editor.

Using the Macro Action

A macro is used in an application in precisely the same way a custom block is used. The only difference is that you write a macro file outside Application Express and then include the file as a command block in the application by using the Macro action.

To add an external program file as a Macro command block in an application, follow these steps:

1. Select Macro from the action list.

2. When prompted for the name of the external file, enter the full file name, including the drive and directory if the file is stored somewhere other than the current drive and directory. Do not forget to include the file extension, if any.

R:BASE searches the drive and directory for the file. If the file is found, R:BASE merges the external file as a command block in the application file and gives the block the same name as the file (without the extension). Thus, you can merge a file only once in an application to ensure that the block name is unique. If you want to execute the block from more than one menu option, you can always write a custom block to run the merged block (see "Using the Custom Action").

The Macro action enables you to use the same external command file in more than one application. Because the file is separate, you can merge it with any number of applications. This capability—probably the best and most common use of the Macro action—is almost a tradition with R:BASE developers: write a good command file once, and then use it everywhere you can. When you develop the stand-alone file for merging as a macro block, try to make it as generally useful as possible. Prompt for table, column, form, report, and label names rather than using specific names. See "Using the Custom Action" for an example.

If you need to change a macro block, use the techniques described in the "Changing Actions" section of this chapter. When prompted with the Keep/Replace/Delete menu, choose Keep. R:BASE asks whether you want to edit the macro block. Answer Yes to modify the macro block, using the editor. At this point, the macro block is exactly the same as a custom block; it is contained in the application file. An alternate method is to modify the stand-alone file that you merged by using the Macro action; then choose the Replace option and remerge the modified file.

Keep these rules in mind when using the Macro action:

- The stand-alone file must be an ASCII command file. It cannot be encoded and cannot contain command, menu, or screen blocks.

- The stand-alone file must be executable as a stand-alone file. Test the file before merging it into the application. If the file does not work on its own, it will not work in your application.

- The stand-alone file's name must be unique in the application. In other words, if you have named the application MYAPP, the stand-alone file cannot be named MYAPP, too, even if its file extension is something other than APP, APX, or API.

Using the Template Action

A *template* is a special type of file that provides a format for creating a command block. Template files are used only in Application Express. The concept behind a template file is to supply the basic commands and a "form" to fill out for adding the details. R:BASE combines a template's commands with the information provided when the template is installed to create a functional command block.

Take a look at one of the templates supplied with the R:BASE software. The following template file is named SUMDATE.TPL:

Line	Template File
1	%1 Enter the column to total:
2	%2 Enter the table that contains the column:
3	%3 Enter the column that contains the date:
4	CLEAR VARIABLES vdate1, vdate2
5	CLS
6	FILLIN vdate1 USING 'Enter the date to sum or press Enter for + today: ' AT 9 15
7	IF vdate1 IS NULL THEN
8	SET VARIABLE vdate1 = .#DATE
9	SHOW VARIABLE vdate1 AT 9 63
10	ENDIF
11	COMPUTE vdate2 AS SUM %1 FROM %2 WHERE %3 = .vdate1
12	WRITE 'Total for this date: ' AT 11 15
13	SHOW VARIABLE vdate2 AT 11 36
14	WRITE 'Press any key to continue' AT 13 15
15	PAUSE
16	CLEAR VARIABLES vdate1, vdate2
17	RETURN

First, examine the first three lines of the file beginning with %. These lines are the template form. When you use this template in Application Express, these lines are presented as prompts for you to fill in a specific column name that will be totaled, the table containing the column, and a column containing a date for comparison. Figure 8.29 shows what the screen looks like when you use the Template action to include SUMDATE.TPL in an application.

When R:BASE merges the command lines, it substitutes every occurrence of a % value used in the form lines into the command lines. For example, if you enter the column name AMOUNT when prompted for the column to sum, R:BASE substitutes AMOUNT in the commands wherever it finds %1.

Lines 4 through 17 contain the commands to be executed when the option that uses this action is selected during execution of the application. All these commands are described in Appendix C, but the following briefly explains the purposes of the lines:

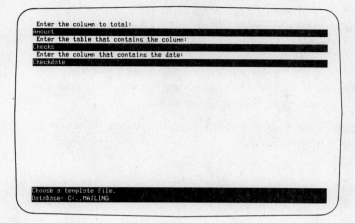

Fig. 8.29

A template file prompts you for the variable data needed to complete the command structure.

Line 4: Clears data from two variables. This command ensures that the date variables do not contain data before the rest of the commands are executed.

Line 5: Clears the entire screen.

Line 6: Prompts the user to enter a specific date. This line tells the following commands which row or rows to use to total the sum column. The date entered is loaded into variable *vdate1*.

Lines 7 and 10: Specifies the beginning and ending of an IF...ENDIF structure. IF structures test the value of a variable. If the tested condition is true, the commands contained between IF and ENDIF are executed. In this IF statement, the variable *vdate1* is tested to determine whether it does not contain a value. The variable might not contain a value if the user pressed Enter when prompted for the date on Line 7.

Line 8: If the variable *vdate1* does not contain a value (IS NULL) as tested in Line 8, the program loads the current date into variable *vdate1* by setting the variable value equal to the system date variable #DATE.

Line 9: Displays the value of *vdate1*. This line is executed only if the test in Line 8 indicates that *vdate1* is null. In this case, it will always be today's date because this line is contained within an IF structure that previously set the variable to today's date.

Line 11: Computes the sum of the column named for the %1 prompt from the table named for the %2 prompt when the column named as the date column for the %3 prompt is equal to the value of the date contained in variable *vdate1*.

Line 12: Displays the message Total for this date: on screen Line 11, starting in screen Column 15.

Line 13: Displays the summed value calculated in command Line 11 on screen Line 11, starting in screen Column 36.

Line 14: Displays the message Press any key to continue on screen Line 13, starting in screen Column 15.

Line 15: Halts execution until a key is pressed.

Line 16: Clears the values from the two variables used in the commands.

Line 17: Returns to the main block of the application.

When the user requests the option to which the Template action is assigned, the screen looks similar to figure 8.30.

Fig. 8.30

When executed, a template file executes just like any other command block.

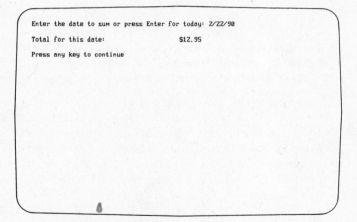

```
Enter the date to sum or press Enter for today: 2/22/90

Total for this date:              $12.95

Press any key to continue
```

Writing Trigger Files

Trigger files are command or application files executed when a form is being used. A trigger file can be executed when the cursor enters or leaves a field. A trigger file provides a great deal of processing power for a form because the file exits the form, performs any kind of calculation you want, and then returns to the form at exactly the point where the trigger was executed.

A trigger file can involve as little as executing a single command such as COMPUTE to find a total, or as much as executing a multi-level application. Although what can be done in a trigger file is limited only slightly, trigger files are usually only a few lines long. They are typically used to calculate a value that the form expressions cannot handle or to skip fields on the form if a certain value is entered in a field. You cannot do the following from a trigger file:

- Run another command or trigger file
- Create or redefine the database structure
- Assign or reassign passwords
- Execute a form
- Start any R:BASE module
- Exit or ZIP ROLLOUT from R:BASE

Using Trigger Files To Load Data

With these limitations in mind, take a look at what you *can* do with a trigger file. Examine first the field-skipping function. In the CHKBOOK database, a form enables you to enter checks, cash, or deposits all on one form. See Appendix D for a description of the CHKBOOK database. This form gives you access to three tables by using a form driven by a dummy table. The dummy table provides a means to enter data without loading it into any table; a trigger file is used for this task. The form provides fields appropriate to any of the three master tables in the database: Checks, Cash, and Deposits. Each table has a similar set of columns, so you can use the same variable entry fields for all three.

Using a dummy table for a form is a way to trick R:BASE. The dummy table is defined for the sole purpose of driving a form. No data is stored in the table except for a single row that is re-edited each time the form is used. You can use trigger files in variable forms only if you predefine the variable for the field that will execute the trigger before you define the form. There also are other limitations on a variable form. To avoid these problems, you can use a dummy table with a regular form rather than a variable form. The example database, CHKBOOK, uses a dummy table so that you can see how it works. You certainly could use a variable form instead, as long as the variables that execute triggers are defined before you create the form.

Tip: Variable forms can be a useful tool in R:BASE. They enable you to do the following:

- Gather data for manipulation or testing by a command file or to load into more than five tables.

- Capture a keystroke (Esc, Enter, PgUp, PgDn, and so on) used within the form to determine the next action.

- Replace a series of FILLIN commands.

- Define a form with more than five screen pages.

Variable form limitations include the following:

- Variable forms must be driven by a command or procedure file, which requires programming.

- You cannot use multi-row entry.

- You cannot password-protect the form.

- You cannot define a custom menu for the form.

For the dummy table, you define a single column named Dummy. The data type does not matter because the column is never used in the form. Add one row to the dummy table containing any data in the column. You then can use the EDIT USING command on the form.

When you define the form, you use a variable field (*vtype*) for entry of a table type code (CH for Checks, CA for Cash, and DE for Deposits). This field later tells the trigger file which table to load. The rest of the form consists of variable entry fields for the check number, date, payee, amount, budget code, and so on.

Three trigger files are used in the form:

- TRIGGER1.CMD executes after entry in the table type code field. The file looks like this:

```
IF vtype = 'CA' OR vtype = 'DE' THEN
   SKIP TO vchkdate
ENDIF
```

This file checks the table type code. If it is CA or DE, the program skips the check number field and continues to the date field.

```
Command: SKIP
```

- TRIGGER2.CMD executes after entry into the date field. The file looks like this:

```
IF vtype = 'CA' OR vtype = 'DE' THEN
    SKIP TO vchknote
ENDIF
```

Similar to the first trigger file, this file skips the payee field, continuing to the notation field if the table type is not CH.

- TRIGGER3.CMD executes after entry into the last field on the form (the budget code). The file looks like this:

```
IF vtype = 'CH' THEN
    INSERT INTO Checks (Budget, Checkdate, Notation, +
    Payee, Amount) VALUES (.vchkbudget, .vchkdate, +
    .vchknote, .vchkpayee, .vchkamount)
ENDIF
IF vtype = 'CA' THEN
    INSERT INTO Cash (Budget, Cashdate, Amount, +
    Notation) VALUES (.vchkbudget, .vchkdate, +
    .vchkamount, .vchknote)
ENDIF
IF vtype = 'DE' THEN
    INSERT INTO Deposits (Budget, Depdate, Amount, +
    Notation) VALUES (.vchkbudget, .vchkdate, +
    .vchkamount, .vchknote)
ENDIF
COMPUTE vdepsum AS SUM Amount FROM Deposits
COMPUTE vchecksum AS SUM Amount FROM Checks
COMPUTE vcashsum AS SUM Amount FROM Cash
SET VARIABLE vbalance = (.vdepsum - (.vchecksum + .vcashsum))
SKIP TO vtype
```

This file loads the data into the appropriate table depending on what table type code was entered. The INSERT command is used to load data directly into a table. The Values list contains the variables defined on the form to gather the data for each table. The last line in the file skips back to the table type field.

The COMPUTE command block recalculates the checkbook balance and places the balance in the variable *vbalance*. This variable also is placed on the form. The command file used to run the form contains the three COMPUTE commands and the SET VARIABLE command. The commands are executed before the form is used so that the current balance is available when the form is started.

Figure 8.31 shows what the form looks like.

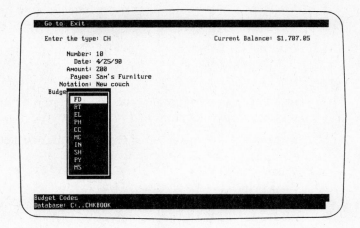

Fig. 8.31

Values calculated in a trigger file.

See Appendix D for more detailed information on the CHKBOOK database and the entry form.

Using Trigger Files To Calculate Data

The second major use of a trigger file is to calculate something that cannot be calculated in the form itself. For example, the CHKBOOK database has a YTDsummary table that contains a summary value for each budget code. This value is a running total. Each time you add a row to one of the master tables (Checks, Cash, or Deposits), you can update the YTDsummary table. YTDsummary contains a row for each budget category, so the table is similar to the Budgets table (see Appendix D). Because the purpose of the YTDsummary table is to hold a year-to-date total for each budget, however, the table also has a total column (Ytdamount). The following trigger file would maintain a running total for each budget category in the YTDsummary table each time you add a row to any of the three tables:

```
IF vytd = Y THEN
    IF vtype = 'DE' THEN
        UPDATE YTDsummary SET Ytdamount = (Ytdamount + +
        .vchkamount) WHERE Budget = .vchkbudget
    ELSE
        UPDATE YTDsummary SET Ytdamount = (Ytdamount − +
        .vchkamount) WHERE Budget = .vchkbudget
    ENDIF
ENDIF
```

This file tells R:BASE to add deposit amounts to whatever was already in Ytdamount and to subtract cash or checks from that amount.

This particular example is not used in the CHKBOOK database as a trigger file because the TRIGGER3.CMD file already is used on the last field on the form. You could incorporate this calculation trigger file by using one of these two methods:

- Add another variable to the form, such as a field that asks whether you want to update the YTDsummary table. In this case, you would need to modify the trigger file to look like this:

```
IF vytd = Y THEN
   IF vtype = 'DE' THEN
      UPDATE YTDsummary SET Ytdamount = (Ytdamount + +
      .vchkamount) WHERE Budget = .vchkbudget
   ELSE
      UPDATE YTDsummary SET Ytdamount = (YTDamount - +
      .vchkamount) WHERE Budget = .vchkbudget
   ENDIF
ENDIF
```

With this additional IF check, the YTDsummary table is updated only if the form user enters Y in the *vytd* field. Of course, in a real application, you would not design your form to give the user a choice in this type of update. The *vytd* field could be labeled with text such as Continue? and then the UPDATE commands could execute, no matter what the response.

- Add the UPDATE trigger file command lines along with the COMPUTE commands to TRIGGER3.CMD to update the checkbook balance variable.

Tip: This section illustrates the use of trigger files that feature one of the most common program control commands—IF...ENDIF. If you want to pursue programming in R:BASE, you should become familiar with the use of the IF...ENDIF structure. Other programming control commands that you will find useful include SWITCH...ENDSW, WHILE...ENDWHILE, and GOTO/LABEL.

Encoding Applications

For any function you want to perform in R:BASE, the program almost invariably provides at least two ways to do the same thing: an easy way and a not-quite-so-easy way. CodeLock provides the second type of functionality for application creation.

CodeLock functioning creates the executable application file in Application Express. What this module provides as a stand-alone utility that Application Express does not offer is the capability to combine two or more of the three building blocks of an application into a single executable file. You write the blocks as individual ASCII files—creating the menus, commands, and screens—and then combine these separate files into a functioning application.

A similar function is performed when you use the Macro action in Application Express to merge a stand-alone command file into an application file. R:BASE (through Application Express) has already built most of the application blocks for you, however. It created menu blocks when you defined menus, it created a command block as the main command section for the application, and it created a screen block if you created a help screen for a menu. You can create each of these blocks separately by using any ASCII text editor (such the R:BASE text editor), and combine them by using CodeLock.

Before using CodeLock, you need at least one command, menu, or screen file to encode. CodeLock has options for encoding or combining all three file types into their appropriate application block types.

The file you want to encode may be the APP file created by Application Express. As mentioned previously, you can edit this file and then encode it again. After you modify the file, you no longer can use Application Express to modify it.

Alternatively, you may want to encode a command file all by itself. The only purpose of this task would be to protect the file from changes. If you create a custom menu file and then call the menu from a command file, you can combine the two to create an executable application file.

You can use CodeLock to combine stand-alone files in a variety of ways. Look at figure 8.1 at the beginning of this chapter. Use this figure as a model for your own custom application, and use CodeLock to merge the parts into one functioning file. Start with a main command block containing the RUN, CHOOSE, and DISPLAY commands that will execute the subsidiary application blocks. In addition, use any other R:BASE commands you need in order to make any calculations, run forms or reports, or add or modify data in your database.

Start CodeLock from Command mode by typing *codelock*. R:BASE displays the CodeLock main menu, as shown in figure 8.32. The menu includes five encoding options and two utility options. The two utility options are similar to processes you have used before—you can display the files in a directory and display the contents of an ASCII file. These options are provided to help you find the files you are going to encode. The encoding options you use depend on the type of source files you want to encode.

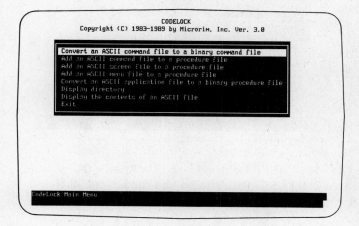

```
                              CODELOCK
              Copyright (C) 1983-1989 by Microrim, Inc. Ver. 3.0

     ┌──────────────────────────────────────────────────────────────────┐
     │ Convert an ASCII command file to a binary command file            │
     │ Add an ASCII command file to a procedure file                     │
     │ Add an ASCII screen file to a procedure file                      │
     │ Add an ASCII menu file to a procedure file                        │
     │ Convert an ASCII application file to a binary procedure file       │
     │ Display directory                                                 │
     │ Display the contents of an ASCII file                             │
     │ Exit                                                             │
     └──────────────────────────────────────────────────────────────────┘



CodeLock Main Menu
```

Fig. 8.32

CodeLock encodes command files or applications.

```
Command: CODELOCK
```

Encoding ASCII Command Files

Use the first option on the menu, Convert an ASCII Command File, when you have a stand-alone command file that you want to protect from changes. R:BASE creates an executable, binary version of the file that you can distribute to other users. Follow these steps:

1. Select the first option on the CodeLock menu.

   R:BASE displays a dialog box (see fig. 8.33).

2. Enter the name of the ASCII file to encode. The file must contain a series of one or more valid R:BASE commands. CodeLock checks for correct syntax. If your file is named OLDFILE.CMD, for example, and is stored on the current drive in directory \APPFILES, type

   \APPFILES\OLDFILE.CMD

3. Enter the name of a backup file. If you want to give your source file and your encoded file the same name and extension, be sure to enter a different name for the backup file. If you want to name the

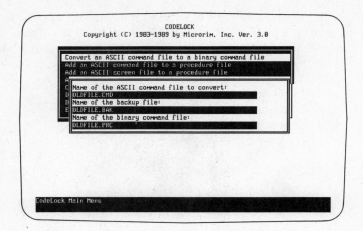

Fig. 8.33

*The CodeLock
dialog box.*

```
                         CODELOCK
              Copyright (C) 1983-1989 by Microrim, Inc. Ver. 3.0

     ┌─────────────────────────────────────────────────────┐
     │Convert an ASCII command file to a binary command file│
     │Add an ASCII command file to a procedure file         │
     │Add an ASCII screen file to a procedure file          │
     │A┌─────────────────────────────────────────┐          │
     │C│Name of the ASCII command file to convert:│          │
     │D│OLDFILE.CMD                               │          │
     │D│Name of the backup file:                  │          │
     │E│OLDFILE.BAK                               │          │
     │ │Name of the binary command file:          │          │
     │ │OLDFILE.PRC                               │          │
     │ └─────────────────────────────────────────┘          │



     CodeLock Main Menu
```

encoded file OLDFILE.CMD, for example, and the source file is
already named OLDFILE.CMD, give the backup file a name like
OLDFILE.BAK.

4. Enter a name for the encoded file. You can give it the same file
   name as the source file, but use a different extension. Otherwise the
   encoded file will be written over the source file.

R:BASE displays the commands on-screen as it checks and encodes them.

To execute the encoded file, type the RUN command at the R> prompt. If
your encoded file is named OLDFILE.PRC, for example, type

   RUN OLDFILE.PRC

Encoding ASCII Application Files

Use the fifth option on the CodeLock menu if you have modified an
Application Express APP file and then need to encode it to create an
executable application file. Follow these steps:

1. Select the fifth option on the CodeLock menu.

   R:BASE displays a dialog box (see fig. 8.34).

2. Enter the name of the ASCII application file to encode. If you have
   modified MAILAPP.APP, for example, and then want to encode it,
   type *mailapp.app*.

3. Enter a name for the encoded file. In this example, because
   Application Express has used the file name MAILAPP.APX in the

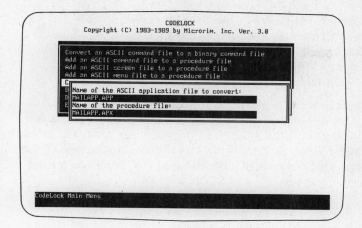

Fig. 8.34

A CodeLock dialog box prompts you for the names of the source file and the encoded application file.

application file (unless you changed the name), you need to give it this name again. If MAILAPP.APX already exists, remove it first by using the File Management options from the Tools menu.

R:BASE checks the command syntax and displays the file as it encodes it.

To execute the encoded file, you can choose it from the Applications pull-down menu (if its extension is APX) or execute it at the R> prompt by using the RUN command. If your application is named MAILAPP.APX, for example, type

   RUN MAILAPP IN MAILAPP.APX

Notice that the main command block in an Application Express-produced file always is given the same name as the application file.

Merging Stand-alone Files into Application Files

Use the second, third, and fourth options from the CodeLock menu to merge stand-alone command, screen, and menu files into a single executable application file.

The second option merges ASCII command files into an application file and makes the result a command block. A command block features $COMMAND as the first line. CodeLock adds this line to the file; your ASCII file should not begin with $COMMAND. You execute command blocks by using the RUN command.

The third option merges ASCII screen files into an application file and makes the result a screen block. A screen block features $SCREEN as the first line of the block. CodeLock adds this line to the file; your ASCII file should not begin with $SCREEN. You execute screen blocks from a command block within the application by using a DISPLAY command.

The fourth option merges ASCII menu files into an application file and makes the result a menu block. A menu block features $MENU as the first line of the block. CodeLock adds this line to the file; your ASCII file should not begin with $MENU. You execute menu blocks from a command block within the application by using a CHOOSE command. A menu block must have a valid format, as follows:

Line 1	Blank or an optional menu block name
Line 2	Menu type and optional title
Lines 3-*n*	Menu option text (If an option contains blanks, the entire option must be enclosed in pipe (I) characters.)
Last line	ENDC

Menu types can be Pull-down, Pop-up, Bar, Column, Row, Chkbox, or Chksort. Application Express uses all these types except Bar, Chkbox, and Chksort. The Bar type is like a pull-down menu except that it cannot have any submenus "pulled down" from the menu options included on it. Chkbox menus are like the menus on which you check off column names. You can choose more than one item from a list. Chksort menus are like the sorting menus used throughout R:BASE.

You also can have option descriptions on the option text lines. For example,

```
IPrint Reportsl IThis option displays the Print Reports menul
IRun Formsl IThis option executes forms for data entryl
```

Tip: Rather than use menu option text, use a # keyword to display certain database items on the menu. You can use the keywords #COLUMNS IN *tblname*, #TABLES, #VIEWS, #TBLVIEWS, #FORMS, #REPORTS, #DATABASE, or #GLOBAL (for defined global variables). When you use a # keyword, it can be the only option on the menu.

The procedure for using any of these three CodeLock options is identical. Follow these steps:

1. Select the second, third, or fourth option on the CodeLock menu.

   R:BASE displays a dialog box similar to figure 8.35.

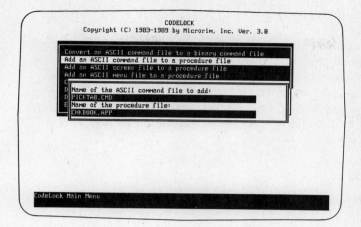

```
                            CODELOCK
             Copyright (C) 1983-1989 by Microrim, Inc. Ver. 3.0

    Convert an ASCII command file to a binary command file
    Add an ASCII command file to a procedure file
    Add an ASCII screen file to a procedure file
    Add an ASCII menu file to a procedure file
  C
  D  Name of the ASCII command file to add:
  D  PICKTAB.CMD
  E  Name of the procedure file:
     CHKBOOK.APP


  CodeLock Main Menu
```

Fig. 8.35

The CodeLock dialog box prompts you for the names of the block file and the application file.

2. Enter the name of the ASCII block file to merge into an application file.

3. Enter a name for the encoded application file. If you have merged a block before in this same session, R:BASE defaults to the name of that application file. Type over the displayed name to change to a different application. Press Enter to accept the name of the application. If the file already contains a block with the same name (the block's file name without the extension), R:BASE asks whether you want to overwrite the existing block. Answer Yes to overwrite the old block with the new block.

If the application file already exists, R:BASE adds the block to the file. If the application file does not exist, R:BASE creates it. R:BASE checks the syntax of the commands in the block and displays the block lines on-screen.

To execute this block in the application, you need a RUN command that looks like this:

    RUN *block_name* IN *application_file_name*

If you execute this command from the R> prompt, the block file executes. If necessary, you can include this RUN command in the main block of the application file, as a menu option's action, for example. (This method is how a Macro or Custom action is executed.)

Summary

In this chapter, you learned how to use Application Express to create an application without programming. You also learned a little about creating your own programs by using the Custom, Macro, and Template actions in Application Express and by examining some trigger files, which are used with forms. Finally, you learned how to combine application command, menu, and screen blocks into an executable application file by using CodeLock—the application encoder.

9

Using Relational Commands

In Chapters 2 and 3, you learned how to define your database so that tables are related. In Chapter 5, you learned how to create relationships by defining a view. In this chapter, you will learn how to create new tables by using the existing relationships between tables. If you learn how to create a good database definition and familiarize yourself with using view structures, you seldom will need to use existing relationships to relate tables. At times, however, you may need to create a table using data from two other tables, and you will not be able to use the views method. These occasions will be rare, but it is a good idea to be familiar with these commands for the infrequent times you will need them.

You can use another method of relating tables that is not included on the R:BASE menus with its full power: the SELECT command. This may be the only R:BASE command that you will use in Command mode, because nearly all other R:BASE functions are handled through the menu structures. You should become familiar with SELECT, even though its syntax diagram indicates that it is a very complex command. The description of SELECT in this chapter should provide enough information for you to get started with the command.

R:BASE provides two methods to relate tables:

- Using defined views that enable you to look at data from more than one table. Creating and using views is discussed in Chapter 5.

- Using relational commands to create new tables made up of data from existing tables. Unlike views, these new tables occupy storage space in your database.

This chapter discusses how to use the relational commands and gives situations in which you may want to create a new table containing redundant data instead of using a view definition.

395

The relational commands discussed in this chapter, except SELECT, are available through the Tools option of the main menu. SELECT is covered later in the chapter. The following section examines the relational commands available from the Tools option.

Using Simple Relational Commands

To start the Relational Tools menu, follow these steps:

1. Highlight Tools on the R:BASE main menu.

2. Select Relational Tools.

R:BASE displays the Relational Tools menu, as shown in figure 9.1.

Fig. 9.1

The Relational Tools menu.

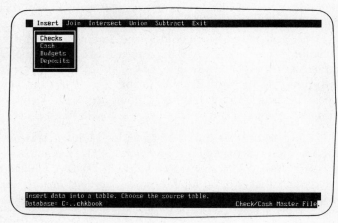

The commands on the Relational Tools menu include the following:

- *INSERT:* Adds data to a table. This command enables you to draw data from a different table in the database. The INSERT command, however, does not create a new table.

- *JOIN:* Creates a new table by combining data from two tables. The new table contains the columns and rows of two other tables. The rows in the new table are drawn from the original tables, based on a comparison of common columns.

- *INTERSECT:* Creates a new table consisting of columns from two tables. The rows added to the new table contain data from two other tables where columns match.

- *UNION:* Creates a new table containing all rows and selected columns from two other tables.

- *SUBTRACT:* Creates a new table containing selected columns and all rows from the second table without a matching common column value in the first table.

Adding Data

The INSERT command adds rows to a table. The data added can come from three sources: another table, the table to which the data is being added, keyboard entry, or global variables.

On the Relational Tools menu, you can use either of the first two methods. You can use the third method, keyboard entry, if you enter the command from the R> prompt. See the INSERT command syntax in Appendix C.

Adding Data from Tables

You can add data to a table from another table or from the table being added to. Follow these steps:

1. Highlight Insert on the Relational Tools menu.

2. Select the source table—the table that contains the data you want to add.

3. Select the columns from the source table. Press F2 when you are finished selecting columns.

4. Select the destination table—the table that is to receive the data. The destination can be the same table as the source table or a different table.

5. Select from the destination table the columns that will receive the data from the source table. Press F2 when you are finished.

   The screen looks similar to the screen shown in figure 9.2. Each menu in the figure relates to Steps 2 through 5, from left to right.

   The columns in the destination table must match the columns from the source table for number of columns and data types. The column names do not need to be the same, as long as the data will fit into the columns of the destination table.

   R:BASE displays a menu for sorting and condition setting, as shown in figure 9.3.

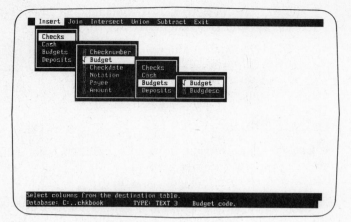

Fig. 9.2

Selecting destination columns for the data.

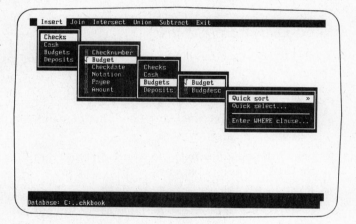

Fig. 9.3

Sorting the data to be inserted.

6. To sort the data, select Quick Sort. Then choose the columns and sort order (ascending or descending). The screen appears similar to figure 9.4. This sort procedure is standard in R:BASE (see Chapter 1 for details). When you are finished, press F2 to return to the Sort/ Condition menu.

7. To set conditions, select Quick Select.

   R:BASE displays the condition-building screen. Select the columns and comparison operators, and enter the comparison data for any conditions you want placed on the rows to be added to the destination table. After you enter the conditions, press F2 to return to the Sort/Condition menu. (See Chapter 1 for more information.)

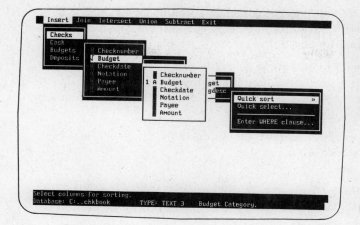

Fig. 9.4

Choosing the columns to sort by and the order of the sort.

8. To enter a WHERE clause, select Enter WHERE Clause. This process has the same effect as condition building, so do one or the other, but not both. When you have completed the WHERE clause, press Enter to return to the Sort/Condition menu.

9. Press F2 to execute the INSERT command.

   R:BASE executes the command and displays a message on the status of the execution, similar to the following message:

   ```
   Successful INSERT operation, 5 rows generated.
   ```

10. Press any key to return to the Relational Tools menu.

If the table receiving the data is protected by a password, you must have a user password that gives you INSERT privileges.

If you have defined a rule that prevents duplicate entries in the table and you are adding data to the column protected by the rule, the INSERT command will fail. To get around this problem, set Rules to Off when using INSERT (if you are the database owner).

Adding Data from the Keyboard or Variables

If you use the INSERT command at the R> prompt, you can enter the data from the keyboard or use global variables. The following INSERT command adds literal data:

```
INSERT INTO Mail_list (Firstname, Lastname) +
VALUES (John, Smith)
```

In the Mail_list table, the Idno column is an autonumber column. When you add the first and last names, R:BASE assigns the next available number to the Idno column. The rest of the columns are blank (null).

INSERT is most useful in command files. You can gather data from a variety of sources or calculate values before loading the data into a table. You can use several methods to get information from a user without a data entry form.

The following series of commands puts information into global variables that are used in the INSERT command.

```
FILLIN vfirst USING 'Enter the first name: '
FILLIN vlast USING 'Enter the last name: '
INSERT INTO Mail_list (Firstname, Lastname) +
VALUES (.vfirst, .vlast)
```

This set of commands can be repeated to add many rows. The FILLIN command enters data into a global variable (see Appendix C). These commands are useful only in a command file.

Another way to fill a variable is through a dialog box (see Appendix C). Examine this series of commands:

```
DIALOG 'Enter the first name:' vfirst vendkey1 1
IF vfirst FAILS THEN
     QUIT
ELSE
     DIALOG 'Enter the last name:' vlast vendkey2 1
ENDIF
IF vlast EXISTS THEN
     INSERT INTO Mail_list (Firstname, Lastname) +
     VALUES (.vfirst, .vlast)
ENDIF
```

This time, the first dialog box prompts for the first name. If nothing is entered, the program ends. If data is entered, the second dialog box prompts for the last name. Again, the variable is checked. If data is entered, the INSERT command is executed.

Several ways exist to accomplish the same task; these examples show you how to use some programming commands to gather data and add the data to a table.

Joining Tables

Use JOIN to create a new table if you want to copy a portion of the data from each of two tables into a third table. You can choose the type of comparison (equal, not equal, and so on) for selecting rows. For this purpose, JOIN has a special WHERE clause unlike the standard WHERE clause. The comparison is performed on the columns you specify from each source table.

The JOIN command has features that INTERSECT lacks:

- All columns are combined in the new table.

- The comparison can be between columns that do not have the same name.

- The comparison can be equal, not equal, greater than, greater than or equal, less than, or less than or equal.

Using Join from the Relational Tools menu is simply a matter of choosing the two source tables, the columns to compare, and the comparison operator, and then entering the name for the new table.

JOIN is useful when you want to combine data from two tables, but you do not have a common column linking the tables. In addition, JOIN is necessary when you want to use a nonequal comparison, such as combining data only when the two column values are not equal or when the first table's column value must be greater than the second column's value.

Intersecting Tables

INTERSECT creates a new table from the data in two source tables. A table created by INTERSECT has the same characteristics as a view, except that the two source tables must have a common column for comparison instead of a link between two similar columns. The rows with equal values in the common columns are included in the new table. Rows that do not have matching values are excluded.

Because INTERSECT extracts the same data as a view definition, you use this command only if a subsequent process requires a table rather than a view. If you want to combine data from more than five tables, for example, you can combine two or more of the tables and then use these combined tables in a view definition.

Using INTERSECT consists of choosing the two source tables and the columns from the tables to include in the destination table (one of the columns must be in both source tables). Then you enter the new table name. You can omit the second source table's columns; R:BASE automatically includes any column in the second table that has a matching column name in the first table.

Forming Unions between Tables

UNION combines all data and rows from two tables into a third table. A common column must exist between the two source tables. However, all rows are included without regard to matching values.

Suppose that you have two tables containing name and address information—one table for customers and one for creditors. If you move your place of business, you must send notes to both customers and creditors. You can extract the data twice (sending it out to a file for mail merge operations with a word processor), or you can combine the information and send it out once. The JOIN command looks like this:

```
UNION customers WITH creditors FORMING Movemail
```

One common column must exist in both tables. If a common column does not already exist, you can add a dummy column to each table to act as the common column. The dummy column does not even need to contain data, because a match is not required. In the example, you can give the name and address columns the same name in both tables so that all names and addresses will be included in the new table.

Subtracting Tables

SUBTRACT is useful for finding out what is not happening. Suppose that you have a budget table and another table with checks written (as in the CHKBOOK database). You can use SUBTRACT to find out which credit categories have not had a check written during the month. To do this, you also use a command named PROJECT, as follows:

```
*( Get the beginning and ending dates for the month )
  FILLIN vbegin USING 'Enter the month starting date: '
  FILLIN vend USING 'Enter the month ending date: '
*( Separate the month's checks into a table )
  PROJECT Tempchecks FROM Checks USING * +
    WHERE Checkdate >= .vbegin AND Checkdate <= .vend
*( Find out which budget categories were not paid )
  SUBTRACT Tempchecks FROM Budgets FORMING Notpaid
*( Display the unpaid budget categories )
  SELECT Budget Budgdesc Budgamount FROM Notpaid
*( Display a message and wait until a key is pressed )
  WRITE 'Press any key to continue.'
  PAUSE
*( Get rid of the temporary tables )
  REMOVE TABLE Tempchecks
  REMOVE TABLE Notpaid
```

If you are new to R:BASE programming, this series of commands may look complicated. The comment lines tell you what is happening in each step of the command file. Comment lines start with an asterisk and an open parenthesis and end with a close parenthesis. See Chapter 8 for more information on programming in R:BASE.

Using the SELECT Command

The SELECT command is the most versatile and complex of the R:BASE commands. Its general use is the selection and display of data from one or more tables in the database. The power of SELECT, however, is far more extensive than that statement implies.

SELECT can create an on-the-fly view. You learned about views in Chapter 5, where you created views by using options from the R:BASE menus. SELECT creates a temporary view for the immediate display of the data. The command can be recalled to execute again, or even saved in a command file for repetitive execution.

You can use SELECT as a clause in other commands. Wherever R:BASE command syntax calls for a SELECT clause, you can use the basic SELECT command syntax. The following list tells you which commands use SELECT as a clause and explains what the SELECT clause does in each command:

• *CREATE VIEW:* Selects the data to be included in a stored view.

- *DECLARE CURSOR:* Defines a path through a table, setting a pointer (cursor) to the current row.

- *INSERT:* Selects data to be added to another table from the same table or a different table.

- *QUERY:* Alternative menu-driven form of CREATE VIEW.

Some commands use parts of the SELECT syntax as their basic selection criteria. If you know how the SELECT command works, you can use the same syntax techniques in these commands:

- *BROWSE:* Selects data to be displayed in the default tabular format.

- *EDIT:* Selects data to be edited and displays it in the default tabular format.

Finally, you can use a special form of SELECT, called a sub-SELECT, in any command's WHERE clause to develop a list of data items for comparison.

If you look at the SELECT command syntax, you see that it is a maze of multilevel options. The syntax is confusing and hard to read, but you should learn about this powerful command. Examine the lines in figure 9.5.

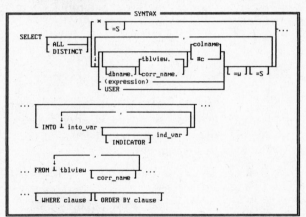

Fig. 9.5

A diagram of the SELECT command syntax.

On the main line of the diagram, you must have the command SELECT, a list of one or more columns or expressions or an asterisk to signify all columns, and the keyword FROM followed by a table or view name.

You can have these clauses:

- *INTO:* Loads the selected columns' data into variables. See "Using INTO Clauses."

- *WHERE:* Compares data in one or more columns to limit the selected rows. See "Using WHERE Clauses."

- *ORDER BY:* Sorts the data by one or more columns. See "Using ORDER BY Clauses."

The following sections describe each of these syntax parts in more detail.

Naming Tables

The keyword FROM and a table or view name are required for R:BASE to know where the data is. The loop in this part of the syntax shows that more than one table or view can be named. Each table or view name is separated from the others with a comma.

If more than one table or view is named, you should assign in the command a correlation name (corr_name) to each table or view. You use the correlation name (or *alias*) with the column names to identify which table or view contains the data you want. If a column name is unique to a table or view, you can omit the correlation name.

Suppose that you want to display data from the Checks table and Budgets table. These tables share the column Budget, so you must assign correlation names to each. The FROM part of the command looks like this:

```
FROM Checks T1, Budgets T2
```

You enter the column names first, so keep in mind what the correlation names for your tables will be.

Defining Columns

The Column section of the syntax starts with two mutually exclusive options: All and Distinct. All displays all rows that meet the conditions set in any other clause in the command. Distinct displays only unique rows that meet the conditions. Unique rows are unduplicated data in any columns displayed by the command.

The next part of Columns tells R:BASE which columns to include. To display all columns, enter an asterisk. If you want to name each column, enter the correlation name followed by the column name. The correlation name can be skipped if the column is unique to one table in the FROM list. In this column list, you tell R:BASE to get the values from four columns:

```
CheckNum, T1.Budget, Budgetdesc, Amount
```

CheckNum and Amount are unique to the Checks table, so you do not have to include the correlation name. Budgetdesc is unique to the Budgets table, so again no correlation name is required. Budget, however, is common to both tables. The correlation name for the Checks table is specified because you want the data related to items in Checks, not necessarily all items in Budgets. This designation limits the rows because common data for Budget must be in Checks, and any Budget values only in Budgets will not be included.

If you are familiar with your tables, you can take a short cut by entering # followed by a number corresponding to a column's position in the table. For example, to include the first, third, and fourth columns, enter the column list like this:

    #1, #3, #4

You can include an expression in the column list just as if the expression were a column. The expression usually, but not necessarily, includes at least one column from any table in the FROM list. An expression used in the column list is like a temporary computed column; the expression calculates something for you when the command executes. The expression can be a mathematical calculation, a text string, or a date or time calculation. You can use any of the SuperMath functions, the system variables (#DATE, #TIME, #PI), literal values, columns, or global variables. Expressions always must be enclosed in parentheses. Here are a few examples of valid expressions:

(items * cost): Displays the multiplication of two columns

('The net amount is: '): Displays the literal text string inside the quotation marks

(enddate - startdate): Calculates the integer number of days difference between the two DATE column values

USER simply displays the current user password.

The option dbname.tblview. or dbname.corr_name. is an SQL convention that makes the SELECT command ANSI-standard. The database named must be the open database and other databases cannot be named. Without dbname, a table or view name can be combined with a column name rather than a correlation name.

If you specify a column or expression, you can adjust the display width by adding = and a width to each. For example, Integer columns are displayed in a nine-character field. If you know that your values have no more than three digits, add =3 next to the Integer column name. If you do not leave sufficient display width for a column, R:BASE displays the field filled with asterisks.

You also can total the entire set of values for a column by appending = S to each column you want added. If you select all columns, you can add = S to the asterisk, and R:BASE provides a total for all numeric columns:

SELECT * = S

Finally, note the loop back in the Column syntax. This loop simply shows that you can repeat the looped part of the syntax diagram as many times as you want. Each iteration of the loop is separated from the next with a comma. The following Column list includes several of the features:

CheckNum = 4, T1.Budget, Budgetdesc = 20, ('The Amount is: ') + Amount = S

By taking each part of the Column syntax by itself, you quickly will understand how each part is used:

- *Checknum = 4:* Displays the data in Checknum limited to a width of four characters.

- *T1 Budget:* Displays the data in the Budget column only from the table assigned to correlation T1.

- *Budgetdesc = 20:* Displays the data in the Budgetdesc column limited to a width of 20 characters.

- *('The Amount Is:'):* Displays the text The Amount Is: before the next column's data.

- *Amount = S:* Displays the data in the Amount column and, after all data is displayed, provides the total of all amounts at the end of the display.

Using INTO Clauses

INTO loads into variables the data extracted by the rest of the SELECT command. After the SELECT command is executed, these global variables can be manipulated in any way a variable can be used. Including INTO suppresses display; the variables are loaded with values, but no data is shown. The Column list specifies the order and number of data items that will be loaded into the variable list. The first Column item's data is loaded into the first variable, the second item's data into the second variable, and so on. A *data item* is a column, variable, or expression included in the Column part of the syntax. The number of variables must match the number of Column items.

The variables that receive the data are called *into_vars*. A second variable, following the INDICATOR keyword, is used to store the status of the data in the *into_var*. For example, if the value loaded is null, the value of the INDICATOR variable is −1. If a value exists, the INDICATOR variable's value is 0. If the value was too long for the variable, the INDICATOR variable's value is an integer showing the actual length of the data.

Tip: When using INTO, limit the data to a single row. Otherwise, the results loaded into the variables may not be what you expect.

Using WHERE Clauses

The WHERE clause for the SELECT command is the standard R:BASE WHERE clause. The WHERE clause limits the rows acted on by the command. For the syntax of a WHERE clause, see Appendix B.

WHERE-clause processing uses column indexes if they are defined for a column specified in the clause. (See Chapter 3 for information on defining an index for a column.) Indexed columns speed the processing of a WHERE clause if the following conditions are met:

- The comparison operator is =, IS NULL, or BETWEEN.
- The WHERE clause contains more than one condition.
- At least one indexed column is compared in the WHERE clause.

A WHERE clause consists of a series of conditions connected by a comparison operator. Each condition causes some restriction on the rows used by the command. A condition accomplishes this restriction by comparison of items, the comparison being determined by the comparison operator inserted between the first and second items.

For example, the command

    SELECT * FROM Checks WHERE Checknumber >= 20

displays all columns from the checks table where the value of Checknumber is greater than or equal to zero.

The first item in the condition is usually a column contained in any table or view named in the FROM clause of the SELECT command. However, the first item also can be a literal value or an expression.

Using Comparison Operators

The comparison operator determines the effect of the comparison. Should the first and second items be equal? Not equal? Of some other relationship? Table 9.1 lists the comparison operators.

Table 9.1
Using Comparison Operators

Operator	Meaning
=	Equal. Item 1 and Item 2 must be equal.
<>	Not equal. Item 1 and Item 2 must not be equal.
>	Greater than. Item 1 must be greater than Item 2.
>=	Greater than or equal to. Item 1 must be greater than or equal to Item 2.
<	Less than. Item 1 must be less than Item 2.
<=	Less than or equal to. Item 1 must be less than or equal to Item 2.
BETWEEN	Item 1 is always a column, and its value must be within the listed range of values that comprise Item 2. For example, this condition selects rows only when the date value is a day in March: Datecolumn BETWEEN 03/01/90, 03/31/90.
NOT BETWEEN	Item 1 is always a column, and its value must not be within the listed range of values that comprise Item 2. This condition, for example, selects all rows except those with a date value in March: Datecolumn NOT BETWEEN 03/01/90, 03/31/90.
CONTAINS	Item 1 is always a column, and its value must contain the value indicated by Item 2. For example, *ed* is contained in *Editor* and *Fred*.
NOT CONTAINS	Item 1 is always a column, and its value must not contain the value indicated by Item 2.
IN	Item 1's value matches one of the values indicated in Item 2. For example, this condition selects all rows with an ID number of 1, 2, or 5: Idnumber IN (1, 2, 5).
NOT IN	Item 1's value should not match any of the values indicated in Item 2.

Table 9.1—*continued*

Operator	Meaning
LIKE	Item 1's value must be similar to Item 2. For example, this condition selects rows where a last name is Browne: Lastname LIKE 'Brown'.
NOT LIKE	Item 1 must not be similar to Item 2.

In addition to comparing Item 1 and Item 2, the WHERE clause can contain conditions that stand by themselves. Table 9.2 lists these conditions.

Table 9.2
Using Stand-alone Comparison Operators

Operator	Meaning
IS NULL	Item 1 must not contain a value (no Item 2 exists).
IS NOT NULL	Item 1 must contain any value (no Item 2 exists).
COUNT = value	Item 1 is the COUNT of rows. Item 2 is the row number. The row selected depends on the sort order.
LIMIT = value	Item 1 is a LIMIT on the number of rows. Item 2 is the number of rows to include. The rows included depend on the sort order. If this condition is included in a WHERE clause, this condition should be the last in the clause.

Item 1 can be a column in one or more of the tables specified in the command, and if allowed by the comparison operator, Item 1 also can be a literal value or an expression.

Specifying Item 1

When a column is specified for Item 1 and if the column is contained in more than one table used by the command, you must include the table name or the correlation (alias) name. You use the names in the same way:

tablename.columnname
aliasname.columnname

To specify the Budget column from the Budgets table, for example, (assuming that the Budgets table was assigned the correlation name T1) either of these specifications works:

Budgets.Budget
T1.Budget

The column in the WHERE clause does not have to be included in the command's column list. The column can be some other column in any table named in the command.

When a literal value is specified in a condition for Item 1, the value can be entered directly, or the value can be contained in a variable. In this case, you precede the variable name with a dot to tell R:BASE to use the value of the variable, not the variable name. This feature is useful especially in command files, when the value is extracted from another source, such as keyboard entry. The variable even can contain a column name.

When an expression is specified as Item 1, the expression can contain column names, SuperMath functions, and arithmetic operators. In other words, the expression can be any valid arithmetic, mathematical, or concatenation expression.

Specifying Item 2

Item 2 in a condition can be a column name, literal value, expression, value list, or a sub-SELECT. Unless Item 2 is a value list or a sub-SELECT, the requirements and rules are the same as described for Item 1.

Value lists are used with the IN and NOT IN comparison operators. Each of these values can be a literal value or a list of dotted variables. The format of a value list is

(value1, value2, value3, ...)

If Item 2 is a value or a value list, text values can use the R:BASE wild-card characters % (substitute for a single character) and _ (substitute for one or more characters). The following example shows wild-card characters in text values:

textcolumn LIKE 'PART-_'

This expression finds all rows where the text column contains "PART-" followed by any one or more characters.

For information on sub-SELECTs, see "Using Sub-SELECT," later in this chapter.

Connecting Conditions

You can connect a series of conditions by using any of the connecting operators. The following list gives the connecting operators and tells what each means:

- *AND:* Both conditions—the condition following and the condition before AND—must be true.

- *OR:* The condition before or after the OR must be true.

- *AND NOT:* The condition following the AND NOT must be false, and the condition before AND NOT must be true.

- *OR NOT:* The condition following OR NOT must be false, and the condition before OR NOT must be true.

By default, R:BASE follows *AND precedence*—processing all AND and AND NOT conditions before any OR or OR NOT conditions. This precedence can be changed to processing from left to right. Change the SET AND status from On to Off. See Appendix B for information on changing the R:BASE environment.

Another method of overriding the AND precedence is to use parentheses in the WHERE clause. As in mathematical expressions, parentheses force R:BASE to evaluate the expression in parentheses before items not contained in parentheses. The innermost parenthetical item in nested parentheses is evaluated first. Consider these examples of processing order:

```
WHERE column1 = 1 AND column2 = 1 OR column2 = 3
WHERE column1 = 1 AND (column2 = 1 OR column2 = 3)
```

In this example, the parentheses change which rows are selected. The following numbers are the data:

	column1	column2
row1	1	2
row2	1	3
row3	2	2
row4	2	3

The first WHERE clause selects row1, row2, and row4. The second WHERE clause selects row1 and row2. The second WHERE clause gets less data because the part of the clause contained in parentheses is evaluated first and selects all rows; then the rest of the clause is evaluated, eliminating any row that does not have a 1 in column1.

Using ORDER BY Clauses

The ORDER BY clause for the SELECT command sorts the rows on which the command acted. ORDER BY clauses can use only columns contained in the tables named in the command. When a column is specified in an ORDER BY clause, and the column is contained in more than one table used by the command, you must include the table name or the correlation alias (name) to tell R:BASE which table or view to use. Use names this way:

tablename.columnname
aliasname.columnname

To specify the Budget column from the Budgets table, assuming that the Budgets table was assigned the correlation name T1, either of these specifications works:

Budgets.Budget
T1.Budget

The column in the ORDER BY clause does not have to be included in the command's column list. The column in the clause can be a column in any table named in the command.

If not otherwise specified, R:BASE sorts in ascending order—A to Z, 1 to higher numbers. You can reverse the sort order by including DESC next to the column name (you can specify ASC, but you do not need to). The following ORDER BY clause sorts by state in ascending order. Under state, the ZIP codes are sorted in descending order:

ORDER BY State, Zipcode DESC

Using Sub-SELECT

A sub-SELECT is a SELECT command contained in a WHERE clause following the IN, NOT IN, ALL, ANY, or SOME WHERE clause operators. The purpose of the sub-SELECT is to create a value list as Item 2 in a condition. The following describes the sub-SELECT operators:

- *IN:* The result of the condition must be that the requested data is contained in the list.

- *NOT IN:* The requested data must not be in the list.

- *ALL:* The result of the condition must be that all the requested data items in the list match the comparison column.

- *ANY:* The data list must contain at least one data item that matches the comparison column.

- *SOME WHERE:* SOME WHERE is equivalent to ANY.

Here is an example of a sub-SELECT:

```
SELECT * FROM Checks WHERE Budget NOT IN +
(SELECT Budget FROM Budgets)
```

This SELECT command displays all columns from the Checks table that have a Budget code which is not entered in the Budgets table. R:BASE develops the value list by selecting all Budget codes from Budgets. R:BASE then compares the Budget column in Checks to that list. If a Budget code in Checks is not in the list, the row is displayed.

Two restrictions exist on what can be used in the SELECT command when it is used as a sub-SELECT:

- Do not use =S (sum the column) or =w (change the display width) with any column name in the sub-SELECT.

- Do not use an INTO clause to load the derived data into variables in the sub-SELECT.

You can have another sub-SELECT in a sub-SELECT's WHERE clause—this condition is called *nesting*. You also can use a GROUP BY SELECT to make the data list a summary of data in the sub-SELECT table.

Grouping Data

You can have the SELECT command group together similar sets of data by using the GROUP BY syntax of the command. The syntax is similar to the SELECT syntax described previously, except for the following differences:

- In addition to the other Column items, you can include a grouping function (sel_func) before a column name to calculate the sum, average, minimum, maximum, or count of the column within the group.

- Omit the ORDER BY clause; the GROUP BY clause replaces the ORDER BY clause.

- Add a GROUP BY clause to specify how to group and sort the data.

Figure 9.6 shows the complete syntax of GROUP BY SELECT.

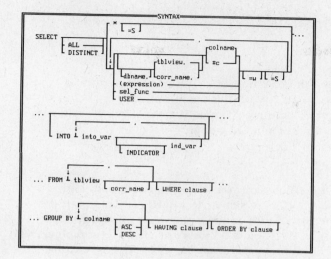

Fig. 9.6

A diagram of the GROUP BY SELECT command syntax.

If you compare this syntax to the earlier SELECT syntax diagram, you will find the addition of the Select function in the Column section of the diagram and the omission of the ORDER BY clause (replaced by the GROUP BY clause).

This section describes these two modifications of the diagram; the rest of the diagram for GROUP BY SELECT is explained in the sections for SELECT earlier in this chapter.

Using Functions

The grouping functions enable you to perform simple arithmetic calculations on the column data as it is grouped together by the GROUP BY clause. The grouping functions follow:

- *SUM:* Adds the values of the column in all the rows to present one summed value for each group.

- *AVG:* Presents the average of the values of the column within the group.

- *MIN:* Presents the minimum value of the column within the group.

- *MAX:* Presents the maximum value of the column within the group.

- *COUNT:* Counts the occurrences of the column values within the group.

- *COUNT (*):* Counts the number of rows within the group.

The following GROUP BY SELECT uses the MIN and MAX functions:

```
SELECT Budget, MIN Amount, MAX Amount FROM Checks +
GROUP BY Budget
```

Notice that you can name the column more than once to perform a different function on the column. With this command, all rows with the same value in the Budget column are grouped together, and the minimum and maximum values in the Amount column are presented.

Setting Group Conditions

When you use the GROUP BY syntax, you can set special conditions with the HAVING clause. HAVING is similar to a WHERE clause, but the conditions are set on the rows in the group rather than on all rows in the table. In other words, HAVING acts on the rows after the grouping takes place, rather than on the raw data from the table. This is a subtle distinction, but try setting the conditions for a GROUP BY SELECT in a WHERE clause and then try the same conditions in the HAVING clause. Look at this series of SELECT commands:

```
SELECT Budget ‹ Amount FROM Checks
```

The first SELECT shows the data contained in the table. The following data is displayed:

```
Budget      Amount
------      -------
    FD      $200.00
    FD      $100.00
    FD      $100.00
    FD       $12.95
    RT      $565.00
```

Then issue this command:

```
SELECT Budget SUM Amount FROM Checks GROUP BY Budget +
WHERE COUNT = 1
```

The second SELECT limits the rows to the first row in the table with a WHERE clause. The following is displayed:

```
Budget  SUM(Amount)

    FD      $200.00
```

Then enter this command:

```
SELECT Budget SUM Amount FROM Checks GROUP BY Budget +
HAVING COUNT = 1
```

The third SELECT limits the rows generated by the GROUP BY clause for each of the summarized rows. In this case, the COUNT = 1 condition operates on each summarized row, not all rows in the table. The following is displayed:

```
Budget    SUM(Amount)

   FD       $412.95
   RT       $565.00
```

Summary

This chapter explained how to use the R:BASE relational commands. The chapter included information on INSERT, JOIN, INTERSECT, UNION, SUBTRACT, and SELECT. You learned how to use INSERT, JOIN, INTERSECT, UNION, and SUBTRACT from the Relational Tools menu. Then you learned about using the SELECT command through Command mode at the R> prompt.

10

Importing and
Exporting Data

Sometimes you may want to send data from a database to another software system, or you may want to move data from another system into a database. Many people who use a database also have a spreadsheet system, such as Lotus, that is useful for producing "what if" types of reports. To simplify sending data back and forth between software products, Microrim developed the GATEWAY import/export utility. GATEWAY makes moving data in and out of R:BASE in a variety of file formats a simple procedure.

With GATEWAY, you can create files in the following formats:

- Lotus 1-2-3 and Symphony
- dBASE III and III PLUS
- DIF file format products such as VisiCalc
- Multiplan SYLK files
- ASCII delimited and fixed field

In addition, you can import data from files with any of these formats, and from PFS:File forms as well. Note that you can read dBASE files directly in R:BASE by using the ATTACH command or by selecting dBASE File from the Databases pull-down menu on the R:BASE main menu.

Using GATEWAY

You can start GATEWAY in any of the following ways:

- From the Tools pull-down menu, choose Import/Export.

- At the R> prompt, type *gateway*.

419

- From Prompt By Example, choose Option 7, R:BASE and Operating System Utilities, from the PBE main menu. Then choose Import/ Export from the R:BASE and Operating System Utilities menu.

- At the DOS prompt, type *gateway*.

```
Command: GATEWAY
```

Regardless of how you start GATEWAY, R:BASE displays the GATEWAY main menu shown in figure 10.1. The Import and Export options are the most important—they are the operational part of GATEWAY. The Disk Management and Settings options provide the convenience of not having to leave GATEWAY to change the database operating environment or to find the name of a file you want to import, for example.

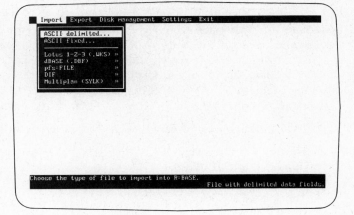

Fig. 10.1

The GATEWAY main menu with the Import options shown.

Exporting Files

In addition to enabling you to bring new data into R:BASE from other systems, the GATEWAY import/export utility enables you to move data back and forth between R:BASE and other systems. You may want to move data back and forth like this if the other system provides some special tools or calculation abilities that R:BASE does not have, or if you just feel more comfortable manipulating data with the other system. The export function of GATEWAY is covered first in this chapter for that reason.

If you choose to export data, you see the options shown in figure 10.2.

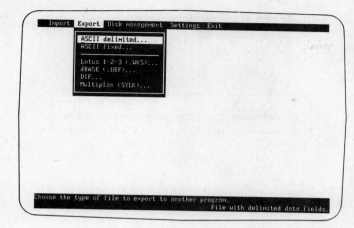

Fig. 10.2
Options for
exporting.

When you choose an export file type, R:BASE creates a DOS file in a format compatible with the system or format you select. If you choose Lotus, for example, Lotus can read the file created with no further modification. As far as the other system is concerned (such as Lotus), the file you create with GATEWAY is the same as if it were created by the other system.

To export data to a file, highlight the file type in which you want to send the data and press Enter. The next few sections describe the general operation of exporting. See "Specifying Export Characteristics," later in this chapter, for specific information on file types.

Naming Files, Databases, Tables, and Columns

When you export data, you need to tell R:BASE where to put the data in the new format. You also must specify the database, table, and columns that the data is coming from. R:BASE displays a dialog box for the name of the export file. To export data, follow these steps:

1. Enter a valid DOS file name for the export data (see fig. 10.3). If you are sending data to a system that uses a specific extension for its files (such as WKS for Lotus), use the appropriate extension. Include a drive and directory path if you want to store the file on a drive or directory other than the current one.

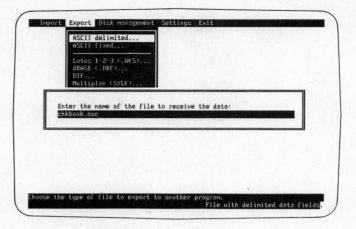

Fig. 10.3

Entering the export file name.

Next, R:BASE needs to know where the data is that you want to export. As figure 10.4 shows, R:BASE displays a dialog box with a variety of prompts to determine the exact data you want to export. The first prompt is for the database.

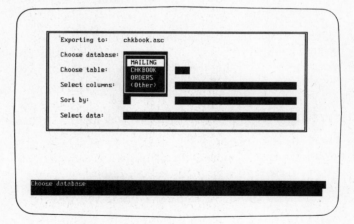

Fig. 10.4

Specifying the database to export from.

2. Choose the database that contains the data you want to export. If the database is stored on a drive and directory other than the current one, choose the (Other) option to enter a database name with a drive and directory path.

   After you select the database, R:BASE lists the tables and views contained in the database (see fig. 10.5).

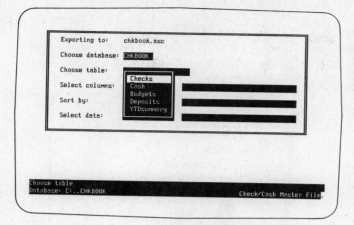

Fig. 10.5

Selecting the table containing the export data.

3. Highlight the table containing the data you want to export and press Enter.

   R:BASE then prompts you for the columns from the table, as shown in figure 10.6.

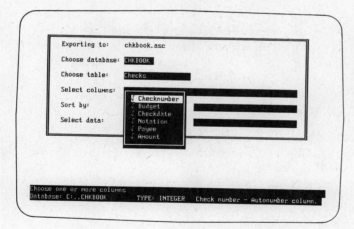

Fig. 10.6

Specifying the columns for export.

4. Highlight each column you want to include and press Enter to place a check mark next to the columns you want to select. To select all columns, press Shift-F6. After you select the columns, press F2.

You now are at a point where you can export the data. However, you may want to export the data in a specific order or limit the rows exported. The next two sections describe how to use these options.

Sorting Data

You can sort the data as it is exported to the file. Sorting in GATEWAY is exactly the same as sorting anywhere else in R:BASE. R:BASE asks for the sort column and the sort order for that column—ascending or descending (see fig. 10.7).

Fig. 10.7

Sorting the export data.

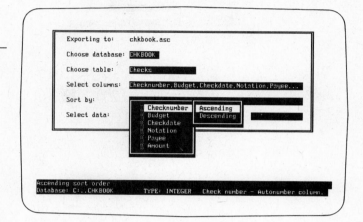

Select a column to sort by and select the sort order. For the Date_mailed table, for example, you may want to sort the data by the Idno column and then the Maildate column. After you select the sort columns and order, press F2.

Limiting Data with WHERE Clauses

You can specify exactly which rows to export by using the standard R:BASE condition builder. After you select the data to be sorted or choose not to sort data, R:BASE displays the condition builder.

Choose a column on which conditions are to be set, select the comparison operator, and then enter the comparison value. You may, for example, want to export only rows for a specific budget type. In this case, choose Budget for the column and = for the comparison operator. Then enter the budget code (such as FD for food) as the comparison value. Figure 10.8 shows how this condition looks.

Choose (Done) from the connecting operator list after you set the conditions.

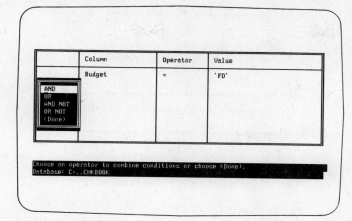

Fig. 10.8

*Setting
conditions.*

Specifying Export Characteristics

R:BASE asks for specific information, depending on the export file type you
select. The following sections describe the requirements for each file type.
After you specify these characteristics for your export file, you are ready to
send the data to the file.

For all export file types, you also can limit the rows by count to export
only a sample of the data. When R:BASE asks whether you want to
export all rows, answer No and then enter the maximum number of rows
to export. This happens after you answer the file-specific prompts
described in the next few sections.

For ASCII file types, R:BASE also asks whether you want to end each
exported row with a carriage return/line feed character. Using this
character is a good idea because most programs that read ASCII delimited
files expect to find a CR/LF at the end of each record.

Exporting to ASCII Delimited Files

Enter the delimiter character that you want to use to divide the data on
each import file line into columns. The default delimiter character is a
comma. See "Importing ASCII Delimited Files," later in this chapter, for
more information.

After you choose the ASCII delimited file type and enter the file, table, and
columns on the Export screen, R:BASE prompts you for the delimiter
character (see fig. 10.9). Enter the delimiter character that you want to
divide the column data or press Enter to accept the comma as the
delimiter.

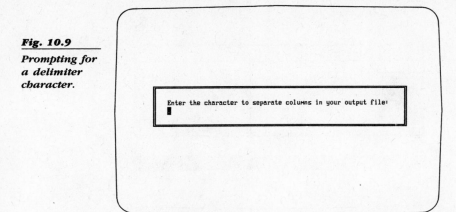

Fig. 10.9

*Prompting for
a delimiter
character.*

Exporting to ASCII Fixed-Field Files

ASCII fixed-field files are DOS files containing ASCII data with each piece
of the data in a fixed location in each record. See "Importing ASCII Fixed-
Field Files," later in this chapter, for more information on fixed-field
formats.

For ASCII fixed-field files, you need to indicate the size of each field (see
fig. 10.10). R:BASE sends the data for each column to a fixed position field
in the file. To change the default lengths as shown on-screen, type over
the length for each field you want to change. These changes appear at the
bottom of the screen on a row of sample data.

Fig. 10.10

*Changing the
width of the
data fields.*

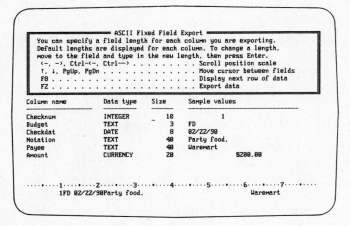

Exporting to Lotus and Symphony

For Lotus and Symphony files, you need to determine whether to export column names to the spreadsheet file. If you do export column names, you also need to enter the spreadsheet row or column for the column names. To send the column names to Row 1 in the spreadsheet, for example, press 3 (see fig. 10.11).

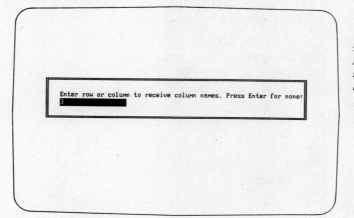

Fig. 10.11

Naming the spreadsheet label area.

If you do not send the column names as data, you need to tell R:BASE how to orient the data—by row or column. Choose Row or Column to specify the orientation. Finally, R:BASE prompts you to specify the upper-left cell to receive data (see fig. 10.12). If you put your column names in Row 3, for example, then you may want the data to start in cell A4.

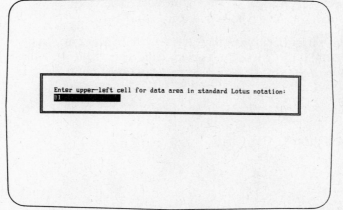

Fig. 10.12

Specifying where to place the data in a Lotus or Symphony file.

Row orientation means that all column data is sent to the export system file row-by-row from the table. *Column orientation* exports all data in all rows from the first column, moves to the next column and exports all data in all rows from that column, and so on.

Lotus and Symphony use a different set of data types than R:BASE. However, most data types are similar enough that R:BASE can guess the correct data type. Table 10.1 lists the R:BASE data type and the Lotus/Symphony data type that R:BASE chooses for the data.

Table 10.1
R:BASE to Lotus/Symphony Data Types

R:BASE Data Type	Lotus/Symphony Data Type
Currency	Currency
Date	Date exported using the @DATE function
Double	General
Integer	General
Note	Text
Real	General
Text	Text
Time	Text

The data formats exported as the Lotus/Symphony General data type are in the same format as in R:BASE.

Exporting to dBASE

R:BASE column names are exported as dBASE column names. If the column name is not valid for dBASE, R:BASE displays a message. You need to rename the invalid column names before you can export the data.

dBASE uses a different set of data types than R:BASE. Most data types are similar enough that R:BASE can guess the correct data type. Table 10.2 lists the R:BASE data type and the dBASE data type that R:BASE chooses for the data.

Table 10.2
R:BASE to dBASE Data Types

R:BASE Data Type	dBASE Data Type
Currency	Numeric (length, 15)
Date	Date (length, 8)
Double	Numeric (default length, 10)
Integer	Numeric (length, 10)
Note	Memo (creates a separate file with the same file name and the extension DBT)
Real	Numeric (default length, 10)
Text	Character (maximum length, 254 characters)
Time	Character (length set by the R:BASE TIME format)

If you have a decimal number (Real or Double), R:BASE enables you to specify the length and number of decimal places for the exported data.

dBASE character fields can contain only 254 characters, whereas R:BASE Text columns can contain up to 1,500 characters. If your Text columns are longer than 254 characters, the data is truncated in dBASE. To prevent truncation, split your Text columns into multiple columns with fewer than 254 characters in each column (a difficult process), or change the Text data type to Note so that R:BASE exports long Text fields as dBASE Memo files.

dBASE also limits the total number of fields to 128; R:BASE enables you to include up to 400 fields. If you attempt to export more than 128 columns, R:BASE simply ignores all columns beyond the maximum 128.

dBASE does not recognize B.C. dates. If any of your Date columns contain B.C. dates, those columns are exported to dBASE as null values.

Exporting to DIF (VisiCalc) Files

DIF files are the standard format for VisiCalc as well as several other software products. If the software to which you want to export data accepts the DIF format, you can use the VisiCalc option to export data.

R:BASE only needs to know whether you want to export column names as DIF labels. Answer Yes or No, depending on whether you want to include the column names as labels in the exported data.

Exporting to SYLK (Multiplan) Files

Multiplan is a spreadsheet format, so you need to enter the upper-left cell for the data in standard Multiplan notation. If you want to export the data so that the upper-left corner begins at Row 2, Column 3, for example, you should type *r2c3*.

A Multiplan spreadsheet is limited in the amount of data it can hold. Be sure that the data you want to export is suitable for the Multiplan format.

Multiplan uses a different set of data types than R:BASE. Most are similar enough that R:BASE can guess the correct data type. Table 10.3 lists the R:BASE data type and the Multiplan data type that R:BASE chooses for the data.

Table 10.3
R:BASE to Multiplan Data Types

R:BASE Data Type	Multiplan Data Type
Currency	Dollar
Date	General
Double	General
Integer	Integer
Note	Continuous
Real	General
Text	General
Time	General

Completing the Export

After you specify the characteristics for your export file, you can export the data to the file by pressing F2. R:BASE displays a screen showing the count of rows as they are exported (see fig. 10.13). If any errors occur, R:BASE displays a message and halts the export if the error is fatal (for example, column names are invalid). The export continues if the error is not fatal (for example, if you try to export too many columns for the export file type).

You now have completed the export process. You can exit from R:BASE and load the exported data using the appropriate software program.

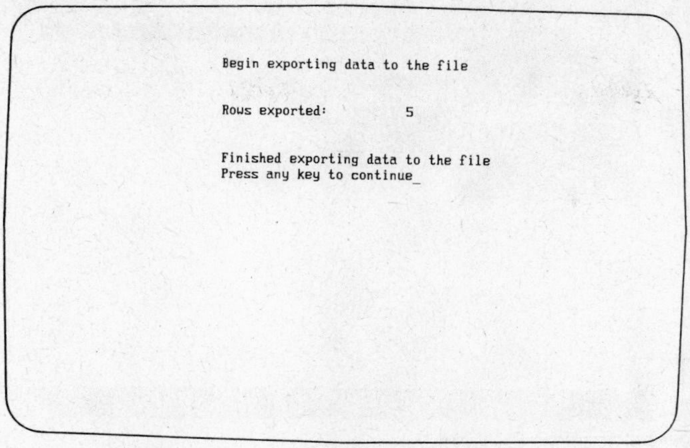

```
Begin exporting data to the file

Rows exported:          5

Finished exporting data to the file
Press any key to continue_
```

Fig. 10.13
*A row count
indicating the
number of
rows exported.*

Importing Files

After you export data and modify it by using the appropriate software, you
can bring the data back into R:BASE. You also can import new data into
R:BASE. The process for importing is similar to the process for exporting.
You can import the same types of files that you can export, and you can
import PFS:File forms as well. You simply name the file to import and then
specify the database and table to receive the imported data. Neither the
database nor the table needs to exist for the import. If you want, R:BASE
creates a new database and/or table for you from the import data, enabling
you to import data from other systems without going through the database
definition process.

Naming Files

The next few sections describe the general process of importing data. See
"Specifying Import Characteristics" for specific details on the different
file types.

You begin the import by choosing the type of file you want to import
from the Import pull-down menu. If you choose a file type that has a
specific extension—such as WKS for 1-2-3 files—R:BASE prompts you with
a list of files with that extension (see fig. 10.14). If the file you want to
import to is on the list, highlight the file name and press Enter. If the file
is on a different drive or directory, you can choose Other and then enter
the file name in the dialog box that R:BASE displays. If the file type you
choose does not have an identifying extension, R:BASE displays a dialog
box instead of a list of files.

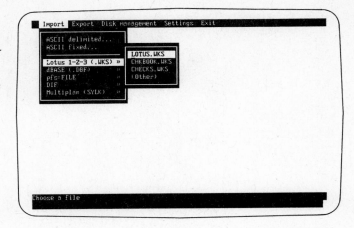

Fig. 10.14

Choosing the file where the import data is to be placed.

After you name the file to import, R:BASE displays the Import dialog box, where you answer several prompts to specify exactly how to import the data (see fig. 10.15).

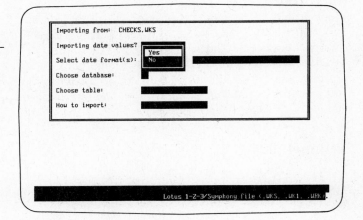

Fig. 10.15

The Import dialog box.

Setting Date Formats

The first prompt in the Import dialog box asks whether the data to import contains dates. You must specify the date format used in the import data so that R:BASE can recognize the date fields when it encounters them. If you are not sure about the format, answer Yes and select all the date formats to ensure that date values can be imported. Figure 10.16 shows the Date Format Selection list. To select a date format, highlight the format and press Enter to place a check mark beside that format, or press Shift-F6 to select all the formats. After you select the date formats, press F2.

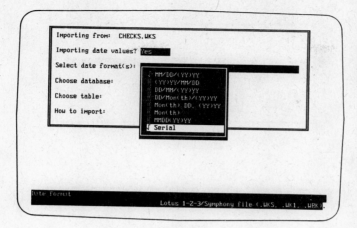

Fig. 10.16

Indicating the date formats.

Choosing Databases and Tables

Next, R:BASE prompts you with a list of databases on the current drive and directory (see fig. 10.17). Choose a database from the list to import the data to an existing database. You also can choose Other to enter a database name with a drive and directory path if the database resides on a different drive and directory, or New to have R:BASE create a new database for you.

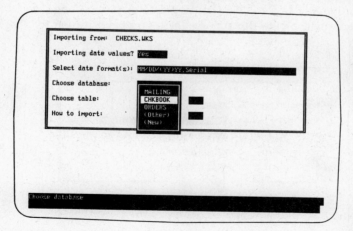

Fig. 10.17

Choosing a database to receive the import data.

R:BASE then asks you for the name of the table. If you choose an existing database, R:BASE displays a list of the tables that includes an additional option: (New) (see fig. 10.18). If you choose to create a new database, R:BASE shows only the (New) option. Use (New) when you want to create a new table for the import data.

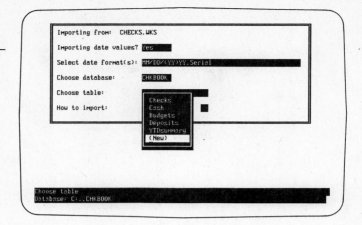

Fig. 10.18

*Choosing a
table to
receive the
data.*

If you choose an existing table with passwords assigned, R:BASE asks for a
password before you can import data into the database. Enter a password
that enables you to use Insert privileges. See Chapter 3 for information on
defining passwords for a database.

In addition, R:BASE asks whether you want to append the new data to
existing data, replace the existing data with new data, or overwrite the
entire table with a new structure and new data (see fig. 10.19). The
Append option adds the data to the table. Replace deletes the existing data
and then adds the new data. Overwrite acts just as if you have chosen to
create a new table.

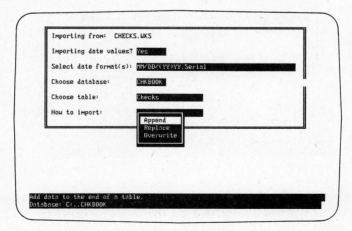

Fig. 10.19

*Importing into
an existing
table.*

If you select the (New) option instead of an existing table, R:BASE prompts
you for the new table name (see fig. 10.20).

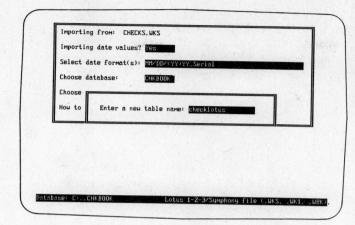

Fig. 10.20
Entering a
table name
for a new
table.

At this point, R:BASE asks specific questions about the type of file you are importing. The following sections on specific file types provide the information you need to answer these questions.

Specifying Import Characteristics

You can import the following types of files:

- ASCII delimited
- ASCII fixed field
- Lotus 1-2-3 or Symphony
- dBASE III or dBASE III PLUS
- PFS:File
- DIF (for example, VisiCalc)
- Multiplan (SYLK)

Importing ASCII Delimited Files

ASCII delimited files are DOS files containing ASCII data with each piece of data (equivalent to a column) separated from other parts with a delimiter character. To import data from ASCII delimited files, you must specify the delimiter. The delimiter often is a comma, but it can be any character that uniquely separates each part of the data. The following data is delimited with a pipe character (|):

```
100|Jones|Fred|'Marketing Manager'|10000.00
200|Smith|Henrietta|'Director of Operations'|15000.00
```

If you tell R:BASE that the delimiter character is a pipe character (|), R:BASE divides the data into columns wherever it finds that character in the record. Each file record becomes one R:BASE row.

If the file contains double quotation marks around text strings, you need to change the Quotes character in R:BASE before importing data if you do not want the quotation marks included in your data. The R:BASE default Quotes character is a single quote ('). You change the character in R:BASE by using the Characters option on the Settings menu before starting GATEWAY.

After you specify the delimiter character, press F2 to load the sample data.

Importing ASCII Fixed-Field Files

ASCII fixed-field files are DOS files containing ASCII data, with each piece of data in a fixed location in each record. An ASCII fixed format looks similar to the following:

```
100Jones    Fred        Marketing Manager    10000.00
200SmithfieldHenrietta  Director of Operations  15000.00
```

R:BASE reads one record and displays it on-screen so that you can mark where each field begins and ends. You mark the fields in much the same way that you mark fields in forms and reports: by using the S and E letters to mark the start and end of the field. Figure 10.21 shows how this data appears when marked with S and E characters.

Fig. 10.21

Marking the beginning and end of fixed-field data.

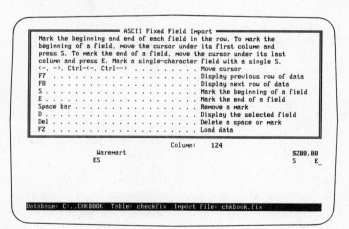

After you mark the fields, press F2.

Importing Lotus and Symphony Files

Because Lotus and Symphony are spreadsheet programs, the data may not be oriented in a database format. Spreadsheets are column-oriented and databases are row-oriented, as the following example illustrates:

Spreadsheet

	January	*February*	*March*
Region 1	100.00	200.00	150.00
Region 2	150.00	175.00	200.00

Database

Area	*Month*	*Sales Amount*
Region 1	January	100.00
Region 2	January	150.00
Region 1	February	200.00
Region 2	February	175.00
Region 1	March	150.00
Region 2	March	200.00

When importing data from a spreadsheet format to a database format, you need to tell R:BASE that the spreadsheet data is column-oriented and that it can find the spreadsheet column names (January, February, and so on) in the first row. For this example, you specifically tell R:BASE to import the column names as data. You also tell R:BASE that the column names are located in Row 1.

If you do not want to include the spreadsheet column names as data, you simply tell R:BASE that the data is oriented by column. For this example, however, the column names are definitely a part of the data you need in the database, so you should include these column names as data.

You also need to enter the range of the data in standard Lotus notation, entering the upper-left corner of the data area followed by the lower-right corner. For this example, you would enter the data range as A2..D3 (the labels are on Row 1). Figure 10.22 shows how you enter the cell range in the dialog box.

After you specify the label and data range, press F2 to load the data.

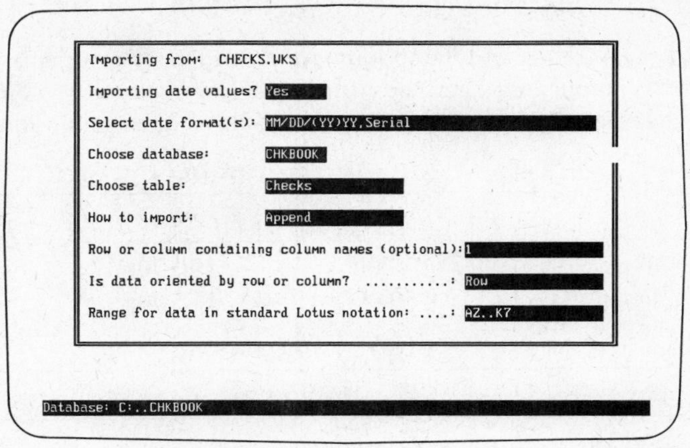

Fig. 10.22

Entering the data range in standard Lotus notation.

```
Importing from:  CHECKS.WKS
Importing date values? Yes
Select date format(s): MM/DD/(YY)YY,Serial
Choose database:      CHKBOOK
Choose table:         Checks
How to import:        Append
Row or column containing column names (optional):1
Is data oriented by row or column? ...........: Row
Range for data in standard Lotus notation: ....: AZ..K7

Database: C:..CHKBOOK
```

Importing dBASE Files

The only additional information you need to provide when importing a dBASE file is whether you want to import deleted data. You may want to import deleted data if your dBASE application did not need the data but you want to return the deleted data to R:BASE.

Note that you can read from and write to dBASE files directly by using the ATTACH command or by choosing dBASE Files from the Databases pull-down menu on the R:BASE main menu.

After answering this prompt, press F2 to import the data.

Importing PFS:File Forms

You can import PFS:File data created with a PFS:File form. Each entry in the form becomes an R:BASE database row. R:BASE does not ask any questions about PFS:File, so you press F2 to continue.

Importing DIF (VisiCalc) Files

The DIF file import requires that VisiCalc files be exported in DIF format before you can import these files. (You also can use the DIF import option with any other program that creates DIF files.)

You specify the data area (as opposed to labels or headings) on the VisiCalc side when you export to DIF format. Press F2 to continue.

Importing SYLK (Multiplan) Files

Multiplan is a spreadsheet system similar to Lotus or Symphony. To understand how spreadsheets are oriented, review "Importing Lotus and Symphony Files," earlier in this chapter.

You must create a SYLK format file in Multiplan by exporting from that product. When you import the SYLK file into R:BASE, you specify the top left and bottom right cell coordinates of the data area, entering them in standard Multiplan format. Type *1r2c1*, for example, to specify the upper-left corner as cell coordinate Row 2, Column 1. You use the same format to specify the bottom right cell coordinate. Press F2 to continue to the next step.

Dealing with Sample Data

If you are importing into an existing R:BASE table, you do not need to deal with the sample data as long as no errors occur when you load the data. If errors occur, you need to make corrections, as described in "Correcting Import Errors," later in this chapter.

If you are defining a new table with the imported data, R:BASE displays a sample row on-screen (see fig. 10.23). R:BASE provides default column names and its best guess at data types and column lengths. On this screen, you can enter the column names you want by typing over the default names, change the data types as needed, and specify lengths for Text columns.

```
 Data  Date format  Exit

 Column name      Data type   Size   Sample values
 ─────────────────────────────────────────────────
 COL10001         TEXT         10     1
 COL10002         TEXT          3     FD
 COL10003         DATE                02/22/90
 COL10004         TEXT         40     Party food.
 COL10005         TEXT          4     W
 COL10006         CURRENCY            $200.00




 Change the name, data type, or size of a column.
 Database: C:..CHKBOOK  Table: checkfix  Import file: chkbook.fix
```

Fig. 10.23

Completing the table definition using sample data.

When you are satisfied with the definition, press Alt-D to display the Data pull-down menu (see fig. 10.24). If you choose to load data, R:BASE displays the data-loading screen, which is similar to the data-exporting screen in figure 10.13. However, in the data-loading screen, R:BASE indicates whether any rows have been rejected because of errors. The next section explains how to deal with data exceptions.

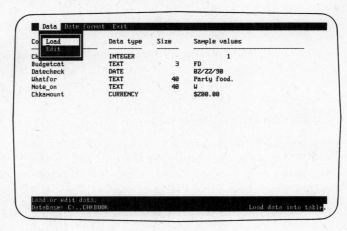

Fig. 10.24

The Data pull-down menu.

If all rows have been loaded properly, you are finished. R:BASE returns you to the GATEWAY main menu. Exit from GATEWAY to check your imported data.

You use the other two options on the Data menu as follows:

- *Date format*: Changes the date format selected earlier. You may need to change the date format if you find that your import data has an additional date format or a different format from the one selected, or if R:BASE displays the same menu for selecting date formats as described previously in "Setting Date Formats." Select the date formats you want. R:BASE changes any data matching the date formats you select to the Date data type.

- *Exit:* Ends the import without loading the data into a table.

Correcting Import Errors

If any exception rows are noted when you load data, R:BASE displays another screen with sample data. This time, any problem area is highlighted in the sample values column (see fig. 10.25).

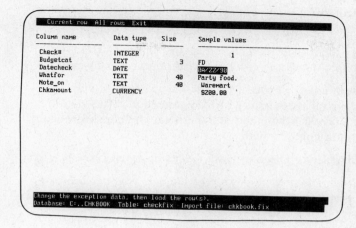

Fig. 10.25

Errors highlighted for correction.

Exceptions are any errors that occur when data is imported. The most common type of error is that the data from the import system is not valid for the data type of the R:BASE column into which the data is to be imported. Other common exceptions include data that is too long to fit into a Text column in the table, date formats that were not selected when you specified the import characteristics, or an attempt to import field names with data.

Note that you can tell R:BASE to ignore exceptions when importing or to store the exceptions in another file for later handling.

After you correct the highlighted errors, press Alt-C to deal with the current row or Alt-A to deal with all exception rows. Figure 10.26 shows the pull-down menu for dealing with all rows. The options for dealing with only the current row are similar.

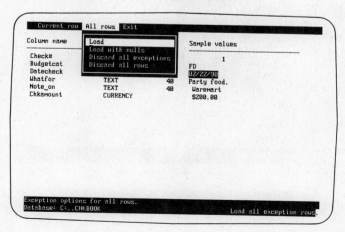

Fig. 10.26

The All Rows pull-down menu.

The options on the All Rows menu follow:

- *Load:* Loads all rows with valid data. If rows exist with exceptions, R:BASE ignores them. The Load option also is on the Current Row menu. R:BASE loads the current row if no exceptions exist.

- *Load with Nulls*: Loads all rows. If a row has exceptions, the columns with errors are loaded with no value (null). This option also is on the Current Row menu. R:BASE loads the current row and fills any exception columns with null values.

- *Discard All Exceptions*: Discards rows that contain exceptions.

- *Discard All Rows*: Discards all rows regardless of whether the row contains an exception. This option also is on the Current Row menu as Discard Row.

"Using the Settings Menu," later in this chapter, provides information on using an exception file—a file that temporarily holds the exception data while you decide how to handle it.

Using the Disk Management Options

The Disk Management pull-down menu from the GATEWAY main menu contains options for using DOS commands in GATEWAY (see fig. 10.27). These options are identical to the ones displayed when you choose the Disk Management option from the Tools pull-down menu on the R:BASE main menu. See Chapter 11 for information on these options.

Fig. 10.27

The Disk Management pull-down menu.

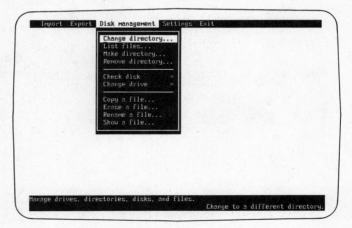

Using the Settings Menu

The Settings pull-down menu shown in figure 10.28 contains options for manipulating the database environment that are useful when importing and exporting data.

Fig. 10.28

The Settings pull-down menu.

The options on the Settings menu are as follows:

- *Set Rules*: Turns on or off rule-checking by R:BASE. If you are importing data that violates a rule you have defined, you may want to turn off rule-checking temporarily while loading the data.

- *User Password*: If you are working with a database with passwords assigned, use this option to enter a password that enables you to load or unload data. If you are going to create a new table or database, you need to enter the owner password.

- *Autonumbering*: Turns on or off autonumbering. If you are importing data with values for an autonumber column, you may want to turn off autonumbering temporarily; otherwise, R:BASE renumbers the imported columns for you.

- *Exceptions*: This option has two functions. First, you can remove exception processing by choosing No so that you do not have to deal with exception data (see "Correcting Import Errors," earlier in this chapter). Second, you can change the name of the default exception file (EXCEPT.DAT) to another file name. The exception file holds the invalid rows until they are edited or discarded; the exception file is erased when you finish using it. You may want to change the exception file name if you want to save the invalid rows to edit outside of GATEWAY. You may, for example, want to use the source system's editing facilities rather than deal with the errors in GATEWAY. Figure 10.29 shows you how to rename the exception file.

Fig. 10.29

***Renaming the
exception file.***

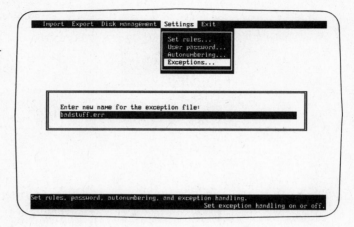

Summary

In this chapter, you learned how to export and import data from other software systems, by using R:BASE's import/export utility.

You learned how to export the following file types:

- ASCII delimited and fixed-field files
- dBASE II, III, and III PLUS files
- Lotus and Symphony files
- DIF files (such as those produced by VisiCalc)
- SYLK files (such as those produced by Multiplan)

You learned how to import these same file types, as well as PFS:File forms.

You learned that you can create new tables by using the Import function, and add data to existing tables. You also learned how to work with errors in imported data.

11

Managing Your Database

Database management includes all functions that help you keep your database in good condition, without modifying your database structure or data. This chapter discusses the following management tools available in R:BASE:

- Backing up and restoring your database
- Using DOS commands in R:BASE
- Executing other programs from within R:BASE
- Setting a user password

Starting the Tools Menu

Most of the database management options are available from the Tools menu, which you reach from the R:BASE main menu. To start the Tools menu, highlight Tools on the R:BASE main menu. Figure 11.1 shows the Tools menu with the Tools option highlighted.

This chapter describes the following options:

- Back Up Database
- Maintenance
- Disk Management
- Access to DOS
- User Password

The following options are discussed in other chapters of this book:

- Import/Export (Chapter 10)
- Relational Tools (Chapter 9)
- Editor (Chapter 8)
- Settings (Appendix B)

445

Fig. 11.1

The Tools menu.

Backing Up and Restoring Your Database

The first option on the Tools menu is Back Up Database. This option is first because regularly making a backup copy of the database is so important. If you have been working with computers for any length of time, you probably have experienced data loss at least once. Data loss can occur because of a number of reasons. Sometimes a hardware malfunction causes bad sectors on your hard disk. Unexpected power failures can cause problems. Even dust or smoke in the air can cause a disk drive malfunction.

Regularly backing up your database is a good idea. (Remember that a backup onto the hard disk is the same as not backing up at all.)

Smart computer users perform complete backups of the hard disk on a regular schedule. For a full backup, you can use the DOS BACKUP command. If you want to back up only your database, R:BASE provides several commands specifically designed for backing up the database:

BACKUP: Backs up the database to multiple floppy disks. Use this backup if your database backup file may require more than one floppy disk.

UNLOAD: Backs up the database in the same way as BACKUP, but you must store the backup file on a single floppy disk only.

RESTORE: Recreates a database from a backup file stored on multiple floppy disks by the BACKUP command.

INPUT: Recreates a database backed up with UNLOAD.

The Tools menu's Back Up Database option uses the BACKUP and RESTORE commands to make a backup of your entire database. The Maintenance menu provides a list of options that enable you to back up selected database items. Figure 11.2 shows the Maintenance menu.

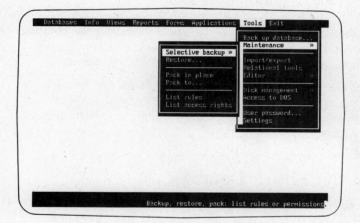

Fig. 11.2

The Maintenance menu.

The Maintenance menu gives you the following options:

- *Selective Backup:* Enables you to make a backup of the data in a single database item: a table, all forms, all reports, all labels, or the structure of the database only. See "Backing Up Selectively," later in this chapter.

- *Restore:* Recreates a backed-up database item from a file created with the Selective Backup option or by the BACKUP command used at the R> prompt. See "Restoring Your Database," later in this chapter.

- *Pack in Place:* Compresses a database without making a backup copy. See "Packing Your Database," later in this chapter.

- *Pack To:* Compresses a database and makes a second copy of the database (all three database files are recreated and the second copy is a usable database). See "Packing Your Database," later in this chapter.

- *List Rules:* Lists the rules defined for the database. This option is on the Maintenance menu because if you restore data to a table, you may violate a data entry rule. If, for example, you make a backup of a table that has a rule requiring unique values in a column and then attempt to restore the data without first removing the existing rows, you would be duplicating rows—thereby violating the rule. You can turn off rule-checking on the Settings menu. See Chapter 3 for information on defining and listing rules and Appendix B for information on changing rule-checking status.

- *List Access Rights:* Lists the table passwords assigned for the database. This option is on the Maintenance menu because it is important for you to know what passwords will be stored in the backup file.

You may not want the passwords to become public (a backup file is an ASCII file that anyone can read). You may want to revoke passwords temporarily to maintain privacy. See Chapter 3 for information on defining and listing access rights.

Backing Up the Entire Database

The quickest and easiest method of making a backup is to back up the entire database. This type of backup is your insurance against data loss if someone inadvertently erases your database files, for example. You should back up your entire database on a regular schedule (and more often if you make a lot of changes to the data or the structure). You also can back up portions of the database by using the Selective Backup options. See "Backing Up Selectively," later in this chapter.

If you are backing up to a floppy disk, be sure to have enough blank, formatted floppy disks available for the backup files. Then follow these steps to back up:

1. Press Alt-T to display the Tools pull-down menu.

2. Select Back Up Database.

   If you do not have an open database, R:BASE presents a list of databases from which to choose. Choose the database and then the access method: Read or Write. To back up a database, you only need Read access. If you assigned an owner password, you need to enter the password as well.

3. Enter the complete drive, path, and file name. If backing up to a floppy disk drive, be sure to include the drive designation and have a formatted floppy disk already inserted into the drive.

R:BASE makes a backup copy of the entire database. For information on the contents of a backup file, see "Backing Up Table Data" and "Backing Up Structures," later in this chapter.

Backing Up Selectively

R:BASE enables you to back up the data or the structure, or both the data and structure. To make a secure backup, you usually back up data and structure so that you can restore both if you lose your database files because of a hardware error.

Backing up data only is a handy way to transfer data from one database to another. Suppose that your office is large enough to have several PCs but the office is not ready for a network. You can have the same database on several PCs with different people adding data to each copy of the database. Then you can use a backup copy to consolidate the data into one master database. In this case, you can create the database structure on one PC, make a backup of the structure only to transfer the structure to a second PC, and then use the database backup to move data from one PC to the other. Another use for a data backup is to transfer data from your office to your home computer and back again.

You can make selective backups of the data or the structure for the following:

- The structure and/or data for an entire database
- The structure and/or data for a single table in the database
- The structure and data for the forms table SYSFORM
- The structure and data for the reports table SYSREP
- The structure and data for the labels table SYSLABEL

Backing Up Data

Data backups send only the data, with some environment commands, to the backup file. The structure of the item being backed up is not included. When you restore a data file, the table structure must exist already in the database. If you are backing up to a floppy disk, be sure to have enough blank, formatted floppy disks available for the backup files.

To make a backup of table data, follow these steps:

1. Press Alt-T to display the Tools pull-down menu.

2. Select Maintenance.

3. Select Selective Backup.

   If you do not have an open database, R:BASE presents a list of databases from which to choose. Choose the database and then the access method—Read or Write. To back up a database, you only need Read access. If you assigned an owner password, you need to enter the password as well.

4. Select Table.

   R:BASE displays a list of the tables in the database.

5. Select the table you want to back up.

6. Enter the complete drive, path, and file name. If you are backing up to a floppy disk drive, be sure to include the drive designation and have a formatted floppy disk already in the drive.

   R:BASE displays the Selective Backup choices.

R:BASE backs up the data from the table. If the data fills the first floppy disk, R:BASE asks for another disk. When the backup is finished, you return to the Tools menu.

Data backups create a series of Insert commands in the file. The following text shows sections of the file as they would appear if you looked at the file (the file is an ASCII file so you can type the file or call it into the editor).

Because the backup file contains a series of commands, you can see that R:BASE creates a command file when R:BASE backs up data. Also, the backup file is an ASCII file, so you can edit the data or commands if you need to make adjustments before reloading the data into the database. Also, you can use a data file to move data from one database to another. If, for example, you keep a sales database that is updated by order entry personnel and a payroll database that is maintained by accounting, you can use a backup file to move sales figures from the sales database to the payroll database for calculation of commissions.

The first section contains R:BASE environment-setting commands. These commands define the environment for this particular database. Because the backup file will load data, you must change certain settings from the standard operating environment. At the end of the file, these settings return to their status prior to the backup file creation. See Appendix B, "Customizing R:BASE," for information on what these settings do.

```
SET QUOTES=NULL
SET QUOTES='
SET DELIMIT=NULL
SET DELIMIT=','
SET SEMI=NULL
SET SEMI=';'
SET PLUS=NULL
SET PLUS='+'
SET SINGLE=NULL
SET SINGLE='_'
SET MANY=NULL
SET MANY='%'
SET CASE OFF
SET AUTOSKIP OFF
SET REVERSE ON
SET BELL OFF
SET NULL '-O-'
SET DATE SEQUENCE MMDDYYYY
SET TIME SEQUENCE HHMMSS
SET CURRENCY '$' PREF 2 B
SET TOLERANCE 0.
SET ZERO OFF
```

The following set of commands are for controlling multiple-disk backup files. These commands ask whether the restore from this file should proceed. These are all programming commands. See Chapter 8 and Appendix C for information on programming commands.

```
CLEAR VAR YESNO
SET VAR YESNO = 'E'
WHILE YESNO NE 'Y' AND YESNO NE 'y' THEN
   FILLIN YESNO USING 'This is disk 1, proceed with restore? (Y/N)?'
   IF YESNO EQ 'n' OR YESNO EQ 'N' THEN
     RETURN
   ENDIF
ENDW
```

The following set of commands make up a load data-block. These commands tell R:BASE the name of the file that should receive the data, and has the data for each row in the table. A *load* block loads data directly into a table. Notice that all text values are enclosed in single quotation marks:

```
LOAD Mail_list
NONUM
1,'John','Doe','A.','1105 Kentucky Ave.','Apt.2','Chicago','IL','50606'
2,'Fred','Roe','B.','999 Ventnor',-0-,'Indianapolis','IN','40404'
3,'Mary','Brown',-0-,'434 Pacific','#404','Fort Wayne','IN','40322-9033'
END
```

The last set of commands are the environment commands that reset
the date and time formats. See Appendix B for information on the
environmental settings:

```
SET VAR YESNO = 'E'
SET DATE FORMAT 'MM/DD/YY'
SET TIME FORMAT 'HH:MM:SS'
SET DATE SEQUENCE MMDDYY
SET TIME SEQUENCE HHMMSS
```

The procedure for making a backup copy of your forms, reports, or
labels is identical. If you are backing up to a floppy disk, be sure to have
enough blank, formatted floppy disks available for the backup files.

R:BASE backs up the structure and data of the system table containing the
forms, reports, or labels. If the backup file fills the first floppy disk, R:BASE
asks for another. When the backup is finished, you return to the Tools
menu.

Backing Up Structures

A *structure* is the definition of a database item. When you create a table in
a database, you are creating the structure of that table. The structures of
forms, reports, labels, views, rules, and passwords are tables created by
R:BASE when you define the first of any of these database items.

If you want to back up only the structure so that you can recreate a
database, you want to use the Selective Backup option—Structure Only.

To back up the structure of the database, follow these steps:

1. Select Maintenance from the Tools menu.

2. Select Selective Backup.

3. Select Structure Only.

   R:BASE prompts you for the name of the backup file.

4. Enter the drive, directory path, and file name. If you are backing up
   to a floppy disk drive, be sure to include the drive designation and
   have a formatted floppy disk in the drive.

5. Press F2.

R:BASE backs up the entire database structure.

Again, you have the environment commands at the beginning of the file just like a data backup.

The environment commands are followed by a CREATE SCHEMA command to recreate the database and a series of CREATE TABLE commands to redefine the tables. *CREATE TABLE* defines a table and the table's columns in the database. *CREATE TABLE* does the same thing as the Database Definition module: it creates table structures. See Chapter 3 for information on table creation and Appendix C for information on the CREATE TABLE command. The commands look like this:

```
CREATE SCHEMA  AUTHOR MAILING PUBLIC
CREATE TABLE Codes_mail          +
     ( Mailcode         TEXT     (2),  +
       Maildesc         TEXT     (40) )
CREATE TABLE When_mailed         +
     ( Idno             INTEGER , +
       Mailcode         TEXT     (2),  +
       Maildate         DATE     )
CREATE TABLE Mail_list           +
     ( Idno             INTEGER , +
       Firstname        TEXT     (30), +
       Lastname         TEXT     (30), +
       Middleinit       TEXT     (2),  +
       Address1         TEXT     (25), +
       Address2         TEXT     (25), +
       City             TEXT     (15), +
       State            TEXT     (2),  +
       Zipcode          TEXT     (10), +
       CSZ_line       = +
     (   City + ',' &    State &    Zipcode ) TEXT (27) )
```

Notice the use of continuation characters (+) at the end of lines to continue the command to second and subsequent lines.

A structure backup is useful for restoring a table or database structure if the structure becomes damaged (sometimes computers do this for no apparent reason, or you inadvertently introduce a computer virus to your machine). A structure backup also provides an easy way to create a new database with similar tables by using the backup file. In the section on data backups, you learned that you can use a backup file to move data from one database to another. In the same manner, you can use a structure backup to recreate the table structure in the second database so that you have a table to move the data to. Again, this is an ASCII file that you can edit.

Restoring Your Database

After you make a backup, you can recreate the data or structure from the commands in the file. If you are restoring a table structure, remove the table from the database before restoring. Use the REMOVE command to do this. If you are restoring table data, delete the rows from the table first. Use the DELETE ROWS command to do this. Alternatively, use the Info option to edit the table, highlight Edit, and then select Delete All Rows.

If you are restoring an entire database, restore the database to a different drive or directory than the original or delete the original database by using the ERASE command (see "Using DOS Commands," later in this chapter). Follow these steps:

1. Select Maintenance from the Tools menu.

2. Select Restore.

   R:BASE displays a list of files on the current directory. Choose the file name you want, or choose Other if the file is located on a directory other than the current one.

   R:BASE prompts you for the backup file name. Enter the entire drive, directory path, and file name. R:BASE prompts you for the first disk (even if the backup copy is stored on the hard disk).

3. Press Y to continue with the restore.

   R:BASE recreates the data, the structure, or both from the backup file.

Packing Your Database

If you have been adding and deleting rows or creating and removing tables, the disk space taken up by the database continues to grow. Space used by a row that is deleted is not copied over with another row and space used by a table is not written over when the table is removed. Occasionally, you should use one of the Pack options to recover this space.

```
Commands: PACK, RELOAD
```

There are two methods for recovering space: pack-in-place or pack-and-copy. The first method is most useful if you make regular backups and you do not need another copy of the database. The second method creates a copy of the database (not a backup file, but a real database) and removes the unused space in the copy.

The pack-in-place method is preferable because a backup of your database takes up less space than a copy. To pack a database, follow these steps:

1. Back up your entire database. You can use the Selective Backup option to make individual backup files for each database item, or you can use the Back Up Database option to back up the entire database in one file.

2. Select Maintenance from the Tools menu.

3. Select Pack in Place.

   If you do not have an open database, R:BASE presents a list of databases from which to choose. Choose the database and then choose the access method: Read or Write. To back up a database, you only need Read access. If you have assigned an owner password, you will need to enter it as well.

   R:BASE displays a message asking whether you have made a backup copy of your database.

4. Press Y and then Enter to continue with the in-place pack.

   R:BASE displays a series of messages showing the tables that are being packed, followed by messages for each index reload.

   If you check the size of the database before and after packing, you should find a substantial savings in disk space, depending on how much unused space was occupied by deleted rows and tables.

Using DOS Commands

Many of the most useful DOS commands are available from within R:BASE. DOS commands enable you to manipulate and maintain your drive and directory structure and to deal directly with DOS files.

The DOS commands available in R:BASE are provided in the Disk Management option of the Tools menu. You use the Access to DOS option to execute a program or batch file outside of R:BASE. The Access to DOS option uses the ZIP command.

When you select Disk Management, the Disk Management menu is displayed (see fig. 11.3). The first group of options deals with directory management. The second group of options deals with memory space, RAM, and drive. The third group of options deals with DOS files.

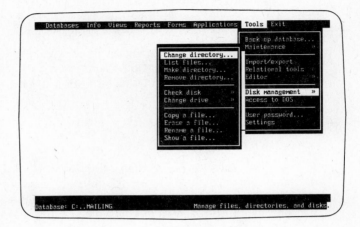

Fig. 11.3

The Disk Management options.

Maintaining Directories

Directories are partitions of your disk drive media. You can have directories on hard drives, virtual drives (pseudo-drives created in memory over 640K), or floppy disks.

The general procedure for using any of these disk management options follows:

1. Press Alt-T to display the Tools pull-down menu.

2. Select Disk Management.

   R:BASE displays the Disk Management options.

3. Select the option you want to use.

Depending on the option you select, R:BASE prompts you with a dialog box for additional information. The directory management options are described in the next few sections.

Changing Directories

The Change Directory option on the Disk Management menu changes the current directory to another existing directory. R:BASE prompts you for a directory path. Choose a directory from the menu or choose Other to enter the directory path in a dialog box. Enter the directory using this format:

\FIRSTDIR\SECNDDIR\THIRDDIR.

Substitute your own directory path.

Listing Files

The List Files option on the Disk Management menu lists the DOS files on the current directory or on the specified directory. R:BASE prompts you for a directory path. Choose a directory from the menu or choose Other to enter the directory path in a dialog box. With the List Files option, you also can specify a drive. Enter the path using this format:

C:\FIRSTDIR\SECONDDIR

Also, you can specify a specific file. You can use the wild-card characters with the List Files option. R:BASE's default wild-card characters for DOS options are an asterisk (*) to replace one or more characters and a question mark (?) to replace a single character. Using wild cards enables you to manipulate multiple files with a single command. You can type

C:\RBFILES\RBASE.*

to list all files in directory C:\RBFILES with the name RBASE and any extension.

You can type

\MYDATAB*.RBF

to list all files in directory \MYDATAB that have the extension RBF. These are database files.

You can type

MYDB?.RBF

to list all files in the current directory that begin with MYDB, have any character for fifth (and last) character in the name, and have the extension RBF. R:BASE should list three files (if they exist): MYDB1.RBF, MYDB2.RBF, and MYDB3.RBF. These are the three files that make up a database.

You can change the wild-card characters to the DOS standard wild cards by using the Settings menu. See Appendix B for information on customizing environment settings.

Creating Directories

The Make Directory option on the Disk Management menu creates a new directory. R:BASE prompts you for the directory path to create. Enter the path using the format

    \FIRSTDIR\NEWDIR

or

    \NEWDIR

Removing Directories

The Remove Directory option on the Disk Management menu removes an existing directory if no files exist in the directory. R:BASE prompts you for the directory path to remove. Choose a directory from the menu or choose Other to enter the directory path in a dialog box. Enter the path using the format

    \FIRSTDIR\OLDDIR

This path removes the subdirectory \OLDDIR.

Commands: CHDIR, CHDRV, DIR, MKDIR, RMDIR

Checking Memory and Disk Space

Sometimes you need to know how much memory or disk space you have available. Alternatively, you want to find out which drive is current or you want to change to a different drive.

Checking Memory

The Check Disk option on the Disk Management menu displays the available disk space on the specified drive and the amount of random access memory (RAM) available.

R:BASE prompts you for a drive letter by listing all possible drive designations, A through Z, for your computer. The display looks similar to figure 11.4.

Changing Drives

The Change Drive option on the Disk Management menu displays the current drive (if no drive is specified) or changes to the specified drive.

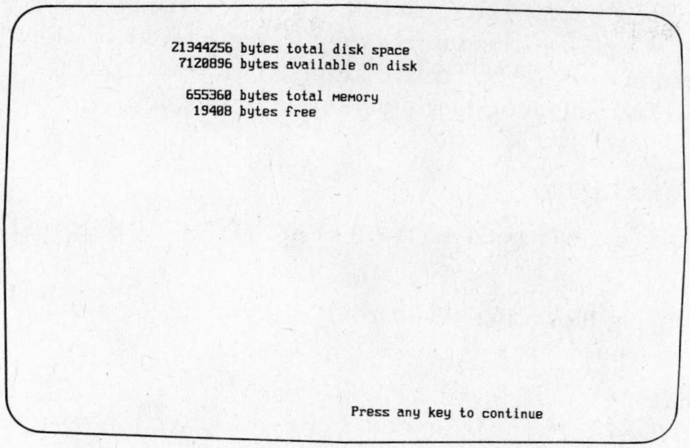

```
        21344256 bytes total disk space
         7120896 bytes available on disk

          655360 bytes total memory
           19408 bytes free
```

Fig. 11.4

CHKDSK tells you how much memory and disk space you have available.

```
                Press any key to continue
```

R:BASE prompts you for a drive with a list of all possible drive designations, A through Z, for your computer. Choose the drive you want to change to.

Commands: CHDRV, CHKDSK

Working with Files

You can manage DOS files by using the third group of options on the Disk Management menu. The options are copying, erasing, renaming, and displaying files. These options enable you to work with the DOS files while remaining in R:BASE.

Copying Files

The Copy a File option on the Disk Management menu makes a copy of a DOS file. You enter the source file name and the copy file (destination) name. You can copy to a different drive and directory if needed. R:BASE prompts you for the name of the file you want to copy with a menu of all files on the current directory and the name for the destination file. You can copy a file to a different directory and give the destination file the same name as the original source file. Consider the following example:

Source file: MYDATA.DAT
Destination file: C:\OTHERDIR\MYDATA.DAT

You can use this option with wild-card characters. R:BASE's default wild-card characters for DOS options are an asterisk (*) to replace one or more characters and a question mark (?) to replace a single character. To make copies of all three database files, consider the following example:

>   Source file: MYDATA?.RBF
>   Destination file: MYDATA?.BAK

This creates a set of three files named MYDATA1.BAK, MYDATA2.BAK, and MYDATA3.BAK

Use caution when copying files using wild cards. Consider the following source and destination names:

>   Source file: MYDB?.RBF
>   Destination file: MYDATA?.RBF

Because the source file name is shorter than the destination file name, R:BASE (really, DOS because R:BASE uses DOS routines for these options) copies MYDB1.RBF to MYDATA.RBF, then copies MYDB2.RBF to MYDATA.RBF, and finally copies MYDB3.RBF to MYDATA.RBF. All you end up with is a single file containing the last copied file.

You can change the wild-card characters to the DOS standard wild cards by using the Settings menu. See Appendix B for information on customizing environment settings.

Erasing Files

The Erase a File option on the Disk Management menu removes a file (or files if you use wild-card characters). R:BASE prompts you for the name of the file to erase with a menu of all files on the current directory. Choose a file or Other to enter a file name in a dialog box. You can enter a drive and directory path with the file name and use wild-card characters in the file name.

Use the List Files option before erasing files using wild-card characters. Enter the file name with List Files using the same wild-card characters to ensure that the files you want to erase are the only files that match the file name you enter. Suppose that you want to erase a database (three files). If you enter the file name with wild cards by typing

>   MYDATA?.*

you will not only erase MYDATA1.RBF, MYDATA2.RBF, and MYDATA3.RBF (the three database files), but you also will erase files named MYDATA.APP, MYDATA.APX, and MYDATA.API (if you had created an application with this name). Because the ? wild card means any character, ? also means any null value.

Renaming Files

The Rename a File option on the Disk Management menu changes the name of a file. R:BASE prompts you for the original file name with a menu of all files on the current directory. Choose a file or Other to enter a file name in a dialog box. Then enter the new name for the file. You can use wild cards with the Other option. If you do use wild cards, use the List Files option first to find out if there are any files that match the file name using wild cards that you do not want to rename. See "Erasing Files," earlier in the chapter.

Displaying Files

The Show a File option on the Disk Management menu displays an ASCII file. R:BASE prompts you for the name of the file with the file menu. You can include a drive and directory path with the file name by using the Other option.

If the file is not an ASCII file, you will see a lot of strange characters, but nothing intelligible. R:BASE will not stop you from displaying a non-ASCII file, but it will not be particularly useful.

```
Commands: COPY, ERASE, RENAME File, TYPE
```

Running External Programs

You can execute other programs from within R:BASE by using the Access to DOS option on the Tools menu. The Access to DOS option sends control to the DOS prompt. From there, you can execute other programs. After you exit from the other program and return to the DOS prompt, type *exit* to return to R:BASE.

```
Command: ZIP
```

Use of the ZIP command from the Tools menu is limited to executing small programs in DOS. If you want to switch between R:BASE and a word processor, for example, you need to use ZIP at the R> prompt. Type

    ZIP ROLLOUT wordpgm

The Rollout option modifies what R:BASE retains in memory. Without Rollout, the currently-open database, configuration settings, and other parts of memory are held by R:BASE. This will not leave much memory for your other program to run. If the program you want to execute requires a large amount of memory, use the Rollout option.

You easily can find out if the program requires the Rollout option. Try exiting from R:BASE by using the Access to DOS option. Start your other program. If you get a message telling you that you have insufficient memory to load the second program, you probably will need to use the Rollout option with ZIP. Use caution, however, because you may not get a memory warning until you load your program and even modify data in that program. To return to R:BASE, type exit at the DOS prompt.

Setting User Passwords

When you are dealing with maintenance options such as backups, the person selecting the options must enter the database owner name. This option enables you to enter any user password, but in general, the user must enter the owner name to use the options on the Tools menu. Follow these steps to set the user password:

1. Press Alt-T to display the Tools pull-down menu.

2. Select User Password.

   If you do not have an open database, R:BASE displays a list of databases from which you can choose. Choose the database and then choose the access method—Read or Write. To back up a database, you only need to use Read access.

   R:BASE prompts you for a password.

3. Enter the password that you need for the process that you want to perform. If you are making backup copies, enter the owner password (if one has been assigned to the database).

Summary

This chapter described the process for backing up your database files, using the DOS commands in R:BASE, and using the Access to DOS option to execute other programs while remaining in R:BASE.

If you followed this book from beginning to end, you have used all the R:BASE tools you need to create and use your database. The appendixes contain other items of interest. In particular, refer to Appendix C for a complete list of R:BASE commands and Appendix B for information on customizing the R:BASE working environment.

Installing R:BASE

This appendix describes system requirements, installation procedures, and start-up procedures for R:BASE 3.1.

Installing a Single-User System

You can use R:BASE 3.1 on a stand-alone PC without any other requirements than installation and modifying your system start-up files, CONFIG.SYS, and AUTOEXEC.BAT.

To use R:BASE 3.1 on a stand-alone computer, you will need an IBM or 100 percent IBM-compatible computer with a minimum of 640K of RAM (480K available) and a hard disk with at least 7M of free space for the complete R:BASE software package or 4.9M for the program files only. You will need DOS Version 3.1 or higher if you are installing from 5 1/4-inch disks. If you are installing from 3 1/2-inch disks, you will need DOS Version 3.2 or higher for PC-style computers, or DOS Version 3.3 or higher for PS/2-style computers.

You can check memory and disk space by typing *chkdsk* at the DOS prompt. Your display will look similar to figure A.1.

Note the lines saying 12288308 bytes available on disk and 550560 bytes free. These tell you whether you have sufficient disk space and available memory. On the display, for example, the computer has 12,288,308 bytes on disk. This is about 12M. The computer also has 550,560 bytes of free memory. This translates to approximately 550K of available memory. Your computer should have sufficient disk and memory space to install R:BASE.

R:BASE uses up to 8M of expanded memory under LIM EMS 3.2 and higher, or 32M using LIM EMS 4.0 or higher. You can use extended memory as a virtual disk with the R:BASE −V startup option.

*The CHKDSK
command
provides
memory and
disk space
data.*

```
C:\>chkdsk
Volume DISK1VOL1   created Aug 29, 1989 3:05p

  19344256 bytes total disk space
     53248 bytes in 3 hidden files
     49152 bytes in 22 directories
  10815488 bytes in 445 user files
    143360 bytes in bad sectors
  12283008 bytes available on disk

    655360 bytes total memory
    550560 bytes free

C:\>_
```

If you do not have sufficient memory (480K), and you do have an EGA or
VGA graphics board, you can use a special program that comes with
R:BASE to use the memory available on the graphics board. Before starting
R:BASE, type *rvmx on* at the DOS prompt. If you leave R:BASE and want
to use a program that requires graphics, type *rvmx off* to free the board's
memory for graphics use.

Installing a Multiuser System

Multiuser R:BASE installation enables you to share a database among several
users on a local area network. The installation process is almost identical
to that described in "Installing a Single-User System," with these
exceptions:

- You must be logged on and linked to the network's server. If you do
  not know how to do this, stop the installation by pressing Esc and
  check with your network administrator before continuing. The safest
  procedure, of course, is to let the network administrator perform the
  installation.

- R:BASE asks for your server drive and the network directory on
  which you want to install R:BASE.

To use R:BASE on a local area network, each workstation that will execute
R:BASE must have at least 640K of RAM (480K available). You can install
and use R:BASE from the network server, although it is preferable to
install R:BASE on each workstation. In this case, the workstation must have
the minimum requirements of a single-user computer (see the information
on system requirements in the "Installing a Single-User System" section).

If you do not have sufficient memory (480K) and you do have an EGA or VGA graphics board, you can use a special program that comes with R:BASE to use the memory available on the graphics board. Before starting R:BASE, type *rvmx on* at the DOS prompt. If you leave R:BASE and want to use a program that requires graphics, type *rvmx off* to free the board's memory for graphics use.

Microrim has tested R:BASE on the following networks:

AT&T Starlan
Banyan Networks and Banyan Vines
Novell Netware
3COM 3+, Etherlink, and Etherlink Plus
IBM Token Ring and IBM PC NET

R:BASE also works successfully on networks not tested by Microrim, but Microrim does not guarantee the operation of R:BASE on networks that it has not tested.

R:BASE automatically installs as a multiuser system, but you will need to purchase a LAN pack version of R:BASE to allow more than one user access to a shared database. The basic R:BASE configuration handles one user on a local area network.

You can install R:BASE on the network server or, preferably, on each workstation that will be using R:BASE. The database to be shared must be on a network drive that is accessible to the workstations. With the basic R:BASE 3.1 configuration, only one user can access a database at a time. R:BASE also comes in a LAN pack that can be used simultaneously by up to six users. Even the basic one-user version can be installed as multiuser. As many users as you want can use the R:BASE software; only access to an individual database is limited to one user at a time.

If you plan to purchase a LAN pack to add to your initial configuration, or you plan to use R:BASE with the basic single-user configuration on a LAN, see the installation instructions that come with R:BASE.

Installing the Program

The installation process is almost identical, whether you install from the 5 1/4-inch or 3 1/2-inch disks and whether you are installing R:BASE as a single-user or multiuser system.

Follow these steps to install R:BASE:

1. Start your computer.

2. Insert R:BASE Disk 1 into a floppy disk drive (usually drive A).

3. Type *a:install* and press Enter.

4. Follow the instructions on-screen. The first few screen pages contain instructions and may contain documentation update information. Press any key to page through these instructions.

5. INSTALL prompts you for the drive on which the files are to be installed. R:BASE displays those drives it detects for your computer. Drive C is highlighted. Choose the drive for R:BASE installation.

6. INSTALL displays a dialog box prompting you for the subdirectory into which R:BASE will be installed. It defaults to \RBFILES on the drive you selected in Step 5. Press Enter to accept \RBFILES or type a different directory name. The directory does not need to exist on your computer; R:BASE will create it for you.

7. INSTALL gives you two options:

   • Install parts of the system
   • Install the entire system

   If this is your first R:BASE installation, you probably want to install the entire system. This includes demo tutorial and sample files used to illustrate R:BASE concepts.

8. If you chose to install only selected parts of R:BASE, the install program displays a list of possible parts to install (see fig. A.2). You must install Program Files. The rest of the selections are optional. Press Y next to each part you want to install. This will change the No to Yes. After you select all the parts you want, press Enter to continue.

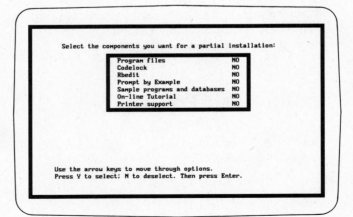

Fig. A.2

Choosing parts for installation.

```
Select the components you want for a partial installation:

           Program files                    NO
           Codelock                         NO
           Rbedit                           NO
           Prompt by Example                NO
           Sample programs and databases    NO
           On-line Tutorial                 NO
           Printer support                  NO


    Use the arrow keys to move through options.
    Press Y to select; N to deselect. Then press Enter.
```

9. If you chose to install the entire system in Step 7 or the Sample Programs and Database and the On-line Tutorial in Step 8, INSTALL asks for the directories for each of these parts. The default directories are \RBFILES\SAMPLES and \RBFILES\TUTORIAL. Press Enter at each directory prompt to accept the defaults or enter different directory names for these parts. In either case, INSTALL creates the directories if they do not exist.

   Note: You must have 7M available to install the entire system or 4.9M to install all required program files (no samples or tutorial).

10. If you chose to install the entire system in Step 7 or Printer Support in Step 8, INSTALL displays a list of printer files from which to choose. Select as many of the printers as you think you may be using with R:BASE. To do this, press Y when the printer name is highlighted to change No to Yes. After you select the printers, press Enter to continue.

    Note: You must select at least one printer file.

11. INSTALL asks if you want to add a PATH to your R:BASE directory to your AUTOEXEC.BAT file. Press Enter to accept Yes or backspace over the Yes and type *no* to modify your own AUTOEXEC file. See "Modifying the System Files" for more information.

12. INSTALL asks if you want to allow it to modify your CONFIG.SYS file. Again, you can let INSTALL do this for you or modify the file yourself. See "Modifying the System Files" for information.

13. INSTALL asks you to insert the next disk. It then copies the files you have requested to the correct drive and directory. If you are installing only parts of the system, not all disks will be requested. Be sure to note the disk number when INSTALL prompts you for a new disk.

14. After all files are copied, INSTALL makes backup copies of your AUTOEXEC.BAT and CONFIG.SYS files and then modifies the files as needed (if you asked INSTALL to do so in Steps 11 and 12).

15. INSTALL asks you to insert Disk 1 again and press a key. It then decompresses the installed files. Because the files come in a compressed format, you can use only the install program to copy them to your computer; do not attempt to use the DOS COPY or DISKCOPY commands.

16. Press any key twice to exit to DOS.

17. Restart your computer to load the modifications to your CONFIG.SYS and AUTOEXEC.BAT files. If you bypassed modifications to these files, see the next two sections.

18. You now can start R:BASE (see "Starting R:BASE").

Modifying System Files

In the installation procedure, you were asked whether you wanted to modify your system files: CONFIG.SYS and AUTOEXEC.BAT. If you chose to bypass this step during installation, you can modify the files yourself by using any ASCII text editor.

Modify your CONFIG.SYS file to contain the following:

```
FILES = 20
BUFFERS = 16
```

Modify your AUTOEXEC.BAT file to contain a PATH command, or add the following to your PATH command:

```
PATH = C:\RBFILES
```

If you chose to install R:BASE on a directory other than the default C:\RBFILES, substitute that directory.

Starting R:BASE

Start R:BASE by typing *rbase* at the DOS prompt. Without startup options, R:BASE starts with a blue background and white foreground, and displays the R:BASE main menu (see fig. A.3).

Fig. A.3

The R:BASE main menu.

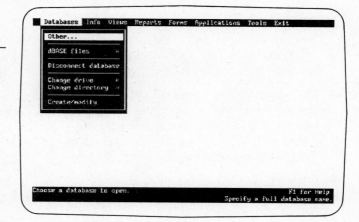

Using Start-up Options

You can modify the way that R:BASE starts, using any or all of the start-up options shown in figure A.4.

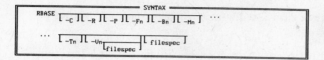

Fig. A.4

The start-up command syntax.

You use the start-up options as follows:

- −F*n*: Set a foreground color. The default color is white.
- −B*n*: Set a background color. The default color is blue.

Substitute a color number in place of the *n*. If you change colors while in R:BASE, use the color names exactly as shown. The following lists the valid colors and their numeric codes:

Background Colors	Foreground Colors
0 = Black	All background colors plus:
1 = Blue	8 = Gray
2 = Green	9 = Light Blue
3 = Cyan	10 = Light Green
4 = Red	11 = Light Cyan
5 = Magenta	12 = Light Red
6 = Brown	13 = Light Magenta
7 = Light Gray	14 = Yellow
	15 = White

Descriptions of the rest of the start-up options follow:

- −C: Starts R:BASE in Command mode.

- −P: Starts R:BASE in the menu system set in the configuration file (the R:BASE main menu—the default—or Prompt By Example).

  Command mode shows the R> at the left margin. Enter commands by typing them. See Appendix C for a complete list of commands and their syntax. Prompt By Example is the R:BASE command-building module. Select a command to execute and R:BASE will prompt you for the parameters you need to complete the command. As the command is created, it is displayed at the top of the screen. This is a good way to learn R:BASE commands.

- −R: Suppresses the display of the Microrim logo at startup. It takes a few seconds to draw the logo on-screen. Startup is a little faster if the logo is omitted.

- −M*n*: Sets the monitor for monochrome graphics.

  Use the −M option if your system uses monochrome graphics. Substitute 1 for the *n* if your system is non-color; use 2 if it is something other than non-color.

- −T*n*: Turns off automatic test for monitor type and substitutes a specific monitor type.

  Use the −T option if the display does not look correct when you start R:BASE without the options. R:BASE attempts to set the display mode for your system configuration, but if your system has a non-IBM display board, you may need to use −T to correct the display. Substitute 0 for the *n* for a color display; use 1 for monochrome, and use 2 for other non-IBM displays.

- −V*n* [filespec]: Specifies a sort file name. Substitute 0 for the *n* to use the file anywhere that R:BASE can find room. Use 1 to use the file in EMS memory; use 2 to use the file on the hard disk, or use 3 to use the file in the base 640K of memory. To use expanded or extended memory, your system must have more than 640K.

- Filespec: Names a start-up file.

  A start-up file must contain R:BASE commands. These commands execute after you start R:BASE. A start-up file is a handy method for setting start-up colors or for opening a specific database. The following start-up file, for example, sets colors, changes the default quotes character, and opens a database:

```
SET COLOR FORE BLACK
SET COLOR BACK RED
SET QUOTES="
CONNECT MAILING
```

You can mix and match the start-up options and place them in any order on the command line. If you always use a certain set of the options, you may want to create a batch file containing the R:BASE command and the start-up options you always want.

Starting R:BASE Multiuser

The process for using R:BASE to share a database on a local area network is the same as described in the preceding section. The only difference is that when you install R:BASE as a multiuser system, a switch called Multi is set to On. You can change this switch to Off while in R:BASE, but if you do so, you must reopen the database. Also, if anyone is sharing the database, you will not be able to switch Multi to Off. To set Multi to On or Off, start R:BASE and choose Settings from the Tools pull-down menu. See Appendix B, "Customizing R:BASE," for information on using the Settings menu.

There are many other considerations when using R:BASE for multiuser access to a single database. R:BASE handles the data-sharing necessary for multiuser access better than most database management systems. You may have special needs or considerations, however, beyond the scope of this book's purpose (assistance for the beginning user). See the "Transaction Processing and Multiuser" section of commands in Appendix C and Microrim's documentation on multiuser processing (see also the R:BASE 3.1 Installation Guide and Chapter 5 in the reference manual).

R:BASE prevents conflicting changes to data in Multiuser mode in a variety of ways: concurrency control, locking, and resource waiting. Depending on the task being performed, R:BASE will provide one or more of these methods of data protection. Following are definitions of the three multiuser data-protection methods:

- *Concurrency Control:* R:BASE tracks the changes made by all users when data is being edited. If more than one user changes the same data, R:BASE notifies the last user who made changes for confirmation of the changes. Checking for changes is performed by default at the row level. By changing the verify level using the SET VERIFY command, users can force data-checking at the column level.

- *Locking:* R:BASE locks out second and subsequent users from database changes when a first user issues any command that changes the database structure or data other than editing. R:BASE locks at the database level if the structure is being changed or at the table level when the data is being changed (for example, when deleting rows, as opposed to modifying data contained in a row). Users can manually lock a table by using the SET LOCK command. Users can lock a database by using the SET MULTI command (setting Multi to Off).

- *Resource Waiting:* Used with locking techniques, resource waiting notifies second and subsequent users if a database or table is locked, and enables the user to retry access to the resource (database or table) at periodic intervals (the default wait period is approximately four seconds). Users can change the wait period by using the SET WAIT command.

B

Customizing R:BASE

This appendix contains information about using the R:BASE environmental settings, creating user-defined function keys, and recording and playing back script keystroke files.

Changing the R:BASE Environment

The following sections provide a synopsis of the options available from the Settings menu. To use the Settings menu, follow these steps:

1. Choose Settings from the Tools pull-down menu on the R:BASE main menu. Alternatively, type *set* at the R> prompt.

    R:BASE displays the Settings menu (see fig. B.1).

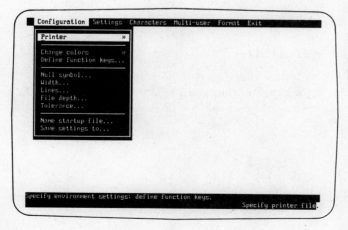

Fig. B.1

The Settings menu.

2. Highlight the menu option to display the pull-down menu for each Settings category.

3. Highlight the Settings option and press Enter.

4. Enter the new settings parameter. See the tables in this appendix for the default and valid values for each setting.

The Settings are divided into general groups by type, as follows:

- *Configuration:* Sets printers, colors, function keys, the null symbol, screen width and depth, file depth, decimal number tolerance, start-up file, and configuration file. See table B.1.

- *Settings:* Sets On and Off status for a variety of functions. See table B.2.

- *Characters:* Defines characters that R:BASE recognizes as special. See table B.3.

- *Multiuser:* Sets parameters for using R:BASE on a network. See table B.4.

- *Format:* Defines the display format for dates, times, and currency values. See table B.5.

To define the configuration by using the SET command, follow these steps:

1. Go to command mode.

2. Type *set*, followed by the SET keyword and the parameters needed for the keyword. See the tables for the default values and valid values for each setting.

Defining Configuration

The Configuration options set the working environment for R:BASE. The following table describes each option and the keyword to use with the SET command to execute the option at the R> prompt.

Table B.1
Using Configuration Options

Option	Keyword	Description
Printer	PRINTER	Selects a printer control file to provide custom printer type styles in reports and labels. When you installed R:BASE, you selected one or more printer files. You can switch between printers by using this option. The default is the first printer selected during installation. Normal text will print without choosing a printer.
Change Colors	COLOR DIALOG MENU FIRST	Provides a color palette for determining foreground (FORE) and background (BACK) colors. The default is white on a blue screen (COLOR), black on a cyan dialog box (DIALOG FORE and BACK), black on gray menus (MENU FORE and BACK), and red initial letters for options (FIRST).
Not On Settings Menu	EXPLODE	Determines how a dialog box is drawn. If on, the box expands outward from the center. If off, the box appears instantly. Default is Off.
Define Function Keys	None	Enables you to define keystrokes to be executed after you press a single key. Not a SET command. Press Ctrl-F1 to display the Script/Key menu.
Null Symbol	NULL	Sets a one- to four-character symbol to represent null values. Default is -0-.
Width	WIDTH	Controls the width of display for the screen or printer when using the COMPUTE, CROSSTAB, DISPLAY, SELECT, TYPE, or UNLOAD commands. Default is 79.
Lines	LINES	Sets the number of lines to display on-screen. Default is 20.

Table B.1—*continued*

Option	Keyword	Description
File Depth	FILES	Determines the maximum number of command files to have open at any one time. Default is 5.
Tolerance	TOLERANCE	Defines how closely numeric testing is to match. By making the tolerance higher, "fuzzy" comparisons can be made. Default is 0.
Name Startup File	None	Provides the name of a command file to execute when you start R:BASE. Default is RBASE.DAT.
Save Settings To	None	Saves all currently defined settings to a configuration file. R:BASE reads the configuration file on startup and restores all settings as they are stored in the file. Default is RBASE.CFG.

Setting the Operating Environment

The Settings options give you control over how the system operates. Table B.2 lists the Settings options, the SET command keyword, and the description of each option. Many of these settings have an On or Off status only. Others need one or more parameters that are described.

Table B.2
Using Settings Options

Option	Keyword	Description
Error Messages	ERROR MESSAGES	Controls whether to display or suppress error messages. Default is On.
Status Messages	MESSAGES	Controls whether to display or suppress standard status messages. Default is On.
Bell	BELL	Enables you to determine whether the computer bell sounds on errors. Default is On.

Option	Keyword	Description
Insert/ Overwrite	INSERT	Controls the use the of the Ins key to toggle between Insert and Overwrite mode. Default is On.
Zero	ZERO	Controls how null numeric values are to be used in expressions. If on, nulls are considered zero; if off, nulls are ignored. Default is Off.
Headings	HEADINGS	Determines whether headings are displayed with the SELECT and TALLY commands. Default is On.
Clear	CLEAR	Controls clearing of the internal buffer. If on, the buffer is cleared after each transaction; if off, the buffer is filled to capacity before clearing. Default is On.
Autoskip	AUTOSKIP	Controls how the cursor moves in a form. If on, the cursor skips to the next field when the current field is filled. Default is Off.
Reverse Video	REVERSE	Determines whether the field the cursor is in is displayed in reverse video. Default is On.
Case Sensitivity	CASE	Directs R:BASE to ignore or use case (upper- and lowercase) differences in comparisons. Default is Off.
Echo	ECHO	Determines whether command syntax is sent to the current output device when commands are executed from a command file. Default is Off.
Layout	LAYOUT	Determines whether or not the Layout features are saved when you edit a table using tabular edit. Default is On.
CGA	CGA	Helps to suppress "snow' when using a CGA graphics card, however, setting CGA to ON slows redisplay of menus. Default is Off.

Table B.2—*continued*

Option	Keyword	Description
Rules	RULES	Controls whether R:BASE uses defined data-entry rules when data is entered or modified. Default is On.
Application Break	ESCAPE	Determines whether the Esc key exits from a command file or application or is ignored. The Ctrl-Break key is enabled. Default is On.
AND Precedence	AND	Controls how AND and OR connecting operators are processed. If on, ANDs are processed before ORs; if off, conditions are processed from left to right. Default is On.
Scratch Files	SCRATCH	Enables R:BASE to create a temporary disk file on the database directory during sorting. If on, it stores on the database drive and directory; if off, it stores on the current drive and directory. Default is On.
Sort	SORT	Sorts small parts of the data and then recombines the data with unsorted rows (if on). Used with extremely large sorts to optimize sorting. Default is Off.
Not on the Settings Menu	COMPAT	Enables R:BASE 3.1 to use R:BASE 2.x databases without conversion. Default is Off.
Not on the Settings Menu	LOOKUP	Tells R:BASE how many form lookups to store in memory. Default is 5

Redefining Characters

Certain punctuation characters have a special meaning for R:BASE. The Characters options enables you to redefine the characters used in special circumstances. Table B.3 lists the characters, the SET keyword for the character, and describes how the character is used in R:BASE.

Table B.3
Using Characters Options

Option	Keyword	Description
Many Wildcard	MANY	Replaces one or more characters in file management or comparisons on text strings. Default is %.
Single Wildcard	SINGLE	Replaces a single character in file management or comparisons on text strings. Default is _
Quotes	QUOTES	Encloses text strings that contain spaces. Default is '.
Command Separator	SEMI	Separates multiple commands on the same entry line. Default is ;.
Continuation	PLUS	Continues a command line across two or more screen lines. Default is +.
Delimit	DELIMIT	Separates individual data items in an input string. Default is ,.
Blank	BLANK	Provides spaces in text strings. Default is a space.

Controlling Multiuser Processing

When using R:BASE on a local area network, you need to tell R:BASE that the database will be shared by two or more users. The multiuser options control this use. Table B.4 lists the multiuser options, provides the SET command keyword, and describes how the option is used.

Table B.4
Multiuser and Transaction Processing

Option	Keyword	Description
Set Multi	MULTI	Turns on or off multiuser processing. Reopens the database after changing the setting. Default is Off.
Network ID	NAME	Specifies a network ID for a user. No default.
Verify	VERIFY	Determines how data checking is performed when more than one user is editing data with a form. ROW checks after each row is saved; COLUMN checks after each column is modified. Default is COLUMN.
Wait Time	WAIT	Specifies the number of seconds to wait between attempts to access a database resource. Default is 4.
Auto-Refresh Interval	REFRESH	Defines how often to refresh the screen for a data-entry form. Refreshing enables a user to see changes made by another user. Default is 0.
Not on Settings Menu	TRANSACT	Turns transaction processing on and off. Default is Off.
Not on Settings Menu	MAXTRANS	Sets the maximum number of users in transaction processing. Default is Off.
Not on Settings Menu	AUTOCOMMIT	Turns automatic commitment of transactions in transaction processing on and off. Default is Off.

Setting Formats

The Format options enable you to determine how to enter and display currency amounts, dates, and times. Table B.5 lists the format options, the SET keyword, and a description of each option's use.

Table B.5
Using Format Options

Option	Keyword	Description
Date Output Format	DATE FOR	Defines a maximum 30-character format to display dates. Default is MM/DD/YY.
Date Input Sequence	DATE SEQ	Defines the entry sequence of the month, day, and year for dates. Default is MMDDYY.
Time Output Format	TIME FOR	Defines a maximum 20-character format to display times. Default is HH:MM:SS.
Time Input Sequence	TIME SEQ	Defines the entry sequence of the hours, minutes, and seconds for times. Default is HHMMSS.
Currency Symbol	CURRENCY	Defines the symbol to be used when displaying currency values. Default is $.
Currency Location	CURRENCY	Defines the location of the currency symbol. Default is at the beginning.
Currency Digits	CURRENCY	Defines how many decimal digits to include in the currency format. Default is 2.
Currency Format	CURRENCY	Defines one of the following standard display formats: A—999.999.999,99 B—999,999,999.99 (default) C—999 999 999,99

Defining Keys and Scripts

Like many other products, R:BASE provides a way for you to define a single key or key combination (such as Alt-F1 or Ctrl-A) to play back a series of keystrokes. In addition, R:BASE provides the capability to record keystrokes in a file that you can play back later to repeat a process. This section describes how to define and use a key or key combination and how to record and play back scripts.

Creating User-Defined Keys

If a function key or key combination (such as Alt-F1) is not used by R:BASE, you can define the key with any series of keystrokes you want. This is called a *key map*. You may want to define a key map for actions you do often. You can define a key map anywhere in R:BASE. Whatever processing is taking place is suspended while you enter the key definition.

Follow these steps to define a key map:

1. Press Ctrl-F1. This displays the Script/Key menu as a pop-up menu on the center of the screen (see fig. B.2).

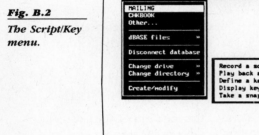

Fig. B.2

The Script/Key menu.

2. Highlight the Define a Key Map option and press Enter. R:BASE prompts you for a key to define and the definition in a dialog box (see fig. B.3).

3. Press the key or key combination that you want to define. Press Alt-F3, for example, to define a series of keystrokes that will execute whenever you press this key combination.

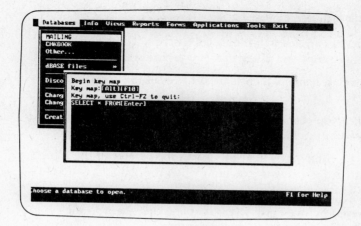

4. Enter the keystrokes you want to replay when you use the key. This may be a command that you use often or a series of menu selections that take you to a specific place in one of the R:BASE modules.

5. Press Ctrl-F2 to end the key definition. This returns you to the Script/Key menu.

6. Press Ctrl-F2 again to leave the menu.

A key map you define is not saved permanently unless you choose to do so. You can save permanently any defined key maps by using the Key Maps option on the Settings menu. You reach the Settings menu through the Tools menu. From the Tools pull-down menu, choose Settings. This displays a new screen with the Settings menu option displayed across the top of the screen. Highlight Configuration and choose Save Settings To. R:BASE prompts you for a configuration file name. All environment settings including key maps will be saved in the configuration file. Whenever you start R:BASE from the same directory as the configuration file, the settings in the file will become the default settings for R:BASE.

After you define a key, you recall the keystrokes stored in the key definition by pressing the key combination. If you defined Alt-F1 to contain the words SELECT * FROM, for example, then pressing Alt-F1 will type these words just as if you were entering them from the keyboard. In this particular case, you should be in Command mode. When defining a key map, be sure that when you press the key combination to recall it, that key combination will make sense to R:BASE. The SELECT * FROM combination would not work, for example, if you were on the R:BASE main menu.

Creating Playback Scripts

You also can record keystrokes in a file called a script. The main differences between a script and a key map are as follows:

- A script is given a name, which is used to recall the script keystrokes.

- The keystrokes you record in a script are executed at the same time they are stored in the file.

- A script can be named as a start-up option for several of the R:BASE modules so that the script is executed when the module is started (only from Command mode).

- Scripts are saved permanently without you saving them in the configuration file, as required with key maps.

```
Commands: PLAYBACK, RECORD
```

Follow these steps to record a script:

1. Press Ctrl-F1 to display the Script/Key menu.

2. Choose the Record a Script option.

   R:BASE prompts you for the name of the script file (see fig. B.4).

3. Enter the DOS file name you want to give the script.

   R:BASE leaves the Script/Key menu. You now are recording keystrokes in the script file.

Fig. B.4

Naming a script file.

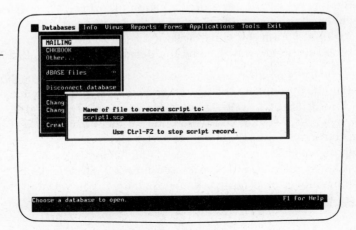

4. Continue with the process you want to record.

5. When you want to close the script, press Ctrl-F2.

R:BASE signals that recording is over, as shown in figure B.5. Press any alphanumeric key to continue with your task.

As an alternative, at the R> prompt you can start recording a script by typing *record*, followed by a script file name. When you want to end recording, type *record* without a file name.

To play back a script, use the Script/Key menu and choose the Play Back a Script option. Enter the script file name (see fig. B.6). The script file then takes over the keyboard. All keystrokes recorded in the script will be executed just as if you were entering them from the keyboard.

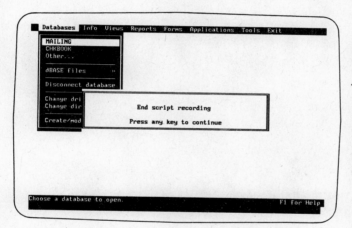

Fig. B.5

When you finish recording, R:BASE confirms that recording is halted. Press any key to continue.

Fig. B.6

Entering the script's DOS file name to play back a script.

If the script you recorded contains commands to be executed at the R> prompt, you can type *playback*, followed by the file name of the script.

Summarizing R:BASE Commands

This appendix shows the syntax and briefly describes the use of all R:BASE commands.

General-Use Commands

General use commands are those commands that you can use at the R> prompt or within R:BASE command or procedure files. You can access some of the commands through the R:BASE menu structures.

Structure-Development Commands

You use structure development commands to create and maintain the structure of tables, forms, reports, and labels; to define rules, views, and column indexes; and to create new tables from existing tables.

For information on table definition, indexing, passwords, and rules, see Chapter 3. For information on views, see Chapter 5. For information on forms, see Chapter 6. For information on reports and labels, see Chapter 7. For information on creating new tables from existing tables, see Chapter 9.

ALTER TABLE

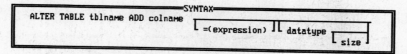

The ALTER TABLE command changes the structure of an existing table by adding a new column to it. You can define the column's data type and an expression to create a computed column.

AUTONUM

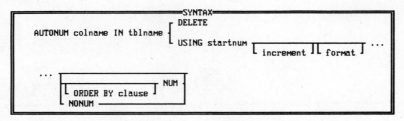

The AUTONUM command specifies that R:BASE number a column automatically when new rows are entered. DELETE removes autonumbering from the column's definition. NUM numbers existing rows, and NONUM creates the autonumber definition without renumbering existing rows. Alternatively, you can use RBDEFINE to assign autonumbering through the menu-driven Database Definition module.

COMMENT ON

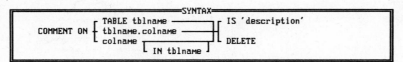

COMMENT ON applies a description of up to 80 characters to a column or table. DELETE removes an existing description. You also can add comments by using RBDEFINE.

CREATE INDEX

CREATE INDEX defines a column to be stored in summary form with pointers to each indexed row.

CREATE SCHEMA

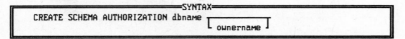

CREATE SCHEMA creates a database ready for the addition of tables. You must follow it always with one or more CREATE TABLE commands, or you can use RBDEFINE to create tables through the menu-driven Database Definition module. You can assign an owner password when you create the database.

CREATE TABLE

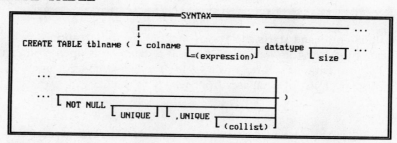

CREATE TABLE defines the structure of a table. With this command, you can define the columns for the table and create a limited set of rules. Alternatively, you can use RBDEFINE to create a table through the menu-driven Database Definition module.

CREATE VIEW

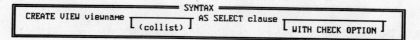

The CREATE VIEW command relates the data of two or more tables or provides a subset of the columns or rows of a single table. Alternatively, you can use QUERY, which creates a view through the menu-driven Views module. QUERY does not create a permanent view, but CREATE VIEW does.

DROP

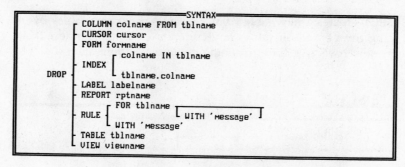

DROP removes columns, tables, forms, reports, views, indexes, labels, rules, and the cursor.

FORMS

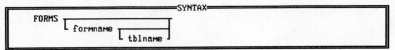

The FORMS command starts the Forms module for the creation or modification of a custom data-entry form. If a database is open, you can specify a form name or a form and a table. If a database is not open, R:BASE displays a list of databases from which to select.

GRANT

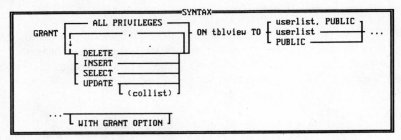

GRANT assigns user-access rights to tables and views. Alternatively, you can use RBDEFINE to assign passwords through the menu-driven Database Definition module.

INTERSECT

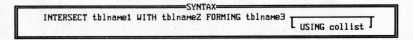

INTERSECT creates a new table from data in two existing tables by combining rows based on values in a common column. The new table contains only rows that have matching common column values.

JOIN

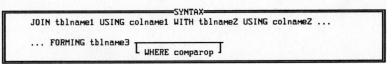

JOIN creates a new table from data in two existing tables by combining rows and adding rows to the new table, based on a comparison of values contained in a column in each source table. The columns do not have to be common, but must have a compatible data type. The new table contains rows in which the two columns have the relationship specified by the comparison operator.

LIST

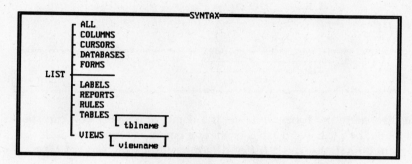

The LIST command lists any of the specified database structures in the open database.

LIST ACCESS

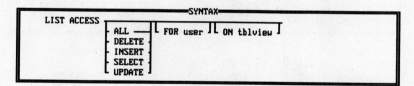

LIST ACCESS lists the assigned user passwords and their access privileges.

PROJECT

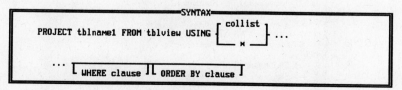

PROJECT creates a new table from data in another table. The new table contains the specified columns and the rows meeting the WHERE clause criteria.

RBDEFINE

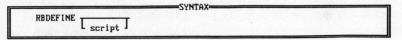

RBDEFINE starts the Database Definition module. If a database is open, R:BASE displays the Database Create/Modify menu. If no database is open, R:BASE displays the Database Building menu.

RBLABELS

RBLABELS starts the Labels module. If a database is open, you can specify a label name, or a label and table or view name as options. If a database is not open, R:BASE displays a list of databases from which to select.

REDEFINE

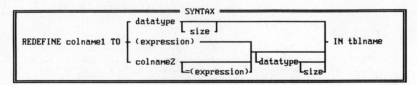

REDEFINE changes the structural definition of a column.

RENAME

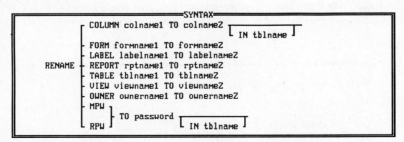

RENAME changes the name of the specified database structure in the open database.

REPORTS

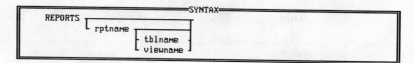

REPORTS starts the Reports module. If a database is open, you can specify a report name, or a report and table or view name as options. If a database is not open, R:BASE displays a list of databases from which to select.

REVOKE

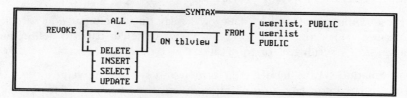

REVOKE removes access privileges from a user.

RULES

RULES creates data-entry and modification rules. Alternatively, you can use RBDEFINE to create rules through the menu-driven Database Definition module.

SUBTRACT

SUBTRACT creates a new table from two existing tables, adding rows to the new table based on the comparison of a common column in the two source tables. The new table contains only those rows from the second table that do not exist in the first table.

UNION

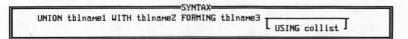

UNION creates a new table from two existing tables, combining all rows from both tables as long as there is at least one column common to both tables. Matching common columns form a single row and unmatched columns are given their own rows.

Select and Display Commands

Use these commands to select data for display on the tabular edit screen, to compute values from data, to create views to select data, to define and use a keystroke script file, or to create ad hoc or saved reports.

For information on the tabular edit screen and computing values, see Chapter 4. For information on creating views, see Chapter 5. For information on reports and labels, see Chapter 7. For information on ad hoc reporting through SELECT, see Chapter 9. For information on creating and using keystroke script files, see Appendix B.

BROWSE

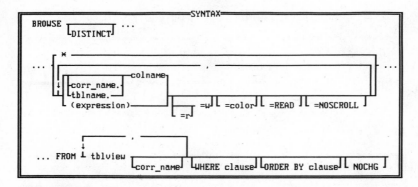

The BROWSE command displays the selected columns and rows from one or more tables in a tabular format. You cannot make any modifications when using BROWSE. This command has almost the same syntax as EDIT. The only difference is that BROWSE starts in non-edit mode. With the NOCHG clause, you cannot switch to Edit mode after the data is displayed. If you extract the data from a view, you cannot make any modifications with EDIT or BROWSE. After the data is displayed, the menu enables you to modify the format of the displayed data.

COMPUTE

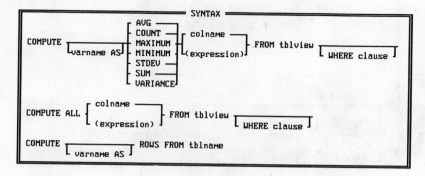

COMPUTE calculates the sum, average, minimum, maximum, count, standard deviation, or variance of a column. The ALL option performs all of these calculations.

CROSSTAB

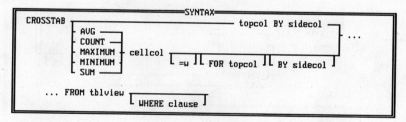

CROSSTAB displays a cross-tabular format of correlated data from a table, calculating the sum, average, minimum, maximum, or count of a column related to two other columns.

PLAYBACK

The PLAYBACK command substitutes keyboard entry for the recorded keystrokes contained in the script file. See "RECORD."

QUERY

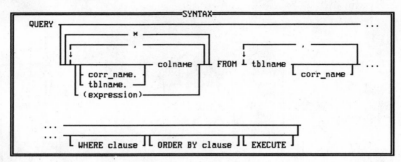

QUERY creates a temporary view structure from one or more tables. After you create the view, you can execute the EDIT or BROWSE command. If the data is from a single table, use the EDIT command so that you can edit the data. If the data is from two or more tables, execute the BROWSE command to display the data. Use QUERY with no arguments to start the menu-driven Views module.

SELECT

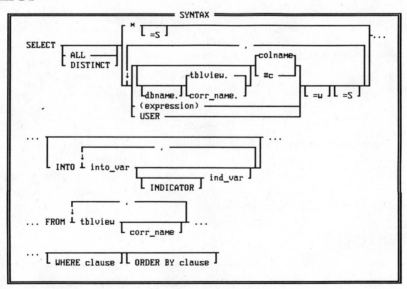

SELECT creates a temporary view structure from one or more tables and then displays the data.

If you use SELECT as a clause in another command (SELECT clause syntax), the command selects rows to be acted on by a data-modification command. See DELETE, INSERT, and UPDATE. You can place the selected data in a global variable with the INTO clause.

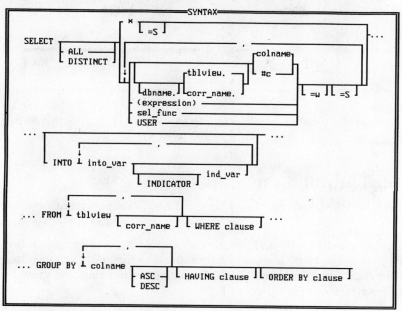

The GROUP BY SELECT command summarizes data based on the value of a column (a condition) and calculates the sum, average, minimum, maximum, or count of one or more grouped columns.

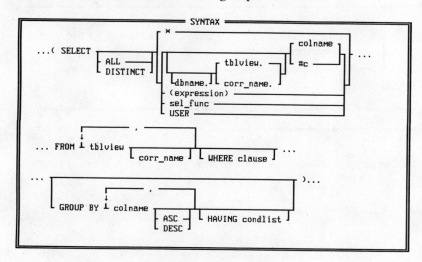

Used as a sub-SELECT in a WHERE clause, SELECT creates a list of values for comparison. See "WHERE."

TALLY

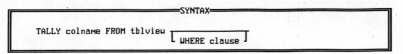

TALLY counts the number of occurrences of each unique column value in a table or view. You limit the rows with a WHERE clause.

Printer/Output Commands

Printer/output commands control where and how data is printed or displayed.

For information on reports and labels, see Chapter 7. For information on programming commands, see the "Programming Commands" section, later in this appendix, and Chapter 8. For information on defining and using keystroke script files, see Appendix B.

LBLPRINT

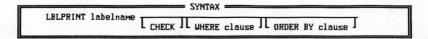

The LBLPRINT command prints the specified custom labels to the current output device. See "RBLABELS."

NEWPAGE

NEWPAGE sends a form-feed character (new page) to the current output device.

OUTPUT

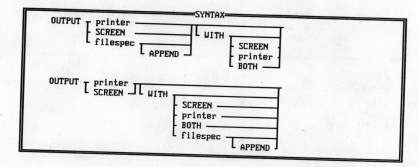

OUTPUT sets the current output device: printer, screen, file, or a combination of any of the three.

PRINT

The PRINT command prints the specified custom report to the current output device. See "REPORTS." You also can set conditions on or sort data with the PRINT command.

RECORD

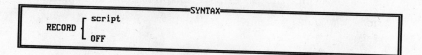

RECORD stores keystrokes/commands in the specified script file at the same time the keystrokes/commands are executed. See "PLAYBACK."

SHOW VARIABLE

SHOW VARIABLE displays a single global variable as the specified screen row and column, or all system and global variables.

SNAP

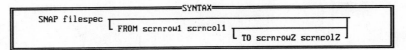

SNAP stores the current screen image in a file. You then can redisplay the screen image by using the DISPLAY command.

WRITE

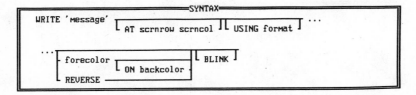

WRITE sends the specified message line to the current output device. If the output device is the screen, you also can specify the screen row.

Data-Entry and Modification Commands

You use data entry and modification commands to enter and modify data in your database.

For information on using tabular edit, see Chapter 4. For information on forms, see Chapter 6.

DELETE

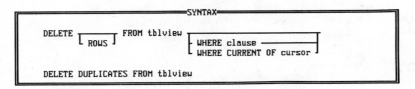

DELETE removes one or more rows from a table or view. If no WHERE clause is included, all rows are removed.

DRAW

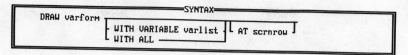

DRAW displays a variable-only form on-screen at the specified screen row.

EDIT

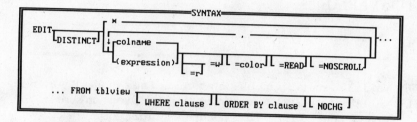

EDIT starts the menu-driven Info/Views module. If you specify a table or single-table view, you can edit data. If you specify a multitable view, you can browse only. See "BROWSE." After R:BASE displays the data, you can modify the format by using the menu options.

EDIT USING

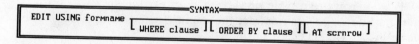

EDIT USING starts a custom form in Edit mode. See "ENTER" and "FORMS."

EDIT VARIABLE

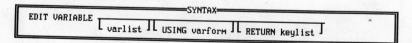

EDIT VARIABLE starts a variable-only form in Edit mode. Before using EDIT VARIABLE, use DRAW to display the form layout on-screen. You then can edit the variables defined for the form.

ENTER

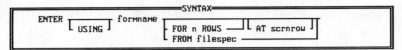

ENTER starts a custom form in Enter mode. See "EDIT USING" and "FORMS."

ENTER VARIABLE

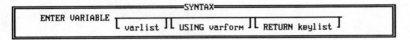

ENTER VARIABLE starts a variable-only form in Enter mode. Before using ENTER VARIABLE, use DRAW to display the form layout on-screen. You then can enter values for the variables defined in the form.

INSERT

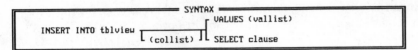

INSERT adds rows to a table or view. You can enter the data on the command line or you can extract the data from the same table or another table by using the SELECT clause.

LOAD

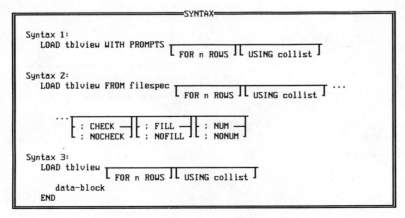

LOAD adds rows to a table. You can use LOAD in the following ways:

- *With Prompts:* R:BASE prompts you with the column names and data types.

- *From a File:* The data in the DOS file must be in an ASCII delimited file format.

- *In a Data Block:* R:BASE prompts you with an L>. You must enter each column's data separated by spaces or a comma from other column's data.

For all methods of using LOAD, you can specify a maximum number of rows that you will enter and which columns you will enter.

UPDATE

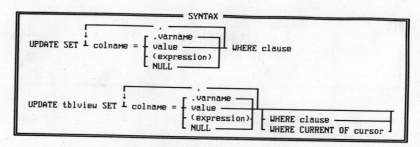

UPDATE modifies existing data in a table. You can change data in as many columns as you want. You specify the rows that you want to change for all tables by using a WHERE clause only (this changes data in any table that contains the specified column and meets the conditions) or by limiting the change to a specific table.

Environment Commands

Environment commands control how R:BASE is used—specifying a database, using menus, exiting, and setting the operating environment.

For information on defining and opening databases, see Chapters 1 through 4. For information on using menus in R:BASE, see Chapter 1. For information on customizing R:BASE, see Appendix B. For information on defining and using variables, see Chapters 6 through 9.

ATTACH

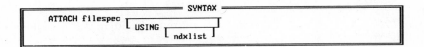

ATTACH connects a dBASE III, III PLUS, or IV database file to an R:BASE database. You can attach dBASE index files as well for dBASE III and III PLUS files.

CONNECT

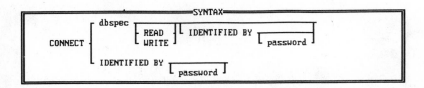

CONNECT opens a database for use. You may specify the owner password on the command line. READ opens the database for display only; you cannot perform any modifications of structure or data.

DETACH

Removes access to a previously attached dBASE database file.

DISCONNECT

DISCONNECT closes the currently open database and writes all data to the database. EXIT also closes a database.

EXIT

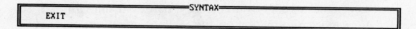

EXIT leaves R:BASE and closes the database.

MENU

MENU displays the R:BASE main menu.

PROMPT

PROMPT starts the R:BASE command-building module—Prompt By Example. See Chapter 1 for more information on Prompt By Example.

SET

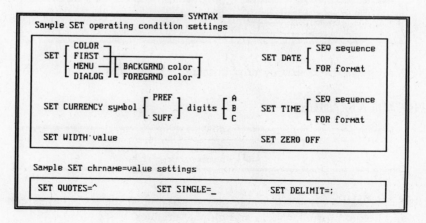

SET is a multipurpose environment definition command. Depending on the keyword you use, you can vary the operating conditions as needed. Used without a keyword, SET takes you to the Settings menu, where you can modify any of the operating conditions by using the menu system. The syntax diagram shows all the various operating modifiers: characters; on/off switches; basic values; colors; and currency, date, and time formats. See Appendix B for more information on the Settings menu options.

SET VARIABLE

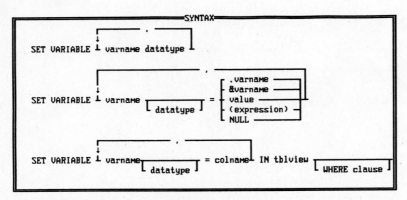

SET VARIABLE defines one or more global variables. See the "Programming Commands" section for more information. See also "FETCH."

SHOW

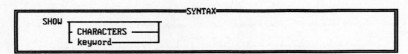

SHOW displays the operating environment. See "SET."

SHOW VARIABLE

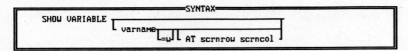

SHOW VARIABLE displays a single global variable as the specified screen row and column, or all system and global variables.

Backup and Restore Commands

Use Backup and Restore commands to make backup copies of your database and to import and export data.

For information on importing and exporting data, see Chapter 10. For information on backups, see Chapter 11.

BACKUP

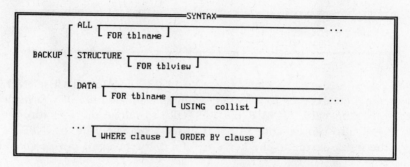

BACKUP sends the structure, data, or both to a specified DOS file. BACKUP will write the file across more than one floppy disk. BACKUP has the same syntax as the UNLOAD command, which writes to only a single floppy disk. The file BACKUP creates consists of a series of R:BASE commands. If you are backing up the structure, the file includes the commands that build a database structure. If you are backing up data, the file includes one or more LOAD data-block commands. The file is a DOS ASCII file that you can edit with R:BASE editor or any word processor that creates ASCII files. You specify the file by using an OUTPUT command before the BACKUP command.

COPY

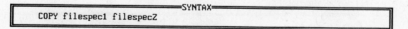

COPY creates duplicates of DOS files.

GATEWAY

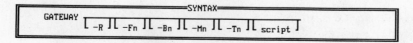

GATEWAY starts the import/export utility. This is a menu-driven module that can export R:BASE data to ASCII fixed-field and delimited files; Lotus 1-2-3; Symphony; Lotus Transfer (T-A-C); SYLK (Multiplan format); DIF (Visicalc format); and dBASE II, III, and III PLUS. GATEWAY can import data from any of these file structures, in addition to PFS:File. You can execute the FileGateway module independently from DOS.

INPUT

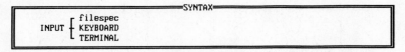

```
                          ═══SYNTAX═══
          ┌ filespec
    INPUT ┤ KEYBOARD
          └ TERMINAL
```

INPUT executes the commands contained in the specified file. Use INPUT to recreate a database or to load data from an unloaded file. If you made a database backup with BACKUP, use RESTORE to reload the structure or data. INPUT also can execute an ASCII format command file, or INPUT can return the input device to the keyboard if a different input device (file) is in control.

PACK

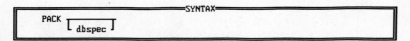

```
                          ═══SYNTAX═══
    PACK ┌────────┐
         └ dbspec ┘
```

PACK reorders and compresses a database. Use PACK if you have deleted tables or rows from your database. Before using PACK, back up your database by using BACKUP or UNLOAD.

RELOAD

```
                          ═══SYNTAX═══
    RELOAD dbspec
```

RELOAD reorders and compresses a database, but makes a second copy of the database while doing so. This is an alternative to backing up with BACKUP or UNLOAD. Be sure that you have sufficient disk space for two copies of your database.

RESTORE

RESTORE recreates a database from a backup file created with BACKUP. You can use BACKUP and RESTORE for backups on multiple floppy disks.

UNLOAD

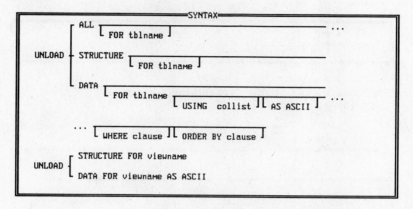

Used with OUTPUT, UNLOAD backs up the database structure, data, or both to a DOS ASCII file. See "BACKUP."

Housekeeping Commands

Use housekeeping commands to manage your drive, directories, and files. For information on using help screens, see Chapter 1. For information on DOS commands, see Chapter 11.

CHDIR

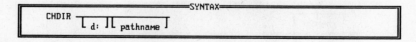

CHDIR displays or changes the current DOS directory to the specified directory. The directory already must exist. See "MKDIR."

CHDRV

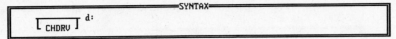

CHDRV changes the current drive to the specified drive. If you do not specify a drive, CHDRV displays the current drive.

CHKDSK

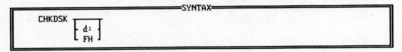

CHKDSK displays the available disk and memory space.

DIR

DIR displays the DOS files on the specified directory.

ERASE

ERASE removes a DOS file. You cannot erase files that contain an open database.

HELP

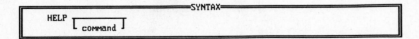

The HELP command starts the Help module—a menu-driven set of help screens for R:BASE commands. If you specify a command, HELP displays the help screens for that command only.

MKDIR

MKDIR creates a directory on the specified drive and directory or in the current directory.

RENAME File

RENAME changes the name of a DOS file. Do not rename only one of the database RBF files. If you rename the database, be sure to rename all three files or your database will not be usable.

RMDIR

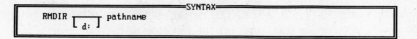

RMDIR removes a directory.

TYPE

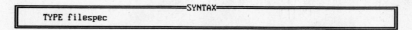

TYPE outputs a DOS ASCII file to the current output device.

Command Clauses

Many R:BASE commands use the ORDER BY and WHERE clauses. You use these clauses in the same way for every command. For more information on these clauses, see Chapter 9.

ORDER BY

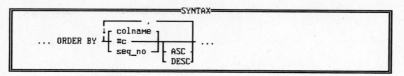

ORDER BY sorts the rows by the specified column or columns. You also can specify ascending or descending sort order.

WHERE

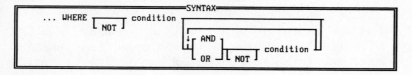

WHERE sets conditions on the rows to limit the data being acted on by the command. A WHERE clause consists of one or more conditions connected with AND, OR, AND NOT, or OR NOT. A condition is a comparison between a column on the left side of the operator, a comparison operator, and a value on the right side of the operator. Some alternative conditions include checking for the existence of any value (IS NULL and IS NOT NULL), a specific row (COUNT =), limiting the number of rows to include by count (LIMIT =), creation of a comparison list with a sub-SELECT, specifying a range of values (BETWEEN), or comparing all or part of a text value (LIKE and CONTAINS).

Structured Query Language

Structured Query Language (SQL) is a standard control language developed for use with relational databases. R:BASE includes the complete ANSI-standard set of SQL commands. Each command listed in this section is described elsewhere under the heading appropriate to the command use. The commands are listed here so that you will know when you are using an SQL command. Command use within R:BASE for SQL is the same as any R:BASE command; you need not, as some other database management systems require, start any special environment to use the SQL command language.

All of these commands are described elsewhere in this appendix.

Data-Definition Commands

Data-definition commands are described in the "Structure-Development Commands" section, earlier in this appendix. These commands enable you initially to describe and then change the structure of your database.

ALTER TABLE

Modifies an existing table by adding a column.

COMMENT ON

Adds descriptive comments to tables or columns.

CREATE INDEX

Creates a pointer to the data values for a column to enhance access speed.

CREATE SCHEMA

Creates the initial database structure.

CREATE TABLE

Creates a table.

CREATE VIEW

Creates a query definition (view).

DROP INDEX

Removes an existing key for a column.

DROP TABLE

Removes a table.

DROP VIEW

Removes a view.

Data-Manipulation Commands

Data-manipulation commands provide command-driven data entry and modification. These commands are described in the "Data-Entry and Modification Commands" section, earlier in this appendix.

DELETE

Removes one or more rows from a table.

INSERT

Adds one or more rows to a table.

SELECT

Selects columns and rows for display. If you use SELECT as a clause, it selects rows for deletion, insertion, or modification.

UPDATE

Modifies values of one or more columns in one or more rows.

Data-Security Commands

Data-security commands provide command-driven password protection for your database. These commands are described in the "Structure-Development Commands" section, earlier in this appendix.

CONNECT

Gains access to a database.

DISCONNECT

Closes and stores a database.

LIST ACCESS

Lists existing passwords by user.

GRANT

Assigns password-protection to a table.

REVOKE

Removes user privileges (password access) from a table.

Programming-Control Commands

You generally use programming-control commands within command or application files. See the "Programming Commands" section, later in this appendix, for a description of each command. In addition, see Chapters 8 and 9 for more detailed information on programming.

——comment

Provides internal documentation for the program.

CLOSE

Releases the memory used by a cursor pointer.

DECLARE CURSOR

Defines a cursor pointer to rows in a table or view.

DROP CURSOR

Removes a defined cursor pointer.

FETCH

Extracts data pointed to by a cursor and places the values in global variables.

OPEN

Specifies the cursor pointer to use in subsequent commands.

Programming Commands

Programming commands provide custom programming features using the R:BASE language. These commands include the following:

- Program control for repetitive processing
- Custom menus

- Pointers for multirow processing
- Screen and keyboard control
- Variable setting and use

For information on programming, see Chapters 8 and 9.

BEEP

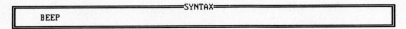

BEEP sounds the computer's bell, even if BELL is set off.

CHOOSE

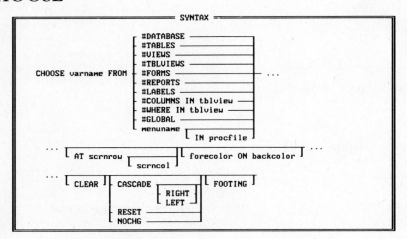

Used with a # keyword, CHOOSE displays a pop-up menu containing the specified database items. With a menu name, CHOOSE displays the specified custom menu file. Custom menu files have a specific structure.

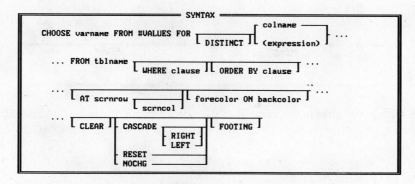

CHOOSE creates and displays a pop-up menu containing data from a single column in the specified table. The WHERE and ORDER BY clauses limit and sort the data to be displayed.

For both types of CHOOSE commands, you can specify the position of the pop-up menu on-screen (AT), choose foreground and background colors, choose to clear the menu from the screen (CLEAR), cascade the pop-up menu from the last displayed menu (CASCADE), or suppress the standarad message lines at the bottom of the screen (FOOTING).

CLEAR

CLEAR removes global variables: all variables, specified variables, or all variables *except* the listed variables.

CLOSE

CLOSE halts use of a specific cursor pointer (see DECLARE CURSOR). CLOSE frees some memory space, but does not remove the cursor definition.

CLS

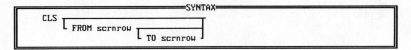

CLS clears the screen. To clear specific screen rows, enter FROM and TO screen line numbers. CLS affects only screen display. See "NEWPAGE."

CODELOCK

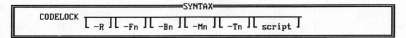

CODELOCK starts the R:BASE application-encoding module. Use this module to convert an ASCII application file into an executable procedure file. You also can use CODELOCK to secure ASCII command files by creating an executable binary, non-editable version of the file. CODELOCK has facilities for creating a procedure file by merging separate ASCII command, screen, and menu files into a single, encoded procedure file. You can execute CODELOCK independently from DOS.

COMMENT

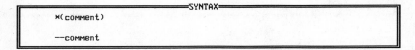

COMMENT comments serve to document your command and application files internally. You can use either or both of the comment formats in any executable file. R:BASE ignores everything within a comment.

DECLARE CURSOR

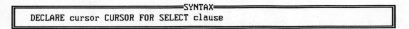

DECLARE CURSOR sets a path to a series of rows in a table. The path is pointed to by a cursor. The cursor contains the definition of the path to follow. See "FETCH."

DIALOG

```
                              ═══SYNTAX═══
  DIALOG 'message' response endkey lines
```

DIALOG displays a dialog box on-screen with the specified message as a prompt for entry. The data entered in the box is stored in the global variable that you specify in place of the response parameter. The variable you specify in place of endkey will hold the ending keystroke (Enter, F2, Esc, or F1). The parameter lines specify how many 50-character lines you can use for the entry (up to 15). The SET keyword EXPLODE determines whether R:BASE draws the box instantly (EXPLODE OFF) or explodes outward from the center of the box (EXPLODE ON). You can set dialog box foreground and background colors by using SET DIALOG.

DISPLAY

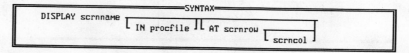

```
                              ═══SYNTAX═══
  DISPLAY scrnname
                   └ IN procfile ┘└ AT scrnrow ┐
                                        └ scrncol ┘
```

DISPLAY shows a DOS ASCII file's contents, a screen block in a procedure file, or a screen snapshot file created with the SNAPSHOT command.

DROP CURSOR

```
                              ═══SYNTAX═══
  DROP CURSOR cursor
```

DROP CURSOR removes a cursor definition from memory. See "DECLARE CURSOR."

EXPRESS

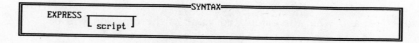

```
                              ═══SYNTAX═══
  EXPRESS
         └ script ┘
```

EXPRESS starts the R:BASE application-building module—Application Express. This menu-driven module leads you through the steps of creating a custom application.

FETCH

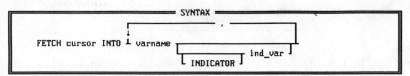

FETCH loads data from the cursor-defined row into the specified global variables and moves the cursor pointer to the next row indicated by the cursor definition. See "DECLARE CURSOR."

FILLIN

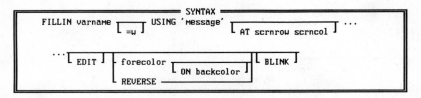

FILLIN prompts you for a value from the keyboard and stores the value in a global variable. The USING message appears as a prompt for the value. You can specify the screen row and column at which the message is displayed. The screen cursor is positioned at the end of the message.

Functions

You use R:BASE SuperMath functions in expressions. These functions provide a variety of arithmetic, mathematical, string, and logical calculations. R:BASE calculates the function value based on the arguments included with the function. You can use functions in computed column expressions, to calculate the value of a global variable, or to calculate the value of a column.

The following tables provide a description for each function, the syntax for the function, and what the calculated value of the function will be.

Table C.1
Using Arithmetic and Mathematical Functions

Function/Syntax	Description
Absolute Value ABS(*value*)	Absolute value; a positive number regardless of whether *value* is negative or positive.
Difference DIM(*value1,value2*)	Positive difference between the first and second value.
Exponent EXP(*power*)	Returns *e* raised to the power (where *e* = 2.71828182845905).
Logarithmic Values LOG(*value*)	Log base of *e*, as determined by value.
LOG10(*value*)	Log base 10 of *value*.
Square Root SQRT(*value*)	Square root of *value*.
Average LAVG(*valuelist*)	Average of the values in *value_list*.
Minimum LMIN(*valuelist*)	Minimum value in *value_list*.
Maximum LMAX(*valuelist*)	Maximum value in *value_list*.
Modulus MOD(*value1,value2*)	Remainder (modulus) of *value1/value2*.
Sign SIGN(*value1,value2*)	Replaces the sign (positive or negative) of *value2* with the sign of *value1*.
Next Autonumber Value NEXT(*table,column*)	Next autonumber value for the specified column and table.

Table C.2
Using Trigonometric Functions

Function/Syntax	Description
Sine	
SIN(*angle*)	Sine of *angle*
ASIN(*argument*)	Arcsine of *angle*
SINH(*angle*)	Hyperbolic sine of *angle*
Cosine	
COS(*angle*)	Cosine of *angle*
ACOS(*argument*)	Arccosine of *angle*
COSH(*angle*)	Hyperbolic cosine of *angle*
Tangent	
TAN(*angle*)	Tangent of *angle*
ATAN(*argument*)	Arctangent of *angle*
ATAN2(*angle1,angle2*)	Arctangent of the coordinate angle specified by *angle1* and *angle2*
TANH(*angle*)	Hyperbolic tangent of *angle*

Using Table C.3
Using Numeric Conversions

Function/Syntax	Description
AINT(*real number*)	Removes the decimal part of the number, leaving an integer value with the original data type.
ANINT(*real number*)	Rounds the decimal part to the nearest integer, leaving the number the original data type.
INT(*real number*)	Truncates the decimal part, returning an integer number.
NINT(*real number*)	Rounds the number to the nearest whole number, returning an integer number.
FLOAT(*integer*)	Converts an integer to a decimal number.

Table C.4
Using Date Functions

Function/Syntax	Description
RDATE(mm,dd,yy)	Converts the three integer values into a valid date
JDATE(*date*)	Provides the julian date format YYDDD for the given date
IDAY(*date*)	Returns the integer day
IDWK(*date*)	Returns the integer day of the week
IMON(*date*)	Returns the integer month
IYR(*date*)	Returns the integer year
TDWK(*date*)	Returns the text day of the week
TMON(*date*)	Returns the text month

Table C.5
Using Time Functions

Function/Syntax	Description
RTIME(hh,mm,ss)	Converts the three integer values into a valid time
IHR(*time*)	Returns the integer hours
IMIN(*time*)	Returns the integer minutes
ISEC(*time*)	Returns the integer seconds

Table C.6
Using Financial Functions

Function/Syntax	Description
Future Value FV1(*payment,interest,periods*)	Future value of a series of equal payments, with interest, over the specified number of periods.
FV2(*present value,interest,periods*)	Future value of the present value based on the accumulation of interest over the specified number of periods.
Present Value PV1(*payment,interest,periods*)	Present value of a series of equal payments at the specified interest rate and periods.
PV2(*future value,interest,periods*)	Present value given a future value, with interest over the specified number of periods.
Payments PMT1(*interest,periods,present value*)	Payment amount needed to pay off the present value over the specified periods at the given interest rate.
PMT2(*interest,periods,future value*)	Payment amount needed to attain the future value given the interest rate and number of periods.
Periodic Interest Rate RATE1(*future value,present value,periods*)	Rate to attain the future value from the specified present value over the given number of periods.
RATE2(*future value,payment,periods*)	Rate to attain the future value given the specified payments over the given number of periods.
RATE3(*present value,payment,periods*)	Rate to return the specified payment given the present annuity value and the number of periods.

Function/Syntax	Description
Number of Periods TERM1(*present value,interest,* *future value*)	Number of periods to attain the future value based on the given present value and interest rate.
TERM2(*payment,interest,future* *value*)	Number of periods to attain the future value given the payments and interest.
TERM3(*payment,interest,present* *value*)	Number of periods to pay off the present value given the payment amount and interest rate.

Table C.7
Using Keyboard and Operating System Functions

Function/Syntax	Description
SET Keyword Value CVAL(*keyword*)	Returns the SET keyword's current value.
Environment Variable ENVVAL(*environment variable*)	Returns the value of a variable defined in your computer's CONFIG.SYS file.
Key Value CHKKEY(0)	Returns 1 if keystrokes exist in the type-ahead buffer. Returns 0 if no keystrokes are available.
GETKEY(0)	Gets the text value of the first keystroke in the type-ahead buffer.
LASTKEY(0)	Gets the text value of the last key pressed.

Table C.8
Using Logical Comparison Functions

Function/Syntax	Description
IFEQ(*value1,value2,return1,return2*)	Compares *value1* and *value2*. If they are equal, returns the value of *return1*; otherwise, returns the value of *return2*.
IFLT(*value1,value2,return1,return2*)	Compares *value1* and *value2*. If *value1* is less than *value2*, returns the value of *return1*; otherwise, returns the value of *return2*.
IFGT(*value1,value2,return1,return2*)	Compares *value1* and *value2*. If *value1* is greater than *value2*, returns the value of *return1*; otherwise returns the value of *return2*.

Table C.9
Using Text Functions

Function/Syntax	Description
Retrieving Text Strings SGET(*text,number,position*)	Retrieves the *number* of characters in *text* starting at *position*.
SLEN(*text*)	Returns the length of text.
SLOC(*text,string*)	Finds the starting location of *text* in *string*.
SSUB(*text,n*)	Finds the *n*th substring within *text*. You must separate the substrings with commas.
Modifying Values in Text Strings SFIL(*character,number*)	Fills a text string with the *character*, repeated *number* times.

Function/Syntax	Description
SMOVE(*text,position1, number,string,position2*)	Moves *number* characters from *string* starting in *position2* into *text* starting in *position1*.
SPUT(*text,string,position*)	Moves *string* into *text* at *position*.
STRIM(*text*)	Trims trailing blanks from *text*.
ULC(*text*)	Makes *text* all lowercase.
LUC(*text*)	Makes *text* all uppercase.
ICAP1(*text*)	Makes *text* initial caps on the first word with lowercase for subsequent letters.
ICAP2(*text*)	Makes *text* initials caps for all words.
Positioning Text Strings CTR(*text,width*)	Centers *text* in *width* characters.
LJS(*text,width*)	Left-justifies *text* in *width* characters.
RJS(*text,width*)	Right-justifies *text* in *width* characters.

Table C.10
Using Text Conversions

Function/Syntax	Description
Change to Text CTXT(*value*)	Converts *value* to a Text data type
Change to ASCII Integer ICHAR(*character*)	Returns the ASCII integer value of *character*
Change Integer to Text CHAR(*integer*)	Returns the text value of *integer*

GOTO

```
                        ═══SYNTAX═══
    GOTO lblname
```

GOTO sends control to the command following the specified label.

IF...ENDIF

```
                        ═══SYNTAX═══
    IF condlist THEN        IF condlist THEN
        then-block             then-block
    ENDIF                  ELSE
                               else-block
                           ENDIF
```

IF...ENDIF executes the commands contained between IF and ENDIF if the specified comparison is true. Include ELSE to execute commands between IF and THEN if the comparison is true or to execute commands between ELSE and ENDIF if the comparison is false.

LABEL

```
                        ═══SYNTAX═══
    LABEL lblname
```

LABEL specifies a place to send control to by a GOTO command.

NEWPAGE

```
                        ═══SYNTAX═══
    NEWPAGE
```

NEWPAGE clears the screen or sends a form feed character to the printer if the current output device is PRINTER.

OPEN

```
                        ═══SYNTAX═══
    OPEN cursor
```

OPEN makes a defined cursor pointer available for use.

PAUSE

PAUSE halts processing of a command file until you press a key to continue.

QUIT

QUIT exits from a command file. If you include a TO, the specified command file is executed after you exit.

RBEDIT

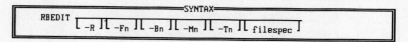

RBEDIT starts the R:BASE text editor. You can use the editor for ASCII files or recorded scripts (see "RECORD" and "PLAYBACK"). The editor has text search and replace, as well as text copy and move capabilities. You can execute RBEDIT from DOS.

RETURN

RETURN returns control to where the program was executed. If you execute the program by a RUN or INPUT command entered from the R> prompt, the program terminates and returns to the R> prompt. If you execute the program from another command or procedure file, the program returns to the calling command or procedure file.

RUN

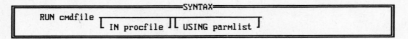

RUN executes a command file or a block in a procedure file.

SET ECHO

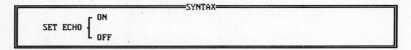

If SET ECHO is on, R:BASE sends the executing commands in a command file to the current output device. The default is Off. SET ECHO is a useful debugging tool because you can see the commands as they execute. Therefore, you know which command has a problem if an error occurs.

SET ERROR

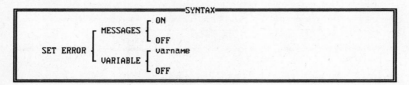

Using SET ERROR with VARIABLE defines a system error variable. The variable assumes the error number of the command that executes.
By checking the value of this variable after a command executes, you can determine whether an error occurred and, if so, what that error is. The ERRMSG database that comes with R:BASE contains all error messages and their numeric values.

You can use SET ERROR with MESSAGES to turn on or off error message display.

SET VARIABLE

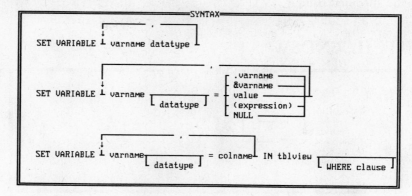

SET VARIABLE defines a global variable and assigns a value to the variable.

SHOW ERROR

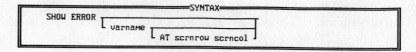

SHOW ERROR displays the error message related to the current error value contained in the system error variable. See "SET ERROR VARIABLE."

SHOW VARIABLE

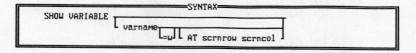

SHOW VARIABLE displays a single global variable as the specified screen row and column, or all system and global variables.

SKIP

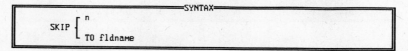

Used in form trigger files, SKIP skips the next *n* field or skips to the field with the specified name.

SWITCH...ENDSW

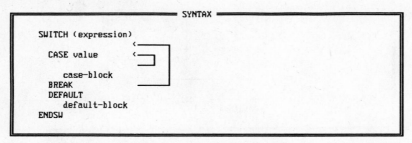

SWITCH..ENDSW defines a variable to compare. Each CASE section in the command block makes a comparison of the value of a variable and, if the comparison is true, executes the commands following the CASE line. If none of the CASE comparisons are true, R:BASE executes the commands following the DEFAULT line. A BREAK command (used only in SWITCH and WHILE structures) marks the end of each CASE block of commands.

WHENEVER

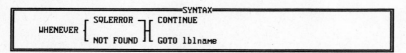

WHENEVER sets error-checking on SQL commands (SQLERROR) or database searches (NOT FOUND). If an error occurs, control passes to the label specified by the GOTO. The CONTINUE option turns off error-checking set with a previous WHENEVER command.

WHILE...ENDWHILE

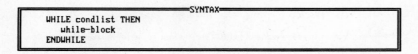

WHILE...ENDWHILE executes the commands contained in the while-block as long as the conditions specified on the WHILE line are true or until a BREAK command exits the WHILE loop.

ZIP

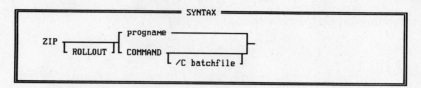

ZIP temporarily exits from R:BASE to execute the specified program or batch file. With the ROLLOUT option, R:BASE saves the environment and database, and then resets and reopens the database on return to R:BASE. ROLLOUT frees sufficient memory to execute large application programs. Without ROLLOUT, the database and its environment are saved in memory, enabling you to execute only small programs or DOS batch files. To execute batch files, use the COMMAND /C option.

Transaction-Processing and Multiuser Commands

You use transaction-processing commands to group and control functions that update the data in the database. With transaction processing turned on, you can collect a series of commands in a single batch that you can execute or cancel. You can increase greatly the speed of modifications by grouping and then executing all changes with a single command.

Multiuser commands set the environment for multiple users accessing the same database simultaneously. Multiuser commands are useful only if you install R:BASE on a local area network with a database resident on a shared drive.

After each command in this section, you are told whether that command is a transaction-processing command or a multiuser command.

Multiuser and transaction processing are topics that are not covered in this book. For more information, see your R:BASE documentation.

COMMIT

Commits all transactions executed since the last COMMIT.

(transaction-processing command)

ROLLBACK

Returns the database to its state prior to the last set of transactions. In other words, ROLLBACK negates any transactions executed since the last COMMIT.

(transaction-processing command)

SET AUTOCOMMIT

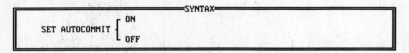

With TRANSACT ON, SET AUTOCOMMIT turns on or off automatic commitment of transactions to the database. With TRANSACT OFF, use the COMMIT command to commit transactions to the database.

(transaction-processing command)

SET LOCK

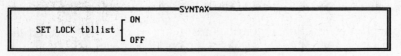

SET LOCK locks the table or tables, preventing access by users other than the user issuing the command.

(multiuser command)

SET MAXTRANS

With TRANSACT ON, SET MAXTRANS specifies the number of users that you will allow to access the database during transaction processing.

(transaction-processing command)

SET TRANSACT

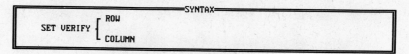

SET TRANSACT sets transaction processing on or off. In multiuser, all users must first set TRANSACT to On and then connect to the database.

(transaction-processing command)

SET VERIFY

```
                          ═══════SYNTAX═══════
    SET VERIFY ┌ ROW
               └ COLUMN
```

SET VERIFY sets the verify level for form use. COLUMN checks for changes made by other users for each column in a form. ROW checks only when you save a row to the database.

(multiuser command)

SET WAIT

```
                              ═══SYNTAX═══
  SET WAIT n
```

Sets the number of seconds to wait before retrying access to a database resource. If a table is locked (SET LOCK), for example, and another user wants to use the table, the WAIT period specifies how often R:BASE rechecks to determine if the table is available.

(multiuser command)

Example Databases

This appendix describes every part of the two sample databases used in this book. After reading the chapters in this book and the information in this appendix, you should be able to reproduce the sample databases.

This book used two databases: MAILING and CHKBOOK. The MAILING database elements were covered in detail in Chapters 3 through 7. The CHKBOOK database illustrated some of the advanced features, but was not created in the chapters. If you want to recreate CHKBOOK, the information for doing so is in this appendix.

The Mailing Database

The MAILING database contains three tables related by common columns. In Chapters 3 through 7, you learned how to create the tables, define a view, create two types of forms, and create two types of reports.

In Quick Start 4, you also used the MAILING database in an application.

The following sections describe all of the items that make up the MAILING database.

Tables

Type *list* at the R> prompt to list all user-defined tables and views, as well as the system tables (see fig. D.1).

See Chapter 3 for information on defining tables and Chapter 5 for information on defining views.

Following are the tables and views that you created:

- *Mail_list:* Master table listing people and their addresses.

```
Tables in the Database Mailing

Name           Columns    Rows     Name          Columns    Rows

SYSINFO           7        17      Codes_mail       2         2
SYSRULES          4         1      When_mailed      3         5
SYSREP            3        64      SYSFORM          3        176
SYSLABEL          3        31      SYSVIEWS         3         1
Q_mail           14        N/A     Mail_list       10         3
```

Fig. D.1

LIST TABLES displays all tables and views in the MAILING database.

- *Codes_mail:* Master table containing mailing codes (types of mailings sent) and descriptions of those codes.

- *When_mailed:* Detail table using data from Mail_list and Codes_mail showing specific items mailed to whom on what days.

- *Q_mail:* View definition that combines data from Mail_list and When_mailed.

R:BASE creates the following tables after you define parts of a database:

- *SYSINFO:* System-generated table that contains expressions for computed columns and autonumbering definitions.

- *SYSRULES:* System-generated table that contains rule definitions.

- *SYSFORM:* System-generated table that contains data entry forms.

- *SYSREP:* System-generated table that contains reports.

- *SYSVIEWS:* System-generated table that contains view definitions.

- *SYSLABEL:* System-generated table that contains label definitions.

Columns

The LIST *tblname* command displays the columns contained in the table. For each column, R:BASE displays the data type, indexing status, expression (if it is a computed column), and autonumbering status.

See Chapters 2 and 3 for information on defining tables, the columns that make up each table, autonumbering columns, computed columns, data entry rules, and passwords.

Column definitions for all user-defined tables follow, as shown in figure D.2, D.3, and D.4.

```
Table: Mail_list
Read Password: No
Modify Password: No

Mailing List Master Table

Column definitions
# Name              Type      Index Expression
1 Idno              INTEGER   ⋈    Autonumbering
            Identification number - Autonumber column
2 Firstname         TEXT      30
            First name
3 Lastname          TEXT      30
            Last Name
4 Middleinit        TEXT      2
            Middle Initial
5 Address1          TEXT      25
            Address Line 1
6 Address2          TEXT      25
            Address Line 2
7 City              TEXT      15
            City+

8 State             TEXT      2
            State
9 Zipcode           TEXT      10
            Zip Code
10 CSZ_line         TEXT      27        (   City + ',' &
                                        State &   Zipcode )
            Complete City, State, Zip

Current number of rows:     3
```

Fig. D.2

Mail_list is the database's master table.

```
Table: Codes_mail
Read Password: No
Modify Password: No

Mailing type codes and descriptions

Column definitions
# Name              Type      Index Expression
1 Mailcode          TEXT      2 ⋈
            Mailing Type Code
2 Maildesc          TEXT      40
            Mailing Code Description

Current number of rows:     2
```

Fig. D.3

Codes_mail describes the types of mailings.

Fig. D.4

When_mailed shows what was mailed and to whom.

```
Table: When_mailed
Read Password: No
Modify Password: No

Mailings by Id Number

Column definitions
#  Name              Type      Index  Expression
1  Idno              INTEGER    *
2  Mailcode          TEXT       Z  *
3  Maildate          DATE
             Date Mailed

Current number of rows:        3
```

Rules

If you type *list rules* at the R> prompt, R:BASE displays data entry rules (see fig. D.5).

Fig. D.5

LIST RULES shows all the defined data entry rules.

```
(RULES    ) ON  Check data validation RULES
MESSAGE :  Value for Idno must be unique.
TABLE :  Mail_list     the row is added or changed if the WHERE clause SUCCEEDS
WHERE :  Idno NOT IN ( SELECT Idno FROM Mail_list )

MESSAGE :  Value for Idno must exist in Idno in Mail_list
TABLE :  When_mailed   the row is added or changed if the WHERE clause SUCCEEDS
WHERE :  Idno IN ( SELECT Idno FROM Mail_list )
```

See Chapter 3 for information on defining rules by using menus and prompts.

Views

The LIST VIEW *viewname* command shows the definition for a view. The following view list shows the command structure defining the view:

```
View: Q_mail
SELECT FROM Mail_list #T1, When_mailed #T2 WHERE (#T1.Idno
    = #T2.Idno)
```

See Chapter 5 for information on defining views by using menus and prompting.

Forms

The LIST FORMS command displays a list of the forms in the database:

```
Form        Table                  Form Description
--------    ------------------     ------------------------------------
Codeform    Codes_mail             Entry/Edit Form for Mailing Codes
Mailings    Mail_list              Form for Mail_list table.
Maillist    Mail_list              Form for Mail_list table.
```

See Chapter 6 for information on defining forms.

Codeform is a multirow entry form used to enter or edit data in the Codes_mail table. Its design is a modification of the Quick form you created in Quick Start 4. The modification changed the form from a single-table, single-row form to a single-table, multirow form. Figure D.6 shows the form layout.

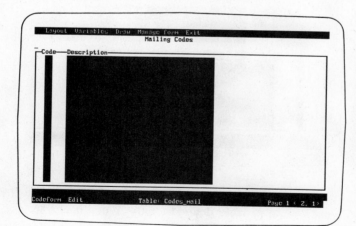

Fig. D.6

Codeform provides entry and editing for multiple rows in a multirow region.

Mailings is a single-table form; it is the simplest form format, using a single table and a single screen page. Figure D.7 shows the form layout.

Maillist is a multitable form with a multirow region defined for the second table. Figure D.8 shows the layout of the multitable form. Notice that the

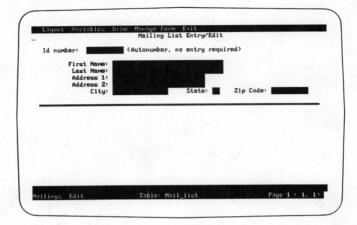

Fig. D.7

Mailings is a single-table, single-page form.

top part of the form is similar to Mailings because this form was developed as an extension of the simpler Mailings form. A table was added and a multirow region created to allow entry into multiple rows in the second table.

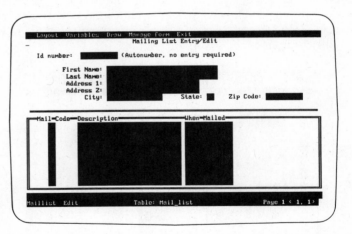

Fig. D.8

Maillist is a multitable form with a multirow region for the second table.

Maillist has the following lookup variable defined for the When_mail (second) table:

vdesc = Maildesc IN Codes_mail WHERE Mailcode = Mailcode

Reports

The LIST REPORTS command displays a list of the reports in the database:

```
Report      Table / View         Report Description
--------    ------------------   ------------------------------
Mailrep     Q_mail               Mailing Report
Mailings    Q_mail               Mailing report grouped by person
```

R:BASE produced Mailrep as a Quick report. Mailrep is a row-oriented report that enables you to print a large amount of data in an 80-column format. Figure D.9 shows the report layout.

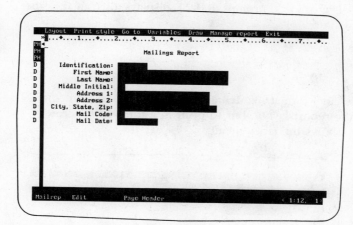

Fig. D.9

Mailrep prints data from a view.

Mailings is a breakpoint report format, breaking the data into groups based on the value of the Idno column in the Q_mail view. Figure D.10 shows the report layout.

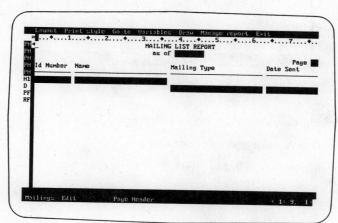

Fig. D.10

Mailings shows a simple way to use report breakpoints.

Mailings has the following variables defined. The first variable is a concatenation variable that places all of the name data into a single field. The second variable is a lookup variable to draw the mailing code description from the Codes_mail table:

```
vfullname = (Firstname & Middleinit & Lastname)
vdesc = Maildesc IN Codes_mail WHERE Mailcode = Mailcode
```

See Chapter 7 for information on defining reports.

Labels

If you type *list labels* at the R> prompt, R:BASE displays a list of the label templates in the database:

```
Label       Table / View          Label Description
--------    ------------------    ------------------
M_labels    Mail_list             Mailing Labels.
```

M_labels is a simple label format. Its definition tells R:BASE to print the data as shown on the report layout, but to print in a three-label-across format. Figure D.11 shows the label layout.

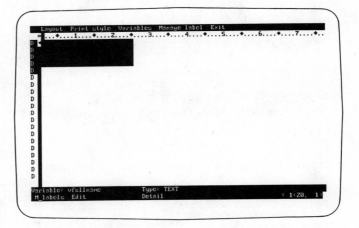

Fig. D.11

Label formats are similar to report formats except that data can be printed in a variety of label sizes.

M_labels has the following concatenation variable defined:

vfullname = (Firstname & Middleinit & Lastname)

See Chapter 7 for information on defining labels.

Applications

See Quick Start 4 for an example application using the MAILING database.

The Checkbook Database

The CHKBOOK database has four tables. Three of the tables are used to hold information on checks, cash, and deposits. The fourth table is a year-to-date summary of data contained in the other three tables.

The CHKBOOK database is not described in detail in this book; only parts of it are used to illustrate concepts in Part IV. The following sections describe all of the items that make up the CHKBOOK database.

Tables

The LIST command lists all user-defined tables and views, as well as the system tables (see fig. D.12).

Fig. D.12

LIST TABLES displays all tables and views in the CHKBOOK database.

```
Tables in the Database CHKBOOK

Name          Columns  Rows    Name          Columns  Rows

SYSINFO          7      22      Checks           6       6
SYSRULES         4       3      Cash             5       4
Budgets          2       8      Deposits         5       4
SYSFORM          3     181      YTDsummary       2       8
SYSREP           3      21      Dummy            1       1
```

The tables that you create for the database follow:

- *Checks:* Contains check numbers, pay-to, notation, amount, and budget code for checks written.

- *Cash:* Contains pay-to, notation, amount, and budget code for cash withdrawals.

- *Deposits:* Contains source, notation, amount, and budget code for deposits.

- *YTDsummary:* Contains a computed summary value for each budget category for Checks, Cash, and Deposits.

- *Dummy:* Contains a single column named Dummy. This table is used to drive a form that loads data into all of the master tables. See the "Forms" section, later in this chapter.

See Chapter 3 for information on defining tables.

The following tables are created by R:BASE when you define parts of a database.

- *SYSINFO:* System-generated table that contains expressions for computed columns and autonumbering definitions.

- *SYSRULES:* System-generated table that contains rule definitions.

- *SYSFORM:* System-generated table that contains data-entry forms.

- *SYSREP:* System-generated table that contains reports.

Columns

The LIST *tblname* command displays the columns contained in the table. For each column, R:BASE displays the data type, indexing status, expression (if it is a computed column), and autonumbering status. Figures D.13 through D.16 show the column definitions for all user-defined tables.

See Chapters 2 and 3 for information on defining tables, the columns that make up each table, autonumbering columns, computed columns, data-entry rules, and passwords.

Fig. D.13

Checks contains information on checks written.

```
Table: Checks
Read Password: No
Modify Password: No

Check/Cash Master File.

Column definitions
# Name          Type       Index Expression
1 Checknumber      INTEGER    *     Autonumbering
                Check number - Autonumber column.
2 Budget           TEXT       3 *
                Budget Category.
3 Checkdate        DATE
                Date check was written.
4 Notation         TEXT      40
                Notation on check.
5 Payee            TEXT      40
                Who check was written for.
6 Amount           CURRENCY
                Amount of check.

Current number of rows:    10
```

```
Table: Deposits
Read Password: No
Modify Password: No

Deposit Table.

Column definitions
# Name              Type      Index Expression
1 Budget            TEXT    3 ×
2 Depdate           DATE
          Deposit Date.
3 Amount            CURRENCY
4 Notation          TEXT    40
5 DepNumber         INTEGER   ×      Autonumbering
          Deposit Number - Autonumber column.

Current number of rows:     4
```

Fig. D.14

Deposits contains information on money deposited.

```
Table: Cash
Read Password: No
Modify Password: No

Cash Entries.

Column definitions
# Name              Type      Index Expression
1 Budget            TEXT    3 ×
2 Cashdate          DATE
          Date cash withdrawn/expended.
3 Amount            CURRENCY
4 Notation          TEXT    40
5 Cashnumber        INTEGER   ×      Autonumbering
          Cash Number - Autonumber column.

Current number of rows:     4
```

Fig. D.15

Cash contains information on cash withdrawals.

```
Table: Dummy
Read Password: No
Modify Password: No

Dummy table for Alltabs form.

Column definitions
# Name              Type      Index Expression
1 Dummy             TEXT    8
          Dummy column for Alltabs form.

Current number of rows:     1
```

Fig. D.16

Dummy is used in the Alltabs form.

Rules

If you type *list rules* at the R> prompt, R:BASE displays data entry rules
(see fig. D.17).

Fig. D.17

*LIST RULES
shows all
the defined
data-entry
rules.*

```
(RULES    ) ON  Check data validation RULES
MESSAGE : Value for Budget cannot be null.
  TABLE : Checks    Row is added or changed if condition SUCCEEDS
  WHERE : Budget IS NOT NULL

MESSAGE : Value for Budget cannot be null.
  TABLE : Deposits   Row is added or changed if condition SUCCEEDS
  WHERE : Budget IS NOT NULL

MESSAGE : Value for Budget cannot be null.
  TABLE : Cash    Row is added or changed if condition SUCCEEDS
  WHERE : Budget IS NOT NULL
```

See Chapter 3 for information on defining rules by using menus and
prompts.

Forms

Type *list forms* to display a list of the forms in the database:

```
Form      Table               Form Description
--------  ------------------  -----------------------------
Checks    Checks              Check entry form
Cash      Cash                Cash entry form
Deposits  Deposits            Deposit entry form
Alltabs   Dummy               All table variable entry form
```

Figures D.18 through D.21 show each of these forms.

The Checks form is a multirow, single-table form (see fig. D.18).

Other special features include help messages for each entry field and a
pop-up menu available when the cursor is in the Budget field. This pop-up
menu displays all budget categories available in the Budgets table.

The Cash form is similar to the Checks form (multirow, single-table). The
Cash form has no variables or expressions (see fig. D.19). It also has a pop-
up menu defined for the Budget field.

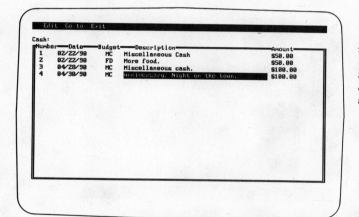

```
 Edit  Go to  Exit
Checks:
Number──Date────Budget──Pay-to/Notation═══════════════════Amount═══
 1     02/22/90   FD    Waremart                        $200.00
                        Party food.
 2     02/22/90   FD    Safeway                         $100.00
                        Party.
 3     02/22/90   MC    Bank check                      $100.00
                        Miscellaneous cash
 4     02/20/90   FD    Safeway                         $12.95
                        Food
 5     03/05/90   RT    Rent                            $565.00
                        George Willis
 7     04/28/90   SH    Fred Jones                      $100.00
                        Lawn mower.
 8     05/02/90   SH    Tires R Us                      $100.00
                        New tires for bike.
 9     04/20/90   IN    Allnation Insurance             $225.00
                        Initial insurance payment.
10     04/25/90   SH    Sam's Furniture                 $200.00
                        New couch
```

Fig. D.18

Using Checks to enter or edit checks.

```
 Edit  Go to  Exit
Cash:
Number──Date────Budget───Description═══════════════════Amount═══
 1     02/22/90   MC    Miscellaneous Cash              $50.00
 2     02/22/90   FD    More food.                      $50.00
 3     04/28/90   MC    Miscellaneous cash.             $100.00
 4     04/30/90   MC    Anniversary. Night on the town. $100.00
```

Fig. D.19

Using Cash to enter or edit cash withdrawals.

The Deposits form is similar to the Cash form (multirow, single-table) and, like Cash, has no variables or expressions. The Deposits form also has a pop-up menu defined for the Budget field (see fig. D.20).

The last form, Alltabs, illustrates the use of trigger files in a form (see fig. D.21). See "Writing Trigger Files" in Chapter 8 for a complete explanation of how to use trigger files and the related commands.

See Chapter 6 for information on defining forms.

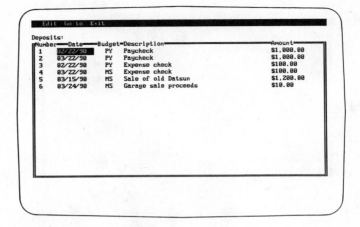

Fig. D.20

Using Deposits to enter or edit bank deposits.

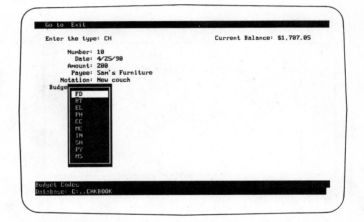

Fig. D.21

Using the Alltabs form to enter Checks, Cash, and Deposits with the help of trigger files.

Reports

Type *list reports* to display a list of the reports in the database:

Report	Table / View	Report Description
Checks	Checks	MTD Check List
Deposits	Deposits	MTD Deposit List
Cash	Cash	MTD Cash List

All of the list reports have a similar format. They each use a single breakpoint, breaking on the Budget column. Figure D.22 shows the same Checks report.

```
                         CHECK SUMMARY

Budget Category      /    Check#    Payee/Notation          Amount
FD Food/Groceries
                          1 Waremart                       $200.00
                            Party food.
                          2 Safeway                        $100.00
                            Party.
                          4 Safeway                         $12.95
                            Food
                                                       _____
IN Insurance                                              $312.95
                          9 Allnation Insurance            $225.00
                            Initial insurance payment.
                                                       _____
MC Miscellaneous Cash                                     $225.00
                          3 Bank check                     $100.00
                            Miscellaneous cash
                                                       _____
RT Rent Payment                                           $100.00
                          5 Rent                           $565.00
                            George Willis
                                                       _____
SH Small Household Expense                                $565.00
                          8 Tires R Us                     $100.00
                            New tires for bike.
                          7 Fred Jones                     $100.00
                            Lawn mower.
                         10 Sam's Furniture                $200.00
                            New couch
                                                       _____
                                                          $400.00

Total Check Amount        $1,602.95
```

Fig. D.22

The Checks report groups the checks into Budget categories.

See Chapter 7 for information on defining reports.

Programs

The CHKBOOK database, while not a complete application, uses some programming techniques. See "Writing Trigger Files" in Chapter 8 for illustrations of a special command file named a trigger file that is used in a form. The following shows the command files used with the database:

- *ALLTABS.CMD:* Executes the Alltabs form for multitable entry. See "Forms," earlier in this chapter.

```
SET MESSAGES OFF
SET ERROR MESSAGES OFF
RUN calcbal.cmd
EDIT USING alltabs
SET MESSAGES ON
SET ERROR MESSAGES ON
CLEAR ALL VARIABLES
```

- *CALCBAL.CMD:* A trigger file that also is executed when the report is used. This execution of the file initializes the account balance displayed on the Alltabs form.

- *YTDSUM.CMD:* Summarizes the amounts from Checks, Deposits, and Cash, and places the summarized-by-budget values in the YTDsummary table. With a few more lines of code, the summary also can be done by budget within month.

The complete listing for YTDSUM.CMD follows:

```
*( Generate YTD Summary for Each Budget Category )
*( Set ZERO so null values will be interpreted as 0 )
SET ZERO ON
*( Predefine the variables and set vbudget with a value )
SET VARIABLE vbudget CURRENCY
SET VARIABLE vbudget TEXT = 'XX'
*( Set a pointer to the budget table )
DECLARE cursor1 CURSOR FOR SELECT Budget FROM Budgets ORDER+
  BY Budget
*( Put the budget code into variable vbudget )
OPEN cursor1
*( Process budget codes until there are no more to process )
WHILE vbudget IS NOT NULL THEN
  *( Clear the variable and then put the budget category
    into vbudget )
  CLEAR VARIABLE vbudget
  FETCH cursor1 INTO vbudget
  *( If no other budgets exist then break from the WHILE loop )
  IF vbudget FAILS THEN
    BREAK
  ENDIF
  *( Find the total amount for this budget category -
    positive for deposits and negative for checks and cash )
  COMPUTE vdepsum AS SUM Amount FROM Deposits +
    WHERE Budget = .vbudget
  COMPUTE vchecksum AS SUM Amount FROM Checks +
    WHERE Budget = .vbudget
  COMPUTE vcashsum AS SUM Amount FROM Cash +
    WHERE Budget = .vbudget
  SET VAR vbalance =  (.vdepsum - (.vchecksum + .vcashsum))
  *( Write the total to the YTDsummary table )
  UPDATE YTDsummary SET Ytdamount = .vbalance +
    WHERE Budget = .vbudget
  *( Go to the top of the WHILE loop to process another
    budget code )
```

```
ENDWHILE
*( All budgets complete so quit )
*( Remove the cursor pointer )
DROP CURSOR cursor1
RETURN
```

As a beginner, you should not expect to be able to understand this command file completely. Each of the lines starting with *(are comments that explain what the next command or set of commands will do. The key features of this command file follow:

- Using DECLARE to set a pointer to each budget category sequentially and FETCH to load the pointed to value into a variable.

- Using WHILE to repeat a set of commands for each budget category.

- Using COMPUTE to calculate the total amount for each budget category in each table.

- Using UPDATE to change the summary value in the YTDsummary table.

- Using GOTO to direct R:BASE to pass control to another part of the command file.

With the exception of COMPUTE and UPDATE, this command file illustrates the use of programming control commands. You can use COMPUTE and UPDATE as stand-alone commands. You used COMPUTE in Chapter 4 and UPDATE in Chapter 8.

What's New in R:BASE Version 3.0

Throughout R:BASE's history, Microrim (R:BASE's developer), has continually improved on the R:BASE program and added features to it that are even more powerful and easy to use. This combination of power and ease-of-use culminates in the R:BASE 3.0 design.

The most evident change is the new graphics-like user interface. In addition, many programming commands have been added, and the existing commands have been expanded to make R:BASE fully ANSI-standard compatible.

Note that you can use prior R:BASE version databases directly by turning on Compatibility mode (see the SET tables in Appendix C for details). In addition, R:BASE software includes conversion programs for both databases and applications developed in R:BASE 2.0 and 2.1.

This appendix lists, briefly, the tools that come with R:BASE 3.0 and then the new or enhanced features of the product.

Tools and Utilities

R:BASE 3.0 is a menu-driven system with the following tools and utilities:

- On-line help obtained anywhere in the system by pressing the F1 function key.

- Most of the utilities and tools available through the R:BASE main menu—no commands are needed.

- Menu-driven modules for building databases, applications, forms, reports, and labels.

- Data transfer capability for moving data to and from other products through R:BASE's data import/export utility.

- Easy-to-use Query By Example module that enables you to quickly combine, sort, view, edit, and save data.

- MS-DOS commands available from within R:BASE, both through the menu system and as commands.

- Fully ANSI-standard Structured Query Language in addition to a complete set of programming commands. SQL commands are available through the menu system, which leads you step-by-step through the command-building process, or you can enter them directly in Command mode. R:BASE's SQL, because it is ANSI-standard, will teach you how to use SQL in high-level languages such as FORTRAN, Pascal, and C. Microrim also sells a system called the Program Interface, which enables you to use R:BASE commands in a stand-alone fourth-generation language. The current version of Program Interface may not yet be compatible with R:BASE 3.0.

- Application compilation through the CodeLock utility, R:BASE's command and application encoder. This utility does two things. First, it enables R:BASE to execute application files (called *procedures*) and, second, it encrypts the commands in an application to protect them from inadvertent changes.

- ASCII file editor.

- Transaction processing for saving modifications to the database and then committing or revoking the modifications with a single command.

If you are moving up to R:BASE 3.0 from an earlier R:BASE version, you will be interested in knowing what is new with this version. The R:BASE documentation set contains a lengthy guide for previous R:BASE users called the *R:BASE 3.0 for R:BASE Users Guide*.

Features

The new features in R:BASE 3.0 follow:

- *New Conversions.* DOS programs DBCONV-3 and APCONV-3 convert existing R:BASE 2.0 databases and applications to R:BASE 3.0.

- *New Query By Example.* Module for requesting data from one or more sets of data stored in a database.

- *Revised SELECT Command.* Upgraded for full SQL compatibility.

- *New Menu Systems.* A new user interface makes R:BASE easier to use for novices and experienced users. The menus now all use the same set of function keys and have the same look to make the product consistent between modules.

- *Revised Structured Query Language.* Two SQL commands were added—CONNECT/DISCONNECT and COMMENT ON. All existing SQL commands have been revised for complete ANSI-standard SQL compatibility.

- *Revised Forms Module.* New features make forms more powerful. Pop-up menus display data. Includes help lines for individual fields. Enables you to execute command files from a form. Includes NEXT function for automatic numbering and variable-only forms with addition of the EDIT VARIABLE, ENTER VARIABLE, and DRAW commands to use them. Enables you to create a quick form from R:BASE. Executes a form from the Forms module.

- *Revised Reports Module.* New features make reports more powerful. Includes printer tables for easy font changes and picture formats for individual fields. Enables you to create quick reports from R:BASE.

- *Revised Programming Language.* In addition to extension of the SQL capability, several commands have been added: AUTONUM to number rows, DIALOG to create dialog boxes, SKIP to use with forms trigger files, SNAP to take snapshots of the screen, SWITCH/ CASE for comparisons, and WHENEVER for error processing.

- *Revised Editor.* Addition of Search and Search and Replace capability.

- *New SuperMath Functions.* The following SuperMath functions have been added: CHKKEY checks the value of the last keystroke; GETKEY returns the value of the last keystroke; ENVVAL returns the value of a DOS environment variable; NEXT returns the next available number for a column defined for autonumbering; SSUB returns a value from a text string by position—used with the new two-dimensional menu type.

- *Revised Environment.* The Settings menu system has been revised and the following SET keywords have been added: AND determines the precedence of AND/OR operations in WHERE clauses, IF...ENDIF, WHILE...ENDWHILE, and SWITCH...ENDSW. AUTOCOMMIT turns automatic commitment of transactions on or off. COMPAT enables you to work with R:BASE 2.0 databases. DIALOG sets colors for dialog boxes. EXPLODE determines how dialog boxes are drawn—exploding or immediate display. FILES sets the number of open files allowed at one time. FIRST sets the color of initial characters on menu options. INSERT sets the Ins key toggle on or off. MAXTRANS sets the maximum number of transaction processing users. MENU sets menu colors. NAME sets a network ID. PRINTER names the printer control file. REFRESH sets how often form data is refreshed to display current information. TRANSACT turns transaction processing on or off. Some characters have been revised: the default QUOTES character is now ', SINGLE wild card is %, and MANY wild card is _.

- *New Transaction Processing.* Enables batch control of transactions so that you can revoke or enter a set of data modification commands to the database. COMMIT adds transactions to the database. ROLLBACK revokes transactions and returns the database to a previous state. SET TRANSACT turns transaction processing off and on. SET MAXTRANS sets the maximum number of transaction processing users. SET AUTOCOMMIT turns automatic commitment of transactions on or off.

- *Reading and writing dBASE files.* R:BASE can now directly read from and write to dBASE database files either through the Database option on the Main Menu or through the ATACH and DETACH commands.

Index